Tony Rein
_513-_
_703-2613_

STEPHENS' C# PROGRAMMING WITH VISUAL STUDIO® 2010 24-HOUR TRAINER

Stephens' C# Programming with Visual Studio® 2010 24-Hour Trainer

Stephens' C# Programming with Visual Studio® 2010 24-Hour Trainer

Rod Stephens

Wiley Publishing, Inc.

Stephens' C# Programming with Visual Studio® 2010 24-Hour Trainer

Published by
Wiley Publishing, Inc.
10475 Crosspoint Boulevard
Indianapolis, IN 46256
www.wiley.com

ISBN: 978-0-470-59690-6

Manufactured in the United States of America

10 9 8 7 6 5 4 3 2

For general information on our other products and services please contact our Customer Care Department within the United States at (877) 762-2974, outside the United States at (317) 572-3993 or fax (317) 572-4002.

Wiley also publishes its books in a variety of electronic formats. Some content that appears in print may not be available in electronic books.

Library of Congress Control Number: 2010922567

ABOUT THE AUTHOR

 **ROD STEPHENS** started out as a mathematician, but while studying at MIT, discovered how much fun programming is and has been programming professionally ever since. During his career, he has worked on an eclectic assortment of applications in such fields as telephone switching, billing, repair dispatching, tax processing, wastewater treatment, concert ticket sales, cartography, and training for professional football players.

Rod is a Microsoft Visual Basic Most Valuable Professional (MVP) and has taught introductory programming at ITT Technical Institute. He has written more than 20 books that have been translated into languages from all over the world, and more than 250 magazine articles covering C#, Visual Basic, Visual Basic for Applications, Delphi, and Java. He is currently a regular contributor to DevX (www.DevX.com).

Rod's popular *C# Helper* web site (www.csharphelper.com) contains tips, tricks, and example programs for C# programmers. His *VB Helper* web site (www.vb-helper.com) receives several million hits per month and contains similar material for Visual Basic programmers.

You can contact Rod at RodStephens@csharphelper.com or RodStephens@vb-helper.com.

CREDITS

ACKNOWLEDGMENTS

THANKS TO Bob Elliott, Kevin Kent, Kim Cofer, Sara Shlaer, and all of the others who work so hard to make producing any book possible.

CONTENTS

INTRODUCTION

SO YOU WANT to learn Visual C# programming? Excellent choice!

Visual C# is a powerful, all-purpose programming language that lets you build robust applications that run on the desktop or over the Web. Visual C# provides all of the tools that you need to build a huge variety of applications such as:

➤ Database applications

➤ Point of sales systems

➤ Web applications

➤ Two- and three-dimensional graphics programs

➤ Image processing and photo manipulation systems

➤ Computer-aided design (CAD) systems

➤ Document layout and printing systems

➤ Hardware control systems

➤ High-performance games

➤ Much, much more

In case you ever need to mention it at parties, C# is pronounced "see sharp." It's written C# because the number sign (#) is the closest most keyboards can get to the musical sharp symbol (♯).

Of course there are some problems that you won't be able to solve even with Visual C#. If you want a program that picks the winning number on a roulette wheel or that can predict stock prices, you may have better luck using tarot cards (or a degree in economics), but for tractable problems Visual C# is a great choice.

This book is a self-paced guide to Visual C# programming in the Visual Studio environment. It uses short, easy-to-follow lessons, reinforced by step-by-step instructions, screencasts, and supplemental exercises to help you master Visual C# programming quickly and painlessly. It explains how to write Visual C# programs that interact with the user to read inputs, calculate results, and display outputs. It shows how to read and write files, make printouts, and use databases.

This book won't make you an expert, but it will give you a solid understanding of how to write Visual C# programs. When you've finished reading this book and working through the Try It sections, you'll be able to write non-trivial programs of your own. You may not be able to accurately pick winning lottery numbers (if you do, please let me know!), but you will be able to build some useful programs. And you'll be ready to learn more about specialized topics such as database programming, file processing, and graphics.

WHO THIS BOOK IS FOR

This book is for anyone who wants to learn how to write programs using Visual C#. Whether you want to move into a lucrative career as a software developer, add a few new skills to your resume, or pick up a fascinating new hobby, this book can get you started.

This book does *not* assume you have any previous programming experience. It assumes you can turn your computer on and surf the Web, but that's about it for previous qualifications. It is suitable as a first programming book for high school or college students, but its self-paced, hands-on approach also makes it ideal if you're trying to learn to program on your own.

I say all this because I don't want to receive a bunch of flaming e-mails complaining that the material in this book is too basic. So I'm warning you right now: If you've been programming in C++ or Visual Basic for 16 years, don't blame me if a lot of this material seems pretty simple to you. Don't waste your time complaining; go find a more advanced book.

WHAT THIS BOOK COVERS (AND WHAT IT DOESN'T)

This book explains Visual C# programming. It explains how to write, debug, and run desktop applications that interact with the user and the computer. It shows how to understand object-oriented concepts, perform calculations, manipulate files and strings, produce printouts, and interact with simple databases.

Programming in any language is an enormous topic, however, so this book doesn't cover everything. It doesn't explain how to design databases, build cryptographically secure web applications, create multithreaded programs that run on multiple cores or computers, or build Xbox games. All of those tasks are possible using Visual C#, however, and after you finish this book you'll be ready to move on to more advanced books that cover those topics.

To make everything fit into a single book, I had to make some tough choices about what to include and what to omit. This book focuses on desktop applications because, if you want to learn C# programming, then you probably have a computer that can run applications. It doesn't cover ASP.NET programming using C# not because it's a bad thing to learn, but because it's a less self-contained learning environment. Visual Studio will let you build ASP.NET web applications, but unless you have a web server that supports ASP.NET, you won't be able to exercise the full power of ASP.NET.

Similarly there are many ways to approach database programming. In this book, I've tried to give you a taste of database programming without being completely overwhelming. The book's lessons explain how to use Visual Studio wizards to get simple database applications up and running quickly and how to use LINQ to perform simple database queries. Database programming is an enormous topic, however, and no general programming book can hope to cover it in its entirety.

No introductory book can cover every programming topic. However, the topics this book does cover give you a good foundation of fundamental programming skills that you can use as a base for further study.

THE WROX *24-HOUR TRAINER* APPROACH

Educators have known for many years that different people use different learning styles most effectively. Personally, I learn best by watching and doing. However, different students may learn best by:

➤ Reading a textbook

➤ Looking at non-written material such as pictures and graphs

➤ Listening to an instructor lecture

➤ Watching someone demonstrate techniques

➤ Doing exercises and examples

Good instructors try to incorporate material that helps students with all of these learning styles. Combining text, lecture, demonstration, discussion, and exercises lets every student pick up as much as possible using whichever methods work best.

Like a good instructor, this book uses materials that address each learning style. It uses text and figures to help visual learners, screencasts that provide visual demonstrations and auditory instruction, step-by-step instruction to help you do it yourself, and exercises for independent study.

The book is divided into small, bite-sized lessons that begin with a discussion of a particular concept or technique, complete with figures, notes, tips, and other standard fare for instructional books. The lessons are short and tightly focused on a single task so you can finish each one in a single sitting. You shouldn't need to stop in the middle of a lesson and leave concepts half-learned (at least if you turn off your phone).

After describing the main concept, the lesson includes a Try It section that invites you to perform a programming exercise to solidify the lesson's ideas.

The Try It begins with a high-level overview. It then contains several subsections:

➤ **Lesson Requirements** describes the exercise so you know what should happen.

➤ **Hints** gives pointers about possible confusing aspects of the problem (if they're needed).

➤ **Step-by-Step** provides a numbered series of steps that show how to solve the problem.

A screencast on the accompanying DVD shows me (the author) working through the Try It problem. Additional commentary at the end of the screencast highlights extensions of the lesson's main concepts.

After the Try It's Step-by-Step section, the lesson concludes with extra exercises that you can solve for further practice and to expand the lesson's main ideas. I recommend that you at least skim the exercises and ask yourself if you think you could do them. Solutions to all of the exercises are available for download on the book's web site.

WEB SITES

Actually the book has two web sites: Wrox's version and my version. Both sites contain the book's source code.

To find the Wrox web page, go to `www.wrox.com` and search for the book by title or ISBN. Once you've found the book, click the Download Code link on the book's detail page to obtain all the source code for the book. Once you download the code, just decompress it with your favorite compression tool. Alternatively, you can go to the main Wrox code download page at `http://www.wrox.com/dynamic/books/download.aspx` to see the code available for this book and all other Wrox books.

To find my web page for the book, go to `www.CSharpHelper.com/24hour.html`.

The following list summarizes each lesson's structure.

>   Lesson text
>
>   Try It
>
>>   Lesson Requirements
>>
>>   Hints (if needed)
>>
>>   Step-by-Step
>
>   Exercises

The one thing that a good classroom experience has that this book doesn't is direct interaction. You can't shout questions at the instructor, work as a team with fellow students, or discuss exercises with other students.

Although the book itself can't help here, there are at least three things you can do to get this kind of interaction. First, join the Wrox P2P (peer-to-peer) discussion forum for this book. As the section "p2p.wrox.com" later in this introduction says, you can join the discussion forum to post questions, provide answers, see what other readers are doing with the book's material, and generally keep tabs on book-related topics. (You can join other Visual C# discussion groups on the Web, too, but this one is dedicated to this book and you know I'll be watching it.)

Second, you can browse or subscribe to my blog at `blog.CSharpHelper.com` to see new example programs, articles, and commentary. Many of the entries describe tips, tricks, and short example programs that demonstrate techniques that you may find useful for your Visual C# programs.

Finally, if you get stuck on an exercise or some other program you're working on, e-mail me at `RodStephens@CSharpHelper.com`. I won't solve the exercises for you, but I'll try to clarify problems or give you any hints you need so you can solve them yourself.

GETTING THE MOST OUT OF THE BOOK

This book provides a lot of tools that you can use to best match your learning style but you have to use them. If you learn best by reading text, spend more time on the text. If you like step-by-step instructions, focus on the Try It's step-by-step exercise. If you learn best by watching and listening, focus on the screencasts.

Then, after you've finished a lesson, use the exercises to verify that you've mastered the material.

And don't be afraid to invent programs of your own. Just because an idea isn't in the book doesn't mean it wouldn't make good practice.

HOW THIS BOOK IS STRUCTURED

This book is divided into six sections, each containing a series of short lessons. The lessons are generally arranged in order with later lessons depending on earlier ones, so you should study the lessons more or less in order, at least until sections V and VI. The lessons in sections V and VI cover slightly more specialized topics and their order is less critical. (However, you should still probably study "Programming Databases, Part 1" before you study "Programming Databases, Part 2," but you can study them before or after reading the lesson on printing.)

PERSISTENT PROGRAMS

A number of the lessons work with the SimpleEdit example program. This program starts as a simple form containing a few controls in Lesson 3 and grows into a serviceable word processing application before all is done.

Each time a lesson asks you to add to this program, it tells you to copy the previous version. If you skip a step, you may not have the necessary version available. In that case, you can download the version you need from the book's web site.

For example, the instructions for Lesson 6's Exercise 1 say to copy the version you built for Lesson 5, Exercise 5. If you skipped that exercise, you can download the Lesson 5 material from the book's web site and use the version of SimpleEdit that it contains.

Section I: The Visual Studio IDE and Controls

The lessons in this section explain how to use the Visual Studio integrated development environment (IDE) and how to use the controls that make up a user interface. These form the foundation on which you build everything else in a Visual C# program.

Lesson 1, "**Getting Started with the Visual Studio IDE,**" explains Visual Studio. It describes some of the IDE's useful features and shows how to build a simple program and run it. From the very first lesson, you'll be able to build a program!

Lesson 2, "**Creating Controls,**" explains what controls are, what they are for, and how to use them. It shows how to add controls to a form to make a user interface. In Visual C# programs, controls are critical for getting the job done.

Lesson 3, "**Making Controls Arrange Themselves,**" explains how to use control properties to make controls automatically rearrange themselves at run time to take full advantage of the available space. When the user resizes a form, the controls can automatically move and resize as needed.

Lesson 4, "**Handling Events,**" explains what events are. It shows how to catch events to respond to user actions so the user can interact with the program.

Lesson 5, "**Making Menus,**" explains how to add main menus and context menus to an application, and how to respond when the user selects a menu item. By responding to menu events, the program gives the user an easy and well-understood way to control the application.

Lesson 6, "**Making Tool Strips and Status Strips,**" explains how to build tool strips and status strips, and how to handle their events. Tool strips provide a faster method for the user to control the application than menus, while status strips provide useful feedback to let the user know what the program is doing.

Lesson 7, "**Using RichTextBoxes,**" explains the `RichTextBox` control and shows how to manipulate it with code. The `RichTextBox` allows the user to enter text and, if the program provides the right tools, lets the user format the text with different fonts, colors, bullets, and other text decorations.

Lesson 8, "**Using Standard Dialogs,**" explains standard dialogs. It shows how to use them to display messages and questions, change fonts and colors, browse for folders, and let the user select files for opening and saving.

Lesson 9, "**Creating and Displaying New Forms,**" explains how code can display new instances of forms and interact with the controls on those forms. This is important for more complicated programs that cannot do everything they need to on a single form.

Lesson 10, "**Building Custom Dialogs,**" explains how to use new forms as custom dialogs. It shows how to use the `Form` object's `ShowDialog` method, how to assign a dialog's return result, and how to interpret that result.

Section II: Variables and Calculations

The lessons in this section deal with variables and calculations. They explain what variables are and how a program can use them to calculate results. The lessons in Section I explain how to make controls that let the user enter information. The lessons in this section explain how to take that information and do something with it.

Lesson 11, "**Using Variables and Performing Calculations,**" explains how to declare and use variables and constants, and how to perform simple calculations. It also shows how to convert information from one data type to another. For example, it shows how to take an age entered by the user and convert it from the textual value "47" into the numeric value 47. (It's a small distinction to a person but a huge one to a program.)

Lesson 12, "Debugging Code," explains techniques for finding and fixing bugs. It shows how to set breakpoints in the code, step into and over routines, examine and modify variable values, and use watches. Almost every nontrivial program starts with a bug or two. This lesson shows how to find those bugs.

Lesson 13, "Understanding Scope," explains how scope restricts a variable's accessibility to pieces of code. It also explains why a programmer should restrict scope as much as possible.

Lesson 14, "Working with Strings," explains how to combine, manipulate, and format strings. It explains the String class's ToString and Format methods that let you build nicely formatted string to show the user.

Lesson 15, "Working with Dates and Times," explains how to use date and time values. It explains the Date and TimeSpan classes, and shows how to use and format them.

Lesson 16, "Using Arrays and Collections," explains single- and multi-dimensional arrays and collection classes such as Collection and ArrayList. It explains how to declare and initialize arrays and collections.

Lesson 17, "Using Enumerations and Structures," explains how to use more advanced data types such as structures and enumerations. These help make the code easier to understand, debug, and maintain.

Section III: Program Statements

The lessons in the previous sections explain how to let the user control the program by raising events, to get data entered by the user in controls, to place that data in variables, and to perform simple calculations. The lessons in this section explain how to perform more complex calculations. They explain how to control the program's flow, make decisions, and repeat operations. While controls and message boxes are some of the more visible pieces of an application, these statements let the program do most of its work.

Lesson 18, "Making Choices," explains how programmers can control the flow of code with if, switch, nested if, and cascading if statements. These statements let the program take different actions depending on the situation.

Lesson 19, "Repeating Program Steps," explains looping code that uses for, foreach, do, and while statements. It explains how to use these statements to iterate through a series of integer values, arrays, and lists, and how to break out of loops.

Lesson 20, "Reusing Code with Methods," explains how a programmer can write functions and why functions are important. It explains the syntax of declaring functions, defining return values, and using parameters passed by value or reference.

Lesson 21, "Handling Errors," explains how to use try blocks to handle unexpected errors. It also explains how to throw errors to tell other parts of the program that something has gone wrong.

Lesson 22, "Preventing Bugs," explains bug proofing techniques that make it easier to detect and correct bugs. It explains how to use `Assert` statements to validate inputs and results so you can catch bugs quickly rather than letting them remain hidden in the code.

Section IV: Classes

Structures, enumerations, and functions are all programming abstractions that let you think about pieces of the program at a higher level. When you call the `CalculateInterest` function, you don't need to know how it works, just that it does.

The ultimate programming abstraction is the class. A class lets you think about data and functions packaged as a single unit. For example, a `Customer` class might include data (name, employee ID, office number) together with functions (`ScheduleWork`, `PrintPaycheck`).

The lessons in this section deal with classes. They explain how to create and use classes and how to use more advanced class features such as generics and operator overloading.

Lesson 23, "Defining Classes," explains how to define classes. It explains the three fundamental characteristics of object-oriented classes (inheritance, encapsulation, and polymorphism) and how classes provide them. It explains how to build simple properties and methods.

Lesson 24, "Initializing Objects," explains constructors, destructors, and initializers, and shows how to use them to make creating objects easier.

Lesson 25, "Fine-Tuning Classes," explains how you can overload and override class methods. These techniques let you make classes more flexible and easier to use.

Lesson 26, "Overloading Operators," explains operator overloading. This technique lets you define the behavior of operators such as +, *, and % for objects other than numbers.

Lesson 27, "Using Interfaces," explains what a class interface is and how to build one. Just as a program's user interface defines the features that a user sees, a class interface defines the features that a class must have to implement the interface.

Lesson 28, "Making Generic Classes," explains how to build new generic classes. Whereas Lesson 16 shows how to use generic collection classes such as `Hashtable` to work with different kinds of data, this lesson explains how you can build your own generic classes and methods.

Section V: System Interactions

Earlier lessons explain how to let a program interact with the user. The lessons in this section explain methods a program can use to interact with the operating system and other programs.

Lesson 29, "Reading and Writing Files," explains how a program can read and write files. It explains how to use streams to manipulate the text in a file all at once or in pieces, for example, one line at a time.

Lesson 30, "Using File System Classes," explains ways in which a program can use classes to find, examine, and manipulate directories and files. It describes file handling classes such as `DriveInfo`, `DirectoryInfo`, `Directory`, and `FileInfo`.

Lesson 31, "Printing," explains how to create printouts. It tells how to draw simple shapes and text on one or more pages sent to the printer.

Lesson 32, "Using the Clipboard," explains how to move text, images, and file drop lists in and out of the clipboard. Using the clipboard in this way is somewhat crude, but it's simple and flexible, allowing your program to interact with many others without understanding anything about how those other applications work.

Lesson 33, "Providing Drag and Drop," explains how a program can use drag-and-drop to interact with other programs. It explains how to start a drag, provide "drag over" feedback, and handle a drop. Like the clipboard, drag-and-drop lets your programs interact with others without knowing how the other programs work.

Section VI: Specialized Topics

The lessons presented in the earlier sections cover topics that are generally useful for a large variety of programs. Whether you are writing a sales tax calculator, an invoice tracking system, or a word guessing game, techniques such as handling events, debugging code, using `if` statements, and printing will be useful to you.

This section introduces topics that are more specialized so you might not need them in every program you write. For example, localizing your application for different locales is important for some applications but not for every program you write.

Each of the lessons in this section gives a sense of what its topic is about and provides enough detail to get started, but the lessons cannot cover their topics in complete detail due to the topic's length and complexity.

Lesson 34, "Localizing Programs," explains how to make programs that can run in multiple cultures. It shows how to use different text and images for different locales and discusses some of the other issues an international application must address.

Lesson 35, "Programming Databases, Part 1," explains how to use Visual Studio wizards to build a simple database application quickly. It shows how to display the data in a database and save any changes that the user makes.

Lesson 36, "Programming Databases, Part 2," explains slightly more advanced database features than those covered by Lesson 35. It explains how to make the simple programs described in Lesson 35 search, filter, and sort their results.

Lesson 37, "LINQ to Objects," explains how you can use Language-Integrated Query (LINQ) to filter and extract values from collections and other enumerable lists into new ones. This lets you perform database-like queries on data stored in program objects instead of an actual database.

Lesson 38, "LINQ to SQL," explains how you can use LINQ to manipulate database entities as if they were objects inside the program. It lets your program treat records in tables as if they were instances of classes, and provides an alternative database strategy to the one used in Lessons 35 and 36.

Lesson 39, "Drawing with GDI+," provides more detail about drawing with Graphic Device Interface (GDI+) functions. Previous lessons, notably Lesson 31, used GDI+ functions to draw.

These functions let you draw lines, rectangles, polygons, ellipses, curves, text, and other shapes on windows, bitmaps, and printouts. Those lessons provided only the bare minimum needed to demonstrate their topics. This lesson provides more detail so you can generate more complex graphics.

Lesson 40, "Making WPF Applications," explains Windows Presentation Foundation (WPF), a framework for building Window applications that provides an alternative to the Windows Forms applications described so far in this book. WPF applications provide new tools and approaches that let you build applications that are potentially more interactive and engaging.

Lesson 41, "Printing with WPF," explains one way you can generate printouts in WPF applications. It shows how to print an image of a WPF visual object, a much different method than the event-driven technique used by the Windows Forms approach described in Lesson 31.

Appendices

This book's appendices summarize useful information for handy reference.

Appendix A, "Glossary," explains common programming terms that you may encounter while studying Visual C# programming.

Appendix B, "Control Summary," summarizes each of the standard controls provided by Visual C#. You can use it to help select the right control for your needs.

Appendix C, "What's on the DVD?", goes into more detail about using the DVD that comes with the book.

WHAT YOU NEED TO USE THIS BOOK

To get the most out of this book, you need to install Visual Studio 2010 and Visual C#.

You don't need any fancy version of Visual Studio or Visual C# Professional Edition. In fact, the Professional Edition, Team System Development Edition, and Team System Team Suite versions don't really add all that much that you're likely to want to use for a long time. Mostly they add support for performing unit tests, managing test cases, profiling code, building code libraries, and performing other tasks that are more useful for programming teams than they are for individuals, particularly beginners. In short, to work through this book, the Express Editions should be good enough.

The following list describes some links that you may find useful for learning about and installing different Visual Studio products:

➤ **Visual C# Express Edition home page** (www.microsoft.com/express/vcsharp): This page contains information about Visual C# Express Edition and provides a download link.

➤ **Visual C# Developer Center** (msdn.microsoft.com/vcsharp): This page contains links to Visual C# information such as downloads, "getting started" articles, and other resources.

➤ **Visual Studio Developer Center** (msdn.microsoft.com/vstudio): This page contains links to Visual Studio information such as downloads, "quick tour" articles, and other resources.

➤ **Visual Studio Express Edition home page** (www.microsoft.com/express/product): This page contains information about Express Editions of Visual Studio products such as Visual Basic, Visual C#, Visual C++, and Visual Web Developer.

At a minimum, visit the Visual C# Express Edition home page (www.microsoft.com/express/vcsharp) and download and install Visual C# Express Edition. You should also occasionally check the Visual C# home page for service packs and extra tools that may be available.

Running any version of Visual Studio will require that you have a reasonably fast, modern computer with a large hard disk and lots of memory. For example, I'm fairly happy running my Intel Core 2 system at 1.83 GHz with 2GB of memory and a huge 500GB hard drive. That's a lot more disk space than necessary but disk space is relatively cheap, so why not buy a lot?

You can run Visual Studio on much less powerful systems but using an underpowered computer can be extremely slow and frustrating. Visual Studio has a big memory footprint, so if you're having performance problems, installing more memory may help.

Of course, buying a superfast quad-core desktop system with 6GB of RAM and 1TB of disk space will give you outstanding performance, but it will add dramatically to the $0 you're spending on Visual C# Express Edition.

CONVENTIONS

To help you get the most from the text and keep track of what's happening, we've used several conventions throughout the book.

> **SPLENDID SIDEBARS**
>
> Sidebars such as this one contain additional information and side topics.

 Boxes with a warning icon like this one hold important, not-to-be forgotten information that is directly relevant to the surrounding text.

The pencil icon indicates notes, tips, hints, tricks, and asides to the current discussion. They are offset and placed in italics like this.

 References such as this one tell you when to look at the DVD for screencasts related to the discussion.

As for styles in the text:

➤ New terms and important words are *italicized* when they are introduced. You can also find many of them in the glossary in Appendix A.

➤ Keyboard strokes look like this: [Ctrl]+A.

➤ URLs, code, and e-mail addresses within the text are shown in monofont type as in `www.vb-helper.com`, `x = 10`, and `RodStephens@CSharpHelper.com`.

`We use a monofont type with no highlighting for most code examples.`

`We use bold to emphasize code that's particularly important in the present context.`

The code editor in Visual Studio provides a rich color scheme to indicate various parts of code syntax such as variables, comments, and Visual C# keywords. That's a great tool to help you learn language features in the editor and to help prevent mistakes as you code. However, the colors don't show up in the code in this book.

SOURCE CODE

As you work through the examples in this book, you may choose either to type in all the code manually or to use the source code files that accompany the book. (I like to type in code when I work through a book because it helps me focus on it so I get a better understanding.)

Many of the examples in the book show only the code that is relevant to the current topic and may be missing some of the extra details that you need to make the example work properly. To fill in the missing pieces, you may need to write your own code or download the book's code.

All of the source code used in this book is available for download on the book's web sites. As I indicated earlier in this introduction, either go to the Wrox web site (`www.wrox.com`) and search for the book or visit my web page for the book `www.CSharpHelper.com/24hour.html`. Any updates to the code will be posted in both of these places.

At the Wrox web site, because many books have similar titles, you may find it easiest to search by ISBN; this book's ISBN is 978-0-470-59690-6.

ERRATA

The Wrox editors and I make every effort to ensure that there are no errors in the text or in the code. However, no one is perfect, and mistakes do occur. If you find an error in one of our books, like a spelling mistake or faulty piece of code, we would be very grateful for your feedback. By sending in errata you may save another reader hours of frustration and at the same time you will be helping us provide even higher quality information.

To find the errata page for this book, go to `http://www.wrox.com` and locate the title using the Search box or one of the title lists. Then, on the book details page, click the Book Errata link. On this page you can view all errata that has been submitted for this book and posted by Wrox editors. A complete book list including links to each book's errata is also available at `www.wrox.com/misc-pages/booklist.shtml`.

If you don't spot "your" error on the Book Errata page, go to `www.wrox.com/contact/techsupport.shtml` and complete the form there to send us the error you have found. We'll check the information and, if appropriate, post a message to the book's errata page and fix the problem in subsequent editions of the book.

P2P.WROX.COM

For author and peer discussion, join the P2P forums at `p2p.wrox.com`. The forums are a Web-based system for you to post messages relating to Wrox books and related technologies, and to interact with other readers and technology users. The forums offer a subscription feature to e-mail you topics of interest of your choosing when new posts are made to the forums. Wrox authors, editors, other industry experts, and your fellow readers are present on these forums.

At `p2p.wrox.com` you will find a number of different forums that will help you not only as you read this book, but also as you develop your own applications. To join the forums, just follow these steps:

1. Go to `p2p.wrox.com` and click the Register link.

2. Read the terms of use and click Agree.

3. Complete the required information to join as well as any optional information you wish to provide and click Submit.

4. You will receive an e-mail with information describing how to verify your account and complete the joining process.

You can read messages in the forums without joining P2P but in order to post your own messages, you must join.

Once you join, you can post new messages and respond to messages other users post. You can read messages at any time on the Web. If you would like to have new messages from a particular forum e-mailed to you, click the Subscribe to this Forum icon by the forum name in the forum listing.

For more information about how to use the Wrox P2P, be sure to read the P2P FAQs for answers to questions about how the forum software works as well as many common questions specific to P2P and Wrox books. To read the FAQs, click the FAQ link on any P2P page.

SECTION I
The Visual Studio IDE and Controls

The lessons in this section of the book explain how to use the Visual Studio integrated development environment (IDE). They explain how to use the IDE to create forms, place controls on the forms, and set control properties. These lessons describe some of Visual C#'s most useful controls and give you practice using them.

You can do practically all of this in the IDE without writing a single line of code! That makes Visual C# a great environment for rapid prototyping. You can build a form, add controls, and run the program to see what it looks like without ever creating a variable, declaring a function, or getting stuck in an infinite loop.

The lessons in this section explain how to get that far. A few of these lessons show how to add a line or two of code to a form to make it a bit more responsive, but for now the focus is on using the IDE to build forms and controls. Writing code (and fixing the inevitable bugs) comes later.

- ▶ **LESSON 1:** Getting Started with the Visual Studio IDE

- ▶ **LESSON 2:** Creating Controls

- ▶ **LESSON 3:** Making Controls Arrange Themselves

- ▶ **LESSON 4:** Handling Events

- ▶ **LESSON 5:** Making Menus

- ▶ **LESSON 6:** Making Tool Strips and Status Strips

- ▶ **LESSON 7:** Using RichTextBoxes

- ▶ **LESSON 8:** Using Standard Dialogs

- ▶ **LESSON 9:** Creating and Displaying New Forms

- ▶ **LESSON 10:** Building Custom Dialog

1

Getting Started with the Visual Studio IDE

The Visual Studio integrated development environment (IDE) plays a central role in Visual C# development. In this lesson you explore the IDE. You learn how to configure it for Visual C# development, and you learn about some of the more useful of the IDE's windows and what they do. When you finish this lesson, you'll know how to create a new project. It may not do much, but it will run and will prepare you for the lessons that follow.

Visual Studio *is a development environment that you can use with several programming languages including Visual C#, Visual Basic, Visual C++, and F#. C# is a high-level programming language that can read inputs, calculate results, display outputs to the user, and perform other operations typical of high-level programming languages.*

Visual C# is the combination of C# used in the Visual Studio development environment. You can use a text editor to write C# programs without Visual Studio, but it's a lot of work and is not the focus of this book.

Visual C# and C# go together like politicians and bickering: if you mention one, most people assume you're also talking about the other. Most people simply say C#, so this book does, too, unless there's a reason to distinguish between C# and Visual C#.

The .NET Framework also plays an important role in C# programs. It includes classes that make performing certain tasks easier, runtime tools that make it possible to execute C# programs, and other plumbing necessary to build and run C# programs.

Normally you don't need to worry about whether a feature is provided by Visual Studio, the C# language, or the .NET Framework. They all go together in this book, so for the purposes of this book at least you can ignore the difference.

INSTALLING C#

Before you can use C# to write the next blockbuster first-person Xbox game, you need to install it. So if you haven't done so already, install C#.

You can install the Express Edition at www.microsoft.com/express/Windows. If you think you need some other version (for example, you're working on a big project and you need test management, source code control, and other team programming tools), go to msdn.microsoft.com/vcsharp and install the version that's right for you.

It's a big installation, so it could take a while.

TALKIN' 'BOUT MY GENERATION

Developers talk about different generations of programming languages ranging from the very primitive to quite advanced. In a nutshell, the different generations of languages are:

➤ **1GL** — Machine language. This is a series of 0s and 1s that the machine can understand directly.

➤ **2GL** — Assembly language. This is a translation of machine language into terse mnemonics that can be easily translated into machine language. It provides no structure.

➤ **3GL** — A higher-level language such as FORTAN or BASIC. These provide additional structure (such as looping and subroutines) that makes building complex programs easier.

➤ **4GL** — An even higher-level language or development environment that helps build programs, typically in a specific problem domain.

➤ **5GL** — A language where you specify goals and constraints and the language figures out how to satisfy them. For example, the database Structured Query Language (SQL) allows you to use statements like SELECT FirstName FROM Employees. You don't need to tell the database how to get the names; it figures that out for you.

Visual Studio provides code snippets that let you copy standard chunks of code into your program, IntelliSense that helps you select and use functions and other pieces of code, refactoring tools that help you rearrange and restructure your code, and more. That makes Visual C# a 4GL (or perhaps a 3.5GL depending on how high your standards are).

CONFIGURING THE IDE

When you first run Visual Studio, it asks how you want to configure the IDE. You can pick settings for general development, Visual Basic, Visual C#, and so forth. Because you're going to be focusing on C# development, select that option.

These settings determine such things as what keystrokes activate certain development features. You can certainly write C# programs with the Visual C++ settings but we may as well be on the same page, so when I say, "Press F5," the IDE starts your program instead of displaying a code window or whatever Visual C++ thinks F5 means.

If you ever want to switch to different settings (for example, if you got carried away during installation and selected the general settings and now want the C# settings), you can always change them later.

To change the settings later, open the Tools menu and select Import and Export Settings to display the Import and Export Settings Wizard. You can use this tool to save your current settings, reload previously saved settings, or reset settings to default values.

To reset settings, select the Reset All Settings option on the wizard's first page and click Next.

On the next page, indicate whether you want to save your current settings. When you've made your choice, click Next to display the page shown in Figure 1-1. Select the Visual C# Development

FIGURE 1-1

Settings choice and click Finish. (Then sit back and wait. Or better still, go get a coffee because this could take a while. Visual Studio has a lot of settings to reset, and it could take several minutes depending on how fast and busy your computer is.)

BUILDING YOUR FIRST PROGRAM

Now that you've installed C#, you're ready to get started. Launch Visual Studio by double-clicking its desktop icon or by selecting it from the system's Start menu.

To create a new project, press [Ctrl]+[Shift]+N to display the New Project dialog box shown in Figure 1-2. Alternatively, you can open the File menu, expand the New submenu, and select Project.

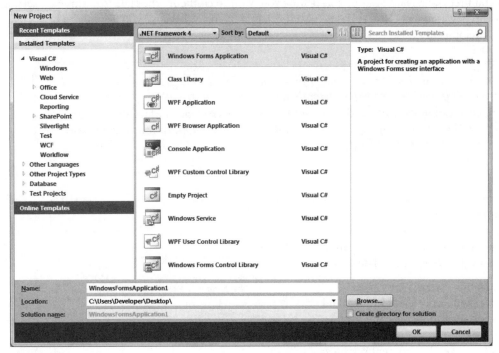

FIGURE 1-2

Expand the Visual C# project type folder on the left and select the template for the type of project that you want to build on the right. For most of this book, that will be a Visual C# Windows Forms Application.

Below the list of project types, you need to enter several pieces of information.

➤ **Name** — This is the application's name. Visual Studio creates a folder with this name to hold the program's files. It also sets some key values in the project to this name.

➤ **Location** — This is where you want Visual Studio to put the project's folder.

➤ **Solution Name** — If the Create Directory for Solution box is checked (which it is by default), Visual Studio creates a folder with this name at the location you entered. It then places the application's folder inside the solution's folder.

So if the Create Directory for Solution box is checked, you get a filesystem layout that looks like this:

SolutionFolder

    SolutionFiles

ApplicationFolder

ApplicationFiles

If the Create Directory for Solution box is not checked, you get a filesystem layout that looks like this:

ApplicationFolder

ApplicationFiles

An application contains a single program. A solution can contain several applications. A solution is useful when you want to build applications that go closely together. It's particularly useful if you want to build a library of routines plus an executable program to test the library.

The applications you build in this book are single programs so they don't really need to be inside a separate solution folder. Most of the time, I uncheck the Create Directory for Solution box to keep my filesystem simpler.

By default, Visual Studio places new projects in your Projects folder at some obscure location such as C:\Users\MyUserName\Documents\Visual Studio 2010\Projects. Later it can be hard finding these projects in Windows Explorer (for example, to make a copy).

To make finding projects easier, set the location to something more intuitive such as the desktop or a folder on the desktop. The next time you create a new project, Visual Studio will initialize the location textbox to this same location, so from now on it'll be easy to find your projects.

If you open the New Project dialog box while you have another project open, you'll see an additional dropdown that lists the choices Create New Solution and Add to Solution. The first choice closes the current solution and creates a new one. The second choice adds the new application to the solution you currently have open. Normally you'll want to create a new solution.

After you display the New Project dialog box and enter a Name, Location, and Solution Name, click OK. The result should look like Figure 1-3.

If you have previously edited a project, you can quickly reload it from the File menu's Recent Projects submenu. You can also load a solution into the IDE by double-clicking the solution's .sln *file.*

FIGURE 1-3

The rest of this lesson deals with the features available in Visual Studio, some of which are displayed in Figure 1-3. Before you launch into an inventory of useful features, however, press F5 or open the Debug menu and select Start Debugging to run your new program. Figure 1-4 shows the result. Admittedly this first program isn't very fancy, but by the same token you didn't need to do much to build it.

This first program may not seem terribly impressive but there's a lot going on behind the scenes. C# has built a form with a bunch of useful features, including:

FIGURE 1-4

➤   A resizable border and draggable title bar.

➤   Minimize, maximize, and close buttons in the upper-right corner.

➤   A system menu in the upper-left corner that contains the commands Restore, Move, Size, Minimize, Maximize, and Close.

➤   An icon in the system taskbar.

➤   The ability to use [Alt]+[Tab] and Flip3D ([Win]+[Tab]) to move between the application and others.

➤   Other standard window behaviors. For example, if you double-click the form's title bar it maximizes (or restores if it is already maximized), and if you press [Alt]+F4, the form closes.

Unless you're an absolute beginner to Windows, you probably take all of these features for granted, but providing them is actually a lot of work. Not too long ago you would have had to write around 100 lines of code to handle these sorts of issues. Now Visual Studio automatically builds a form that handles most of these details for you.

You can still get in and change the way things work if you want to (for example, you can set a form's minimum and maximum sizes) but usually you can ignore all of these issues and concentrate on your particular application, not the Windows decorations.

A SUITABLE EXECUTABLE

Whenever you run a program in the IDE, Visual Studio builds an executable program, normally in the project's `bin\Debug` subdirectory. You can run the executable by simply double-clicking it, for example, in Windows Explorer.

That doesn't mean the executable is suitable to run on any old computer. If you copy that file to another computer, it won't run unless the .NET Framework runtime libraries have been installed there. If that computer has Visual Studio installed, you're all set, but if it doesn't you'll need to install the redistributable yourself.

To install these libraries, go to Microsoft's download web page `www.microsoft.com/downloads` and search for ".NET Framework redistributable." Pick the version that matches the one you're using (version 4.0 if you're using Visual C# 2010) and install it on the target computer.

Now you can copy C# executables onto the system and run them.

COPYING PROJECTS

Sometimes you may want to copy a project. For example, you might want to save the current version and then make a new one to try things out. Or you may want to give a copy of the project to a friend or your programming instructor.

To make a copy, you might look in the File menu and see the Copy As commands. Don't be tempted! Those commands copy single files, not the entire project. Later when you try to open one of those files, you'll discover that Visual Studio cannot find all of the other project pieces that it needs and you'll be left with nothing usable.

To correctly copy a project, find the solution or application folder in Windows Explorer and copy the project's *entire* directory hierarchy. Alternatively, you can compress the project directory into a compressed or zipped file and then copy that. Just be sure that whatever copying method you use brings along *all* of the project's files.

Note that you can delete the `bin` and `obj` subdirectories if you like to save space. Visual Studio will re-create them when it needs them later.

Compressing a project into an archive is very useful because it keeps all of its files together in a package. In particular, if you ever need to e-mail a project to someone (for example, if you e-mail me at RodStephens@CSharpHelper.com *for help), you can remove the* bin *and* obj *directories, compress the project folder, and e-mail the package as a single file. (If you're sending the project to your instructor as part of an assignment, rename the compressed file so it contains your name and the name of the assignment, for example,* RodStephens6-1.zip.*)*

EXPLORING THE IDE

The Visual Studio IDE contains a huge number of menus, toolbars, windows, wizards, editors, and other components to help you build applications. Some of these, such as the Solution Explorer and the Properties window, you will use every time you work on a program. Others, such as the Breakpoints window and the Connect to Device dialog box, are so specialized that it may be years before you need them.

Figure 1-5 shows the IDE with a simple project loaded with some of the IDE's most important pieces marked. The following list describes those pieces.

1. **Menus** — The menus provide all sorts of useful commands. Exactly which commands are available, which are enabled, and even which menus are visible depends on what kind of editor is open in the editing area (#4). Some particularly useful menus include File (opening old projects and creating new ones), View (finding windows), Project (adding new forms and other items to a project), Debug (build, run, and debug the project), and Format (arrange controls on a form).

2. **Toolbars** — The toolbars provide shortcuts for executing commands similar to those in the menus. Use the Tools menu's Customize command to determine which toolbars are visible.

3. **Solution Explorer** — The Solution Explorer lists the files in the project. One of the most important is Form1.cs, which defines the controls and code for the form named Form1. If you double-click a file in the Solution Explorer, the IDE opens it in the editing area.

4. **Editing Area** — The editing area displays files in appropriate editors. Most often you will use this area to design a form (place controls on it and set their properties) and write code for the form, but you can also use this area to edit other files such as text files, bitmaps, and icons.

5. **Toolbox** — The Toolbox contains controls and components that you can place on a form. Select a tool and then click and drag to put a copy of the tool on the form. Notice that the Toolbox groups controls in tabs (All Windows Forms, Common Controls, Containers, Menus & Toolbars, and so on) to make finding the controls you need easier.

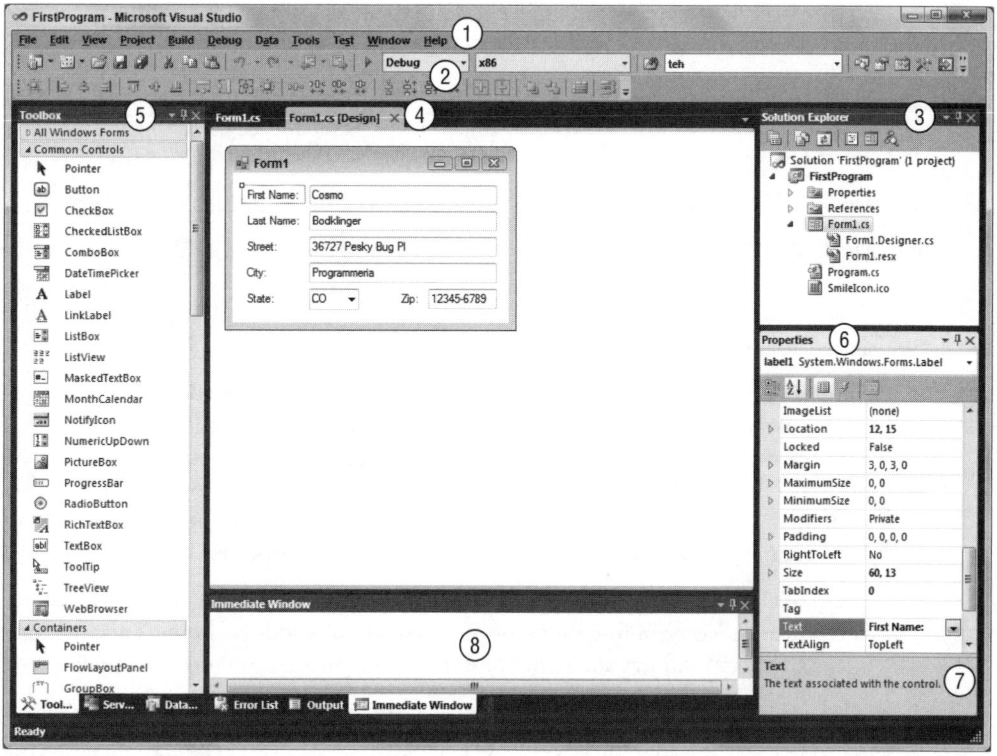

FIGURE 1-5

6. **Properties Window** — The Properties window lets you set control properties. Click a control on the Form Designer (shown in the editing area in Figure 1-5) to select it, or click and drag to select multiple controls. Then use the Properties window to set the control(s) properties. Notice that the top of the Properties window shows the name (`label1`) and type (`System.Windows.Forms.Label`) of the currently selected control. The currently selected property in Figure 1-5 is `Text`, and it has the value `First Name:`.

7. **Property Description** — The property description gives you a reminder about the current property's purpose. In Figure 1-5, it says that the `Text` property gives the text associated with the control. (Duh!)

8. **Other Windows** — This area typically contains other useful windows. The tabs at the bottom let you quickly switch between different windows.

Figure 1-5 shows a fairly typical arrangement of windows but Visual Studio is extremely flexible so you can rearrange the windows if you like. You can hide or show windows; make windows floating or docked to various parts of the IDE; make windows part of a tab group; and make windows automatically hide themselves if you don't need them constantly.

If you look closely at the right side of the title bar above one of the windows in Figure 1-5, for example, the Properties window, you'll see three icons: a dropdown arrow (▾), a thumbtack (📌), and an **X** .

If you click the dropdown arrow (or right-click the window's title bar), a menu appears with the following choices:

➤ **Float** — The window breaks free of wherever it's docked and floats above the IDE. You can drag it around and it will not re-dock. To make it dockable again, open the menu again and select Dock.

➤ **Dock** — The window can dock to various parts of the IDE. I'll say more about this shortly.

➤ **Dock as Tabbed Document** — The window becomes a tab in a tabbed area similar to #8 in Figure 1-5. Unfortunately, it's not always obvious which area will end up holding the window. To make the window a tab in a specific tabbed area, make it dockable and drag it onto a tab (described shortly).

➤ **Auto Hide** — The window shrinks itself to a small label stuck to one of the IDE's edges and its thumbtack icon turns sideways (-=) to indicate that the window is auto-hiding. If you float the mouse over the label, the window reappears. As long as the mouse remains over the expanded window, it stays put, but if you move the mouse off the window, it auto-hides itself again. Select Auto Hide again or click the sideways thumbtack to turn off auto-hiding. Auto-hiding gets windows out of the way so you can work in a bigger editing area.

➤ **Hide** — The window disappears completely. To get the window back, you'll need to find it in the menus. You can find many of the most useful windows in the View menu, the View menu's Other Windows submenu, and the Debug menu's Windows submenu.

The thumbtack in a window's title bar works just like the dropdown menu's Auto Hide command does. Click the thumbtack to turn on auto-hiding. Expand the window and click the sideways thumbtack to turn off auto-hiding. (Turning auto-hiding off is sometimes called *pinning* the window.)

The ✕ symbol in the window's title bar hides the window just like the dropdown menu's Hide command does.

In addition to using a window's title bar menu and icons, you can drag windows into new positions. As long as a window is dockable or part of a tabbed window, you can grab its title bar and drag it to a new position.

As you drag the window, the IDE displays little drop targets to let you dock the window in various positions. If you move the window so the mouse is over a drop target, the IDE displays a translucent blue area to show where the window will land if you drop it. If you drop when the mouse is not over a drop target, the window becomes floating.

Figure 1-6 shows the Properties window being dragged in the IDE. The mouse is over the right drop target above the editing area so, as the translucent blue area shows, dropping it there would dock the window to the right side of the editing area.

The drop area just to the left of the mouse represents a tabbed area. If you drop on this kind of target, the window becomes a tab in that area.

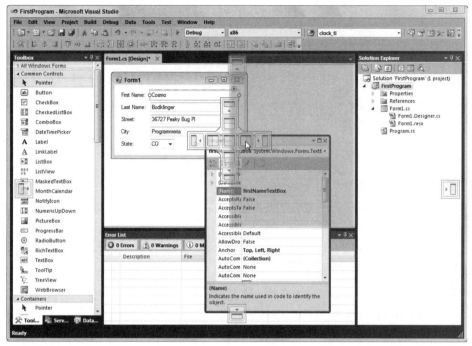

FIGURE 1-6

CUSTOMIZATION MODERATION

Visual Studio lets you move, dock, float, hide, auto-hide, and tabify windows. If you have multiple monitors, you can float a window and move them to other monitors, giving you a larger editing area. It's so flexible that it can present as many different faces as a politician during an election year.

Feel free to customize the IDE to suit your needs, but if you do, keep in mind that your version of Visual Studio may look nothing like the pictures in this book. To minimize confusion, you may want to keep the IDE looking more or less like Figure 1-5, at least until you get a better sense of which tools will be most useful to you.

TRY IT

In this Try It, you prepare for later work throughout the book. You locate web resources that you can use when you have questions or run into trouble. You create and run a program, explore the project's folder hierarchy, and make a copy of the project. You also get a chance to experiment a bit with the IDE, displaying new toolbars, moving windows around, and generally taking the IDE for a test drive and kicking the tires.

Note that the solutions for this lesson's Try It and exercises are not all available on the book's web site. The Try It and some of the exercises ask you to experiment with the IDE rather than producing a finished program, so there's really nothing to download. In later lessons, example solutions to the Try It and exercises are available on the book's web sites.

Lesson Requirements

In this lesson, you:

➤ Find and bookmark useful web resources.

➤ Launch Visual Studio and start a new Visual C# project.

➤ Experiment with the IDE's layout by displaying the Debug toolbar, pinning the Toolbox, and displaying the Output window.

➤ Run the program.

➤ Find the program's executable, copy it to the desktop, and run it there.

➤ Copy the project folder to a new location and make changes to the copy.

➤ Compress the project folder to make a backup.

Hints

➤ When you create a new project, be sure to specify a good location so you can find it later.

➤ Before you compress the project, remove the `bin` and `obj` directories to save space.

Step-by-Step

➤ Find and bookmark useful web resources.

1. Open your favorite web browser.

2. Create a new bookmark folder named C#. (See the browser's documentation if you don't know how to make a bookmark folder.)

3. Go to the following web sites and bookmark the ones you like (feel free to search for others, too):

➤ My C# Helper web site (`CSharpHelper.com`).

➤ This book's web page (`CSharpHelper.com/24hour.html`).

➤ This book's Wrox web page (go to `www.wrox.com` and search for *Stephens' C# Programming with Visual Studio 2010 24-Hour Trainer*).

➤ Visual C# Express Edition MSDN forum (`social.msdn.microsoft.com/ Forums/en-US/Vsexpressvcs/threads`)

➤ Visual C# IDE MSDN forum (`social.msdn.microsoft.com/Forums/en-US/csharpide/threads`)

➤ Visual C# Language MSDN forum (`social.msdn.microsoft.com/Forums/en-US/csharplanguage/threads`)

➤ Visual C# General MSDN forum (`social.msdn.microsoft.com/Forums/en-US/csharpgeneral/threads`)

➤ Launch Visual Studio and start a new Visual C# project.

1. If you don't have a desktop icon for Visual Studio, create one.

   a. Open the Windows Start menu and find Visual Studio. Either browse for it (it's probably in a folder named Visual Studio 2010 and the program is called Visual Studio 2010) or use the menu's search textbox to find it.

   b. Right-click the program, open the Send To submenu, and select Desktop (Create Shortcut).

2. Launch Visual Studio. Double-click the desktop icon or open the system's Start menu and select the Visual Studio 2010 program.

3. Create a new project.

   a. Press [Ctrl]+[Shift]+N or open the IDE's File menu, expand the New submenu, and select Project.

   b. Expand the Visual C# project types folder and select the Windows Forms Application template.

   c. Enter a project name and a good, easy-to-find location like the desktop or a folder named C# Projects on the desktop. Uncheck the Create Directory for Solution box and click OK.

➤ Experiment with the IDE's layout by displaying the Debug toolbar, pinning the Toolbox, and displaying the Output window.

1. Open the Tools menu and select Customize. On the Customize dialog box, select the Toolbars tab and check the box next to the Debug toolbar. Experiment with the other toolbars if you like. Close the dialog box when you're done.

2. If the Toolbox is auto-hiding (it should be after you first install Visual Studio), float the mouse over it until it expands. Click the thumbtack to pin it.

3. To display the Output window, open the View menu and select Output. Grab the Output window's title bar and drag it around. Move it over some drop targets to see where it lands. When you're finished, drop it at the bottom of the IDE as shown in Figure 1-5.

➤ Run the program.

1. Press F5 or open the Debug menu and select Start Debugging.

> **2.** Try out the form's minimize, maximize, and close buttons, and the commands in the form's system menu. Move the form around and resize it. Marvel at the fact that you didn't need to write any code!

➤ Find the program's executable, copy it to the desktop, and run it there.

> **1.** Start Windows Explorer and navigate to the location that you specified when you created the new program.

> **2.** There you should find a folder named after the program. Open that folder and examine the files inside. Notice the .sln file that you can double-click to reopen the solution in Visual Studio. Notice also the bin and obj directories.

> **3.** Enter the bin directory and move into its Debug subdirectory. It contains several files including the executable, named after the program but with the .exe extension. Right-click the executable and select Copy.

> **4.** Right-click the desktop and select Paste to copy the executable to the desktop.

> **5.** Double-click the copy of the executable on the desktop.

➤ Copy the project folder to a new location and make changes to the copy.

> **1.** In Windows Explorer, return to the location where you created the project and you can see the project's folder.

> **2.** Right-click the project's folder and select Copy.

> **3.** Right-click the desktop and select Paste to copy the project folder.

> **4.** Open the copied project folder and double-click the .sln file to open the copied project in Visual Studio. If the form doesn't open in the Form Designer (#4 in Figure 1-5), look in Solution Explorer and double-click the file Form1.cs.

> **5.** In the Form Designer, grab the handle on the form's lower-left corner and resize the form to make it tall and skinny.

> **6.** Run the modified program. Then go back to the original project (which should still be running in another instance of Visual Studio) and run it. Notice that the two versions display forms of different sizes.

➤ Compress the project folder to make a backup.

> **1.** In Windows Explorer, return to the project's folder. Find and delete the bin and obj directories.

> **2.** Move up one level so you are in the location you specified when you created the project and you can see the project's folder. Right-click the folder, expand the Send To submenu, and select Compressed (Zipped) Folder.

> **3.** E-mail copies of your first project to all of your friends and relatives!

 Please select Lesson 1 on the DVD to view the video that accompanies this lesson.

EXERCISES

1. Build a solution that contains two projects. (Create a project named Project1. Check the Create Directory for Solution box and name the solution TwoProjects. Then open the File menu, expand the Add submenu, and select New Project to add a new project named Project2.)

2. This chapter explains only a tiny fraction of the ways you can customize Visual Studio. Try another one by making your own toolbar. Select the Tools menu's Customize command. On the Toolbars tab, click the New button and name the new toolbar MyTools. Then on the Commands tab, drag commands onto the toolbar. Search the command categories for useful tools. The Debug and Format categories contain some useful commands.

3. This chapter also describes only a few of the windows Visual Studio offers. Use the menus to find and display the Output, Immediate, Error List, and Task List windows. Put them all in tabs at the bottom of Visual Studio (#8 in Figure 1-5).

4. Some tools are only available when Visual Studio is in a certain state. Look in the Debug menu's Windows submenu. Then start the program and look there again. Most of those windows are useful only when the program is running and you are debugging it. (I talk about some of them in later lessons.)

5. Later lessons spend a lot of time describing the form and code editors, but Visual Studio includes a lot of other editors, too. To try out the icon editor, open the Project menu and select Add New Item. Open the General category, select Icon File, give the file a good name, and click Add. Use the icon editor to make an icon similar to the one shown in Figure 1-7. Later you can double-click the icon file in the Solution Explorer to reopen the icon in the editor.

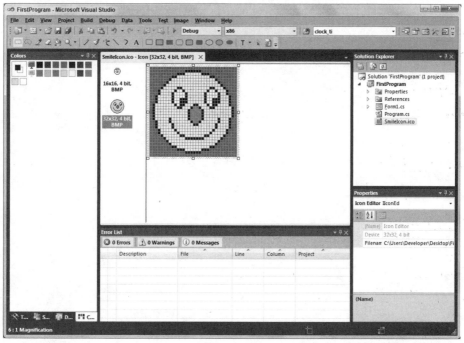

FIGURE 1-7

6.   Make a cursor that looks similar to the icon you built in Exercise 5. After you create the cursor file, right-click below the list of cursor types (initially just "32×32, 1 bit, BMP") and select New Image Type to give the cursor the types "16×16, 24 bit, BMP" and "32×32, 24 bit, BMP." You can copy and paste the images from the icon into the appropriate cursor types. Set each cursor type's hotspot to be the center of the smiley's nose.

> *You can download the solutions to exercises 1, 5, and 6 in the download available on the book's web site at* www.wrox.com *or* www.CSharpHelper .com/24hour.html. *You can find them in the Lesson01 folder.*

Creating Controls

Way back in the computer stone ages, when programmers worked by candlelight on treadle-powered computers and hand-carved wooden monitors, input and output were very simple. The computer wrote text in toxic green on the bottom of a monitor and the text scrolled up as the monitor became full. The user typed on a keyboard to enter text at a single input prompt, and that was about it. Multiple windows performing useful work simultaneously, forms displaying many labels and textboxes, buttons, scrollbars, full-color images, and even mice existed only in the fevered dreams of science-fiction writers.

Today these things are so commonplace that we take them completely for granted. They appear in desktop software, web pages, laptops, handheld computers, and even cell phones.

Building these sorts of objects in the old days would have been extremely difficult, but today it's practically trivial to add them to your application.

You already saw in Lesson 1 how easy it is to make an application (albeit a trivial one) that displays a form that runs independently of the others on the computer. It's almost as easy to use labels, textboxes, buttons, scrollbars, images, menus, popups, and everything else that makes up a modern application.

Visual C# makes all of these objects and more available as controls.

In this lesson, you learn how to add controls to a form. You learn how to size, position, and arrange controls. You also learn how to use a control's properties to change its appearance and behavior at design time and at run time. When you're done with this lesson, you'll be able to build a professional-looking form.

UNDERSTANDING CONTROLS

A *control* is a programming entity that combines a visible appearance on the screen and code to manage it. The code defines the control's appearance and behavior.

For example, a `TextBox` control displays a blank area on the screen where the user can type information. The code inside the control determines how the control draws itself and provides normal textbox features such as multi-line or single-line behavior; scrolling and scrollbars displayed as needed; copy, cut, and paste; a context menu displayed when you right-click the control; the ability to navigate when the user presses the [Tab] key; and much more.

WHAT'S IN A NAME?

By convention, the names of control types (and other types) use *Pascal casing* where multiple words are strung together with the first letter of each word capitalized, for example, TextBox, ProgressBar, Button, and PictureBox.

In addition to controls, Visual C# provides components. A *component* is similar to a control except it has no visible piece on the form. For example, the Timer component acts as a clock to let the program do something at regular intervals. The Timer interacts with the program, but doesn't display anything visible to the user. (Some components such as ErrorProvider and ToolTip may display visible effects on the screen, but the components themselves are not visible on the form.)

The features of controls (and components) fall into three categories: properties, methods, and events.

Properties

A *property* determines the appearance and state of a control. If a Car were a control, its properties would be things like Color, NumberOfCupHolders, CurrentSpeed, and TransmissionType. Your program could set a Car's Color to HotPink (to attract the attention of other drivers) or set its CurrentSpeed to 110 (to attract the attention of the police).

For a programming example, the TextBox control has a Font property that determines the font it uses and a ForeColor property that determines the color of its text.

Methods

A *method* is an action that the control can perform. Your code can call a method to make the control do something. For example, the Car control might have methods such as Start, Stop, EjectPassenger, and OilSlick. Your program could call the OilSlick method to make the car spray oil out the back so you can escape from spies.

For a programming example, the TextBox has a Clear method that blanks the control's text and an AppendText method that adds text to the end of whatever the control is currently displaying.

Events

An *event* occurs when something interesting happens to the control. The control *raises* or *fires* the event to tell the program that something happened. For example, a Car might have RanOutOfGas and Crashed events. The Car control would raise the Crashed event to tell the program that the user had driven it into a tree. The program could then take action such as calling an ambulance and a tree surgeon.

For a programming example, the `TextBox` has a `TextChanged` event that tells the program that its text has changed. When the event occurs, the program could examine the text to see if the user had entered a valid input. For example, if the `TextBox` should hold a number and the user entered "One," the program could beep and change the `TextBox`'s `BackColor` property to `Yellow` to indicate an error.

Later lessons discuss events and the code that handles them in greater detail. This lesson focuses on adding controls to a form, arranging them, and setting their properties.

CREATING CONTROLS

Adding controls to a form is easy. In fact, it's so easy and there are so many different ways to add controls to a form that it takes a while to describe them all.

Start by creating a new project as described in Lesson 1. Open the form in the Form Designer. (If the form isn't already open, double-click it in Solution Explorer.)

The following list describes some of the ways you can put controls on the form:

➤ Click a tool in the Toolbox to select it. Then click and drag on the form. When you release the mouse, Visual Studio creates the control in the area you selected and then selects the pointer in the Toolbox.

➤ Click a tool in the Toolbox to select it. Then hold down the [Ctrl] key while you click and drag on the form to place a copy of the control on the form. When you release the mouse, Visual Studio creates the control in the area you selected and keeps the control's tool selected in the Toolbox so you can make another control of that type.

➤ Double-click a tool in the Toolbox to select it to create an instance of the control on the form at a default size and position. (You'll then probably want to resize and reposition it.)

➤ Select one or more controls that are already on the form. Press [Ctrl]+C to copy them and then press [Ctrl]+V to paste them onto the form. You can even copy and paste from one instance of Visual Studio to another.

➤ Select one or more controls on the form. While holding down the [Ctrl] key, drag the controls to a new location. Visual Studio makes a copy of the controls, leaving the originals where they started.

 There are several ways to select controls on the Form Designer. Click on a control to select only it. Click and drag to select multiple controls.

Hold down the [Shift] or [Ctrl] key while clicking or clicking and dragging to toggle whether controls are in the current selection.

And, if you want to deselect all controls, simply click on the form's surface or press [Esc].

The first method (select a tool and then click and drag to create a control) is probably used most often, but some of the other methods are particularly useful for creating a lot of very similar groups of controls.

For example, the form in Figure 2-1 displays four rows, each of which holds a `Label` and a `TextBox`. You could easily build all of these controls individually, but you can build them even faster by using copy and paste. First place one `Label` and `TextBox` on the form, arrange them next to each other, and give them any property values that you want all of the `Label`s or `TextBox`es to share. (For example, you may want to set their fonts or colors.) Now click and drag to select both controls, copy and paste, and drag the new controls into position. Repeat this two more times and you'll have all of the controls in position. You'll still need to change the `Label`s' text but the basic arrangement will be done without going back and forth to the Toolbox.

FIGURE 2-1

SETTING CONTROL PROPERTIES

After you've added controls to a form, you can use the Properties window to view and change their property values. If you have more than one control selected, the Properties window shows only the properties that the controls have in common.

For example, if you select a `TextBox` and a `Label`, the Properties window shows the `Text` property because both `Label`s and `TextBox`es have a `Text` property. However, it won't display the `Multiline` property because the `TextBox` control has that property but the `Label` control does not.

The Properties window provides special support for many control properties. For example, Figure 2-2 shows the Properties window when a `TextBox` is selected.

Notice that the `Font` property contains its own sub-properties `Name`, `Size`, `Unit`, `Bold`, and so forth. Click the triangle next to a property to expand or collapse it and show or hide its sub-properties.

Also notice in Figure 2-2 the ellipsis to the right of the `Font` property. If you click that ellipsis, the dialog box shown in Figure 2-3 appears. You can use this dialog box to edit the font sub-properties and see a sample of the font.

The Properties window provides appropriate support when it can for other properties. Many properties can hold only certain values. For example, the `Font`'s `Italic`, `Bold`,

FIGURE 2-2

`Strikeout`, and `Underline` sub-properties can only take the values `True` or `False`. The `Font`'s `Unit` sub-property can only take the values `World`, `Pixel`, `Point`, `Inch`, `Document`, and `Millimeter`. In these cases, the Properties window provides a dropdown listing the allowed choices.

Figure 2-4 shows the editor that the Properties window displays when you click the dropdown arrow to the right of a `TextBox`'s `BackColor` property. The Custom tab lets you pick a color from a palette, the Web tab lets you pick standard web page colors, and the System tab lets you pick system colors such as the normal control background color or the menu highlight color.

By using the Properties window's editors and typing in values when there is no editor, you can change a control's appearance and behavior.

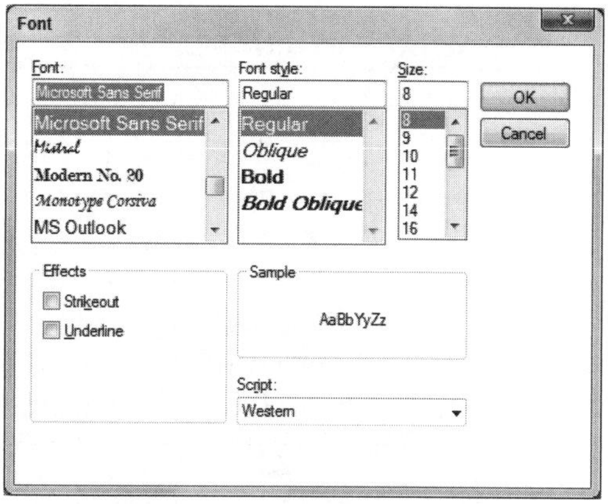

FIGURE 2-3

Control Names

Whenever you create a control, Visual Studio gives it a rather nondescript name such as `label2`, `textBox5`, or `pictureBox1`. Although these names tell you what kind of object the control is, they don't tell you what it is for and that's much more important when you later need to use the control in your code. Names like `firstNameTextBox` and `streetTextBox` are much more meaningful than `textBox3` and `textBox7`.

Note that you don't need to give good names to every control, just the ones that you will need to use in the code. You often don't need to name `Labels`, `GroupBoxes`, and other purely decorative controls.

You can learn more about Microsoft's naming conventions at the web page "Guidelines for Names" at `msdn.microsoft` `.com/library/ms229002.aspx`.

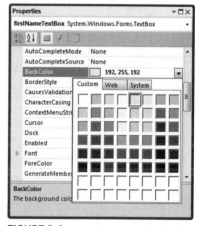

FIGURE 2-4

WHAT'S IN A NAME, REDUX

Earlier in this chapter I said that control *type* names use Pascal casing. By convention, the names of specific instances of controls use *camel casing* where multiple words are strung together with the first letter of each word capitalized, except for the first word. For example, the control type `TextBox` uses Pascal casing and the specific control name `firstNameTextBox` uses camel casing.

It's called camel casing because it sort of looks like a camel lying down: low at the ends with one or more humps in the middle. I guess `stateLabel` would be a dromedary (one-humped) camel, `priceTextBox` would be a Bactrian (two-humped) camel, and `numberOfEmployeesCoveredByPlanTrackBar` would be some sort of camel created by Dr. Seuss.

WHAT'S IN A NAME, PART 3

Most C# developers add a control's type as a suffix to its name as in `firstNameTextBox` or `resultLabel`, but it's becoming more common for developers to use a more generic word such as `Value` or `Field`. The idea is that if you decide to change the type of control that handles the value, you won't need to change the code that refers to the control.

For example, suppose your program uses a `TrackBar` to let the user specify the number of UFO detectors to purchase. If you name this control `numUfoDetectorsValue`, they you won't need to change the code if you later decide to let the user select the value from a `NumericUpDown` control instead of a `TrackBar`.

Some developers even omit the suffix completely as in `numUfoDetectors`, although that can be confusing if you need more than one control to represent a similar concept or you want a variable inside the code that holds the numeric value represented by the control.

For now, I recommend that you stick with the control's full type name as a suffix.

Popular Properties

You'll learn about key control properties as you go along and you can see a summary of key properties for specific controls in Appendix B, but for now Table 2-1 summarizes some of the most useful properties. Note that not all controls have every property. For example, a `Button` cannot display a border so it has no `BorderStyle` property.

TABLE 2-1

PROPERTY	PURPOSE
Anchor	Determines how the control sizes itself to use the available space. This property is described further in Lesson 3.
AutoSize	Determines whether the control automatically resizes itself to fit its contents. This can be `True` or `False`. By default, `Labels` are born with `AutoSize = True`.
BackColor	Determines the control's background color.
BackgroundImage	Determines the image that the control displays.
BorderStyle	Determines whether the control displays a border. This can be `None`, `FixedSingle`, or `Fixed3D`.
Dock	Determines how the control sizes itself to use the available space. This property is described further in Lesson 3.

PROPERTY	PURPOSE
Enabled	Determines whether the control will interact with the user. Many controls display a special appearance when disabled such as being grayed out. This can be `True` or `False`.
Font	Determines the font that the control uses to display text.
ForeColor	Determines the control's foreground color. For controls that display text, this is usually the text's color.
Image	Determines the image that the control displays. (Some controls have `Image`, others have `BackgroundImage`, a few have both, and some cannot display any image. No one said this was completely consistent!)
Items	For controls such as `ListBox` and `ComboBox`, this is the list of items that the user can select.
Location	Gives the control's location in pixels from the upper-left corner of whatever it is in (for now, assume it's in the form). `Location` includes `X` and `Y` subproperties. For example, the value `(10, 20)` means the control is 10 pixels from the form's left edge and 20 pixels from its top edge.
Name	Gives the control a name that your code can use. You should always give a *good* name to any control that you will refer to in code.
Size	Gives the control's width and height in pixels. For example, the value `(75, 30)` means the control is 75 pixels wide and 30 pixels tall.
Tag	This property can hold any value that you want. For example, you might put text or a number in several `Buttons`' `Tag` properties so the code can easily tell the `Buttons` apart.
Text	Many controls have a `Text` property that determines what the control displays. For `Labels` and `TextBoxes`, `Text` determines the text they show (pretty obvious). For controls such as `ComboBoxes` and `ListBoxes`, `Text` determines the control's current selection. For a `Form`, which in some sense is really just another kind of control, `Text` determines what's displayed in the title bar.
TextAlign	Determines how text is aligned within the control.
Visible	Determines whether the control is visible. This can be `True` or `False`. Set it to `False` to hide a control from the user.

If you want some practice with these properties, create a new project and give them a try. Create a `Button` and set its `Text` property. Also click the form and set *its* `Text` property. Change the form's `Font` property and see what happens. You can experiment with some of the other properties such as `Image` and `ForeColor` if you like.

Modifying Properties in Code

This lesson doesn't really go into handling control events very much (that's the subject of Lesson 4) but I do want to explain how to set properties in code. Besides, it's easy, sort of fun, and it'll let you make a program that does something more than just sitting there looking pretty.

First, to make a simple event handler, double-click the control in the Form Designer. That opens the Code Editor and creates an empty event handler for the control's default event. For `Button` controls, that's the `Click` event. Whenever the user clicks the control at run time, it raises its `Click` event and this code executes.

To change a property in code, type the control's name, a dot (or period), the name of the property, an equals sign, and finally the value that you want to give the property. Finish the line of code with a semi-colon. For example, the following statement sets the `Left` property of the label named `greetingLabel` to 100. That moves the label so it is 100 pixels from the left edge of its container.

```
greetingLabel.Left = 100;
```

The following code shows a complete event handler.

```
// Move the Label.
private void moveLabelButton_Click(object sender, EventArgs e)
{
    greetingLabel.Left = 100;
}
```

In this code, I typed the first line that starts with two slashes. That line is a *comment*, a piece of text that is contained in the code but that is not executed by the program. Any text that comes after the // characters is ignored until the end of the current line. You can (and should) use comments to make your code easier to understand.

I also typed the line that sets the `Label`'s `Left` property.

Visual Studio typed the rest when I double-clicked the `moveLabelButton` control. You don't need to worry about the details of this code right now, but briefly the `sender` parameter is the object that raised the event (the `Button` in this example) and the `e` parameter gives extra information about the event. The extra information can be useful for some events (for example, in the `MouseClick` event it tells where the mouse was clicked), but it's not very interesting for a `Button`'s `Click` event.

Simple numeric values such as the 100 used in this example are easy to set in code, but some properties aren't numbers. In that case, you must set them to values that have the proper data type.

For example, a `Label`'s `Text` property is a string so you must assign it a string value. The following code sets the `greetingLabel` control's `Text` property to the string `Hello`.

```
greetingLabel.Text = "Hello";
```

Other property values have more exotic data types such as `Date`, `AnchorStyles`, `Point`, and `BindingContext`. When you set these properties, you must make sure that the values you give them have the correct data types. I'm going to ignore most of these for now, but one data type that is relatively simple and useful is `Color`.

Notice that you must include the string "Hello" in double quotes to tell Visual C# that this is a literal string and not some sort of C# command. If you leave the quotes off, Visual C# gets confused and gives you the error "The name 'Hello' does not exist in the current context."

Over time, you'll get used to messages like this and they'll make sense. In this case, the message just means, "I don't know what the word 'Hello' means."

A control's `ForeColor` and `BackColor` properties have the data type `Color` so you cannot simply set them to strings such as `Red` or `Blue`. Instead you must set them equal to something that also has the type `Color`. The easiest way to do that is to use the colors predefined by the `Color` class. This may seem a bit confusing but in practice it's actually quite easy.

For example, the following two statements set a `Label`'s `ForeColor` and `BackColor` properties to `HotPink` and `Blue`, respectively.

```
greetingLabel.BackColor = Color.HotPink;
greetingLabel.ForeColor = Color.Blue;
```

The following code shows how the MoveButton example program, which is available as part of this lesson's code download on the book's web site, changes several `Label` properties when you click a `Button`.

```
// Change a Label's properties.
private void moveLabelButton_Click(object sender, EventArgs e)
{
    greetingLabel.Left = 100;
    greetingLabel.Text = "Hello";
    greetingLabel.BackColor = Color.HotPink;
    greetingLabel.ForeColor = Color.Blue;
}
```

ARRANGING CONTROLS

The Form Designer provides several tools to help you arrange controls at design time. The following sections describe some of the most useful: snap lines, arrow keys, the Format menu, and the Layout toolbar.

Snap Lines

When you drag a control around on the form, the Form Designer displays *snap lines* that show how the control lines up with the form and other controls. Figure 2-5 shows the Form Designer displaying light blue snap lines indicating that the control is a standard distance (12 pixels) away from the form's top and left edges.

You can drag the control away from this position and, if you do so, the snap lines disappear. When you drag the control close to one of the form's edges, the control jumps to the standard distance and the Form Designer displays the snap lines again.

The Form Designer also displays snap lines to show how controls align. In Figure 2-6, I dragged a second button below the first. Different snap lines show that:

➤ The second button is the standard distance from the form's left edge.

➤ The second button's left and right edges line up with the first button's edges.

➤ The second button is a standard distance (6 pixels) below the first button.

FIGURE 2-5

Other snap lines show how the control contents line up. In Figure 2-7 snap lines show that the Label is the standard distance from the second Button, and that the Label's text baseline lines up with the baseline of the second Button.

For a more realistic example, consider Figure 2-8. In this figure I was laying out a small data entry form, and I wanted all of the labels and textboxes to line up nicely. In this figure, snap lines show that the Street textbox is lined up on the left and right with the other textboxes, is a standard distance from the textboxes above and below, is a standard distance from the form's right edge, and has its baseline lined up with the Street label.

FIGURE 2-6

Arrow Keys

In addition to dragging controls with the mouse, you can move controls by pressing the arrow keys. Select one or more controls and then use the left, right, up, and down arrow keys to move the control(s) one pixel at a time. This method is slower than using the mouse but gives you finer control.

When you move controls with the arrow keys, the Form Designer doesn't display snap lines so you may want to keep an eye on the control's Location property in the Properties window to see where it is.

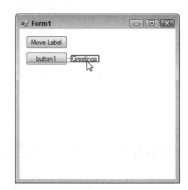

FIGURE 2-7

The Format Menu and Layout Toolbar

The Format menu contains many commands that arrange one or more controls. Table 2-2 summarizes the Format menu's submenus.

FIGURE 2-8

TABLE 2-2

SUBMENU	COMMANDS
Align	Aligns groups of controls on their lefts, middles, rights, tops, bottoms, and centers.
Make Same Size	Makes controls have the same width, height, or both.
Horizontal Spacing	Adjusts the horizontal spacing between controls. It can make the space between controls equal, smaller, larger, or zero.
Vertical Spacing	Works like the Horizontal Spacing submenu except it adjusts the vertical spacing between controls.
Center in Form	Centers the controls vertically or horizontally in their container. If the controls are inside a container like a `Panel` or `GroupBox`, these commands center the controls within the container, not the form.
Order	These commands send a control to the front or back of the stacking order. This is useful if you have controls that overlap so some are behind others.

The Layout toolbar contains the same commands as the Format menu but in a handy toolbar so they're easier to use. The buttons display little pictures that show how they align controls.

How these tools arrange controls depends on how you select the controls. One of the selected controls, normally the first one you select, is the group's dominant control. The dominant control is marked with white boxes while the other controls are marked with black boxes.

When you use an arranging tool, the dominant control determines how the others are arranged. For example, if you select the Format ⇨ Align ⇨ Lefts command, the other controls are moved so their left edges line up with the dominant control's left edge.

To change the dominant control in a selected group, click on the one you want to be dominant (without holding down the [Ctrl] or [Shift] keys).

TRY IT

In this Try It, you get some practice building a user interface. You place controls on a form and arrange them so they line up nicely. You also get some practice setting control properties at design time and changing them at run time.

You can download the code and resources for this Try It from the book's web page at www.wrox.com *or* www.CSharpHelper.com/24hour.html. *You can find them in the Lesson02 folder in the download.*

Lesson Requirements

In this lesson, you:

➤ Add controls to a form and arrange them as shown in Figure 2-9. (Note the form's title and the fact that the form has a non-resizable border.)

➤ Give the key controls names.

➤ Set properties at design time on the result label (at the bottom in Figure 2-9) to make the label:

   ➤ Display its text centered.

   ➤ Show a border.

   ➤ Use a 16-point Comic Sans MS font.

   ➤ Remain invisible until the user clicks one of the buttons.

➤ Make the OK button the form's default button so it fires when the user presses [Enter]. Make the Cancel button the form's cancel button so it fires when the user presses [Esc].

➤ Add code behind the OK button to display the result label with a green background as shown in Figure 2-9.

➤ Add code behind the Cancel button to display the result label with a hot pink background and the text "Operation Canceled."

FIGURE 2-9

Hints

➤ Create the First Name label and textbox first and arrange them. Then copy and paste them to make more labels and textboxes.

➤ Use the Format menu or Layout toolbar to center the buttons and the result label.

Step-by-Step

➤ Add controls to a form and arrange them as shown in Figure 2-9. (Note the form's title and the fact that the form has a non-resizable border.)

   1. Start a new project named NewCustomer. Remember to put it somewhere easy to find.

   2. Use the Properties window to set the form's Text property to "New Customer".

3. Use the Properties window to set the form's `FormBorderStyle` property to `FixedDialog`. (Feel free to experiment with the other values.)

4. Create the First Name `TextBox`.

    a. Click the Toolbox's `TextBox` tool and then click and drag to place a `TextBox` on the form.

    b. Drag the `TextBox` into the form's upper-right corner until the snap lines show that it is a standard distance from the top and right edges of the form.

5. Create the First Name `Label`.

    a. Click the Toolbox's `Label` tool and then click and drag to create the `Label`.

    b. Drag the `Label` to the form's upper-left corner so the snap lines show that the `Label` is a standard distance from the form's left edge and that its baseline aligns with the `TextBox`'s baseline.

    c. To determine the `Label`'s width, you need to set its text. Use the Properties window to set the `Label`'s `Text` property to `"First Name"`.

    d. Click the `TextBox`. Click the drag handle on the `TextBox`'s left edge and drag it until it is a standard distance from the `Label`.

6. Make copies of the `Label` and `TextBox`.

    a. Click and drag to select both the `Label` and `TextBox`.

    b. Press [Ctrl]+C to copy the controls. Press [Ctrl]+V to paste new copies of the controls.

    c. With the new controls still selected, click and drag the `TextBox` until the snap lines show it is a standard distance away from the `TextBox` above and the form's right edge.

    d. Use the Properties window to set the `Label`'s `Text` property to `"Last Name"`.

    e. Repeat this four more times (using appropriate `Text` values) until you have five rows of `Labels` and `TextBoxes`.

7. Make the ZIP `Label`.

    a. Set the bottom `TextBox`'s `Text` property to `12345-6789`. Then use the `TextBox`'s left drag handle to make the `TextBox` smaller so it's a bit bigger than its `Text` value (see Figure 2-9).

    b. Create a `Label` for the ZIP code and set its `Text` property to `ZIP`. Drag it so the snap lines show its baseline aligns with the baseline for the `Label` and `TextBox` on that same line, and it is the standard distance to the left of the `TextBox`.

    c. Use the Properties window to set the `TextBox`'s `TextAlign` property to `Right`.

8. Make the State `ComboBox`.

    a. Use the Toolbox to make a `ComboBox` (see Figure 2-9). Set its `Text` property to `WW` and resize the box so the text fits reasonably well.

b. Drag the ComboBox so the snap lines show its baseline aligns with the Labels on that row and its left aligns with the left edges of the TextBoxes above.

c. With the ComboBox selected, look in the Properties window and click the Items property. Then click the ellipsis (...) button on the right to open the String Collection Editor. Enter CO, AZ, WY, UT, and any other state abbreviations that you want to use and click OK. (If you want to enter "Confusion" and "Denial," you'll need to make the ComboBox wider.)

d. Use the Properties window to set the DropDownStyle property to DropDownList.

The DropDownStyle value Simple displays a TextBox where the user can type and a list below it.

The value DropDown displays a TextBox where the user can type and a drop-down arrow that makes a dropdown list appear.

The value DropDownList is similar to DropDown except the user can select only from the dropdown list and cannot type new values. DropDownList is often the best choice because it prevents the user from typing garbage.

9. Make the Buttons.

a. Double-click the Toolbox's Button tool twice to make two Buttons.

b. Drag one Button so it is a nice distance below the TextBoxes. Drag the other Button so it's aligned horizontally with the first, positioning it some reasonable distance to the side (the exact distance doesn't matter here).

c. Click and drag to select both Buttons. Select Format ⇨ Center in Form ⇨ Horizontally.

d. Use the Properties window to give the Buttons the Text values OK and Cancel.

10. Use the Toolbox to make the result Label. (Don't worry too much about its size and position right now. Just drop it somewhere close to where it is shown in Figure 2-9.)

➤ Give the key controls names.

1. Give the key controls the names shown in Table 2-3. You don't need to give names to the other controls because the program won't need to refer to them. (Actually this example doesn't refer to the TextBoxes or ComboBox either, but a real program certainly would. A form wouldn't contain TextBoxes and ComboBoxes that it won't use.)

TABLE 2-3

CONTROL	NAME
First Name TextBox	firstNameTextBox
Last Name TextBox	lastNameTextBox

CONTROL	NAME
Street TextBox	streetTextBox
City TextBox	cityTextBox
State ComboBox	stateComboBox
ZIP TextBox	zipTextBox
OK Button	okButton
Cancel Button	cancelButton
Result Label	resultLabel

➤ Set properties at design time on the result label (at the bottom in Figure 2-9) to make the label:

  ➤ Display its text centered.

    1. Set the Label's TextAlign property to MiddleCenter. (Use the Properties window's TextAlign editor to select the middle position.)

    2. Set the Label's AutoSize property to False.

    3. Set the Label's Size property to 218, 37. (Or expand the Size property and set the Width and Height sub-properties separately.)

    4. Use the Format menu or Layout toolbar to center the Label on the form.

  ➤ Show a border.

    1. Set the Label's BorderStyle property to Fixed3D.

  ➤ Use a 16-point Comic Sans MS font.

    1. Expand the Property window's Font entry. Set the Name sub-property to "Comic Sans MS". Set the Size sub-property to 16.

  ➤ Remain invisible until the user clicks one of the buttons.

    1. Set the Label's Visible property to False.

➤ Make the OK button the form's default button so it fires when the user presses [Enter]. Make the Cancel button the form's cancel button so it fires when the user presses [Esc].

  1. Click the form and use the Properties window to set the form's AcceptButton property to the accept button okButton.

  2. Similarly set the form's CancelButton property to the cancel button cancelButton.

➤ Add code behind the OK button to display the result label with a green background as shown in Figure 2-9.

  1. Double-click the OK button to create an event handler for its Click event.

2. Type the bold text in the following code so the event handler looks like this:

```
// Create the new customer.
private void okButton_Click(object sender, EventArgs e)
{
    resultLabel.Text = "New User Created";
    resultLabel.BackColor = Color.LightGreen;
    resultLabel.Visible = true;
}
```

➤ Add code behind the Cancel button to display the result label with a hot pink background and the text "Operation Canceled."

1. Double-click the Cancel button to create an event handler for its Click event.

2. Type the bold text in the following code so the event handler looks like this:

```
// Don't create the new customer.
private void cancelButton_Click(object sender, EventArgs e)
{
    resultLabel.Text = "Operation Canceled";
    resultLabel.BackColor = Color.HotPink;
    resultLabel.Visible = true;
}
```

Now run the code and experiment with the program. Notice what happens when you press the [Enter] and [Esc] keys while focus is in a TextBox. See what happens if focus is on one of the buttons.

 Please select Lesson 2 on the DVD to view the video that accompanies this lesson.

EXERCISES

1. Build a checkerboard similar to the one shown in Figure 2-10. (Hints: The squares are PictureBoxes with different background colors. Give the form a bluish background. Finally, use the Format menu or Layout toolbar to align the controls.)

2. Make a tic-tac-toe (or naughts-and-crosses) board similar to the one shown in Figure 2-11. (Hints: Make three labels for each square, named after the rows and columns. For the upper-left square, name them x00Label for the little X label, o00Label for the little Y label, and taken00Label for the big label. Give the smaller labels Click event handlers that set the Text

FIGURE 2-10

property of the big label appropriately. Don't worry about the rules such as not allowing someone to claim a square that is already claimed.)

3. Modify the tic-tac-toe program from Exercise 2 so instead of displaying X or O in each square, it displays a picture. Use your favorite football team logos, a cat and a dog, your picture and your boss's, or whatever. (Hints: Use `PictureBoxes` instead of the large `Labels`. Add two hidden `PictureBoxes` to the form. To set their `Image` properties, click the ellipsis next to the `Image` property in the Properties window, click the Import button, and browse for the image files. Finally, instead of setting a `Label`'s `Text` property, the `Click` event handlers should set the appropriate `PictureBox`'s `Image` property equal to one of the hidden `PictureBox`'s `Image` properties. Set all `PictureBoxes`' `SizeMode` properties to `Zoom`.)

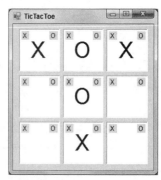

FIGURE 2-11

4. Make a program with a `Label` that says "Move Me" and four `Buttons` with text (0, 0), (200, 200), (200, 0), and (0, 200). Make each `Button` move the `Label` to the corresponding position by setting its `Left` and `Top` properties.

5. The solution to Exercise 4 moves its `Label` in two steps by setting its `Left` and `Top` properties. Modify the program so it sets the `Label`'s `Location` property in a single step using code similar to this:

```
moveMeLabel.Location = new Point(0, 0);
```

6. Build a menu selection form similar to the one shown in Figure 2-12. (Hints: Copy and paste the `Labels` and `TextBoxes` from the Try It program. To set the `PictureBox`'s image, look in the Properties window and click the ellipsis next to the `Image` property. In the Select Resource dialog box, click Import and browse to select a picture. Finally, set the `PictureBox`'s `SizeMode` property to `AutoSize`.)

FIGURE 2-12

 You can download the solutions to these exercises from the book's web page at `www.wrox.com` *or* `www.CSharpHelper.com/24hour.html`*. You can find them in the Lesson02 folder.*

Making Controls Arrange Themselves

Lesson 2 explained how to add controls to a form and arrange them nicely. Using those techniques, you can create forms like the one shown in Figure 3-1.

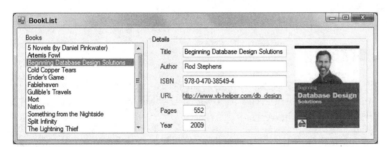

FIGURE 3-1

That form looks okay in Figure 3-1, but what if the user enlarges the form as shown in Figure 3-2? Pretty lame, huh? Although the form is bigger, the areas that contain data are not.

FIGURE 3-2

The URL for the book selected in Figure 3-2 is too long to fit within the `GroupBox`, so it is truncated even though the form has extra wasted space on the right. The `ListBox` isn't big enough to display all of its items even though there's wasted space at the bottom. It would be nice if the controls rearranged themselves to use the available space and display the entire URL and more list items.

Figure 3-3 shows another problem with this form. If the user shrinks the form, the `TextBoxes` and URL `LinkLabel` are chopped off, the Year `Label` and `TextBox` are chopped in half vertically, the `ListBox` doesn't fit, and the cover picture is completely missing.

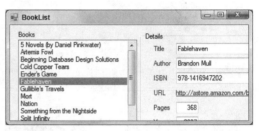

FIGURE 3-3

The program would look nicer if the controls were shrunk so you could at least see their edges. Some of the values still wouldn't fit but at least the form wouldn't look so amateurish. You could even make the form refuse to shrink so it's too short to display the Year controls.

This lesson explains some simple ways you can make controls rearrange themselves to take advantage of whatever space is available, and how to give the form minimum and maximum sizes so the user can't make it completely useless.

RESTRICTING FORM SIZE

Forms (and in fact all controls) have `MinimumSize` and `MaximumSize` properties that you can use to restrict the form's size. Simply set these properties to a width and height (or set their `Width` and `Height` sub-properties) and the form does the rest.

For example, to prevent the user from making the form shown in Figure 3-3 too small, you can set the form's `MinimumSize` property to `663, 233`.

USING ANCHOR PROPERTIES

The `MinimumSize` property prevents the user from making a form too small but it doesn't solve the problem shown in Figure 3-2. When the user resizes a form, it would be nice for controls to change their sizes to match.

The `Anchor` property lets a control resize itself when its container resizes. This property can take one or more of the values `Top`, `Bottom`, `Left`, and `Right`, in any combination. These values indicate that the control's edge should remain the same distance from the corresponding edge of its container.

For example, initially a control's `Anchor` property is set to `Top Left` so it remains the same distance from its container's top and left edges. If you resize the form, the control doesn't move.

For a more interesting example, suppose you place a `TextBox` on a form, set its `Multiline` property to `True`, arrange it so its edges are 12 pixels from the edges of the form, and set its `Anchor` property to `Top`, `Bottom`, `Left`, `Right`. Then when you resize the form, the `TextBox` resizes itself so its edges remain 12 pixels from the form's edges.

If an `Anchor`'s *values don't include either* `Left/Right` *or* `Top/Bottom`, *the control moves to keep itself the same distance from the middle of the form. For example, if a* `Button`'s `Anchor` *property is* `Bottom`, *it moves so it remains the same distance from the horizontal middle of the form.*

This fact lets you keep one or more controls centered. For example, place several `Buttons` *near the bottom of a form and use the Format menu to center them horizontally. Now if you set their* `Anchor` *properties to* `Bottom`, *the group of* `Buttons` *remains centered when the form resizes.*

The `Anchor` *property cannot resize a control such as a* `Label` *or* `LinkLabel` *if that control has* `AutoSize` *set to* `True`. *In that case the control has its own ideas about how big it should be.*

To set the `Anchor` property at design time, you can type a value like `Top, Left, Right` into the Properties window or you can use the Properties window's `Anchor` editor.

To use the editor, click the `Anchor` property in the Properties window. Then click the dropdown arrow to the right to make the editor shown in Figure 3-4 appear. Click the skinny rectangles to select or deselect the anchors that you want to use. (In Figure 3-4 the top, bottom, and left anchors are selected.) When you're finished, press [Enter] to accept your changes or [Esc] to cancel them.

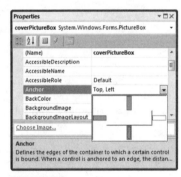

FIGURE 3-4

Using the `Anchor` property, you can solve the problem shown in Figure 3-2. Table 3-1 gives the `Anchor` property values used by the controls to let them take advantage of the form's available space.

TABLE 3-1

CONTROL	`Anchor` PROPERTY
Books `ListBox`	`Top, Bottom, Left`
Details `GroupBox`	`Top, Bottom, Left, Right`
Title `TextBox`	`Top, Left, Right`
Author `TextBox`	`Top, Left, Right`
ISBN `TextBox`	`Top, Left, Right`
URL `LinkLabel`	`Top, Left, Right`
Cover `PictureBox`	`Top, Right`

Now when the form resizes:

➤ The `ListBox` stretches vertically to match the form's height.

➤ The `GroupBox` stretches vertically and horizontally to use as much of the form's width and height as possible.

➤ The `TextBoxes` and `LinkLabel` stretch horizontally to be as wide as possible while still fitting inside the `GroupBox`.

➤ The `PictureBox` moves with the `GroupBox`'s right edge so it leaves as much room as possible to the left for the `TextBoxes` and `LinkLabel`.

Figure 3-5 shows the result. Now the `ListBox` is big enough to show all of its items and the `LinkLabel` is big enough to show the entire URL.

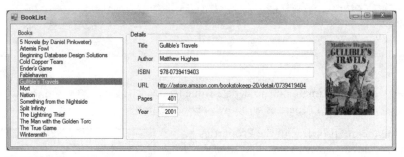

FIGURE 3-5

Note that the `TextBoxes` and `LinkLabel` do *not* stretch horizontally when the form resizes; they stretch when the `GroupBox` that contains them resizes. In this example, when the form stretches, the `GroupBox` stretches, and when the `GroupBox` stretches the `TextBoxes` and `LinkLabel` stretch.

USING DOCK PROPERTIES

The `Anchor` property can handle most of your arranging needs but some combinations of `Anchor` values are so common that Visual C# provides another property to let you handle these situations more easily: `Dock`. The `Dock` property lets you tell a control to attach itself to one of the edges of its container.

For example, a menu typically attaches to the top of a form and resizes horizontally to fill the form when the form resizes. You could provide that behavior by setting the menu's `Anchor` property to `Top`, `Left`, `Right`, but setting `Dock` to `Top` is even easier.

The `Dock` property can take one of six values. `Left`, `Right`, `Top`, and `Bottom` attach the control to the corresponding edge of its container. `Fill` makes the control take up any space left over after any other controls' `Dock` properties have had their way, and `None` detaches the control so its `Anchor` property can take over.

 The `Dock` *property cannot resize a control such as a* `Label` *or* `LinkLabel` *if that control has* `AutoSize` *set to* `True`.

The Dock property processes positioning requests in a first-come-first-served order based on the controls' stacking order on the form. In other words, it positions the first control that it draws first, the second next in whatever space is still available, and so forth.

Normally the stacking order is determined by the order in which you add controls to the form, but you can change the order by right-clicking a control and selecting Bring to Front or Send to Back. However, if you're working with a complicated set of Dock properties and the stacking order gets messed up, it's often easier to delete all of the controls and start over from scratch.

Figure 3-6 shows a form holding five docked Labels (with AutoSize = False). The numbers in the controls' Text properties give the order in which they were created, which is also their stacking order. The following list explains how the form's space was divvied up among the Labels:

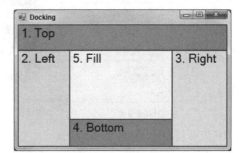

FIGURE 3-6

1. The first Label has Dock = Top, so it took the top part of the form.

2. The second Label has Dock = Left, so it took the left edge of the remaining area (after the first Label was positioned).

3. The third Label has Dock = Right, so it took the right edge of the remaining area.

4. The fourth Label has Dock = Bottom, so it took the bottom edge of the remaining area.

5. The final Label has Dock = Fill, so it fills all of the remaining area.

DOCKED MENUS

In one typical docking scenario, a form contains a MenuStrip with Dock = Top and a container such as a Panel with Dock = Fill so it takes up the rest of the form. All of the other controls are placed inside the Panel.

You can also add ToolStrips, ToolStripContainers, and StatusBars with the appropriate Dock properties to put those controls in their correct places. Figure 3-7 shows a form holding a MenuStrip (Dock = Top), a ToolStripContainer (Dock = Top) containing two ToolStrips, a Panel (Dock = Fill), and a StatusStrip (Dock = Bottom).

FIGURE 3-7

TRY IT

In this Try It, you have a chance to practice using the `Anchor` and `Dock` properties. You build the application shown in Figure 3-8.

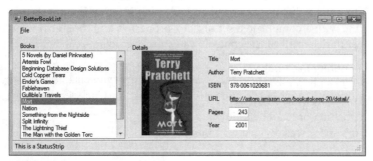

FIGURE 3-8

When the form resizes, the `TextBoxes` and `LinkLabel` stretch horizontally.

When the form resizes, the `PictureBox` also stretches vertically. Notice in Figure 3-8 that the cover image is rather tall and thin. When the `PictureBox` grows taller, it can display a larger version of the cover image. The control displays the image as large as possible without distorting it.

Note that the program you build won't actually do anything except sit there looking pretty and resizing controls when the form resizes. The techniques you need to make it respond to list selections are covered in later lessons.

You can download the code and resources for this Try It from the book's web page at www.wrox.com *or* www.CSharpHelper.com/24hour.html. *You can find them in the Lesson03 folder in the download.*

Lesson Requirements

In this lesson, you:

➤ Create the program's three main controls: a `MenuStrip`, a `Panel`, and a `StatusStrip`. Use `Dock` properties to make these three controls stay in their proper positions.

➤ Add controls to the `Panel`.

➤ Use the `Anchor` property to make the `ListBox` stretch vertically when the form resizes.

➤ Use `Anchor` properties to make the `TextBoxes` and `LinkLabel` stretch horizontally when the form resizes.

➤ Use `Anchor` properties to make the `PictureBox` resize vertically when the form resizes.

Hints

➤ Remember that the `TextBoxes` and `LinkLabel` stretch with the `GroupBox` that contains them, not the form itself. If you don't make the `GroupBox` stretch, the controls it contains won't either.

➤ To make the File menu, add a `MenuStrip` to the form, click it, click the Type Here box that appears, and type **&File**. (The ampersand gives the "F" the underline.) Making the menu do something useful is covered in Lesson 5, so don't worry about it now.

➤ To make the status strip label, add a `StatusStrip` to the form and click it. Click the little dropdown arrow on the `StatusStrip` and select `StatusLabel`. Click the new `StatusLabel` and use the Properties window to set its Text to `"This is a StatusStrip"`.

➤ Add some items to the `ListBox` and add a picture to the `PictureBox`, but don't worry about making the program take any actions.

Step-by-Step

➤ Create the program's three main controls: a `MenuStrip`, a `Panel`, and a `StatusStrip`. Use `Dock` properties to make these three controls stay in their proper positions.

1. Start a new project named BetterBookList. Set the form's `Size` and `MinimumSize` properties to `726, 286`.

2. Add a `MenuStrip` to the form. (Notice that by default the `MenuStrip` has Dock = Top.) Use the `MenuStrip` hint from the "Hints" section of this lesson to create the empty File menu.

3. Add a `Panel` to the form. Set its `Dock` property to `Fill`. Set its `BackColor` property to light green.

4. Add a `StatusStrip` to the form. (Notice that by default the `StatusStrip` has Dock = Bottom.) Use the `StatusStrip` hint from the "Hints" section of this lesson to create the `"This is a StatusStrip"` label.

➤ Add controls to the `Panel`.

1. Add controls to the form in roughly the positions shown in Figure 3-8.

2. Set the `LinkLabel`'s `AutoSize` property to `False` and make it the same size as the `TextBoxes`.

3. Enter some `Text` values in the `TextBoxes` and `LinkLabel` so you have something to look at. Enter enough items in the `ListBox` so they won't all fit when the form is its initial size.

4. Set the `PictureBox`'s `SizeMode` property to `Zoom`. Place a relatively tall, thin image in its `Image` property.

➤ Use the `Anchor` property to make the `ListBox` stretch vertically when the form resizes.

1. Set the `ListBox`'s `Anchor` property to `Top, Bottom, Left`.

➤ Use `Anchor` properties to make the `TextBoxes` and `LinkLabel` stretch horizontally when the form resizes.

1. Set the `GroupBox`'s `Anchor` property to `Top, Bottom, Left, Right`.

2. Set the `TextBoxes`' and the `LinkLabel`'s `Anchor` property to `Top, Left, Right`.

➤ Use `Anchor` properties to make the `PictureBox` resize vertically when the form resizes.

1. Set the `PictureBox`'s `Anchor` property to `Top, Bottom, Left`.

Run the program and see what happens when you resize the form.

 Please select Lesson 3 on the DVD to view the video that accompanies this lesson.

EXERCISES

1. (SimpleEdit) Create a new project named SimpleEdit, putting it somewhere you can easily find so you can add enhancements in later lessons. Give it a `MenuStrip` and `StatusStrip` with appropriate (default) `Dock` values. Add a `RichTextBox` control and set its `Dock` property to `Fill`. (That's all for now. In later lessons you add features to this program.)

2. Make a New Customer dialog box similar to the one shown in Figure 3-9. Make the First Name, Last Name, Street, City, and Email `TextBoxes` resize horizontally when the form resizes. Use the OK and Cancel buttons as the form's accept and cancel buttons, and attach them to the form's lower-right corner.

FIGURE 3-9

3. The `SplitContainer` control displays two areas separated by a splitter. The user can drag the splitter to divide the available space between the two areas. Make a program similar to the one shown in Figure 3-10. Feel free to use a different picture and information. Make the `PictureBox` display its image as large as possible without distortion. Set the bottom `TextBox`'s `MultiLine` property to `True` and make it stretch vertically and horizontally as the form resizes. Make the other `TextBoxes` stretch horizontally. Set the `SplitContainer`'s `Panel1MinSize` and `Panel2MinSize` properties to `100`.

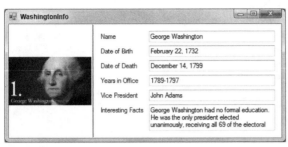

FIGURE 3-10

 You can download the solutions to these exercises from the book's web page at www.wrox.com or www.CSharpHelper.com/24hour.html. You can find them in the Lesson03 folder of the download.

Handling Events

An *event* is something that a control raises to tell the program that something significant has happened. Events are extremely important because they are the main way the user controls the program. When the user clicks buttons, drags sliders, and selects menu items, events tell the program that something has happened so it can take action.

As Lesson 2 briefly explained, when the user clicks a `Button`, the `Button` raises a `Click` event. An *event handler* can *catch* that event and take appropriate action such as displaying a message, performing a calculation, or downloading the latest *Dilbert* comic from the Web.

`Click` is a very useful event, but it's only one of hundreds (if not thousands) of events that your programs can catch.

This lesson explains how you can catch events other than `Click`. It describes some of the most useful events provided by common controls and, as a bonus, explains how you can display messages to the user when events occur.

MAKING EVENT HANDLERS

The easiest way to build an event handler is to double-click a control in the Form Designer. This creates an empty event handler for the control's default event and opens the event handler in the Code Editor. You would then insert the code needed to take whatever action is appropriate.

The following code shows the empty `Click` event handler created for a `Button`:

```
private void crashSystemButton_Click(object sender, EventArgs e)
{

}
```

Probably the most commonly used events are the `Click` events raised by `Buttons`, `ToolStripMenuItems` (which represent menu items), and `ToolStripButtons` (which represent toolbar buttons). For these controls and many others, you almost always want to use the default event handler, so double-clicking them is the easiest way to go.

If you're not ready to write the real event handler code, you can write a place-holder event handler. One easy way to do that is to use `MessageBox.Show` *to display a message. For example, the following code displays a placeholder message for the File menu's Save command:*

```
private void fileSaveMenuItem_Click(object sender, EventArgs e)
{
    MessageBox.Show("File > Save not yet implemented");
}
```

Lesson 8 describes message boxes in greater detail.

Most controls, however, provide dozens of other events that you can catch. To create an event handler for one of these non-default events, select the control in the Form Designer. Then click the lightning bolt icon near the top of the Properties window to make the window list the control's events. Figure 4-1 shows the Properties window displaying some of the events that a `Button` can raise.

To create an empty event handler for an event, simply double-click the event's name in the Properties window's event list.

You can also type the name that you want to give the event handler. When you press [Enter], Visual Studio creates the event handler and opens it in the Code Editor.

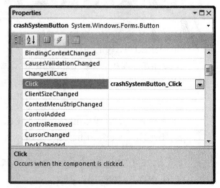

FIGURE 4-1

If your code already contains event handlers that could handle the event, you can click the event and then click the dropdown arrow to the right to select one of those event handlers.

USING EVENT PARAMETERS

All event handlers include parameters that give additional information about the event. Later lessons say more about parameters and how you can use them, but for now you should know that sometimes they can tell you more about the event.

For example, the following code shows a `Button`'s `Click` event handler. The parameters `sender` and `e` give extra information about the event.

```
private void crashSystemButton_Click(object sender, EventArgs e)
{

}
```

In a `Click` event, the `sender` parameter tells you what control raised the event. In this example, that's the `Button` that the user clicked.

The e parameter has the `EventArgs` data type, which doesn't give you a lot of additional information. Fortunately you usually don't need any additional information for a `Button`. Just knowing it was clicked is enough.

Some event handlers, however, provide really useful information. For example, the e parameter provided by the mouse events `MouseClick`, `MouseMove`, `MouseDown`, and `MouseUp` include the X and Y coordinates of the mouse over the control raising the event. Those values are crucial if you're trying to build a drawing application or need to track the mouse's position for some other reason.

The FollowMouse example program shown in Figure 4-2 (and available as part of this lesson's code download) uses a `MouseMove` event handler to make two scrollbars follow the mouse's position. When you click on the area in the center of the form, the program moves the picture of the mouse to that position.

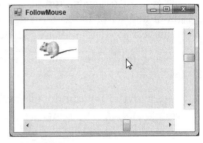

The program's form contains a green `Panel` control that holds a `PictureBox` holding the mouse image. It also contains `VScrollBar` and `HScrollBar` controls. The scrollbars' `Maximum` properties are set to the width and height of the `Panel` so they can hold the coordinates of any point in the `Panel`.

FIGURE 4-2

The program uses two event handlers that track mouse movement and detect mouse clicks.

Tracking Mouse Movement

The program's first event handler, which is shown in the following code, catches the `Panel`'s `MouseMove` event whenever the mouse moves across the `Panel`. Note that the `Panel` raises the event only when the mouse is over the `Panel` itself, not when it is over the `PictureBox` inside the `Panel`.

```
// Move the scrollbars to track the mouse.
private void fieldPanel_MouseMove(object sender, MouseEventArgs e)
{
    mouseHScrollBar.Value = e.X;
    mouseVScrollBar.Value = e.Y;
}
```

The code sets the scrollbars' `Value` properties to the mouse's X and Y coordinates so the scrollbars' thumbs follow the mouse.

Detecting Mouse Clicks

The second event handler, shown in the following code, catches the `Panel`'s `MouseClick` event and moves the `mousePictureBox` control to the mouse's current position.

```
// Move the mouse picture here.
private void fieldPanel_MouseClick(object sender, MouseEventArgs e)
{
    mousePictureBox.Left = e.X;
    mousePictureBox.Top = e.Y;
}
```

REMOVING EVENT HANDLERS

If you delete an event handler's code, the program may still include automatically generated code that attaches the event handler to the control that raises it. When you try to run the program, you'll get an error similar to: "'WindowsFormsApplication1.Form1' does not contain a definition for 'crashSystemButton_Click' and blah, blah, blah..." All this really means is Visual C# is confused.

The Properties window gives you an easy way to safely remove event handlers. *Before* you delete the event handler's code, find the event handler in the Properties window. Right-click the event handler's name and select Reset to break the link between the event handler and the control. Now you can remove the event handler's code safely.

If you already deleted the event handler's code, you can assign a temporary new event handler to the event, reset the event, and then remove the temporary event handler.

Alternatively, you can double-click the error in the Error window to see the automatically generated code that's making Visual C# throw its temper tantrum. The line should look something like this:

```
this.crashSystemButton.Click +=
    new System.EventHandler(this.crashSystemButton_Click);
```

Delete that line and you should be ready to run again.

 Don't fool around inside the automatically generated code. If you accidentally mess up that code, you may remove controls from the form, change properties, or even make the form unloadable so you have to throw it away. Get in, delete that single line, and get out before you do any serious damage.

ADDING AND REMOVING EVENT HANDLERS IN CODE

At design time, you can use the Properties window to attach event handlers to events. Occasionally you may want to attach or detach an event handler from an event at run time.

The following code shows a simple Button Click event handler. When this event handler executes, it displays a message to the user.

```
// Display a message box.
private void clickMeButton_Click(object sender, EventArgs e)
{
    MessageBox.Show("You clicked me!");
}
```

Suppose you have written this event handler but have not attached it to any control at design time. The following code attaches the event handler to the clickMeButton control's Click event:

```
clickMeButton.Click += clickMeButton_Click;
```

The += operator means "add to," so this code adds a new event handler to the clickMeButton .Click event.

After running this code, if the user clicks the clickMeButton, the event handler executes.

The following code removes the event handler from the button's Click event:

```
clickMeButton.Click -= clickMeButton_Click;
```

The -= operator means "subtract from," so this code removes an event handler from the clickMeButton.Click event.

The DynamicEvents example program shown in Figure 4-3 (and available in the Ex4-1 folder of this lesson's code download) lets you add and remove event handlers at run time. Initially the Click Me button does nothing. Click the Attach button to attach an event handler to the Click Me button. Click the Detach button to remove the event handler.

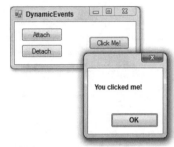

FIGURE 4-3

USEFUL EVENTS

Table 4-1 lists some of the more useful events raised by various controls.

TABLE 4-1

EVENT	MEANING
CheckedChanged	A CheckBox's or RadioButton's checked state has changed.
Click	The user has clicked the control.
FormClosing	The form is about to close. Set the e.Cancel parameter to true to cancel the closing and force the form to remain open.
KeyDown	The user pressed a key down while this control had focus.
KeyPress	The user pressed and released a key while this control had focus.
KeyUp	The user released a key while this control had focus.
Load	The form is loaded but not yet visible. This is the last place you can change the form's appearance before the user sees it.
MouseClick	The user pressed and released a mouse button over the control. Unlike the Click event, this event has parameters that give the click's location.
MouseDown	The user pressed a mouse button down over the control.

continues

TABLE 4-1 *(continued)*

EVENT	MEANING
MouseEnter	The mouse has entered the control.
MouseHover	The mouse has hovered over the control.
MouseLeave	The mouse has left the control.
MouseMove	The mouse has moved while over the control.
MouseUp	The user released a mouse button over the control.
Move	The control has moved.
Paint	The control needs to be redrawn. (This is useful for drawing graphics.)
Resize	The control has resized.
Scroll	The slider on a TrackBar or scrollbar was moved by the user.
SelectedIndexChanged	A ComboBox's or ListBox's selection has changed.
TextChanged	The control's Text property has changed. (This is particularly useful for TextBoxes.)
Tick	A Timer control's Interval has elapsed.
ValueChanged	The value of a TrackBar or scrollbar has changed (whether by the user or by code).

TRY IT

In this Try It, you use event handlers to display color samples as the user adjusts red, green, and blue scrollbars.

Figure 4-4 shows the finished program in action. When you change a scrollbar's value, the label to the right shows the new value and the large label on the far right shows a sample of the color with the selected red, green, and blue color components.

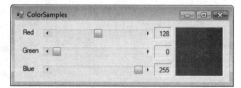

FIGURE 4-4

You can download the code and resources for this Try It from the book's web page at www.wrox.com or www.CSharpHelper.com/24hour.html. You can find them in the Lesson04 folder in the download.

Lesson Requirements

In this lesson, you:

➤ Create the form shown in Figure 4-4. Arrange the controls and set their Anchor properties.

➤ Make an event handler for the red scrollbar that displays all three color values and the color sample.

➤ Attach the event handler to the green and blue scrollbars, as well as the red one.

Hints

This Try It requires a few techniques that haven't been covered yet, but it's not too hard to build with a couple of hints.

➤ A scrollbar's Value property is an integer. To convert it into a string so you can display it in the labels, call its ToString method. For example, the following code makes the redLabel control display the redHScrollBar's Value property:

```
redLabel.Text = redHScrollBar.Value.ToString();
```

➤ The Color class's FromArgb method returns a color with given red, green, and blue color components between 0 and 255. For example, Color.FromArgb(255, 128, 0) returns the color orange (red = 255, green = 128, and blue = 0). Pass this method the values selected by the scrollbars (returned by their Value properties) and assign the result to the sample label's BackColor property.

Step-by-Step

➤ Create the form shown in Figure 4-4. Arrange the controls and set their Anchor properties.

1. Create the controls as shown in Figure 4-4. For the scrollbars, set Minimum = 0, Maximum = 264, SmallChange = 1, LargeChange = 10, and Anchor = Top, Left, Right.

 For some bizarre reason, the largest value that a user can select with a scrollbar is Maximum - LargeChange + 1. *If* Maximum = 264 *and* LargeChange = 10, *the largest selectable value is 264 - 10 + 1 = 255, so these properties let the user select values between 0 and 255.*

➤ Make an event handler for the red scrollbar that displays all three color values and the color sample.

1. Double-click the red scrollbar to create an empty event handler for the control's Scroll event. Type the bold lines in the following code so the event handler looks like this:

```
private void hbarRed_Scroll(object sender, ScrollEventArgs e)
{
    lblRed.Text = hscrRed.Value.ToString();
```

```
lblGreen.Text = hscrGreen.Value.ToString();
lblBlue.Text = hscrBlue.Value.ToString();
lblSample.BackColor =
    Color.FromArgb(hscrRed.Value, hscrGreen.Value, hscrBlue.Value);
}
```

➤ Attach the event handler to the green and blue scrollbars, as well as the red one.

1. In the Form Designer, click the green scrollbar. In the Properties window, click the event button (the lightning bolt). Then click the control's `Scroll` event, click the drop-down arrow to the right, and select the event handler.

2. Repeat the previous steps for the blue scrollbar.

Run the program and experiment with it. Note how the largest value you can select in the scrollbars is 255.

 Please select Lesson 4 on the DVD to view the video that accompanies this lesson.

EXERCISES

1. Build the DynamicEvents example program shown in Figure 4-3. What happens if you click Attach twice? Three times? What happens if you then click Detach once? Five times?

2. Create a form with one `Button` labeled "Stop" and two `Timers`. Set the `Timers'` `Interval` properties to 1000. At design time, set the first `Timer's` `Enabled` property to `True`.

➤ In each `Timer's` `Tick` event handler, disable that `Timer` and enable the other one.

➤ Make one `Timer's` `Tick` event handler also move the `Button` to (10, 10) by setting its `Left` and `Top` properties.

➤ Make the other `Timer's` `Tick` event handler move the `Button` to (200, 200).

➤ In the `Button's` `Click` event handler, set `Enabled = false` for both `Timers`.

Run the program. Experiment with different values for the `Timers'` `Interval` properties. What happens if `Interval = 10`?

3. Make a program similar to the one shown in Figure 4-5. When the user changes the scrollbar values, the program should set the `PictureBox's` `Left` and `Top` properties. Use `Anchor` properties to keep the scrollbars at the form's edges and make the background `Panel` fill most of the form. (Hint: When the form loads and when the `Panel` resizes, set the scrollbars' `Maximum` properties so they match the `Panel's` size. You can use the same event handler for both.)

FIGURE 4-5

4. Make a program similar to the one shown in Figure 4-6.

➤ Use `Anchor` properties to make the buttons stick to the form's lower-right corner. Make the `Buttons` be the form's accept and cancel buttons, and make them display messages saying "OK" or "Canceled."

➤ Make the `CheckBoxes`' `CheckedChanged` events enable or disable the corresponding `GroupBoxes`.

Hint: If you drag a `CheckBox` onto a `GroupBox`, it falls into the `GroupBox`. (Try it and run the program to see why that's bad.) To prevent this, position the `CheckBoxes` first and then position the `GroupBoxes` on top of them. Right-click a `GroupBox` and select Send to Back if you need to move it behind a `CheckBox`.

Hint: The `GroupBoxes` have `Text` set to a blank value. The `CheckBoxes` label the groups.

Hint: Set a `GroupBox`'s `Enabled` property equal to the corresponding `CheckBox`'s `CheckedChanged` value.

FIGURE 4-6

 You can download the solutions to these exercises from the book's web page at www.wrox.com *or* www.CSharpHelper.com/24hour.html. *You can find them in the Lesson04 folder of the download.*

5

Making Menus

In addition to buttons, labels, and textboxes, menus are one of the most common user interface elements in interactive programs.

This lesson explains how to add menus and context menus to forms and catch their events so your program can take action when the user selects menu items.

CREATING MENUS

To create a menu, simply drop a `MenuStrip` control on a form. By default, the `MenuStrip` is docked to the top of the form so you don't really need to position it carefully. Just double-click the Toolbox's `MenuStrip` tool and you're set.

Unlike most controls, the `MenuStrip` appears in the *Component Tray* below the form in addition to on the form itself. Figure 5-1 shows the SimpleEdit program in the Form Designer. Below the form you can see the Component Tray containing a `MenuStrip` and a `StatusStrip`.

When you select a `MenuStrip` in the Form Designer, the menu bar at the top of the form displays a Type Here box. Click that box and type the menu's caption to create a main menu.

If you create a main menu entry and select it, the Form Designer displays a new Type Here box to let you create menu items (see Figure 5-2).

Continue entering text in the Type Here boxes to build the whole menu structure. Figure 5-3 shows the Edit menu for a new version of the SimpleEdit program. Notice that the menu contains several cascading submenus. The Offset submenu is expanded in Figure 5-3.

FIGURE 5-1

You can use the Type Here boxes to create submenus to any depth, although in practice three levels (as in Edit ⇨ Offset ⇨ Subscript) are about all the user can stomach.

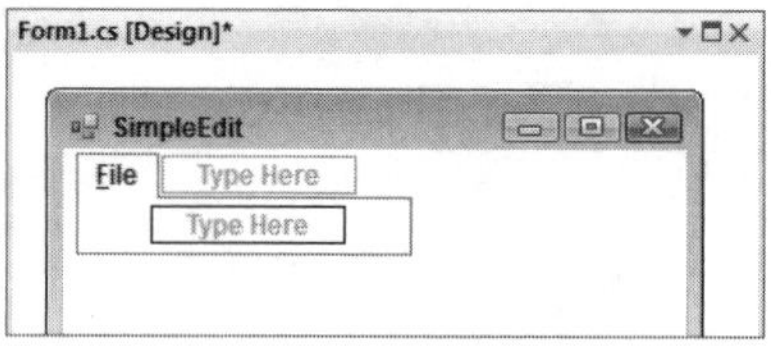

FIGURE 5-2

In addition to menu items, you can place separators, textboxes, and combo boxes in menus. Textboxes and combo boxes are unusual in menus so I won't cover them here. Separators, however, are quite useful for grouping related menu items.

To create a separator, right-click an item, open the Insert submenu, and select Separator. Alternatively, you can create a normal menu item and set its `Text` to a single dash (-).

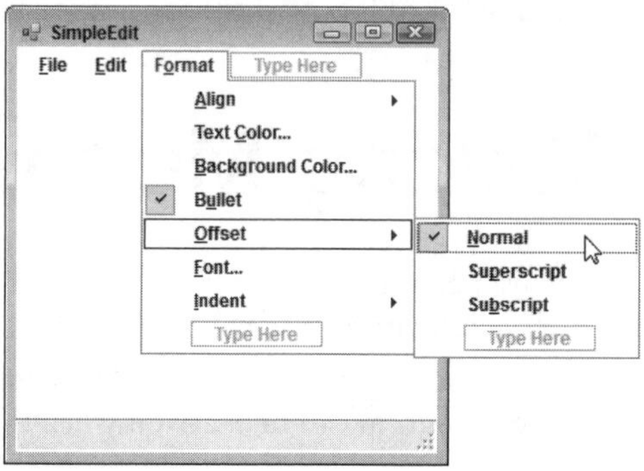

SETTING MENU PROPERTIES

The items in a menu are `ToolStripMenuItems`, and like other controls, they have properties that determine their appearance and behavior.

FIGURE 5-3

Table 5-1 summarizes the most useful `ToolStripMenuItem` properties.

TABLE 5-1

PROPERTY	PURPOSE
Checked	Determines whether the item is checked. In Figure 5-3, the Bullet and Normal items are checked. (See also `CheckOnClick`.)
CheckOnClick	If you set this to `True`, the item automatically toggles its checked state when the user selects it.
Enabled	Indicates whether the item is enabled.
Name	The `ToolStripMenuItem`'s name. Normally you should give a good name to any menu item that makes the program do something at run time so your code can refer to it.
ShortcutKeys	Indicates the item's shortcut key combination (if any). Either type a value such as **Ctrl+C** or click the dropdown arrow to the right to display the shortcut editor shown in Figure 5-4.
Text	The text that the item displays. Place an ampersand before the character that you want to use as the item's accelerator. For example, if you set an item's `Text` to `&Edit`, the item appears as Edit in its menu and the user can activate it by pressing [Alt]+E while the menu is open.

ESSENTIAL ELLIPSES

By convention, if a menu item opens a dialog or requires some other feedback from the user before proceeding, its `Text` should end with an ellipsis (...). If the menu item starts an action immediately, it should not include an ellipsis.

For example, the <u>O</u>pen... menu item displays a file open dialog, so its caption ends with an ellipsis. In contrast, the Edit menu's <u>C</u>opy item immediately copies the selected text so it doesn't need an ellipsis.

Accelerators allow the user to navigate menus with the keyboard instead of the mouse. When the user presses [Alt], the menu's items display underlines below their accelerator keys. For example, the File menu might appear as <u>F</u>ile. The user can then press the accelerator key to open that menu and then use other accelerators to select the menu's items.

FIGURE 5-4

 Recent versions of the Windows operating system typically don't underline menu accelerators until you press the [Alt] key.

You should give accelerators to most if not all of your program's menus, submenus, and menu items. Experienced users can often navigate a menu system faster by using accelerators than they can by using the mouse.

 Be sure not to give the same accelerator character to two menu items in the same menu. For example, in the File menu, don't have <u>S</u>ave and <u>S</u>ave As menu items.

Shortcuts allow the user to instantly activate a menu item. For example, in many programs [Ctrl]+O opens a file and [Ctrl]+S saves the current file. (I remember the difference between accelerators and shortcuts by realizing that "accelerator" and the [Alt] key both begin with the letter "a.")

 Be extra sure not to give two menu items the same shortcut!

HANDLING MENU EVENTS

When the user clicks a menu item, its control raises a `Click` event exactly as a clicked `Button` does, and you can handle it in the same way. You can even create default event handlers in the same way: by double-clicking the control.

CREATING CONTEXT MENUS

A context menu appears when you right-click a particular control. In Visual C# building a context menu is almost as easy as building a form's main menu.

Start by dropping a `ContextMenuStrip` on the form. Like a `MenuStrip`, a `ContextMenuStrip` appears below the form in the Component Tray so you can just double-click the Toolbox's `ContextMenuStrip` tool and not worry about positioning the menu.

Unlike a `MenuStrip`, a `ContextMenuStrip` does not appear at the top of the form. In the Form Designer, you can click a `MenuStrip` either on the form or in the Component Tray to select it. To select a `ContextMenuStrip`, you must click it in the Component Tray. (Immediately after you add a `ContextMenuStrip` to a form, it is selected so you can see it on the form.)

After you select the `ContextMenuStrip`, you can edit it much as you can a `MenuStrip`. The big difference is that a `ContextMenuStrip` does not have top-level menus, just submenu items.

Figure 5-5 shows the Form Designer with a `ContextMenuStrip` selected. By now the menu editor should look familiar.

After you create a `ContextMenuStrip`, you need to associate it with the control that should display it. To do that, simply set the control's `ContextMenuStrip` property to the `ContextMenuStrip` from the dropdown list. To do that, select the control's `ContextMenuStrip` property in the Properties window, click the dropdown arrow on the right, and select the `ContextMenuStrip`. The rest is automatic. When the user right-clicks the control, it automatically displays the `ContextMenuStrip`.

FIGURE 5-5

TRY IT

In this Try It, you create a main menu and a context menu. The main menu includes an Exit command that closes the form. Both menus contain commands that let you change the appearance of a `TextBox` on the form. Figure 5-6 shows the finished program displaying its context menu.

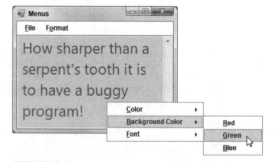

FIGURE 5-6

 You can download the code and resources for this Try It from the book's web page at www.wrox.com or www.CSharpHelper.com/24hour.html. You can find them in the Lesson05 folder in the download.

Lesson Requirements

In this lesson, you:

➤   Create the form shown in Figure 5-6.

➤   Create the following main menu structure (note the accelerator keys and shortcuts):

File

    E<u>x</u>it

F<u>o</u>rmat

    <u>C</u>olor

        <u>R</u>ed   Ctrl+R

        <u>G</u>reen   Ctrl+G

        <u>B</u>lue   Ctrl+B

    <u>B</u>ackground Color

        <u>R</u>ed

        <u>G</u>reen

        <u>B</u>lue

    <u>F</u>ont

        <u>S</u>mall   Ctrl+S

        <u>N</u>ormal   Ctrl+N

        <u>L</u>arge   Ctrl+L

➤   Add code behind the main menu items.

➤   Make the context menu duplicate the main menu's Format submenu.

➤   Attach the context menu items to the event handlers used by the main menu.

➤   Attach the context menu to the `TextBox`.

Hints

➤   The E<u>x</u>it menu item can close the program's form by calling `this.Close()`.

➤   Creating a font isn't trivial (and I haven't covered that yet). It's much easier to keep a sample of a font in a control somewhere on the form and then set the `TextBox`'s `Font` property equal to that control's `Font` property. And what better control to store the font than the menu item itself?

Step-by-Step

➤   Create the form shown in Figure 5-6.

   1.   Create the main menu by double-clicking the Toolbox's `MenuStrip` tool.

2. Add a `TextBox` to the form. Type some text into its `Text` property and set its other properties: `Name = txtContents`, `MultiLine = True`, `Dock = Fill`, `ScrollBars = Both`.

3. Create the context menu by double-clicking the Toolbox's `ContextMenuStrip` tool.

➤ Create the main menu structure.

1. Select the `MenuStrip`. Click the Type Here box and type &File.

2. In the Type Here box below the File menu, type E&xit.

> *By convention, the Exit command uses X as its accelerator. It never has a short-cut because it would be too easy to accidentally close the program while banging your head on the keyboard. (Or if you fat-finger the keys, the keyboard is hit by a flying tennis ball, your cat walks across the keyboard, and so on.)*

3. Click the File item again. In the Type Here box to the right, type F&ormat.

4. Use the Type Here boxes below the Format menu to create the format menu items and their submenus.

5. Use the Properties window to set the font sizes for the Font menu's Small, Normal, and Large items to 6, 9, and 20.

6. Give the Color and Font submenu items appropriate shortcuts.

7. Give the menu items that take action appropriate names. For example, name the Font menu's Small item `formatFontSmallMenuItem`.

➤ Add code behind the main menu items.

1. Double-click the Exit menu item and type the bold line in the following code so the event handler looks like this:

```
private void fileExitMenuItem_Click(object sender, EventArgs e)
{
    this.Close();
}
```

The keyword `this` means "the object currently executing this code," which in this case means the current form, so this line of code tells the current form to close itself.

2. Double-click the Format ➪ Color ➪ Red menu item and type the bold line in the following code so the event handler looks like this:

```
private void formatColorRedMenuItem_Click(object sender, EventArgs e)
{
    contentsTextBox.ForeColor = Color.Red;
}
```

3. Repeat step 2 for the Green and Blue menu items.

4. Repeat step 2 for the Format ➪ Background Color menu items, making them set the TextBox's BackColor property to Pink, LightGreen, and LightBlue.

5. Double-click the Format ➪ Font ➪ Small menu item and type the highlighted line in the following code so the event handler looks like this:

```
private void formatFontSmallMenuItem_Click(object sender, EventArgs e)
{
    contentsTextBox.Font = formatFontSmallMenuItem.Font;
}
```

6. Repeat step 5 for the Normal and Large menu items.

➤ Make the context menu duplicate the main menu's Format submenu.

Do either 1 or 2:

1. Build the structure from scratch. (This is straightforward but slow.)

   a. Click the ContextMenuStrip in the Component Tray to open it for editing.

   b. Use steps similar to the ones you used to build the main menu's structure to build the context menu's structure. End context menu item names with ContextMenuItem as in colorRedContextMenuItem.

2. Copy the Format menu's structure. (This is sneakier and faster, and therefore much cooler!)

   a. Click the MenuStrip in the Component Tray to open it for editing. Expand the Format menu. Click the Color item and then shift-click the Font item to select all of the menu's items. Press [Ctrl]+C to copy the menu items into the clipboard.

   b. Click the ContextMenuStrip in the Component Tray to open it for editing. Press [Ctrl]+V to paste the menu items into the context menu.

   c. Give appropriate names to the new menu items.

➤ Attach the context menu items to the event handlers used by the main menu.

1. Open the ContextMenuStrip for editing. Expand the Color submenu and click the Red item. In the Properties window, click the events button (the lightning bolt) to see the menu item's events. Select the Click event, click the dropdown arrow to the right, and select formatColorRedMenuItem_Click.

2. Repeat step 1 for the ContextMenuStrip's other items, attaching them to the correct event handlers.

➤ Attach the context menu to the TextBox.

1. Click the TextBox. In the Properties window, set its ContextMenuStrip property to the ContextMenuStrip formatContextMenu.

 Please select Lesson 5 on the DVD to view the video that accompanies this lesson.

EXERCISES

1. (SimpleEdit) Copy the SimpleEdit program you started in Lesson 3, Exercise 1 (or download Lesson 3's version from the book's web site at www.wrox.com) and add the menu structure. The following list shows the menu items. The items that display a dash (-) are separators. Note the shortcuts and underlined accelerator keys. Add the code behind the Exit item, but don't worry about the other items yet.

File

New	Ctrl+N
Open	Ctrl+O
Save	Ctrl+S
Save As...	
-	
Print Preview...	Ctrl+P
Print...	
-	
Exit	

Edit

Undo	Ctrl+Z
Redo	Ctrl+Y
-	
Copy	Ctrl+C
Cut	Ctrl+X
Paste	Ctrl+V
Delete	Del
-	
Select All	

Format

    Align

        Left

        Right

        Center

    Color...

    Background Color...

    Bullet

    <u>O</u>ffset

       <u>N</u>ormal

       Su<u>b</u>script

       Su<u>p</u>erscript

    <u>F</u>ont...

    <u>I</u>ndent

       <u>N</u>one

       <u>H</u>anging

       <u>L</u>eft

       <u>R</u>ight

       <u>B</u>oth

Eventually the user will be able to use the Bullet menu item to toggle whether a piece of text is bulleted. To allow C# to toggle this item for you, set the menu item's `CheckOnClick` property to `True`.

Add a `ContextMenuStrip` that duplicates the Format menu and use it for the `TextBox`'s `ContextMenuStrip` property.

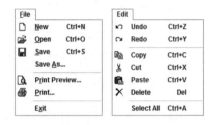

2. (SimpleEdit) Copy the SimpleEdit program you built for Exercise 1 and add images to its menu items. (You can find suitable images files in the `PngFiles` directory of the Lesson 5 downloads available on the book's web site.) Figure 5-7 shows what the menus should look like when you're finished.

3. (SimpleEdit) Copy the SimpleEdit program you built for Exercise 2 and add placeholder routines for the menu items' event handlers. The routines should display simple message boxes indicating what they should really do. For example, the following code shows the File menu's `Save` event handler.

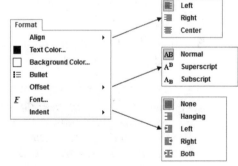

FIGURE 5-7

```
private void fileSaveMenuItem_Click(object sender, EventArgs e)
{
    MessageBox.Show("Save");
}
```

Add placeholders for all menu items (except separators) that do not have submenus. For example, add a placeholder for the Format ➪ Align ➪ Left item but not for Format ➪ Align because it has a submenu.

Attach the context menu's items to the same event handlers except give the context menu's Bullet item its own event handler. (If you make these two share the same event handler, they will interfere with each other in Exercise 4 because of their toggling behavior.)

4. (SimpleEdit) Copy the SimpleEdit program you built for Exercise 3 and add code to manage exclusive selections in the Format menu's Align, Offset, and Indent submenus. For example, the user can select only one of the Align submenu's choices at a time.

Modify the items' placeholder code so when the user selects a choice, the code:

a. Checks the selected submenu item

b. Unchecks the other submenu items.

c. Checks the corresponding context menu item

d. Unchecks the corresponding context menu item

For example, the following code executes when the user selects the Align submenu's Left choice.

```
private void formatAlignLeftMenuItem_Click(object sender, EventArgs e)
{
    formatAlignLeftMenuItem.Checked = true;
    formatAlignRightMenuItem.Checked = false;
    formatAlignCenterMenuItem.Checked = false;
    alignLeftContextMenuItem.Checked = true;
    alignRightContextMenuItem.Checked = false;
    alignCenterContextMenuItem.Checked = false;
    MessageBox.Show("Align Left");
}
```

5. (Simple Edit) Make the Format ⇨ Bullet menu item and the bullet context menu item check and uncheck each other.

You can download the solutions to these exercises from the book's web page at www.wrox.com *or* www.CSharpHelper.com/24hour.html. *You can find them in the Lesson05 folder in the download.*

Making Tool Strips and Status Strips

Not every program needs a tool strip or status strip, but they can make the user's life easier, particularly for complicated programs. This lesson explains how to add tool strips and status strips to your applications.

USING TOOL STRIPS

Usually a tool strip sits below a form's menu bar and typically displays a series of small buttons that let the user easily perform frequently executed tasks. Usually the buttons duplicate functions that are also available in menus, but placing them on the tool strip makes it easier for the user to find and use them.

Place only the most frequently used commands in the tool strip so it doesn't become cluttered.

Recall from Lesson 5 that you should also give most if not all of your menu items accelerators, and you can give the most important commands shortcuts. That means the user can access the most important and useful commands in at least four ways: mouse menu navigation, accelerators, shortcuts, and tool strip buttons.

To create a single tool strip, simply double-click the Toolbox's `ToolStrip` tool. By default, the `ToolStrip` docks to the top of the form so you don't need to position it manually.

Recall from Lesson 3 that docked controls are drawn in their stacking order, which by default is the same as their creation order. To avoid confusion, if a form should contain a main menu and a tool strip, create the menu first so the tool strip appears below it and not above it.

When you select a `ToolStrip`, the Form Designer displays a little icon with a dropdown arrow. Click the arrow to display a list of items that you might want to add to the `ToolStrip` as shown in Figure 6-1.

As you can see from Figure 6-1, you can add the following types of objects to a `ToolStrip`:

➤ Button

➤ Label

➤ SplitButton

➤ DropDownButton

➤ Separator

➤ ComboBox

➤ TextBox

➤ ProgressBar

FIGURE 6-1

The `SplitButton` and `DropDownButton` are new controls that you haven't seen before in the Toolbox so they deserve a little explanation.

The `SplitButton` normally displays a button holding an icon and a dropdown arrow. (You can change its `DisplayStyle` property to make it display text instead of an image, both, or neither.) If the user clicks the button, its `Click` event fires. If the user clicks the dropdown arrow, a menu appears. As is the case with all menus, if the user selects an item, that item's `Click` event fires.

One way you might use a `SplitButton` would be to have the menu items perform some action and then change the button's icon to match the action. Clicking the button would perform the action again.

Another way to think of this would be the button represents a tool and clicking it activates the current tool. Selecting an item from the dropdown menu selects a new tool and activates it.

Like the `SplitButton`, the `DropDownButton` normally displays an icon with a dropdown arrow. (And as is the case with the `SplitButton`, you can use the `DropDownButton`'s `DisplayStyle` property to make it display an image, text, both, or neither.) If the user clicks the dropdown arrow, a menu appears. This control is similar to the `SplitButton` except it doesn't provide a button that the user can click to repeat the previous command.

Although they can contain many different kinds of controls, `ToolStrips` look best when they are not too cluttered and confusing. For example, a `ToolStrip` that contains only `Buttons` and `Separators` is easy to understand and use. `DropDownButtons` and `SplitButtons` are the next easiest controls to understand in a `ToolStrip` and they don't clutter things up too much so you can add them if necessary.

Avoid using `Labels` in a `ToolStrip` to provide status information. Instead place status information in a `StatusStrip`.

USING TOOL STRIP CONTAINERS

A `ToolStripContainer` displays areas on a form's top, left, bottom, and right edges that can hold `ToolStrips`. At run time, the user can drag `ToolStrips` back and forth within and among these areas.

The center of the `ToolStripContainer` is a content panel that can hold one or more other controls.

In a typical configuration for these controls, a form optionally contains a `MenuStrip` and `StatusStrip` docked to the form's top and bottom, respectively. A `ToolStripContainer` is docked to fill the rest of the form, and its content panel contains the rest of the program's controls.

Figure 6-2 shows a form that contains a `MenuStrip` at the top, a `StatusStrip` at the bottom, and a `ToolStripContainer` filling the rest of the form. The `ToolStripContainer` contains three `ToolStrips` and a `RichTextBox` docked to fill its content panel.

FIGURE 6-2

Figure 6-3 shows this program at run time. Here I have dragged two of the `ToolStrips` to the `ToolStripContainer`'s left and right edges.

Two things in Figure 6-2 are of particular note. First, notice the thin rectangles holding arrows on the middle of the content panel's sides. If you click one of these, the control adds room on that edge so you can insert another `ToolStrip`.

The second thing of note in Figure 6-2 is the smart tag shown as a little square holding an arrow in the control's upper-right corner. If you click the smart tag, the smart tag panel shown in Figure 6-4 appears.

In general, smart tags provide quick ways to perform common tasks for a control. In this example, the smart tag panel lets you decide which panels the control should allow. If you uncheck one of the panels, at run time the user cannot drag `ToolStrips` to that edge of the `ToolStripContainer`.

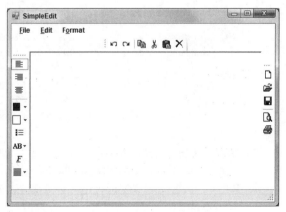

FIGURE 6-3

 You can also determine which panels are available by setting the control's `LeftToolStripPanelVisible`, `RightToolStripPanelVisible`, `TopToolStripPanelVisible`, *and* `BottomToolStripPanelVisible` *properties in the Properties window, but using the smart tag is easier.*

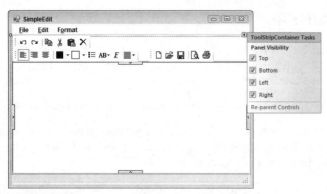

FIGURE 6-4

After you build the `ToolStripContainer`, simply place `ToolStrips` on it and build their items as usual.

USING STATUS STRIPS

A status strip is normally docked to a form's bottom and displays labels, icons, and other controls to give the user a quick summary of the application's status. This area should be reserved for status information and should generally not include buttons and other controls that make the application perform an action. Those commands belong in menus and tool strips.

 Although the current time is sort of a piece of status information, don't add a clock to the status bar. A user who wants a clock can display one in the system's taskbar. The taskbar clock is more convenient because it provides options (such as display format) that you probably don't want to reproduce in your program, and it also can't be hidden by other programs. If the system provides a convenient tool, there's no need for you to reproduce it in your program.

To create a status strip, simply double-click the Toolbox's `StatusStrip` tool. By default, the `StatusStrip` docks to the bottom of the form so you don't need to position it manually.

When you select a `StatusStrip`, the Form Designer displays a little icon with a dropdown arrow similar to the one it displays for a `ToolStrip`. Click the arrow to display a list of items that you might want to add to the `StatusStrip` as shown in Figure 6-5.

As you can see from Figure 6-5, you can add the following types of objects to a `ToolStrip`:

FIGURE 6-5

➤ StatusLabel

➤ ProgressBar

➤ DropDownButton

➤ SplitButton

The only new control, StatusLabel, behaves like a normal Label.

TRY IT

In this Try It, you create a MenuStrip (covered in Lesson 5) and a ToolStrip, both containing commands to change a RichTextBox control's ForeColor and BackColor properties. You also create a StatusStrip to show the currently selected colors. (Yes, I know this is redundant because the values are shown in the ToolStrip and in the text itself.) Figure 6-6 shows the program.

FIGURE 6-6

 You can download the code and resources for this Try It from the book's web page at www.wrox.com *or* www.CSharpHelper.com/24hour.html. *You can find them in the Lesson06 folder in the download.*

Lesson Requirements

In this lesson, you:

➤ Create the form shown in Figure 6-6.

➤ Create the MenuStrip. The menu's hierarchy should be:

File

    Exit

Format

    Text Color

        Black

        Red

        Green

        Blue

    Background Color

        White

        Pink

        Green

        Blue

➤   Initially check the Text Color menu's Black choice and the Background Color menu's White choice.

➤   Give the Background Color menu items `Images` that display samples of the color.

➤   Create the `ToolStrip` with buttons that duplicate the menu hierarchy. The `ToolStrip` should hold two `ToolStripDropDownButtons`.

Name the first tool `ToolStripDropDownButton textColorButton` and make it display the text "A." Give it the items Black, Red, Green, and Blue. Each item should have `ForeColor` property set to its color.

Name the second tool `ToolStripDropDownButton backColorButton` and make it initially display a white color sample. Give it the items White, Pink, Green, and Blue. Make each of these display an `Image` showing a sample of the color.

➤   Give the `StatusStrip` a `ToolStripStatusLabel` named `colorLabel` with `Text = Text Colors`.

➤   Add event handlers.

Make the <u>F</u>ile menu's E<u>x</u>it item close the form.

Make event handlers for each of the Text Color menu items.

   ➤   Set the `RichTextBox` control's `ForeColor` property to the selected color.

   ➤   Set the `ForeColor` property of the `textColorMenuItem` submenu to the appropriate color.

   ➤   Set the `ForeColor` property of the `textColorButton` tool strip button to the appropriate color.

   ➤   Set the `ForeColor` property of the `colorLabel` label to the appropriate color.

   ➤   Check the selected menu item and deselect the other Text Color menu items.

   ➤   Check the corresponding tool strip button and deselect the other Text Color tool strip buttons.

Make event handlers for each of the Background Color menu items.

   ➤   Set the `RichTextBox` control's `BackColor` property to the selected color.

   ➤   Set the `Image` property of the `backColorMenuItem` submenu to display a sample of the appropriate color.

   ➤   Set the `Image` property of the `backColorButton` tool strip button to display a sample of the appropriate color.

   ➤   Set the `BackColor` property of the `colorLabel` label to the appropriate color.

   ➤   Check the corresponding menu item and deselect the other Background Color menu items.

   ➤   Check the selected tool strip button and deselect the other Background Color tool strip buttons.

➤   Use the menu items' event handlers for the corresponding tool strip button event handlers.

DUPLICATE CODE

As you will probably notice, this lesson's Try It includes event handlers that duplicate the same code with minor differences. In general, if large pieces of code do almost the same things with minor changes, then there's probably something wrong with the program's design.

In cases such as this, you should extract the common code into a function. You can use `if`, `switch`, and other C# statements to let the code take different actions for different situations, allowing the same function to handle multiple situations.

Unfortunately, you don't know how to do any of that yet, but you will learn. Lesson 20 explains how to write functions, and Lesson 18 describes statements such as `if` and `switch`. Until then, you're stuck with some duplicate code.

After you read Lessons 18 and 20, you can revisit this code if you like to remove the redundant code, making it easier to maintain in the future. (The process of restructuring existing code to make it more reliable, easier to read, easier to maintain, or otherwise better without changing its functionality is called *refactoring*.)

Hints

➤ Recall that the E<u>x</u>it menu item can close the program's form by calling `this.Close()`.

➤ Place the `RichTextBox` inside the `ToolStripContainer`'s content panel.

Step-by-Step

➤ Create the form shown in Figure 6-6.

   1. Start a new project.

   2. Add a `MenuStrip` to the form.

   3. Add a `StatusStrip` to the form.

   4. Add a `ToolStripContainer` to the form.

   5. Add a `RichTextBox` named `contentRichTextBox` inside the `ToolStripContainer`'s content panel.

➤ Create the `MenuStrip`.

   1. Add the indicated menu items to the `MenuStrip`. Remember to give them good names and appropriate accelerator keys.

➤ Initially check the Text Color menu's Black choice and the Background Color menu's White choice.

   1. Set the Text Color ⇨ Black menu item's `Checked` property to `True`.

2. Set the Background Color ⇨ White menu item's `Checked` property to `True`.

➤ Give the Background Color menu items `Images` that display samples of the color.

1. Set the `Image` properties of these menu items to samples of their colors. (Use Microsoft Paint or some other graphical editor to make small colored images.)

➤ Create the `ToolStrip` with buttons that duplicate the menu hierarchy. The `ToolStrip` should hold two `ToolStripDropDownButtons`.

Name the first tool `ToolStripDropDownButton textColorButton` and make it display the text "A." Give it the items Black, Red, Green, and Blue. Each item should have `ForeColor` property set to its color.

1. Create the `ToolStripDropDownButton`.

2. Below that item, add the items Black, Red, Green, and Blue.

3. Set the `ForeColor` property for each of these items to show its color (that is, set the Black item's `ForeColor` property to black).

Name the second tool `ToolStripDropDownButton backColorButton` and make it initially display a white color sample. Give it the items White, Pink, Green, and Blue. Make each of these display an `Image` showing a sample of the color.

1. Create the `ToolStripDropDownButton`.

2. Below that item, add the items White, Pink, Green, and Blue.

3. Set the `Image` property for each of these items to show samples of their colors.

➤ Give the `StatusStrip` a `ToolStripStatusLabel` named `colorLabel` with `Text = Text Colors`.

1. Create the `ToolStripStatusLabel`. Set its `Name` and `Text` properties.

➤ Add event handlers.

Make the <u>F</u>ile menu's E<u>x</u>it item close the form.

1. Type the bold line of code so the event handler looks like this:

```
private void fileExitMenuItem_Click(object sender, EventArgs e)
{
    this.Close();
}
```

Make event handlers for each of the Text Color menu items.

1. For the Text Color ⇨ Black menu item, type the bold code so the event handler looks like this:

```
private void textColorBlackMenuItem_Click(object sender, EventArgs e)
{
    contentsRichTextBox.ForeColor = Color.Black;
    textColorMenuItem.ForeColor = Color.Black;
    textColorButton.ForeColor = Color.Black;
    colorLabel.ForeColor = Color.Black;
```

```
    textColorBlackMenuItem.Checked = true;
    textColorRedMenuItem.Checked = false;
    textColorGreenMenuItem.Checked = false;
    textColorBlueMenuItem.Checked = false;

    textColorBlackToostripMenuItem.Checked = true;
    textColorRedToostripMenuItem.Checked = false;
    textColorGreenToostripMenuItem.Checked = false;
    textColorBlueToostripMenuItem.Checked = false;
}
```

2. Enter similar code for the other Text Color menu items.

Make event handlers for each of the Background Color menu items.

1. For the Background Color ⇨ White menu item, type the bold code so the event handler looks like this:

```
private void backColorWhiteMenuItem_Click(object sender, EventArgs e)
{
    contentsRichTextBox.BackColor = Color.White;
    backColorMenuItem.Image = backColorWhiteMenuItem.Image;
    backColorButton.Image = backColorWhiteMenuItem.Image;
    colorLabel.BackColor = Color.White;

    backColorWhiteMenuItem.Checked = true;
    backColorPinkMenuItem.Checked = false;
    backColorGreenMenuItem.Checked = false;
    backColorBlueMenuItem.Checked = false;

    backColorWhiteToostripMenuItem.Checked = true;
    backColorPinkToostripMenuItem.Checked = false;
    backColorGreenToostripMenuItem.Checked = false;
    backColorBlueToostripMenuItem.Checked = false;
}
```

2. Enter similar code for the other Background Color menu items.

➤ Use the menu items' event handlers for the corresponding tool strip button event handlers.

1. Click the Properties window's Events button.

2. For each tool strip button:

a. Click the button in the Form Editor.

b. On the Properties window, select the `Click` event. Then click the dropdown arrow to the right.

c. Select the appropriate menu event handler. For example, for the `textColorBlackToolstripMenuItem` tool strip button, select the `textColorBlackMenuItem_Click` event handler.

 Please select Lesson 6 on the DVD to view the video that accompanies this lesson.

EXERCISES

1. (SimpleEdit) Copy the SimpleEdit program you built in Lesson 5, Exercise 5 (or download Lesson 5's version from the book's web site) and add the tool strips, buttons, and separators shown in Figure 6-7. Delete the `RichTextBox` control, add a `ToolStripContainer`, and then re-add the `RichTextBox` inside the `ToolStripContainer`'s content panel.

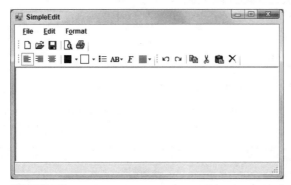

FIGURE 6-7

The black button (fourth from the left on the second tool strip row) is a `ToolStripSplitButton` that lets the user pick a text color. It contains the choices Black, White, Red, Green, and Blue.

The white button next to the text color button is another `ToolStripSplitButton` that lets the user pick a background color. It contains the choices Black, White, Pink, Green, Blue, and Yellow.

The button that says "AB" is a `ToolStripDropDownButton` that provides the same options as the Format menu's Offset submenu: Normal, Superscript, and Subscript.

2. (SimpleEdit) Copy the SimpleEdit program you built for Exercise 1 and add menu item code to manage the new tool strip buttons. Add code to synchronize corresponding menu, context menu, and tool strip button items. For example, the following shows the new code for the Align Left menu item:

```
private void formatAlignLeftMenuItem_Click(object sender, EventArgs e)
{
    formatAlignLeftMenuItem.Checked = true;
    formatAlignRightMenuItem.Checked = false;
    formatAlignCenterMenuItem.Checked = false;
    alignLeftContextMenuItem.Checked = true;
    alignRightContextMenuItem.Checked = false;
    alignCenterContextMenuItem.Checked = false;
    alignLeftButton.Checked = true;
    alignRightButton.Checked = false;
    alignCenterButton.Checked = false;
    MessageBox.Show("Align Left");
}
```

3. (SimpleEdit) Copy the SimpleEdit program you built for Exercise 2 and attach the tool strip buttons to the corresponding event handlers.

4. (SimpleEdit) Copy the SimpleEdit program you built for Exercise 3 and add code to display the appropriate image in the Background, Text Color, Offset, and Indent tool strip buttons. For example, when the user selects Offset Subscript, the `offsetButton` button should show the subscript image.

To make using the foreground and background colors easier, save them in the `foreColorButton` and `backColorButton` buttons' `ForeColor` and `BackColor` properties. For example, the following code shows what the program does when the user selects the red foreground color. It displays the red image in the corresponding menu item, context menu item, and tool strip button. It then saves the color in the `btnFg` button's `ForeColor` property and finishes by displaying a placeholder message.

```
private void foreColorRedToolstripMenuItem_Click(
  object sender, EventArgs e)
{
    formatTextColorMenuItem.Image = foreColorRedToolstripMenuItem.Image;
    textColorContextMenuItem.Image = foreColorRedToolstripMenuItem.Image;
    foreColorButton.Image = foreColorRedToolstripMenuItem.Image;
    foreColorButton.ForeColor = Color.Red;
    MessageBox.Show("Foreground Red");
}
```

5. (SimpleEdit) Copy the SimpleEdit program you built for Exercise 4 and add appropriate tooltips to the program's tool strip buttons. For example, set the `alignLeftButton` button's `ToolTipText` property to "Align Left."

6. Build the Scribbler program shown in Figure 6-8. Give it a `ToolStripContainer` and two `ToolStrips`. Give the first `ToolStrip` buttons representing arrow, line, rectangle, ellipse, scribble, and star tools. Make these tools exclusive choices so if the user selects one, the others deselect. Give the second `ToolStrip` two `ToolStripDropDownButtons` to represent foreground and background colors. Make the entries in each drop-down exclusive choices so if the user selects one, the others deselect.

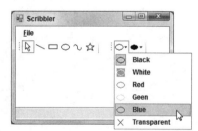

FIGURE 6-8

 You can download the solutions to these exercises from the book's web page at www.wrox.com *or* www.CSharpHelper.com/24hour.html. *You can find them in the Lesson06 folder in the download.*

Using RichTextBoxes

The `TextBox` control lets the user enter text and that's about it. It can display its text in different colors and fonts, but it cannot give different pieces of text different properties. The `TextBox` is intended to let the user enter a simple string, like a name or street address, and very little more.

The `RichTextBox` is a much more powerful control. It can display different pieces of text with different colors, fonts, and styles. It can adjust paragraph indentation and make bulleted lists. It can even include pictures. It's not as powerful as a full-featured word processor, such as Microsoft Word or OpenOffice's Writer, but it can produce a much more sophisticated result than the `TextBox`.

In this lesson you learn more about the `RichTextBox` control and how to use it. You have a chance to experiment with the control, and you use it to add enough functionality to the SimpleEdit program to finally make the program useful.

USING RICHTEXTBOX PROPERTIES

To change the appearance of the text inside a `RichTextBox`, you first select the text that you want to change, and then you set one of the control's properties to modify the text.

To select the text, you use the control's `SelectionStart` and `SelectionLength` properties to indicate where the text begins and how many letters it includes. Note that the letters are numbered starting with 0. (In fact, almost all numbering starts with 0 in C#.) For example, setting `SelectionStart = 0` and `SelectionLength = 1` selects the control's first letter.

After you select the text, you set one of the `RichTextBox`'s properties to the value that you want the text to have.

For example, the following code makes the `RichTextBox` named `rchContent` display some text and color the word "red."

```
contentRichTextBox.Text = "Some red text";
contentRichTextBox.SelectionStart = 5;
contentRichTextBox.SelectionLength = 3;
contentRichTextBox.SelectionColor = Color.Red;
```

Table 7-1 lists properties that you can use to change the text's appearance.

TABLE 7-1

PROPERTY	PURPOSE
SelectionAlignment	Aligns the selection's paragraph on the left, center, or right.
SelectionBackColor	Sets the selection's background color.
SelectionBullet	Determines whether the selection's paragraph is bulleted.
SelectionCharOffset	Determines whether the selection is superscript (offset > 0), subscript (offset < 0), or normal (offset = 0).
SelectionColor	Sets the selection's color.
SelectionFont	Sets the selection's font.
SelectionHangingIndent	The first line in the selection's paragraph is indented normally and then subsequent lines in the paragraph are indented by this amount.
SelectionIndent	All lines are indented by this amount.
SelectionProtected	Marks the selected text as protected so the user cannot modify it.
SelectionRightIndent	All lines are indented on the right by this amount.

The FontFeatures example program shown in Figure 7-1 demonstrates properties that change the appearance of text within a paragraph. These include the SelectionBackColor, SelectionCharOffset, SelectionColor, and SelectionFont.

The ParagraphFeatures program shown in Figure 7-2 demonstrates properties that change the way paragraphs are displayed. These include SelectionIndent, SelectionHangingIndent, SelectionRightIndent, SelectionBullet, and SelectionAlignment.

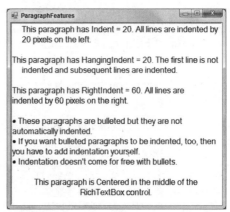

FIGURE 7-1   **FIGURE 7-2**

Both the FontFeatures and ParagraphFeatures sample programs are available as part of the Lesson 7 download at www.wrox.com.

Table 7-2 summarizes four additional properties that change the text displayed by the control that deserve special mention.

TABLE 7-2

PROPERTY	PURPOSE
Text	Gets or sets the control's text without any formatting properties.
Rtf	Gets or sets the control's Rich Text Format (RTF) contents. This includes the text plus RTF formatting codes that define how the text should be displayed.
SelectedText	Gets or sets the selection's text.
SelectedRtf	Gets or sets the selection's text and RTF codes.

GIVING THE USER CONTROL

Allowing the user to change text settings is easy. When the user selects text in the control, the RichTextBox sets its SelectionStart and SelectionLength properties accordingly. All you need to do is set the appropriate property (for example, SelectionColor) and the selected text is updated.

The SetTextProperties example program shown in Figure 7-3 (and available as part of the Lesson 7 code download) uses this technique to let the user control text color, character offset, and paragraph alignment. Select text and then click the tool strip buttons to change the text's properties.

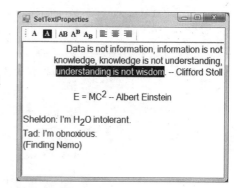

FIGURE 7-3

The following code shows how the SetTextProperties program changes the currently selected text to have a black background and white foreground.

```
private void reverseColorsButton_Click(object sender, EventArgs e)
{
    contentRichTextBox.SelectionBackColor = Color.Black;
    contentRichTextBox.SelectionColor = Color.White;
}
```

The program's other buttons work similarly.

USING RICHTEXTBOX METHODS

Lesson 2 briefly described properties, methods, and events. Other lessons have also worked with many properties and events. In fact, most of the event handlers I've discussed in the lessons so far catch an event and change a property in response.

Though you've worked with many properties and events, the only method you've seen is the form's `Close` method, which makes the form go away. For example, the following code closes the form that executes it:

```
this.Close();
```

The `RichTextBox` provides many new methods that are quite helpful for building a text editing program. Table 7-3 summarizes some of the most useful.

TABLE 7-3

METHOD	PURPOSE
Clear	Clears all text from the control.
Copy	Copies the current selection into the clipboard.
Cut	Cuts the current selection into the clipboard.
DeselectAll	Deselects all text by setting `SelectionLength` = 0.
LoadFile	Loads the control's text from a file with one of various formats such as RTF or plain text.
Paste	Pastes whatever is in the clipboard into the current selection. This can be anything that the `RichTextBox` understands such as text, RTF formatted text, or an image.
Redo	Redoes the previously undone command.
SaveFile	Saves the control's text into a file in one of various formats such as RTF or plain text.
SelectAll	Selects all of the control's text by setting `SelectionStart` = 0 and `SelectionLength` equal to the text's length.
Undo	Undoes the most recent change.

The following code shows how a program can use the `LoadFile` method. The first parameter gives the name of the file, which can be relative to the program's current directory or a full path. The second parameter gives the type of file.

```
rchContent.LoadFile("Test.rtf", RichTextBoxStreamType.RichText);
```

TYPING TIPS

When you type `contentRichTextBox.LoadFile(`, IntelliSense displays a popup showing the parameters that the `LoadFile` method expects, as shown in Figure 7-4. (Visual Studio puts the red squiggly underline below the code in Figure 7-4 because the statement isn't finished yet. Until I finish typing the statement, Visual Studio flags it as an error.)

There are several different *overloaded* versions of the method that take different parameters to choose from. Overloaded versions of a method have the same name but take different parameters.

Use the up and down arrow keys to scroll through the method's available versions.

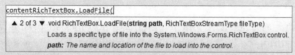

```
contentRichTextBox.LoadFile(
```
▲ 2 of 3 ▼ void RichTextBox.LoadFile(**string path**, RichTextBoxStreamType fileType)
Loads a specific type of file into the System.Windows.Forms.RichTextBox control.
path: The name and location of the file to load into the control.

FIGURE 7-4

As you enter parameters, IntelliSense updates to describe the next parameter that it expects. Figure 7-5 shows the `LoadFile` method after I entered a filename for the first parameter. IntelliSense shows that the next parameter should be a value of type `RichTextBoxStreamType` named `fileType`. IntelliSense even shows a short description of what the value means at the bottom (although it's not super informative).

```
contentRichTextBox.LoadFile("Test.rtf",
```
▲ 2 of 3 ▼ void RichTextBox.LoadFile(string path, **RichTextBoxStreamType fileType**)
Loads a specific type of file into the System.Windows.Forms.RichTextBox control.
fileType: One of the System.Windows.Forms.RichTextBoxStreamType values.

FIGURE 7-5

You could type in `RichTextBoxStreamType` followed by a dot to see a list of available choices, but there's an even easier (that is, better) way to do this: press [Ctrl]+[Space]. That makes IntelliSense display a list of things that you might be trying to type. At this point, IntelliSense is smart enough to guess that you want to type `RichTextBoxStreamType` so it initially selects that type and even displays more information about it, as shown in Figure 7-6.

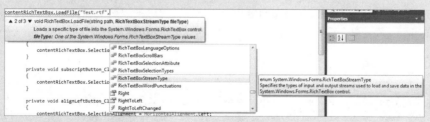

FIGURE 7-6

continues

(continued)

Now you can press [Tab] to make IntelliSense fill in the highlighted value `RichTextBoxStreamType` for you.

Finally, press the "." key to see the list of choices shown in Figure 7-7, pick one, and press [Tab] to add it to the code. Finally add ");" and you're done.

FIGURE 7-7

I know this sounds like a big mess, but with a little practice it becomes surprisingly quick and easy. Typing everything by hand, I can enter the previous `LoadFile` statement in about 30 seconds. With IntelliSense's help, I can type the same line in under 10 seconds.

The following code shows how a program can use the `SaveFile` method. As with `LoadFile`, the first parameter gives the file's name and the second gives its type.

```
contentRichTextBox.SaveFile("Test.rtf", RichTextBoxStreamType.RichText);
```

TRY IT

In this Try It, you add functionality to some of the SimpleEdit program's menu items and tool strip buttons. You use the `RichTextBox` properties and methods to implement the commands in the Edit menu: Undo, Redo, Copy, Cut, Paste, Delete, and Select All. (This also makes the corresponding buttons work at no extra charge.)

Figure 7-8 shows the program with its Edit menu open.

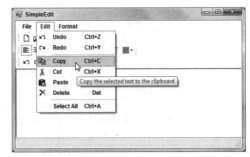

FIGURE 7-8

You can download the code and resources for this Try It from the book's web page at www.wrox.com *or* www.CSharpHelper.com/24hour.html. *You can find them in the Lesson07 folder in the download.*

Lesson Requirements

In this lesson, you:

➤ Copy the SimpleEdit program you built in Lesson 6, Exercise 5.

➤ Add code to handle the Edit menu's commands.

> ➤ Add Undo code.
>
> ➤ Add Redo code.
>
> ➤ Add Copy code.
>
> ➤ Add Cut code.
>
> ➤ Add Paste code.
>
> ➤ Add Delete code.
>
> ➤ Add Select All code.

Hints

➤ For the Delete menu item, simply set the control's `SelectedText` property to an empty string `""`.

Step-by-Step

➤ Copy the SimpleEdit program you built in Lesson 6, Exercise 5. If you skipped that exercise, download the Lesson 6 material from the book's web site at www.wrox.com and use the version it contains.

➤ Add code to handle the Edit menu's commands.

1. Open the program's form in the Form Designer. Click the `MenuStrip`, expand the Edit menu, and double-click the Undo menu item.

2. Replace the placeholder call to `MessageBox.Show` with the following line of code so the event handler looks like this:

```
private void editUndoMenuItem_Click(object sender, EventArgs e)
{
    contentRichTextBox.Undo();
}
```

3. Repeat the previous two steps for the other Edit menu items. The following code shows the new event handlers:

```
private void editUndoMenuItem_Click(object sender, EventArgs e)
{
    contentRichTextBox.Undo();
}
```

```
private void editRedoMenuItem_Click(object sender, EventArgs e)
{
    contentRichTextBox.Redo();
}

private void editCopyMenuItem_Click(object sender, EventArgs e)
{
    contentRichTextBox.Copy();
}

private void editCutMenuItem_Click(object sender, EventArgs e)
{
    contentRichTextBox.Cut();
}

private void editPasteMenuItem_Click(object sender, EventArgs e)
{
    contentRichTextBox.Paste();
}

private void editDeleteMenuItem_Click(object sender, EventArgs e)
{
    contentRichTextBox.SelectedText = "";
}

private void editSelectAllMenuItem_Click(object sender, EventArgs e)
{
    contentRichTextBox.SelectAll();
}
```

When you finish, test the program's new features. One of the RichTextBox's more remarkable features is its ability to paste different kinds of items from the clipboard. For example, copy a picture to the clipboard and then use the program to paste it into the RichTextBox.

 Please select Lesson 7 on the DVD to view the video that accompanies this lesson.

EXERCISES

1. (SimpleEdit) Copy the SimpleEdit program you built for the Try It and add simple code to handle the File menu's New, Open, Save, and Exit commands. For the New command, simply clear the RichTextBox. For the Open and Save commands, just load and save the file "Test. rtf." (The program will create the file the first time you save. If you try to open the file before it exists, the program will crash so don't use Open before you use Save.) Lesson 8 explains how to use file open and save dialogs to let the user pick the file that should be opened or saved.

2. (SimpleEdit) Copy the SimpleEdit program you built for Exercise 1 and add code to handle the Format menu's commands (except for the Font command, which is covered in Lesson 8). Remove the placeholder MessageBox.Show commands. Figure 7-9 shows the program with its Format menu and Align submenu expanded.

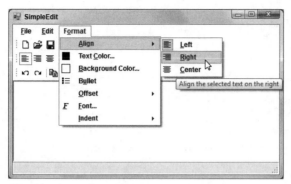

FIGURE 7-9

Hints:

➤ Keep the code that manages the menu items and tool strip buttons. For example, keep the code that makes sure only one alignment menu item and button is selected at a time.

➤ To set the foreground color, use the color stored in `foreColorButton.ForeColor`.

➤ To set the background color, use the color stored in `backColorButton.BackColor`.

➤ Add event handlers to the foreground and background color tool strip menu items. For example, give an event handler to the button that gives the selected text a red foreground color.

➤ Add event handlers to the `foreColorButton` and `backColorButton` buttons so when they are clicked, they apply the current color settings. This lets the user reapply the color setting previously selected by one of the sub-buttons.

➤ Make the indentation commands (None, Hanging, Left, Right, and Both) reset any other indentations. For example, the Hanging command should set the `SelectionIndent` and `SelectionRightIndent` properties to 0 as in the following code:

```
contentRichTextBox.SelectionIndent = 0;
contentRichTextBox.SelectionRightIndent = 0;
contentRichTextBox.SelectionHangingIndent = 20;
```

3. The SimpleEdit program allows only the indentation styles None, Hanging, Left, Right, and Both. It doesn't allow other combinations such as Hanging plus Left. Build a program that uses tool strip buttons to let the user select each of the indentation properties (hanging, left, and right) individually. Provide a fourth button to clear all of the indentation properties.

You can download the solutions to these exercises from the book's web page at www.wrox.com *or* www.CSharpHelper.com/24hour.html. *You can find them in the Lesson07 folder in the download.*

Using Standard Dialogs

A huge number of applications need to display dialogs to let the user select certain standard pieces of information. Probably the most common dialogs let the user select a file to open and select a file to save into. Other dialogs let the user select colors, filesystem folders, fonts, and printers for printing.

Closely related to the print dialog are the print preview dialog (which lets the user see a preview of a printout before sending it to the printer, possibly saving paper if the user then cancels the printout) and the page setup dialog (which lets the user select things like margins before printing).

You could build all of these dialogs yourself (or you will be able to once you've finished reading this book), but why should you? If so many programs need the exact same features, why shouldn't someone build standard dialogs that everyone can use?

Happily that's exactly what Microsoft did.

Visual C# comes with the following standard dialogs that handle these common tasks:

- ➤ ColorDialog
- ➤ FolderBrowserDialog
- ➤ FontDialog
- ➤ OpenFileDialog
- ➤ PageSetupDialog
- ➤ PrintDialog
- ➤ PrintPreviewDialog
- ➤ SaveFileDialog

You might remember that in Lesson 1, I said, "Normally you don't need to worry about whether a feature is provided by Visual Studio, the C# language, or the .NET Framework." That's true here as well, but it's informative to note that these dialogs are actually provided by the .NET Framework not C#. That doesn't change the way you use them, but it means they're the same dialogs used by all .NET languages such as Visual Basic, Visual C++, or JScript.

By building these standard dialogs into the .NET Framework, Microsoft lets programmers using many languages share the same common features.

These dialogs provide some fairly sophisticated features for you automatically with no additional code. For example, the `OpenFileDialog` class lets the user browse through the filesystem to select a file to open. The dialog can automatically verify that the file actually exists so the user cannot type in the name of a non-existent file and click Open.

Similarly, the `SaveFileDialog` class automatically prompts the user if the selected file *does* exist. For example, if the user selects the existing file Test.txt, the dialog displays the message "Test.txt already exists. Do you want to replace it?" If the user doesn't click Yes, the dialog doesn't close. By the time the dialog closes, the user must have picked a file that doesn't yet exist or signed off on destroying the original file.

In this lesson you learn how to display these standard dialogs. You learn how to initialize them to show the user the program's current settings, how to tell whether the user clicked the dialog's OK or Cancel button, and how to use the selections the user made.

This lesson actually cheats a bit on the printing dialogs. Although it explains how to display these dialogs, you can't do anything really useful with them until you know how to print, which is a much more complicated topic. Lesson 31 gets into the details of how to print.

USING DIALOGS IN GENERAL

You can use all of the standard dialogs in more or less the same way. The only differences are in how you initialize the dialogs so they show colors, fonts, files, or whatever, and in how you handle the results.

You can use a standard dialog by following these four steps:

1. Add the dialog to the form.

2. Initialize the dialog to show current settings.

3. Display the dialog and check the return result.

4. Process the results.

Adding the Dialog to the Form

You can add a dialog to a form just as you add any other component such as a `Timer`. Like other components, the dialog appears below the form in the component tray.

The control Toolbox has a Dialogs tab that contains most of the standard dialogs so they are easy to find. The printing-related dialogs are contained in the Printing tab so they're also easy to find (if you know to look there). Figure 8-1 shows the Toolbox's Printing and Dialogs tabs.

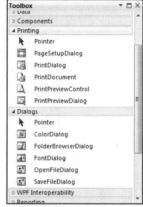

Initializing the Dialog

Most of the standard dialogs start with some initial selection. The `FontDialog` starts with a font selected, the `ColorDialog` starts with a color selected, and so forth. Normally you should initialize the dialog so it shows the user the current settings. For example, a `FontDialog` should show the program's current font.

Usually making these initial selections is easy. Simply set the dialog's key property (`Font`, `Color`, `Filename`) to the value you want to display.

FIGURE 8-1

For example, the following code sets a `ColorDialog`'s `Color` property to the form's current `BackColor` value. (Recall that `this` means the form or other object that is currently executing the code.)

```
backgroundColorDialog.Color = this.BackColor;
```

The only real trick here is in knowing what properties to set. Table 8-1 lists the key properties for the different kinds of dialogs.

TABLE 8-1

DIALOG	KEY PROPERTY
ColorDialog	Color
FolderBrowserDialog	SelectedPath
FontDialog	Font
OpenFileDialog	FileName
SaveFileDialog	FileName

The `PageSetupDialog`, `PrintDialog`, and `PrintPreviewDialog` are a bit different from the others so I won't say anything more about them here. However, printing is covered in more detail in Lesson 31 and Lesson 41.

I just said that you should initialize the dialogs to show current values, but the file open and save dialogs have a special feature that might make you decide to skip this step. When you use these dialogs, they remember the directories they displayed last. That means if the user opens one of these dialogs again, it starts in the same directory it was in last time. In fact, if the user closes and restarts the program, the dialogs still remember where they were last.

If you have several different OpenFileDialogs *(or* SaveFileDialogs*) in the same program, they all share the same idea of where they were last.*

The only reason you might want to initialize these dialogs is if you want the program to separately track more than one file (perhaps different places to save text files, bitmaps, and RTF files). Also note that the OpenFileDialog and SaveFileDialog remember the same directory, so if you want to be able to load from one directory and save into another you might need to store the directories somewhere so you can initialize the dialogs.

Displaying the Dialog and Checking the Return Result

You display all of the standard dialogs by calling their ShowDialog methods. ShowDialog displays the dialog modally and then returns a value to tell you whether the user clicked OK, Cancel, or some other button.

Note that the OK buttons on some of the dialogs don't actually say "OK." The OpenFileDialog's *OK button says "Open," the* SaveFileDialog's *OK button says "Save," and the* PrintDialog's *OK button says "Print." As far as the program is concerned, however, they're all OK buttons, and you test for them all in the same way.*

Your code should test the returned result and, if the user clicked OK, it should do something with the user's selection.

Unfortunately to make that test, you need to use an if statement, and if statements aren't covered until Lesson 18. Luckily this particular use of if statements is quite simple, so I only feel a little guilty about showing it to you now.

The following code shows how a program can display a ColorDialog named backgroundColorDialog. The code calls the ShowDialog method. It then compares the value that ShowDialog returns to the value DialogResult.OK. If the values are equal (that's what == means), the program does whatever is inside the braces (which I've omitted here).

```
if (backgroundColorDialog.ShowDialog() == DialogResult.OK)
{
    . . .
}
```

If the user clicks the Cancel button, then ShowDialog returns the value DialogResult.Cancel, so the if test fails and the program skips the code inside the braces.

If you use IntelliSense to select the OK value on the right in this code, you get System.Windows.Forms.DialogResult.OK *instead of the simpler* DialogResult .OK. *That's okay; IntelliSense just includes more detailed information about where the value is defined. They both represent the same value.*

(If you're curious and you go to the very top of your code, you'll see several using *directives including one that says* using System.Windows.Forms. *That tells the compiler that if it can't find a value such as* DialogResult.OK *locally, it should look in* System.Windows.Forms, *and in this case that's where it will find it.)*

Processing the Results

Finally, if the user clicked OK, the program should do something with whatever the user selected in the dialog. Often this means doing the opposite of the step where you initialized the dialog. For example, suppose a program uses the following code to initialize its ColorDialog:

```
backgroundColorDialog.Color = this.BackColor;
```

Then it would use the following code to set the form's BackColor property to the color that the user selected:

```
this.BackColor = backgroundColorDialog.Color;
```

Putting It All Together

The following code shows the whole sequence for a ColorDialog. The program initializes the dialog, displays it and checks the return value, and processes the result.

```
backgroundColorDialog.Color = this.BackColor;
if (backgroundColorDialog.ShowDialog() == DialogResult.OK)
{
    this.BackColor = backgroundColorDialog.Color;
}
```

This looks a bit more complicated than previous code examples but it's not too bad. The only new part is the if test. The other statements simply set the dialog's Color property equal to the form's BackColor property and vice versa, and you've been setting properties for quite a while now.

USING DIALOG PROPERTIES

Table 8-1 earlier in this chapter listed the dialogs' key properties, but some of the dialogs have other useful properties, too.

For example, the `ColorDialog` has an `AllowFullOpen` property that determines whether the user can click the dialog's Define Custom Colors button to show an area where the user can create new colors. Figure 8-2 shows a `ColorDialog` displaying this area.

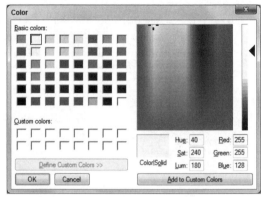

You can learn more about these extra properties by reading the online help. For example, Microsoft's help page for the `ColorDialog` is msdn.microsoft.com/en-us/library/system .windows.forms.colordialog.aspx. You can replace *colordialog* in this URL with the name of another dialog to find its web page.

FIGURE 8-2

Table 8-2 summarizes the `ColorDialog`'s most useful properties.

TABLE 8-2

PROPERTY	PURPOSE
AllowFullOpen	Determines whether the user can create custom colors.
Color	The selected color.
FullOpen	Determines whether the custom color area is open when the dialog appears.

Table 8-3 summarizes the `FolderBrowserDialog`'s most useful properties.

TABLE 8-3

PROPERTY	PURPOSE
RootFolder	The root folder where the dialog starts browsing. This can take values such as `Desktop`, `Favorites`, `History`, and `MyComputer`. The Properties window lets you pick from those values.
SelectedPath	The selected folder.

Table 8-4 summarizes the `FontDialog`'s most useful properties.

TABLE 8-4

PROPERTY	PURPOSE
FixedPitchOnly	Determines if the dialog allows the user to select only fixed-width fonts. This is useful, for example, if you are going to use the font to build a report and you need the characters to all have the same width so columns line up properly.

PROPERTY	PURPOSE
Font	The selected font.
FontMustExist	Determines whether or not the dialog raises an error if the selected font doesn't exist (for example, if the user types "ExtraBold" for the font style and that style isn't available for the selected font).
MaxSize	The largest allowed size for the font.
ShowColor	Determines whether or not the dialog lets the user select a font color. If you set this to True, use the dialog's Color property to see which color was selected.
ShowEffects	Determines whether or not the dialog lets the user select underline, strike-out, and font color. (To select font color, ShowColor and ShowEffects must both be True.)

Table 8-5 summarizes the OpenFileDialog's most useful properties.

TABLE 8-5

PROPERTY	PURPOSE
AddExtension	If this is True and the user selects a filename without an extension, the dialog adds the default extension to the name.
CheckFileExists	If this is True, the dialog won't let the user pick a file that doesn't exist.
CheckPathExists	If this is True, the dialog won't let the user pick a file path that doesn't exist.
DefaultExt	The default file extension.
FileName	The selected file's name.
Filter	The file selection filter. (See the section "Using File Filters" later in this lesson for details.)
FilterIndex	The index of the currently selected filter. (See the section "Using File Filters" later in this lesson for details.)
InitialDirectory	The directory where the dialog initially starts.
ReadOnlyChecked	Indicates whether the user checked the dialog's Read Only box.
ShowReadOnly	Determines whether the dialog displays its Read Only box.
Title	The text displayed in the dialog's title bar.

The `SaveFileDialog` has many of the same properties as the `OpenFileDialog`. See Table 8-5 for descriptions of the properties `AddExtension`, `CheckFileExists`, `CheckPathExists`, `DefaultExt`, `FileName`, `Filter`, `FilterIndex`, `InitialDirectory`, and `Title`.

Table 8-6 summarizes `SaveFileDialog` properties that are not shared with the `OpenFileDialog`.

TABLE 8-6

PROPERTY	PURPOSE
CreatePrompt	If this is `True`, and the user selects a file that doesn't exist, the dialog asks if the user wants to create the file.
OverwritePrompt	If this is `True` and the user selects a file that already exists, the dialog asks if the user wants to overwrite it.
ValidateNames	Determines whether the dialog verifies that the filename doesn't contain any invalid characters.

Table 8-7 summarizes the `PrintDialog`'s most useful property.

TABLE 8-7

PROPERTY	PURPOSE
Document	You set this property to tell the dialog what document object to print. Lesson 31 has more to say about this.

Table 8-8 summarizes the `PrintPreviewDialog`'s most useful property.

TABLE 8-8

PROPERTY	PURPOSE
Document	You set this property to tell the dialog what document object to preview. Lesson 31 has more to say about this.

USING FILE FILTERS

Most of the dialogs' properties are fairly easy to understand. Two properties that are particularly confusing and important, however, are the `Filter` and `FilterIndex` properties provided by the `OpenFileDialog` and `SaveFileDialog`.

The `Filter` property is a list of text prompts and file matching patterns separated by the | character. The items alternate between text prompts and the corresponding filter. The dialog provides a drop-down list where the user can select one of the text prompts. When the user selects a prompt, the dialog uses the corresponding filter to decide which files to display.

For example, consider the following value:

```
Bitmap Files|*.bmp|Graphic Files|*.bmp;*.gif;*.png;*.jpg|All Files|*.*
```

This value represents three file types:

➤ The text prompt "Bitmap Files" with filter `*.bmp`.

➤ The text prompt "Graphic Files" with filter `*.bmp;*.gif;*.png;*jpg`. That filter matches files ending with .bmp, .gif, .png, or .jpg.

➤ The text prompt "All Files" with filter `*.*`.

Figure 8-3 shows an `OpenFileDialog`. The filter dropdown (just above the Open and Cancel buttons) has the text prompt "Graphics Files" selected. (The dialog automatically added the filter in parentheses just to confuse the user.) The dialog is listing the files in this directory that match the filter. In this case, the directory only contains a couple bitmaps and png files, and some other non-graphical files.

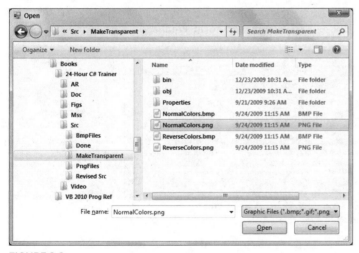

FIGURE 8-3

Once you understand the `Filter` property, the `FilterIndex` property is simple. `FilterIndex` is simply the index of the selected filter, where 1 means the first filter. (Remember in Lesson 7 when I said, "almost all numbering starts with 0 in C#"? This is one of the exceptions.) You can use `FilterIndex` to initially select the filter that you think will be most useful for the user.

The `OpenFileDialog` and `SaveFileDialog` both use the same type of `Filter` and `FilterIndex` properties. In fact, usually if a program displays both of these dialogs, they should use the same `Filter` value. If a program can load .txt and .rtf files, it should probably be able to save .txt and .rtf files.

To carry this idea one step further, you could set the `SaveFileDialog`'s *`FilterIndex` property to the value selected by the user in the* `OpenFileDialog` *under the assumption that a user who loads a .txt file is later likely to want to save it as a .txt file.*

TRY IT

In this Try It, you get to try out all of the standard dialogs except the `PageSetupDialog` (which is hard to use until you're doing actual printing). You initialize, display, and process the results of the dialogs (if the user clicks the OK button).

> *You can download the code and resources for this Try It from the book's web page at* www.wrox.com *or* www.CSharpHelper.com/24hour.html. *You can find them in the Lesson08 folder in the download.*

Lesson Requirements

In this lesson, you:

> ➤ Use `Labels`, `TextBoxes`, and `Buttons` to make a form similar to the one shown in Figure 8-4.

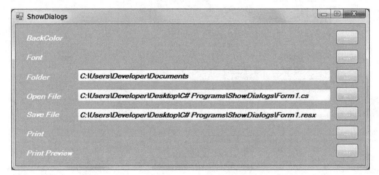

FIGURE 8-4

> ➤ Add `ColorDialog`, `FontDialog`, `FolderBrowserDialog`, `OpenFileDialog`, `SaveFileDialog`, `PrintDialog`, and `PrintPreviewDialog` components to the form.

> ➤ When the user clicks the BackColor button, display the `ColorDialog` but don't allow the user to define custom colors. If the user clicks OK, set the form's `BackColor` property to the dialog's `Color` value.

> ➤ When the user clicks the Font button, display the `FontDialog`, allowing the user to select the font's color. If the user clicks OK, set the form's `Font` property to the dialog's `Font` value and its `ForeColor` property to the dialog's `Color` property.

> ➤ When the user clicks the Folder button, display the `FolderBrowserDialog`. Make the dialog start browsing at MyComputer. If the user clicks OK, make the Folder `TextBox` display the dialog's `SelectedPath` property.

➤ When the user clicks the Open File button, display the OpenFileDialog. Use a filter that lets the user select text files, RTF files, or all files. If the user clicks Open, make the Open File TextBox display the dialog's FileName property and set the SaveFileDialog's FilterIndex equal to the OpenFileDialog's FilterIndex.

➤ When the user clicks the Save File button, display the SaveFileDialog. Use a filter similar to the one used by the OpenFileDialog. If the user clicks Save, make the Save File TextBox display the dialog's FileName property and set the OpenFileDialog's FilterIndex equal to the SaveFileDialog's FilterIndex.

➤ When the user clicks the Print button, display the PrintDialog. Ignore the return result.

➤ When the user clicks the Print Preview button, display the PrintPreviewDialog. Ignore the return result.

Hints

➤ Be sure to initialize each of the dialogs before displaying them.

Step-by-Step

➤ Use Labels, TextBoxes, and Buttons to make a form similar to the one shown in Figure 8-4.

1. Add and arrange the controls in whatever manner you find easiest.

2. Set the Buttons' Anchor properties to Top, Right. Set the TextBoxes' Anchor properties to Top, Left, Right.

➤ Add ColorDialog, FontDialog, FolderBrowserDialog, OpenFileDialog, SaveFileDialog, PrintDialog, and PrintPreviewDialog components to the form.

1. Add the dialogs. They appear in the Component Tray, not on the form.

2. Give the dialogs good names.

➤ When the user clicks the BackColor button, display the ColorDialog but don't allow the user to define custom colors. If the user clicks OK, set the form's BackColor property to the dialog's Color value.

1. To prevent the user from defining custom colors, set the ColorDialog's AllowFullOpen property to False.

2. Use code similar to the following:

```
private void backgroundColorButton_Click(object sender, EventArgs e)
{
    backgroundColorDialog.Color = this.BackColor;
    if (backgroundColorDialog.ShowDialog() == DialogResult.OK)
    {
        this.BackColor = backgroundColorDialog.Color;
    }
}
```

➤ When the user clicks the Font button, display the `FontDialog`, allowing the user to select the font's color. If the user clicks OK, set the form's `Font` property to the dialog's `Font` value and its `ForeColor` property to the dialog's `Color` property.

1. To allow the user to select the font's color, set the dialog's `ShowColor` property to `True`.

2. Use code similar to the following:

```
private void fontButton_Click(object sender, EventArgs e)
{
    formFontDialog.Color = this.ForeColor;
    formFontDialog.Font = this.Font;
    if (formFontDialog.ShowDialog() == DialogResult.OK)
    {
        this.Font = formFontDialog.Font;
        this.ForeColor = formFontDialog.Color;
    }
}
```

➤ When the user clicks the Folder button, display the `FolderBrowserDialog`. Make the dialog start browsing at MyComputer. If the user clicks OK, make the Folder `TextBox` display the dialog's `SelectedPath` property.

1. To start browsing at MyComputer, set the dialog's `RootFolder` property to MyComputer.

2. Use code similar to the following:

```
private void folderButton_Click(object sender, EventArgs e)
{
    if (testFolderBrowserDialog.ShowDialog() == DialogResult.OK)
    {
        folderTextBox.Text = testFolderBrowserDialog.SelectedPath;
    }
}
```

➤ When the user clicks the Open File button, display the `OpenFileDialog`. Use a filter that lets the user select text files, RTF files, or all files. If the user clicks Open, make the Open File `TextBox` display the dialog's `FileName` property and set the `SaveFileDialog`'s `FilterIndex` equal to the `OpenFileDialog`'s `FilterIndex`.

1. Use the filter:

```
Text Files|*.txt|RTF Files|*.rtf|All Files|*.*
```

2. Use code similar to the following:

```
private void openFileButton_Click(object sender, EventArgs e)
{
    if (testOpenFileDialog.ShowDialog() == DialogResult.OK)
    {
        openFileTextBox.Text = testOpenFileDialog.FileName;
        testSaveFileDialog.FilterIndex = testOpenFileDialog.FilterIndex;
    }
}
```

➤ When the user clicks the Save File button, display the SaveFileDialog. Use a filter similar to the one used by the OpenFileDialog. If the user clicks Save, make the Save File TextBox display the dialog's FileName property and set the OpenFileDialog's FilterIndex equal to the SaveFileDialog's FilterIndex.

1. Use the filter:

```
Text Files|*.txt|RTF Files|*.rtf|All Files|*.*
```

2. Use code similar to the following:

```
private void saveFileDialog_Click(object sender, EventArgs e)
{
    if (testSaveFileDialog.ShowDialog() == DialogResult.OK)
    {
        saveFileTextBox.Text = testSaveFileDialog.FileName;
        testOpenFileDialog.FilterIndex = testSaveFileDialog.FilterIndex;
    }
}
```

➤ When the user clicks the Print button, display the PrintDialog. Ignore the return result.

1. Use code similar to the following:

```
private void printDialog_Click(object sender, EventArgs e)
{
    testPrintDialog.ShowDialog();
}
```

➤ When the user clicks the Print Preview button, display the PrintPreviewDialog. Ignore the return result.

1. Use code similar to the following:

```
private void printPreviewDialog_Click(object sender, EventArgs e)
{
    testPrintPreviewDialog.ShowDialog();
}
```

 Please select Lesson 8 on the DVD to view the video that accompanies this lesson.

EXERCISES

1. (SimpleEdit) Copy the SimpleEdit program you built in Lesson 7, Exercise 2 (or download Lesson 7's version from the book's web site) and add the file open and save dialogs for the File menu's Open and Save As commands. Use Filter properties that let the user select RTF files, text files, or all files. Continue using the RichTextBox's LoadFile and SaveFile methods even though they won't really work properly for non-RTF files.

2. (SimpleEdit) Copy the SimpleEdit program you built for Exercise 1 and add a font selection dialog for the Format menu's Font item, and the font tool strip button. If the user selects a font and clicks OK, set the form's font to the selected font.

3. (SimpleEdit) Copy the SimpleEdit program you built for Exercise 2 and add color selection dialogs for the Format menu's Text Color and Background Color items. If the user selects a color and clicks OK for these, set the corresponding menu items' Image properties to the special value null, so they don't display any sample. (Displaying a sample of an arbitrary color is outside the scope of this lesson.)

You can download the solutions to these exercises from the book's web page at www.wrox.com *or* www.CSharpHelper.com/24hour.html. *You can find those solutions in the SimpleEdit folder within the Lesson08 folder.*

Creating and Displaying New Forms

Most of this book so far has dealt with building forms. Previous lessons explained how to add, arrange, and handle the events of controls on a form. They've explained how to work with specific kinds of controls such as MenuStrips, ContextMenuStrips, and ToolStrips. Using these techniques, you can build some pretty nice forms that use simple code to manipulate properties. So far, however, you've only learned how a program can use a single form.

In this lesson you learn how to display multiple forms in a single program. You see how to add new forms to the project and how to display one or more instances of those forms. Once you've mastered these techniques, you can make programs that display any number of forms for all kinds of different purposes.

ADDING NEW FORMS

To add a new form to a project, open the IDE's Project menu and select Add Windows Form to see the dialog shown in Figure 9-1.

Leave the Windows Form template selected, enter a good name for the new type of form, and click Add. After you click Add, Visual Studio adds the new form type to the project. Figure 9-2 shows the new form in Solution Explorer.

Now you can add Labels, TextBoxes, Buttons, MenuStrips, and any other controls you like to the new form.

 Remember, to open a form in the Form Designer, double-click it in Solution Explorer.

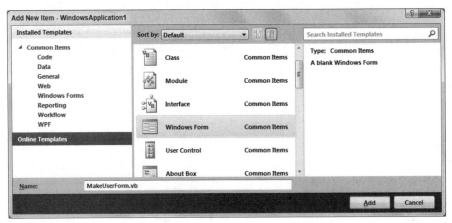

FIGURE 9-1

UNDERSTANDING CLASSES AND INSTANCES

FIGURE 9-2

When you add a new form to the project, you're really adding a new *type* of form, not a new instance of that type. If you add the MakeUserForm type to a project and then run the program, you still only see the original startup form (with the catchy name Form1) and MakeUserForm is nowhere to be seen.

Form types such as Form1 and MakeUserForm are *classes*. They're like blueprints for making copies of the class called *instances*. These are important and sometimes confusing topics so I'm going to explain them briefly now and explain them again in greater detail later in the book in the lessons in Section IV.

A class defines the characteristics of any objects from that class. Your code can use the new keyword to create objects of the class. Once you define the class you can make as many copies — instances — as you like, and every copy is identical in structure to all of the others. Different instances may have different property values but their overall features are the same.

For example, suppose you define a MakeUserForm that has FirstName, LastName, Street, City, State, and ZIP labels and textboxes. Now suppose your program displays two instances of this class. Both of the forms will have the same labels and textboxes, so they have basically the same structure. However, the user can type different values into the two forms.

Your code can also change different instances in various ways. For example, menu items, buttons, and other controls could invoke event handlers that modify the form: change its colors, move controls around, resize the form, or whatever. Here's one of the more potentially confusing features of classes: the code in the event handlers modify the form that is currently running the code.

For example, suppose you build a form that has three Buttons that change the form's BackColor property to red, green, and blue, and then you display three instances of the form. When the user clicks the first form's Red button, the event handler makes the first form red but the other forms are unchanged. The code in the event handler is running in the first form's instance so that's the form it affects.

Hopefully by now you think I've beaten this topic into the ground and you understand the difference between the class (`MakeUserForm`) and the instance (a copy of `MakeUserForm` visible on the screen). If so, you're ready to learn how to actually display forms.

DISPLAYING FORMS

The `new` keyword creates a new instance of a form. If you want to do anything useful with the form, your code needs a way to refer to the instance it just created. It can do that with a *variable*. I'm jumping the gun a bit by discussing variables (they're covered in detail in Lesson 11) but, as was the case when I introduced the `if` statement in Lesson 8, this particular use of the concept is very useful and not too confusing, so I only feel a little guilty about discussing it now.

To declare a variable to refer to a form instance, you enter the form's type followed by whatever name you want to give the new instance. For example, the following code declares a variable named `newUserForm` of type `MakeUserForm`:

```
MakeUserForm newUserForm;
```

At this point, the program has a variable that *could* refer to a `MakeUserForm` object but right now it doesn't refer to anything. At this point the variable contains the special value `null`, which basically means it doesn't refer to anything.

To make the variable refer to a form instance, the code uses the `new` keyword to create the instance and then sets the variable equal to the result. For example, the following code creates a new `MakeNewUser` form and makes the `newUserForm` variable point to it:

```
newUserForm = new MakeUserForm();
```

Now the variable refers to the new form. The final step is to display that form. You can do this by calling the new form's `ShowDialog` or `Show` method.

Technically the variable doesn't hold or contain the form. Instead it contains a reference to the form. The reference is like an address that points to where the form really is in memory. When your code says something like `newUserForm`
`.Show()`, it hunts down the actual form instance and invokes its `Show` method.

For now the distinction is small and you don't need to worry too much about it, but later it will be useful to know that some variables are value types that actually hold their values (`int`, `long`, `double`) and some are reference types that hold references to their values (object references and interestingly `string`).

Lesson 17 says a bit more about this when it discusses structures.

The ShowDialog method displays the form *modally*. That means the form appears on top of the program's other forms and the user cannot interact with the other forms until this form closes.

This is the way dialogs normally work. For example, when you open the IDE's Project menu and select Add Windows Form, the Add New Item dialog displays modally so you cannot interact with other parts of the IDE (the Properties window, Solution Explorer, the menus) until you close the dialog by clicking Add or Cancel.

The following code displays the form referred to by the variable newUserForm modally:

```
newUserForm.ShowDialog();
```

The Show method displays the form *non-modally*. That means the form appears and the user can interact with it or with the program's other forms.

The following code displays the form referred to by the variable newUserForm non-modally:

```
newUserForm.Show();
```

The UserForms example program shown in Figure 9-3 (and available as part of this lesson's code download at www.wrox.com) displays a main form with a New User button. Each time you click the button, the program displays a new MakeUserForm. In Figure 9-3, you can see the main form and two MakeUserForms.

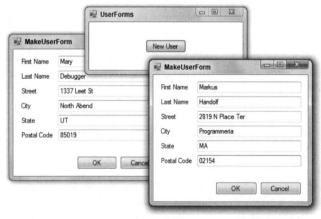

FIGURE 9-3

The following code shows how program UserForms displays a new MakeUserForm when you click its button. The code declares a variable to refer to the form, creates the new form instance, and displays the instance non-modally.

```
private void newUserButton_Click(object sender, EventArgs e)
{
    MakeUserForm newUserForm;
    newUserForm = new MakeUserForm();
    newUserForm.Show();
}
```

Each time you click the button, the event handler executes again. Each time it runs, the event handler creates a new version of the variable named newUserForm, makes a new instance of the MakeUserForm, and displays that instance, so each time you click the button, you get a new form.

FLOOD OF FORMS

The startup form's type Form1 is just like any other form type, so a program can make new instances of it. That means you can create more forms that look just like the startup form if you want.

However, though all forms look about the same to the user, the startup form has a special position in the application. The program keeps running only as long as the startup form exists. If you close that form all of the others close, too.

To avoid confusion, you should generally make the startup form look different from other forms so the user knows that it is special.

CONTROLLING REMOTE FORMS

When you create a new form and make a variable to refer to it, you can later use that variable to manipulate the form. There's just one catch: the techniques described so far don't keep the new form variable around long enough to be useful.

For example, the following code defines the newUserForm variable, makes it point to a new form, and displays the form:

```
private void newUserButton_Click(object sender, EventArgs e)
{
    MakeUserForm newUserForm;
    newUserForm = new MakeUserForm();
    newUserForm.Show();
}
```

When the code finishes executing the event handler, the event handler stops running. If the user clicks the button again, the event handler springs back into action.

Unfortunately, when the event handler stops running, it loses its grip on the newUserForm variable. The next time the event handler runs, it creates a new variable named newUserForm and works with that one.

This is bad for a program that wants to manipulate the new form later. Because the variable is gone, it cannot refer to it to manipulate the form.

The good news is that this is fairly easy to fix. If you move the variable's declaration out of the event handler, the variable exists throughout the program's lifetime. The event handler can make the variable point to a new form, and it can then use the variable later to manipulate that form.

The following code demonstrates this technique. The main form's `Load` event handler creates and displays a new `ColorForm`. When the user clicks the main form's Red button, its event handler changes the remote form's `BackColor` and `ForeColor` properties. The startup form also contains green and blue buttons that have similar event handlers.

```
// The remote form we will manipulate.
ColorForm remoteColorForm;

// Create and display the remote form.
private void Form1_Load(object sender, EventArgs e)
{
    remoteColorForm = new ColorForm();
    remoteColorForm.Show();
}

// Make the color form red.
private void redButton_Click(object sender, EventArgs e)
{
    remoteColorForm.BackColor = Color.Red;
    remoteColorForm.ForeColor = Color.Pink;
}
```

Here the `remoteColorForm` variable is declared outside of the event handlers. The form's `Load` event handler initializes the variable and displays the remote form. The `redButton_Click` event handler uses it. Because the variable is declared outside of the event handlers, they can all use it. (Lesson 13 has more to say about when and where variables are available to the code.)

 In the previous example, I moved the code that creates the `ColorForm` *into the main form's* `Load` *event handler. If that code stayed in a* `Button's` `Click` *event handler, the user could click it a bunch of times and create many different forms. Each time the program created a form, it would make the variable refer to the new one so it would "forget" the previous form. Then the Red button would affect only the most recent form and not any others.*

The RemoteForm example program shown in Figure 9-4 (and available as part of this lesson's code download at www.wrox.com) uses similar code to make its `ColorForm` red, green, or blue.

In addition to modifying a remote form's properties, you can change the properties of the controls on that form. You refer to a control by using the form variable, followed by a dot, followed by the control's name.

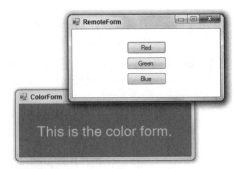

FIGURE 9-4

For example, the bold line in the following code accesses the form referred to by the `remoteColorForm` variable. It locates that form's `messageLabel` control and changes its `Text` property to "I'm red!"

```
private void btnRed_Click(object sender, EventArgs e)
{
    color_form.BackColor = Color.Red;
    color_form.ForeColor = Color.Pink;
    color_form.lblMessage.Text = "I'm red!";
}
```

There's one small catch to this technique: by default the controls on a form are private so no other form can peek at them. You can easily fix this by setting a control's `Modifiers` property to `Public`. Now the other form can see the variable and change its properties.

> *Controls on a form are private to prevent other pieces of code from accidentally messing them up. By making a variable public, you remove this safeguard. In technical terms, you have weakened the form's encapsulation, its ability to hide its internal details from the outside world.*
>
> *In this case, you want to allow access to this label's* Text *property so marking the label as public isn't terribly unreasonable. However, by making the label public you make all of its properties, methods, and events public, not just its* Text *property.*
>
> *A more restrictive approach would be to add a public* SetCaption *method to the* ColorForm. *Then other code would call that method instead of setting the label's text directly. You learn how to build methods such as this one in Lesson 20.*

TRY IT

In this Try It, you create an application similar to the one shown in Figure 9-5. When the user clicks the main form's buttons, the program displays the other forms non-modally.

> *You can download the code and resources for this Try It from the book's web page at* www.wrox.com *or* www.CSharpHelper.com/24hour.html. *You can find them in the Lesson09 folder in the download.*

Lesson Requirements

In this lesson, you:

➤   Create the forms shown in Figure 9-5.

➤   Declare the form variables outside of any event handler.

➤ In the main form's `Load` event handler, add code to create the form instances but don't display the forms.

➤ Add code to the main form's `Button` event handlers to display the corresponding secondary forms non-modally.

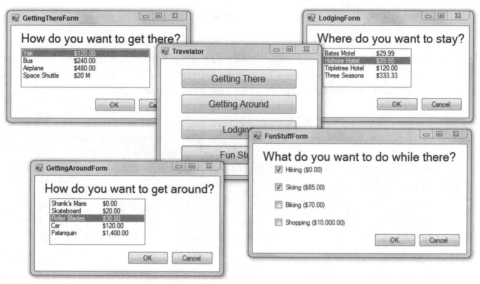

FIGURE 9-5

Hints

➤ Normally every form appears in the taskbar. To avoid cluttering the taskbar with all of the secondary forms, set their `ShowInTaskbar` properties to `False`.

Step-by-Step

➤ Create the forms shown in Figure 9-5.

1. Create the main form.

a. Start a new project. In the Properties window, expand the main form's `Font` property and set its `Size` sub-property to 12.

b. Add the `Buttons`. Center them as a group and set their `Anchor` properties to `None`.

2. Create the `GettingThereForm`.

a. Open the Project menu and select Add Windows Form. Enter the form type name `GettingThereForm` and click Add.

    b.   Set the form's `ShowInTaskbar` property to `False`.

    c.   Add the `Label`, `ListBox`, and `Buttons`. Set the `ListBox`'s `Anchor` property to `Top`, `Bottom`, `Left`. Set the `Buttons`' `Anchor` properties to `Bottom`, `Right`.

3.   Create the `GettingAroundForm`.

    a.   Repeat step 2 for the `GettingAroundForm`.

4.   Create the `LodgingForm`.

    a.   Repeat step 2 for the `LodgingForm`.

5.   Create the `FunStuffForm`.

    a.   Repeat step 2 for the `FunStuffForm`. Leave the `CheckBoxes`' `Anchor` properties with their default values `Top`, `Left`.

➤   Declare the form variables outside of any event handler.

1.   Add the following to the main form's code module outside of any event handlers:

```
// The remote forms.
GettingThereForm theGettingThereForm;
GettingAroundForm theGettingAroundForm;
LodgingForm theLodgingForm;
FunStuffForm theFunStuffForm;
```

➤   In the main form's `Load` event handler, add code to create the form instances but don't display the forms.

1.   Use code similar to the following:

```
// Initialize the forms but don't display them.
private void Form1_Load(object sender, EventArgs e)
{
    theGettingThereForm = new GettingThereForm();
    theGettingAroundForm = new GettingAroundForm();
    theLodgingForm = new LodgingForm();
    theFunStuffForm = new FunStuffForm();
}
```

➤   Add code to the main form's `Button` event handlers to display the corresponding secondary forms non-modally.

1.   Create the `Button Click` event handlers and make each call the corresponding form variable's `Show` method:

```
// Display the getting there form.
private void gettingThereButton_Click(object sender, EventArgs e)
{
    theGettingThereForm.Show();
}

// Display the getting around form.
private void gettingAroundButton_Click(object sender, EventArgs e)
{
```

```
        theGettingAroundForm.Show();
    }

    // Display the lodging form.
    private void lodgingButton_Click(object sender, EventArgs e)
    {
        theLodgingForm.Show();
    }

    // Display the fun stuff form.
    private void funnStuffButton_Click(object sender, EventArgs e)
    {
        theFunStuffForm.Show();
    }
```

 Please select Lesson 9 on the DVD to view the video that accompanies this lesson.

EXERCISES

1. Make a program that displays a `Button` that says "New Form." When the user clicks the `Button`, display a new non-modal instance of the same kind of form. (What happens when you click the new form's button? What happens if you close the new form? What happens if you make several forms and close the original one?)

2. Copy the program you made for Exercise 1 and add a `TextBox` named `valueTextBox` to the form. Before you display the new form, copy the main form's `TextBox` value into the new form's `TextBox`. (Hint: You don't need to set the `TextBox`'s `Modifiers` property to `Public` because the new form is the same kind as the old one. You need to do this only if a form of one type wants to peek at the controls on a form of a different type.)

3. Make a program that displays a `TextBox` and a "New Form" `Button`. When the user clicks the `Button`, display a new form of type `MessageForm` modally.

   The `MessageForm` holds two `Label`s. The first `Label` says "You entered." The second `Label` is blank. When it displays the `MessageForm`, the main program should copy whatever is in its `TextBox` into the `MessageForm`'s second label. (Hint: Now you need to set the label's `Modifiers` property to `Public`.)

4. Build the PickAPicture program shown in Figure 9-6. When the user clicks one of the thumbnail images on the main form, the program displays a `PictureForm` showing the image at full scale. Use whatever images you like. (Hints: Display the thumbnail images in `PictureBoxes` with `ScaleMode` set to `Zoom`. Set the `PictureForm`'s `BackgroundImage` property equal to the `PictureBox`'s `Image` value.)

5. **Extra Credit:** As I've mentioned before, redundant code is usually a sign that the program's structure can be improved. The PickAPicture program from Exercise 4 uses four practically identical event handlers. The only difference is the image that they assign to the `PictureForm`'s background.

FIGURE 9-6

You can improve this program by making all four `PictureBoxes` use the same event handler and making the event handler figure out which image to use.

The event handler's `sender` parameter is the control that raised the event, in this case, the `PictureBox` that the user clicked. The data type of that parameter is object, but you can get a variable of type `PictureBox` that refers to the same object by using the `as` keyword. The `as` keyword tells the program to treat some value (in this case the `sender` parameter) as if it were some other type (in this case a `PictureBox`). The following code shows how you can get a variable that treats the `sender` parameter as a `PictureBox`.

```
PictureBox selectedPictureBox;
selectedPictureBox = sender as PictureBox;
```

Copy the program you built for Exercise 4. Modify the first event handler so it uses the `as` keyword to get a reference to the `PictureBox` that the user clicked, and then uses that `PictureBox` to set the `PictureForm`'s background. Delete the other event handlers and make all the `PictureBoxes` share the modified one.

You can download the solutions to these exercises from the book's web page at www.wrox.com *or* www.CSharpHelper.com/24hour.html. *You can find them in the Lesson09 folder in the download.*

10

Building Custom Dialogs

The standard dialogs described in Lesson 8 make it easy to perform typical chores such as picking files, folders, colors, and fonts. Those dialogs can get you pretty far, but sometimes you may want a dialog that is customized for your application.

For example, you might want to display a dialog where the user can enter a new customer's contact information (name, address, phone number, and hat size). It's unlikely that any predefined standard dialog could ever handle that situation.

Fortunately, it's easy to build custom dialogs. All you need to do is build a new form as described in Lesson 9, add a few buttons, and set a few properties.

In this lesson you learn how to build custom dialogs and make them as easy to use as the standard dialogs that come with Visual C#.

MAKING CUSTOM DIALOGS

Building a custom dialog is pretty easy. Simply add a new form to your project as described in Lesson 9 and give it whatever controls you need.

To allow the user to finish using the dialog, add one or more buttons. Some dialogs have a single OK button. Others have OK and Cancel buttons, or some other combination of buttons. Because you're creating the dialog, you can give it whatever buttons you like.

By convention, the buttons go at the bottom of the dialog in the right corner. Figure 10-1 shows a very simple dialog that contains a single textbox where the user can enter a name.

To make using the dialog easier, you can set the form's `AcceptButton` and `CancelButton` properties. These determine which button is triggered if the user presses [Enter] and [Esc], respectively. Typically the `AcceptButton` triggers the dialog's OK or Yes button and the `CancelButton` triggers the Cancel or No button.

FIGURE 10-1

Often dialogs set other properties to make them behave more like standard dialogs. Some of these include:

➤ *Setting* FormBorderStyle *to* FixedDialog *so the user cannot resize the dialog.*

➤ *Setting* MinimumSize *and* MaxiumSize *to keep the dialog a reasonable size.*

➤ *Setting* MinimizeBox *and* MaximizeBox *to* False *so the user cannot maximize or minimize the dialog.*

➤ *Setting* ShowInTaskbar *to* False *so the dialog doesn't clutter up the taskbar.*

You can make the dialog even easier to use if you set the tab order so the focus starts at the top of the form and works its way down. For example, if the dialog contains Name, Street, City, State, and ZIP textboxes, the focus should move through them in that order.

The user can press [Tab] to move between fields and can press [Enter] or [Esc] when all of the values are filled in. An experienced user can fill in this kind of dialog very quickly.

SETTING THE DIALOG RESULT

A program uses the ShowDialog method to display a dialog. This method returns a value that indicates which button the user clicked. As explained in Lesson 8, the program can check that return value to see what it should do with the dialog's results. The examples in Lesson 8 checked that ShowDialog returned the value DialogResult.OK before processing the user's selections.

The dialog form's DialogResult property determines what value the call to ShowDialog returns. For example, you could use the following code to make the dialog's OK Button set the form's DialogResult property to DialogResult.OK to tell the calling program that the user clicked the OK button:

```
// Return OK to ShowDialog.
private void okButton_Click(object sender, EventArgs e)
{
    this.DialogResult = DialogResult.OK;
}
```

Setting the form's DialogResult property not only determines the return result, but it also closes the dialog so the call to ShowDialog returns and the calling code can continue.

That means you can set the dialog's return result and close the dialog in a single line of code. Typing one line of code should be no real hardship, but believe it or not, there's an even easier way to close the dialog.

If you set a `Button`'s `DialogResult` property, the `Button` automatically sets the form's `DialogResult` property when it is clicked. For example, suppose you set the `cancelButton`'s `DialogResult` property to `DialogResult.Cancel`. When the user clicks the `Button`, it automatically sets the form's `DialogResult` property to `DialogResult.Cancel` so the form automatically closes. That lets you set the return value and close the form without typing any code at all.

If you think setting one `Button` property is still too much work, you can even avoid that, at least for the Cancel button. When you set a form's `CancelButton` property, Visual C# automatically sets that `Button`'s `DialogResult` property to `DialogResult.Cancel`.

Note that when you set the form's `AcceptButton` property, Visual C# does not automatically set the `Button`'s `DialogResult` property. The assumption is that the OK `Button` might need to validate the data the user entered on the form before it decides whether to close the dialog. For example, if the user doesn't fill in all required fields, the OK `Button` might display a message asking the user to fill in the remaining fields instead of closing the dialog.

If you don't want to perform any validation, you can simply set the OK `Button`'s `DialogResult` property to `DialogResult.OK`.

USING CUSTOM DIALOGS

A program uses a custom dialog in exactly the same way that it uses a standard dialog. It creates, initializes, and displays the dialog. It checks the return result and takes whatever action is appropriate.

There's a slight difference in how the program creates the dialog because you can add standard dialogs to a form at run time and you can't do that with custom dialogs. To use a custom dialog, the code needs to create a new instance of the dialog's form as described in Lesson 9.

The following code shows how a program might display a new customer dialog:

```
// Let the user create a new customer.
private void newCustomerButton_Click(object sender, EventArgs e)
{
    // Create and display a NewCustomerForm dialog.
    NewCustomerForm newCustomerDialog;
    newCustomerDialog = new NewCustomerForm();
    if (newCustomerDialog.ShowDialog() == DialogResult.OK)
    {
        // ... Create the new customer here ...
    }
}
```

The code declares a variable to refer to the dialog and makes a new dialog. It displays the dialog by using its `ShowDialog` method and checks the return result. If the user clicks OK, the program takes whatever steps are needed to create the new customer, such as adding a record to a database.

TRY IT

In this Try It, you build and use a simple custom dialog. The dialog lets you enter a name. If you enter a non-blank value and click OK, the main form adds the name you entered to a `ListBox`.

This Try It also gives you a little practice using the `ListBox` control, showing how to add and remove items.

 You can download the code and resources for this Try It from the book's web page at www.wrox.com *or* www.CSharpHelper.com/24hour.html. *You can find them in the Lesson10 folder in the download.*

Lesson Requirements

In this lesson, you:

➤ Create the main form shown on the bottom in Figure 10-2. Make the New Comedian `Button` be the form's `AcceptButton` and the Delete Comedian `Button` be the form's `CancelButton`.

➤ Create the dialog shown on the top in Figure 10-2. Set the `AcceptButton` and `CancelButton` properties in the obvious way.

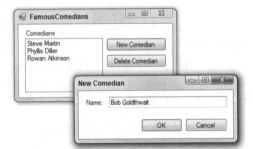

FIGURE 10-2

➤ Make the New Comedian `Button` display the dialog. If the dialog returns `DialogResult.OK`, add the new comedian's name to the `ListBox`.

➤ Make the Delete Comedian `Button` remove the currently selected comedian from the `ListBox`.

➤ When the user clicks the dialog's Cancel button, close the form and return `DialogResult.Cancel`.

➤ When the user clicks the dialog's OK `Button`, check the entered name's length. If the length is 0, display a message asking the user to enter a name. If the length is greater than 0, close the form and return `DialogResult.OK`.

Hints

➤   Use the `ListBox`'s `Items.Add` method to add a new item.

➤   Use the `ListBox`'s `Items.Remove` method to remove the selected item (identified by the `SelectedItem` property).

➤   Check `nameTextBox.Text.Length == 0` to see whether the name entered on the dialog is blank. You can use code similar to the following to take one action if the length is 0 and another if it is not. Notice the new `else` part of the `if` statement. If the condition is true, then the statements after the `if` clause are executed. If the condition is false, then the statements after the `else` clause are executed. (Lesson 18 covers `if` and `else` in more detail.)

```
if (nameTextBox.Text.Length == 0)
{
    ... Display a message here ...
}
else
{
    ... Return DialogResult.OK here ...
}
```

➤   Don't forget to set the `nameTextBox` control's `Modifiers` property to `Public` so the main form's code can use it.

Step-by-Step

➤   Create the main form shown on the bottom in Figure 10-2. Make the New Comedian `Button` be the form's `AcceptButton` and the Delete Comedian `Button` be the form's `CancelButton`.

   1.   Start a new project and add a `Label`, `ListBox`, and two `Buttons` roughly as shown in Figure 10-2.

   2.   Set the `ListBox`'s `Anchor` property to `Top`, `Bottom`, `Left`, `Right`. Set the `Buttons`' `Anchor` properties to `Top`, `Right`.

   3.   Set the form's `AcceptButton` property to the New Comedian `Button`. Set its `CancelButton` property to the Delete Comedian `Button`.

➤   Create the dialog shown on the top in Figure 10-2. Set the `AcceptButton` and `CancelButton` properties in the obvious way.

   1.   Open the Project menu and select Add Windows Form. Enter the name NewComedianForm and click Add.

   2.   Add a `Label`, `TextBox`, and two `Buttons` roughly as shown in Figure 10-2.

   3.   Set the `TextBox`'s `Anchor` property to `Top`, `Left`, `Right`. Set the `Buttons`' `Anchor` properties to `Bottom`, `Right`.

   4.   Set the form's `AcceptButton` property to the OK `Button`. Set its `CancelButton` property to the Cancel `Button`.

➤ Make the New Comedian `Button` display the dialog. If the dialog returns `DialogResult.OK`, add the new comedian's name to the `ListBox`.

1. Create an event handler for the New Comedian `Button`. Use code similar to the following:

```
// Create a new comedian entry.
private void newComedianButton_Click(object sender, EventArgs e)
{
    NewComedianForm newComedianDialog;
    newComedianDialog = new NewComedianForm();
    if (newComedianDialog.ShowDialog() == DialogResult.OK)
    {
        // Add the new comedian.
        comedianListBox.Items.Add(
            newComedianDialog.nameTextBox.Text);
    }
}
```

➤ Make the Delete Comedian `Button` remove the currently selected comedian from the `ListBox`.

1. Create an event handler for the Delete Comedian `Button`. Use code similar to the following:

```
// Remove the currently selected comedian.
private void deleteComedianButton_Click(object sender, EventArgs e)
{
    comedianListBox.Items.Remove(comedianListBox.SelectedItem);
}
```

This makes the `ListBox` remove the currently selected item. Fortunately if there is no selected item, the `ListBox` does nothing instead of crashing.

➤ When the user clicks the dialog's Cancel button, close the form and return `DialogResult.Cancel`.

1. You don't need to do anything else to make this work. When you set the dialog's `CancelButton` property to this `Button`, Visual C# sets the `Button`'s `DialogResult` property to `DialogResult.Cancel` so the button automatically sets the return result and closes the dialog.

➤ When the user clicks the dialog's OK `Button`, check the entered name's length. If the length is 0, display a message asking the user to enter a name. If the length is greater than 0, close the form and return `DialogResult.OK`.

1. Create an event handler for the dialog's OK `Button`. Use code similar to the following:

```
// Make sure the comedian's name isn't blank.
private void okButton_Click(object sender, EventArgs e)
{
    if (nameTextBox.Text.Length == 0)
    {
        MessageBox.Show("Please enter a comedian's name");
    }
```

```
        else
        {
            this.DialogResult = DialogResult.OK;
        }
    }
```

 Please select Lesson 10 on the DVD to view the video that accompanies this lesson.

EXERCISES

1. Make a program that has First Name, Last Name, Street, City, State, and ZIP `Labels` as shown on the ContactInformation form in Figure 10-3. When the user clicks the Edit `Button`, the program should display the Edit Contact Information dialog shown in Figure 10-3 to let the user change the values. If the user clicks OK, the program copies the new values back into the main form's `Labels`.

FIGURE 10-3

Hint: As you would with a standard dialog, initialize the custom dialog before you display it.

2. Sometimes the standard message box given by `MessageBox.Show` is almost perfect but you'd like to change the `Buttons`' text. Create a program that defines the message dialog shown in Figure 10-4.

FIGURE 10-4

The main program should set the `Label`'s text, the dialog's title, and the buttons' text. Make the Accept `Button` return `DialogResult.OK` and make the Decline `Button` return `DialogResult.Cancel`. Make the main form display different messages depending on whether the user clicked Accept or Decline.

Hints:

➤ The light gray area at the bottom of the dialog is a blank label with `AutoSize = False` and `Dock = Bottom`. It's just for decoration.

➤ The question mark icon is displayed in a `PictureBox`.

➤ To give the dialog the right borders and system buttons, set the dialog's properties: `FormBorderStyle = FixedDialog`, `MinimizeBox = False`, and `MaximizeBox = False`.

3. Create a color selection dialog like the one shown in Figure 10-5. The main program's `Buttons` should display the same dialog to let the user select foreground and background colors. Only update the main form's colors if the user clicks OK. Don't worry about initializing the dialog to show the current values before displaying it. (Hint: You built a program that lets the user select colors with scroll bars for Lesson 4's Try It.)

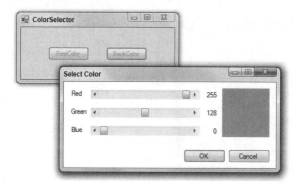

FIGURE 10-5

4. Make a background selection dialog like the one shown in Figure 10-6. When the user clicks the main form's Select Background `Button`, the form displays the dialog. When the user clicks one of the thumbnail images, the dialog displays a border around that image's `PictureBox`. If the user clicks OK, the dialog closes and the main form displays the selected image at full scale.

Hints:

➤ When the user clicks an image, set the `BorderStyle` property to `Fixed3D` for that `PictureBox` and `None` for the others.

➤ To remember which image was selected, place a hidden `PictureBox` on the dialog and set its `Image` property equal to that of the clicked `PictureBox`.

➤ Use the techniques described for Lesson 9, Exercise 5 to use a single event handler for all four `PictureBoxes`.

FIGURE 10-6

 You can download the solutions to these exercises from the book's web page at www.wrox.com *or* www.CSharpHelper.com/24hour.html. *You can find them in the Lesson10 folder in the download.*

SECTION II
Variables and Calculations

You may have noticed that the lessons up to this point haven't done much with numbers, dates, text (other than to just display it), or any other pieces of data. They've mostly dealt with controls and their properties, methods, and events.

Although you can do some fairly impressive things with controls alone, most programs also need to manipulate data. They need to do things like add purchase costs, calculate sales tax, sort appointments by time, and search text for keywords.

The lessons in this section explain how to perform these kinds of tasks. They explain the variables that a program uses to represent data in code, and they show how to manipulate variables to calculate new results.

▶ **LESSON 11:** Using Variables and Performing Calculations

▶ **LESSON 12:** Debugging Code

▶ **LESSON 13:** Understanding Scope

▶ **LESSON 14:** Working with Strings

▶ **LESSON 15:** Working with Dates and Times

▶ **LESSON 16:** Using Arrays and Collections

▶ **LESSON 17:** Using Enumerations and Structures

11

Using Variables and Performing Calculations

Variables hold values in memory so a program can manipulate them. Different kinds of variables hold different types of data: numbers, text, pictures, Halo scores, even complex groups of data such as employee records.

In this lesson you learn what variables are and how to use them. You learn how to define variables, put data in them, and use them to perform simple calculations.

WHAT ARE VARIABLES?

Technically speaking a variable is a named piece of memory that can hold some data of a specific type. For example, a program might allocate 4 bytes of memory to store an integer. You might name those bytes "payoffs" so you can easily refer to them in the program's code.

Less technically, you can think of a variable as a named place to put a piece of data. The program's code can use the variables to store values and perform calculations. For example, a program might store two values in variables, add the values together, and store the result in a third variable.

DATA TYPES

Every variable has a particular *data type* that determines the kind of data that it can hold. In general, you cannot place data of one type in a variable of another. For example, if price is a variable that can hold a number in dollars and cents, you cannot put the string "Hello" in it.

If you like, you can think of a variable as an envelope (with a name written on the outside) that can hold some data, but each type of data requires a different shaped envelope. Integers need relatively small envelopes, singles (which hold numbers with decimal points) need envelopes that are long and thin, and strings need big fat envelopes.

BITS AND BYTES

A *bit* is a single binary digit of memory that can have the value 0 or 1. (The name "bit" comes from "**BI**nary dig**IT**." Or is it "**B**inary dig**IT**?") Generally, bits are grouped into bytes and a program doesn't work with bits directly.

A *byte* is a chunk of memory holding 8 bits. If you view the bits as digits in a binary number, then a byte can hold values between 0 (00000000 in binary) and 255 (11111111 in binary). Groups of bytes make up larger data types such as integers and strings.

A *nibble* is half a byte. Way back in the old days when memory was expensive and computers filled warehouses instead of laps, some programs needed to split bytes and consider the nibbles separately to save space. Now that memory is as cheap as day-old lottery tickets, the nibble is a historical curiosity.

Bigger units of memory include kilobyte (KB) = 1,024 bytes, megabyte (MB) = 1,024KB, gigabyte (GB) = 1,024MB, and terabyte (TB) = 1,024GB. These are often used to measure the size of files, computer memory, flash drives, and disk drives. (Although in some contexts people use powers of 1,000 instead of 1,024. For example, most disk drive manufacturers define a gigabyte as 1,000,000,000 bytes.)

Sometimes the line between two data types is a bit fuzzy. For example, if a variable should hold a number, you cannot put in the string "ten." The fact that "ten" is a number is obvious to a human but not to a C# program.

You can't even place a string containing the characters "10" in a variable that holds a number. Though it should be obvious to just about anyone that "10" is a number, C# just knows it's a string containing two characters 1 and 0, and doesn't try to determine that the characters in the string represent a number.

Programs often need to convert a value from one data type to another (particularly switching between strings and numbers) so C# provides an assortment of data conversion functions to do just that. The section "Type Conversions" later in this lesson describes these functions.

Table 11-1 summarizes C#'s built-in data types. The signed types can store values that are positive or negative while the unsigned types can hold only positive values.

TABLE 11-1

DATA TYPE	MEANING	RANGE
byte	Byte	0 to 255
sbyte	Signed byte	−128 to 127
short	Small signed integer	−32,768 to 32,767
ushort	Unsigned short	0 to 65,535

DATA TYPE	MEANING	RANGE
int	Integer	−2,147,483,648 to 2,147,483,647
uint	Unsigned integer	0 to 4,294,967,295
long	Long integer	−9,223,372,036,854,775,808 to 9,223,372,036,854,775,807
ulong	Unsigned long	0 to 18,446,744,073,709,551,615
float	Floating point	Roughly −3.4e38 to 3.4e38
double	Big floating point	Roughly −1.8e308 to 1.8e308
decimal	Higher precision and smaller range than floating-point types	See the following section, "Float, Double, and Decimal Data Types."
char	Character	A single Unicode character. (Unicode characters use 16 bits to hold data for text in scripts such as Arabic, Cyrillic, Greek, and Thai.)
string	Text	A string of Unicode characters.
bool	Boolean	Can be true or false.
object	An object	Can point to almost anything.

Some of these data types are a bit confusing but the most common data types (int, long, float, double, and string) are fairly straightforward, and they are the focus of most of this lesson. Before moving on to further details, however, it's worth spending a little time comparing the float, double, and decimal data types.

Float, Double, and Decimal Data Types

The computer represents values or every type in binary using bits and bytes, so some values don't fit perfectly in a particular data type. In particular, real numbers such as 1/7 don't have exact binary representations, so the float, double, and decimal data types often introduce slight rounding errors.

For example, a float represents 1/7 as approximately 0.142857149. Usually the fact that this is not exactly 1/7 isn't a problem, but once in a while if you compare two float values to see if they are exactly equal, roundoff errors make them appear different even though they should be the same.

The decimal data type helps reduce this problem for decimal values such as 1.5 (but not non-decimal real values such as 1/7) by storing an exact representation of a decimal value. Instead of storing a value as a binary number the way float and double do, decimal stores the number's digits and its exponent separately as integral data types with no rounding. That lets it hold 28 or 29 significant digits (depending on the exact value) for numbers between roughly −7.9e28 and 7.9e28.

Note that rounding errors can still occur when you combine `decimal` values. For example, if you add 1e28 plus 1e–28, the result would have more than the 28 or 29 significant digits that a `decimal` can provide so it rounds off to 1e28.

The moral of the story is that you should always use the decimal data type for values where you need great accuracy and the values won't get truly enormous. In particular, you should always use `decimal` for currency values. Unless you're Bill Gates' much richer uncle, you'll never get close to the largest value a `decimal` can represent, and the extra precision can prevent rounding errors during some fairly complex calculations.

> *Another interesting feature of the decimal type is that, due to the way it stores its significant digits, it remembers zeros on the right. For example, if you add the values 1.35 and 1.65 as `floats`, you get the value 3. In contrast, if you add the same values as `decimals`, you get 3.00. The `decimal` result remembers that you were working with 2 digits to the right of the decimal point so it stores the result that way, too.*

DECLARING VARIABLES

To declare a variable in C# code, give the data type that you want to use followed by the name that you want to give the variable. For example, the following code creates a variable named `numMistakes`. The variable's data type is `int` so it can hold an integer between –2,147,483,648 and 2,147,483,647.

```
int numMistakes;
```

You can use the equals symbol to assign a value to a variable. For example, the following code sets `numMistakes` to 1337:

```
numMistakes = 1337;
```

As an added convenience, you can declare a variable and give it a value at the same time, as in:

```
int numMistakes = 1337;
```

You can declare several variables of the same type all at once by separating them with commas. You can even initialize them if you like. The following code declares three `float` variables named, x, y, and z and gives them initial values of 1, 2, and –40, respectively:

```
float x = 1, y = 2, z = -40;
```

> *The program must assign a value to a variable before it tries to read its value. For example, C# flags the following code as an error because the second line tries to use x on the right-hand side of the equals sign to calculate y before x has been assigned a value.*
>
> ```
> int x, y;
> y = x + 1;
> ```

LITERAL VALUES

A *literal value* is a piece of data stuck right in the code. For example, in the following statement, numMistakes is a variable and 1337 is a literal integer value:

```
int numMistakes = 1337;
```

Usually C# is pretty smart about using the correct data types for literal values. For example, in the preceding statement C# knows that numMistakes is an integer and 1337 is an integer, so it can safely put an integer value in an integer variable.

Sometimes, however, C# gets confused and assumes a literal value has a data type other than the one you intend. For example, the following code declares a float variable named napHours and tries to assign it the value 6.5. Unfortunately, C# thinks 6.5 is a double and a double won't fit inside a float variable so it flags this as an error.

```
float napHours = 6.5;
```

In cases such as this one, you can help C# understand what data type a literal has by adding a suffix character. For example, the F character in the following code tells C# that it should treat 6.5 as a float not a double:

```
float napHours = 6.5F;
```

Table 11-2 lists C#'s data type suffix characters. You can use the suffixes in either lower- or uppercase.

TABLE 11-2

DATA TYPE	SUFFIX
uint	U
long	L
ulong	UL or LU
float	F
double	D
decimal	M

The int data type doesn't have a literal suffix character. C# assumes a literal that looks like an integer is an int, unless it's too big, in which case it assumes the value is a long. For example, it assumes that 2000000000 is an int because that value will fit in an int. It assumes that 3000000000 is a long because it's too big to fit in an int.

The byte, sbyte, short, and ushort data types also have no literal suffix characters. Fortunately, you can assign an integer value to these types and C# will use the value correctly, as long as it fits.

You can use double quotes to surround `strings` and single quotes to surround `chars` as in the following code:

```
string firstName = "William";
string lastName = "Gates";
char middleInitial = 'H';
```

Sometimes you might like to include a special character such as a carriage return or tab character in a string literal. Unfortunately, you can't simply type a carriage return into a string because it would start a new line of code.

To work around this dilemma, C# provides escape sequences that represent special characters. An *escape sequence* is a sequence of characters that represent a special character such as a carriage return or tab.

Table 11-3 lists C#'s escape sequences.

TABLE 11-3

SEQUENCE	MEANING
\a	Bell
\b	Backspace
\f	Formfeed
\n	Newline
\r	Carriage return
\t	Horizontal tab
\v	Vertical tab
\'	Single quotation mark
\"	Double quotation mark
\\	Backslash
\?	Question mark
\ooo	ASCII character in octal
\xhh	ASCII character in hexadecimal
\xhhhh	Unicode character in hexadecimal

For example, the following code makes a variable that refers to a string that contains quotes and a newline character:

```
string txt = "Unknown value \"ten.\"\nPlease enter a number.";
```

When you display this string in a `MessageBox`, the user sees text similar to the following:

```
Unknown value "ten."
Please enter a number.
```

 When you display text in a `Label` *(or* `MessageBox`*), you can start a new line by using the newline character (*\n*). When you display text in a* `TextBox`*, however, you must start a new line by using the carriage return and newline characters together (*\r\n*). (The* \r\n *sequence also works for* `Labels` *and* `MessageBoxes`*.)*

C# also provides a special *verbatim string literal* that makes using some special characters easier. This kind of value begins with `@"` and ends with a corresponding closing quote `"`. Between the quotes, the literal doesn't know anything about escape sequences and treats every character literally.

A verbatim string literal cannot contain a double quote because that would end the string. It can't even use an escaped double quote because verbatim string literals don't understand escape sequences.

Verbatim string literals are very useful if you need a string that contains a lot of backslashes such as a Windows directory path (C:\Tools\Binary\Source\C#\PrintInvoices) or that needs to describe escape sequences themselves ("Use \r\n to start a new line").

Verbatim string literals can even include embedded new lines (which they represent as \r\n) and tab characters, although those may make your code harder to read.

TYPE CONVERSIONS

C# performs implicit data type conversions where it knows the conversion is safe. For example, the following code declares a `long` variable and sets it equal to the `int` value 6. Because an `int` can always fit in a `long`, C# knows this is safe and doesn't complain.

```
long numBananas = 6;
```

The converse is not always true, however. A `long` value cannot always fit in an `int` variable. Because it cannot know for certain that any given `long` will fit in an `int`, C# won't quietly sit by while your code assigns a `long` value to an `int`.

For example, the following code assigns a value to a `long` variable. It then tries to save that `long` value into an `int` variable. At this point, C# panics and flags the line as an error.

```
long numBananas = 6;
int numFruits = numBananas;
```

In cases such as this, you can use three methods to coerce C# into converting data from one type to another: casting, converting, and parsing.

Casting

To cast a value from one data type to another, you put the target data type inside parentheses in front of the value. For example, the following code explicitly converts the variable numBananas into an int:

```
long numBananas = 6;
int numFruits = (int)numBananas;
```

Casting works only between compatible data types. For example, because double and int are both numbers, you can try to cast between them. (When you cast from a double to an int, the cast simply discards any fractional part of the value with no rounding.) In contrast, the string and bool data types are not compatible with the numeric data types or each other so you cannot cast between them.

Normally a cast doesn't check whether it can succeed. If you try to convert a long into an int and the long won't fit, C# sweeps its mistake under the rug like a politician in an election year, and the program keeps running. The value that gets shoved into the int may be gibberish, but the program doesn't crash.

If the int now contains garbage, any calculations you perform with it will also be garbage so, in many cases, it's better to let your program throw a tantrum and crash. (Lesson 21 explains how to catch errors such as this so you can do something more constructive than merely crashing.)

To make C# flag casting errors, surround the cast in parentheses and add the word checked in front as in the following code:

```
long worldPopulation = 6800000000;
int peopleInWorld = checked((int)worldPopulation);
```

Now when the code executes at run time, the program will fail on the second statement.

If you have several statements that you want to check, you can make a checked block. In the following code, all of the statements between the curly braces are checked.

```
long worldPopulation = 6800000000;
long asiaPopulation = 4000000000;
checked
{
    int peopleInWorld = (int)worldPopulation;
    int peopleInAsia = (int)asiaPopulation;
}
```

The checked *keyword also checks integer calculations for overflow. For example, if you multiply two huge* int *variables together, the result won't fit in an* int. *Normally the program keeps running without complaint even though the result overflowed, so it isn't what you expect.*

If you are working with values that might overflow and you want to be sure the results make sense, protect the calculations with checked.

Converting

Casting only works between compatible types. The `Convert` utility class (which is provided by the .NET Framework) gives you methods that you can use to try to convert values even if the data types are incompatible. These are shared methods provided by the `Convert` class itself, so you don't need to create an instance of the class to use them.

For example, the `bool` and `int` data types are not compatible, so C# doesn't let you cast from one to the other. Occasionally, however, you might want to convert an `int` into a `bool` or vice versa. In that case you can use the `Convert` class's `ToBoolean` and `ToInt32` methods. (You use `ToInt32` because `int`s are 32-bit integers.)

The following code declares two `int` variables and assigns them values. It uses `Convert` to change them into `bool`s and then changes one of them back into an `int`.

```
int trueInt = -1;
int falseInt = 0;
bool trueBool = Convert.ToBoolean(trueInt);
bool falseBool = Convert.ToBoolean(falseInt);
int anotherTrueInt = Convert.ToInt32(trueBool);
```

 When you treat integer values as a Booleans, the value 0 is false and all other values are true. If you convert true *into an integer value, you get –1.*

In a particularly common scenario, a program must convert text entered by the user into some other data type such as an `int` or `decimal`. The following uses the `Convert.ToInt32` method to convert whatever the user entered in the `ageTextBox` into an `int`:

```
int age = Convert.ToInt32(ageTextBox.Text);
```

This conversion works only if the user enters a value that can be reasonably converted into an `int`. If the user enters 13, 914, or –1, the conversion works. If the user enters "seven," the conversion fails.

Converting text into another data type is more properly an example of parsing than of data type conversion, however. So while the `Convert` methods work, your code will be easier to read and understand if you use the parsing methods described in the next section.

Parsing

Trying to find structure and meaning in text is called *parsing*. All of the simple data types (`int`, `double`, `decimal`) provide a method that converts text into that data type. For example, the `int` data type's `Parse` method takes a string as a parameter and returns an `int`; at least it does if the string contains an integer value.

The following code declares a `decimal` variable named `salary`, uses the decimal's `Parse` method to convert the value in the `salaryTextBox` into a `decimal`, and saves the result in the variable:

```
decimal salary = decimal.Parse(salaryTextBox.Text);
```

As is the case with the `Convert` methods, this works only if the text can reasonably be converted into a `decimal`. If the user types "12,345.67," the parsing works. If the user types "ten" or "1.2.3," the parsing fails.

 Unfortunately C#'s conversion and parsing methods get confused by some formats that you might expect them to understand. For example, they can't handle currency characters, so they fail on strings like "$12.34" and "€54.32."

You can tell the `decimal` class's `Parse` method to allow currency values by passing it a second parameter as shown in the following code.

```
decimal salary = decimal.Parse(txt, System.Globalization.NumberStyles.Any);
```

PERFORMING CALCULATIONS

You've already seen several pieces of code that assign a value to a variable. For example, the following code converts the text in the `salaryTextBox` into a `decimal` and saves it in the variable `salary`:

```
decimal salary = decimal.Parse(salaryTextBox.Text);
```

More generally, you can save a value that is the result of a more complex calculation into a variable to the left of an equals sign. Fortunately, the syntax for these kinds of calculations is usually easy to understand. The following code calculates the value 2736 + 7281 / 3 and saves the result in the existing variable named `result`:

```
double result = 2736 + 7281 / 3;
```

The operands (the values used in the expression) can be literal values, values stored in variables, or the results of methods. For example, the following code calculates the sales tax on a purchase's subtotal. It multiplies the tax rate stored in the `taxRate` variable by the `decimal` value stored in the `subtotalTextBox` and saves the result in the variable `salesTax`.

```
salesTax = taxRate * decimal.Parse(subtotalTextBox.Text);
```

Note that a variable can appear on both sides of the equals sign. In that case, the value on the right is the variable's current value and, after the calculation, the new result is saved back in the same variable.

For example, the following code takes x's current value, doubles it, adds `10`, and saves the result back in variable x. If x started with the value `3`, then when this statement finishes x holds the value `16`.

```
x = 2 * x + 10;
```

A variable may appear more than once on the right side of the equals sign but it can appear only once on the left.

The following sections provide some additional details about performing calculations.

Operands and Operators

One issue that confuses some people is the fact that C# uses the data types of an expression's operands to determine the way the operators work. If an expression contains two integers, the operators use integer arithmetic. If an expression contains two floats, the operators use floating-point arithmetic.

Sometimes this can lead to confusing results. For example, the following code tries to save the value 1/7 in the float variable ratio. The values 1 and 7 are integers so this calculation uses integer division, which discards any remainder. Because 1 / 7 = 0 with a remainder of 1, ratio is assigned the value 0, which is probably not what you intended.

```
float ratio = 1 / 7;
```

To force C# into using floating-point division, you can convert the numbers into the float data type. The following code uses the F suffix character to indicate that 1 and 7 should have the float data type instead of int. Now the program performs floating-point division so it assigns ratio the value 0.142857149 (approximately).

```
float ratio = 1F / 7F;
```

Instead of using data type prefixes, you can also use casting to make the program treat the values as floats as in the following code:

```
float ratio = (float)1 / (float)7;
```

Promotion

If an expression uses two different data types, C# *promotes* the one with the more restrictive type. For example, if you try to divide an int by a float, C# promotes the int to a float before it performs the division.

The following code divides a float by an int. Before performing the calculation, C# promotes the value 7 to a float. This is sometimes called *implicit casting*. The code then performs the division and saves the result 0.142857149 in the variable ratio.

```
float ratio = 1F / 7;
```

Operator Summary

C# has many operators for manipulating variables of different data types. The following sections describe the most commonly used operators grouped by operand type (arithmetic, string, logical, and so forth).

Remember that some operators behave differently depending on the data types of their operands.

Arithmetic Operators

The arithmetic operators perform calculations on numbers. Table 11-4 summarizes these operators. The Example column shows sample results. For the final examples, assume that x is an int that initially has value 10.

TABLE 11-4

OPERATOR	MEANING	EXAMPLE
+	Addition	3 + 2 is 5
–	Negation	– 3 is –3
–	Subtraction	3 – 2 is 1
*	Multiplication	3 * 2 is 6
/	Division (integer)	3 / 2 is 1
/	Division (floating point)	3F / 2F is 1.5
%	Modulus	3 % 2 is 1
++	Pre-increment	++x: x is incremented to 11 and then the statement uses the new value 11
++	Post-increment	x++: the statement uses the current value of x (10) and then x is incremented to 11
--	Pre-decrement	--x: x is decrements to 9 and then the statement uses the new value 9
--	Post-decrement	x--: the statement uses the current value of x (10) and then x is decremented to 9

Integer division drops any remainder and returns the integer quotient. The modulus operator does the opposite: it drops the quotient and returns the remainder. For example, 17 % 5 returns 2 because 17 divided by 5 is 3 with a remainder of 2.

The pre- and post- increment and decrement operators return a value either before or after it is incremented or decremented. For example, the following code sets x equal to 10 + y = 20 and then adds 1 to y. When the code finishes, x = 20 and y = 11;

```
int x, y = 10;
x = 10 + y++;
```

In contrast, the following code increments y first and then uses the new value to calculate x. When this code finishes, x = 21 and y = 11.

```
int x, y = 10;
x = 10 + ++y;
```

The decrement operators work similarly except they subtract 1 instead of adding 1.

The increment and decrement operators can be very confusing, particularly when they're in the middle of a complex expression. If you have trouble with them, simply avoid them. For example, the following code gives you the same result as the previous code but without the pre-increment operator:

```
int x, y = 10;
y = y + 1;
x = 10 + y;
```

Logical Operators

The logical operators perform calculations on Boolean (`true` or `false`) values. They let you combine logical statements to form new ones.

Lesson 18 explains how to use these values to perform tests that let a program take action only under certain circumstances. For example, a program might pay an employee overtime if the employee is hourly and worked more than 40 hours in the last week.

Table 11-5 summarizes these operators.

TABLE 11-5

OPERATOR	MEANING
&	And
|	Or
^	Xor
!	Not
&&	Conditional And
||	Conditional Or

The `&` operator returns `true` if and only if both of its operands are `true`. For example, you must buy lunch if it's lunch time *and* you forgot to bring a lunch today:

```
mustBuyLunch = isLunchTime & forgotToBringLunch;
```

The `|` operator returns `true` if either of its operands is `true`. For example, you can afford lunch if you either brought enough money *or* you have a credit card (or both):

```
canAffordLunch = haveEnoughMoney | haveCreditCard;
```

The `^` operator is perhaps the most confusing. It returns `true` if one of its operands is `true` and the other is `false`. For example, you and Ann will get a single lunch check and pay each other back later if either Ann forgot her money and you brought yours, *or* Ann remembered her money and you forgot yours. If neither of you forgot your money, you can get separate checks. If you both forgot your money, you're both going hungry today.

```
singleCheck = annForgotMoney ^ youForgotMoney;
```

The ! operator returns true if its single operand is false. For example, if the cafeteria is *not* closed, you can have lunch there:

```
canHaveLunch = !cafeteriaIsClosed;
```

The conditional operators, which are also called *short-circuit operators*, work just like the regular ones except they don't evaluate their second operand unless they must. For example, consider the following "and" statement:

```
mustBuyLunch = isLunchTime && forgotToBringLunch;
```

Suppose it's only 9:00 a.m. so isLunchTime is false. When the program sees this expression, evaluates isLunchTime, and sees the && operator, it already knows that mustBuyLunch must be false no matter what value follows the && (in this case forgotToBringLunch), so it doesn't bother to evaluate forgotToBringLunch and that saves a tiny amount of time.

Similarly, consider the following "or" statement:

```
canAffordLunch = haveEnoughMoney | haveCreditCard;
```

If you have enough money, haveEnoughMoney is true, so the program doesn't need to evaluate haveCreditCard to know that the result canAffordLunch is also true.

Because the conditional && and || operators are slightly faster, most developers use them when they can instead of & and |.

> *There is one case where the conditional operators may cause problems. If the second operand is not a simple value but is the returned result from some sort of method call, then if you use a conditional operator, you cannot always know whether the method was called. This might matter if the method has side effects: consequences that last after the method has finished like opening a database or creating a file. In that case, you cannot know later whether the database is open or the file is created so the code might become confused.*
>
> *This is seldom a problem and you can avoid it completely by avoiding side effects.*

String Operators

The only string operator C# provides is +. This operator concatenates (joins) two strings together. For example, suppose the variable username contains the user's name. Then the following code concatenates the text "Hello " (note the trailing space) with the user's name and displays the result in a message box:

```
MessageBox.Show("Hello " + username);
```

Lesson 14 explains methods that you can use to manipulate strings: find substrings, replace text, check length, and so forth.

One very non-obvious fact about string operations is that a string calculation does not really save the results in the same memory used by the variable on the left of an assignment statement. Instead it creates a new string holding the result of the calculation and makes the variable refer to that.

For example, consider the following code.

```
string greeting = usernameTextBox.Text;
greeting = "Hello " + username;
```

This code looks like it saves a user's name in variable username *and then tacks "Hello" onto the front. Actually the second statement creates a whole new string that holds "Hello" plus the user's name and then makes* greeting *refer to the new string.*

For many practical applications, the difference is small, and you can ignore it. However, if you're performing many concatenations (perhaps in one of the loops described in Lesson 19), then your program may have performance issues. The StringBuilder *class can help address this issue, but it's a bit more advanced so I'm not going to cover it here. See* msdn.microsoft.com/library/2839d5h5.aspx *for more information.*

Comparison Operators

The comparison operators compare two values and return true or false depending on the values' relationship. For example, x < y returns true if x is less than y.

Table 11-6 summarizes these operators.

TABLE 11-6

OPERATOR	MEANING	EXAMPLE
==	Equals	2 == 3 is false
!=	Not equals	2 != 3 is true
<	Less than	2 < 3 is true
<=	Less than or equal to	2 <= 3 is true
>	Greater than	2 > 3 is false
>=	Greater than or equal to	2 >= 3 is false

Assignment Operators

The assignment operators set a variable (or property or whatever) equal to something else. The simplest of these is the = operator, which you have seen several times before. This operator simply assigns whatever value is on the right to the variable on the left.

The other assignment operators, known as *compound assignment operators*, combine the variable's current value with whatever is on the right in some way. For example, the following code adds 3 to whatever value x currently holds:

```
x += 3;
```

This has the same effect as the following statement that doesn't use the += operator:

```
x = x + 3;
```

Table 11-7 summarizes these operators. For the examples, assume x is a float and a and b are bools.

TABLE 11-7

OPERATOR	MEANING	EXAMPLE	MEANS
=	Assign	x = 10;	x = 10;
+=	Add and assign	x += 10;	x = x + 10;
-=	Subtract and assign	x -= 10;	x = x - 10;
*=	Multiply and assign	x *= 10;	x = x * 10;
/=	Divide and assign	x /= 10;	x = x / 10;
%=	Modulus and assign	x %= 10;	x = x % 10;
&=	Logical *and* and assign	a &= b;	a = a & b;
|=	Logical *or* and assign	a |= b;	a = a | b;
^=	Logical *xor* and assign	a ^= b;	a = a ^ b;

Bitwise Operators

The bitwise operators allow you to manipulate the individual bits in integer values. For example, the bitwise | operator combines the bits in two values so the result has a bit equal to 1 wherever either of the two operands has a bit equal to one.

For example, suppose x and y are the byte values with bits 10000000 and 00000001. Then x | y has bits 10000001.

These are fairly advanced operators so I'm not going to do much with them, but Table 11-8 summarizes them. The shift operators are not "bitwise" because they don't compare two operands one bit at a time, but they are bit-manipulation operators so they're included here.

TABLE 11-8

OPERATOR	MEANING	EXAMPLE
&	Bitwise *and*	11110000 & 00111100 = 00110000
|	Bitwise *or*	11110000 | 00111100 = 11111100
^	Bitwise *xor*	11110000 ^ 00111100 = 11001100
~	Bitwise complement	~11110000 = 00001111
<<	Left shift	11100111 << 2 = 10011100
>>	Right shift (for signed types)	11100111 >> 2 = 11111001
>>	Right shift (for unsigned types)	11100111 >> 2 = 00111001

If the operand has a signed type (sbyte, int, long), then >> makes new bits on the left copies of the value's sign bit (its leftmost bit). If the operand has an unsigned type (byte, uint, ulong), then >> makes new bits 0.

All of these except ~ also have corresponding compound assignments operators, for example, &= and <<=.

Precedence

Sometimes the order in which you evaluate the operators in an expression changes the result. For example, consider the expression 2 + 3 * 5. If you evaluate the + first you get 5 * 5, which is 25, but if you evaluate the * first you get 2 + 15, which is 17.

To prevent any ambiguity, C# defines operator precedence to determine which comes first.

Table 11-9 lists the major operators in order of decreasing precedence. In other words, the operators listed near the beginning of the table are applied before those listed later. Operators listed at the same level have the same precedence and are applied in left-to-right order.

TABLE 11-9

CATEGORY	OPERATORS
Primary	x++, x--
Unary	+, -, !, ++x, --x
Multiplicative	*, /, %
Additive	+, -
Relational	<, <=, >, >=
Equality	==, !=
Logical *and*	&
Logical *xor*	^
Logical *or*	|
Conditional *and*	&&
Conditional *or*	||

The compound assignment operators (+=, *=, ^=, and so forth) always have lowest precedence. The program evaluates the expression on the right, combines it with the original value of the variable on the left, and then saves the result in that variable.

By carefully using the precedence rules, you can always figure out how a program will evaluate an expression, but sometimes the expression can be confusing enough to make figuring out the result difficult. Trying to figure out precedence in confusing expressions can be a great party game (the programmer's version of "Pictionary") but it can make understanding and debugging programs hard.

Fortunately you can always use parentheses to change the order of evaluation, or to make the default order obvious. For example, consider the following three statements:

```
x = 2 + 3 * 5;
y = 2 + (3 * 5);
z = (2 + 3) * 5;
```

The first statement uses no parentheses so you need to use the precedence table to figure out which operator is applied first. The table shows that * has higher precedence than + so * is applied first and the result is 2 + 15, which is 17.

The second statement uses parentheses to emphasize the fact that the * operator is evaluated first. The result is unchanged but the code is easier to read.

The third statement uses parentheses to change the order of evaluation. In this case the + operator is evaluated first so the result is 5 * 5, which is 25.

Parentheses are a useful tool for making your code easier to understand and debug. Unless an expression is so simple that it's obvious how it is evaluated, add parentheses to make the result clear.

CONSTANTS

A constant is a lot like a variable except you must assign it a value when you declare it and you cannot change the value later.

Syntactically a constant's declaration is similar to a variable except it uses the keyword `const`.

For example, the following code declares a `decimal` constant named `taxRate` and assigns it the value `0.09M`. It then uses the constant in a calculation.

```
const decimal taxRate = 0.09M;

decimal subtotal = decimal.Parse(subtotalTextBox.Text);
decimal salesTax = taxRate * subTotal;
decimal grandTotal = subTotal + salesTax;
```

Constants work just like literal values so you could replace the constant `taxRate` with the literal value `0.09M` in the preceding calculation. Using a constant makes the code easier to read, however. When you see the value `0.09M`, you need to remember or guess that this is a tax rate.

Not only can it be hard to remember what this kind of "magic number" means, but it can also make changing the value difficult if it appears in many places throughout the program. Suppose the code uses the value `0.09M` in several places. If the sales tax rate went up, you would have to hunt down all of the occurrences of that number and change them. If you miss some of them, you could get very confusing results.

Note that constants can contain calculated values as long as C# can perform the calculation before the program actually runs. For example, the following code declares a constant that defines the number of centimeters per inch. It then uses that value to define the number of centimeter per foot.

```
const double cmPerInch = 2.54;
const double cmPerFoot = cmPerInch * 12;
```

TRY IT

In this Try It you make some simple calculations. You take values entered by the user, convert them into numbers, do some multiplication and addition, and display the results.

You can download the code and resources for this Try It from the book's web page at www.wrox.com or www.CSharpHelper.com/24hour.html. You can find them in the Lesson11 folder in the download.

Lesson Requirements

In this lesson, you:

➤ Create the form shown in Figure 11-1.

➤ When the user clicks the Calculate `Button`, make the program:

➤ Multiply each item's Quantity value by its Price Each value and display the result in the corresponding Ext. Price textbox.

➤ Add up the Ext. Price values and display the result in the Subtotal textbox.

➤ Multiply the Subtotal value by the entered Tax Rate and display the result in the Sales Tax textbox.

FIGURE 11-1

➤ Add the Subtotal, Sales Tax, and Shipping values, and display the result in the Grand Total textbox.

Hints

➤ It is often helpful to perform this kind of calculation in three separate phases:

1. Gather input values from the user and store them in variables.

2. Perform calculations.

3. Display results.

➤ Use the `decimal` data type for all of the variables because they represent currency.

➤ Lesson 14 has more to say about manipulating and formatting strings but for this Try It it's helpful to know that all data types provide a `ToString` method that converts a value into a string. An optional parameter string indicates the format to use. For this Try It, use the format `"C"` (including the quotes) to indicate a currency format, as in:

```
grandTotalTextBox.Text = grandTotal.ToString("C");
```

Step-by-Step

➤ Create the form shown in Figure 11-1.

1. Create the controls needed for the program shown in Figure 11-1.

a. The Quantity values are `NumericUpDown` controls.

b. All of the other box-like controls are `TextBoxes`.

    c.   The output controls (for the Ext. Price values, Subtotal, Sales Tax, and Grand Total) are `TextBoxes` with `ReadOnly` set to `True`.

    d.   Set the form's `AcceptButton` property to the Calculate button.

2.   Give names to the controls that the program needs to manipulate. That includes the `NumericUpDown` controls and all of the `TextBoxes` except the Item `TextBoxes`, which this program doesn't really use.

➤   When the user clicks the Calculate button, make the program:

    ➤   Multiply each item's Quantity value by its Price Each value and display the result in the corresponding Ext. Price textbox.

    ➤   Add up the Ext. Price values and display the result in the Subtotal textbox.

    ➤   Multiply the Subtotal value by the entered Tax Rate and display the result in the Sales Tax textbox.

    ➤   Add the Subtotal, Sales Tax, and Shipping values, and display the result in the Grand Total textbox.

This is easy to do in three steps:

1.   Gather input values from the user and store them in variables. Because they are already numeric, the code doesn't need to parse the values that come from the `NumericUpDown` control's `Value` properties. The program *does* need to parse the values in `TextBoxes` to convert them into `decimal` values.

```
// Get input values.
decimal quantity1 = quantity1NumericUpDown.Value;
decimal quantity2 = quantity2NumericUpDown.Value;
decimal quantity3 = quantity3NumericUpDown.Value;
decimal quantity4 = quantity4NumericUpDown.Value;
decimal priceEach1 = decimal.Parse(priceEach1TextBox.Text);
decimal priceEach2 = decimal.Parse(priceEach2TextBox.Text);
decimal priceEach3 = decimal.Parse(priceEach3TextBox.Text);
decimal priceEach4 = decimal.Parse(priceEach4TextBox.Text);
decimal taxRate = decimal.Parse(taxRateTextBox.Text);
decimal shipping = decimal.Parse(shippingTextBox.Text);
```

2.   Perform calculations. In this Try It, the calculations are pretty simple. Notice that the code uses a separate variable for each result instead of trying to add them all up at once to keep the code simple.

```
// Calculate results.
decimal extPrice1 = quantity1 * priceEach1;
decimal extPrice2 = quantity2 * priceEach2;
decimal extPrice3 = quantity3 * priceEach3;
decimal extPrice4 = quantity4 * priceEach4;
decimal subtotal = extPrice1 + extPrice2 + extPrice3 + extPrice4;
decimal salesTax = subtotal * taxRate;
decimal grandTotal = subtotal + salesTax + shipping;
```

3. Display results. The program uses `ToString("C")` to display values in a currency format.

```
// Display results.
extPrice1TextBox.Text = extPrice1.ToString("C");
extPrice2TextBox.Text = extPrice2.ToString("C");
extPrice3TextBox.Text = extPrice3.ToString("C");
extPrice4TextBox.Text = extPrice4.ToString("C");
subtotalTextBox.Text = subtotal.ToString("C");
salesTaxTextBox.Text = salesTax.ToString("C");
grandTotalTextBox.Text = grandTotal.ToString("C");
```

 Please select Lesson 11 on the DVD to view the video that accompanies this lesson.

EXERCISES

1. Make a program similar to the one shown in Figure 11-2. When the user checks or unchecks either of the A or B `CheckBoxes`, the program should check or uncheck the result `CheckBoxes` appropriately. For example, if A and B are both checked, the A `&&` B `CheckBox` should also be checked.

The last `CheckBox` is checked at the same time as one of the others. Which one? Does that make sense?

Hint: Set a result `CheckBox`'s `Checked` property equal to a Boolean expression. For example:

FIGURE 11-2

```
aAndBCheckBox.Checked = aCheckBox.Checked && bCheckBox.Checked;
```

Hint: To make a `CheckBox`'s caption display an ampersand, place two in its `Text` property. To display two ampersands, use four in the `Text` property as in "A `&&&&` B."

2. There are lots of ways for a program to get information about the operating system. The following lists three useful values.

➤ `Environment.UserName` — The current user's name.

➤ `DateTime.Now.ToShortTimeString()` — The current time in short format.

➤ `DateTime.Now.ToShortDateString()` — The current date in short format.

Make a program that greets the user when it starts by displaying a message box similar to the one shown in Figure 11-3. (Hint: You'll need to concatenate several strings together.)

3. Make a program to determine whether 12345 * 54321 > 22222 * 33333. In three `Labels`, display the result of 12345 * 54321, the result of 22222 * 33333, and the

FIGURE 11-3

Boolean value 12345 * 54321 > 22222 * 33333. The final value should be true or false. (Hint: Use `ToString` to convert the Boolean result into a string.)

4. Make a program that converts degrees Celsius to degrees Fahrenheit. It should have two `TextBoxes` with associated `Buttons`. When the user enters a value in the Celsius `TextBox` and clicks its `Button`, the program converts the value into degrees Fahrenheit and displays the result in the other `TextBox`. Make the other `Button` convert from Fahrenheit to Celsius. (Hint: °F = °C * 9 / 5 + 32 and °C = (°F – 32) * 5 / 9.) (What's special about the temperature –40° Celsius?)

5. Make a money converter that converts between U.S. dollars, British pounds, Euros, Japanese yen, Indian rupees, and Swiss francs. Make constants for the following conversion factors (or go online and look up the current exchange rates):

    ```
    // Exchange rates in USD.
    const decimal eurPerUsd = 0.68M;
    const decimal gbpPerUsd = 0.63M;
    const decimal jpyPerUsd = 89.16M;
    const decimal inrPerUsd = 47.24M;
    const decimal chfPerUsd = 1.03M;
    ```

    To make the constants usable by every event handler in the program, place these declarations outside of any event handler. (Right after the end of the `Form1` routine would work.)

    Make a `TextBox` and `Button` for each currency. When the user clicks the `Button`, the program should:

    ➤ Get the value in the corresponding `TextBox`.

    ➤ Convert that value into U.S. dollars.

    ➤ Use the converted value in U.S. dollars to calculate the other currency values.

    Display the results. (Note that these event handlers contain a lot of duplicated code, which is not good programming practice. Lesson 20 explains how you can make a function to perform the duplicated work for the event handlers.)

6. Make a program similar to the one you made for Exercise 5 but make this one convert between inches, feet, yards, miles, centimeters, meters, and kilometers.

You can download the solutions to these exercises from the book's web page at www.wrox.com *or* www.CSharpHelper.com/24hour.html. *They can be found the Lesson11 folder in the download.*

12

Debugging Code

A *bug* is a programming error that makes a program fail to produce the correct result. The program might crash, display incorrect data, or do something completely unexpected such as delete the wrong file.

In this lesson you learn how to use the excellent debugging tools provided by Visual Studio's IDE to find bugs in C#. You learn about different kinds of bugs and you get to practice debugging techniques on some buggy examples that you can download from the book's web site.

DEFERRED TECHNIQUES

Unfortunately at this point in the book you don't know enough about writing code to be able to understand and fix certain kinds of bugs. For example, a program crashes if it tries to access an array entry that is outside of the array, but you won't learn about arrays until Lesson 16.

So why does this lesson cover debugging when you don't even know all of the techniques you need to cause and fix certain kinds of bugs? It makes sense for two reasons.

First, the previous lesson was the first part of the book where you were likely to encounter bugs. Whenever I teach beginning programming, students start seeing bugs as soon as they write code that performs calculations like those covered in Lesson 11. These kinds of bugs are easy to fix if you know just a little bit about debugging but can be extremely frustrating if you don't.

Second, it turns out that you don't need to know more advanced techniques to learn simple debugging. Once you learn how to track down simple bugs, you can use the same techniques to find more advanced bugs. (If you learn to swim in 3 feet of water, you can later use the same techniques to swim in 10 feet or 100 feet of water.)

Later, when you know more about C# programming and can create more advanced bugs, that same knowledge will help you fix those bugs. When you know enough to have array indexing errors, you'll also know enough to fix them.

DEBUGGING THEN AND NOW

Back in the bad old days, programmers often fixed bugs by staring hard at the code, making a few test changes, and then running the program again to see what happened. This trial-and-error approach could be extremely slow because the programmer didn't really know exactly what was going on inside the code. If the programmer didn't have a good understanding of what was really happening, the test changes often didn't help and may have even made the problem worse.

Visual Studio's IDE provides excellent tools for debugging code. In particular, it lets you stop a program while it is running and see what it's doing. It lets you follow the program as it executes its code one line at a time, look at variable values, and even change those values while the program is still running.

The following sections describe some of Visual Studio's most useful debugging tools.

SETTING BREAKPOINTS

A *breakpoint* stops code execution at a particular piece of code. To set a breakpoint, open the Code Editor and click the gray margin to the left of the code where you want to stop. Alternatively, you can place the cursor on the line and press F9. The IDE displays a red circle to show that the line has a breakpoint.

Figure 12-1 shows a breakpoint set on the following line of code:

```
decimal grandTotal = subtotal + salesTax + shipping;
```

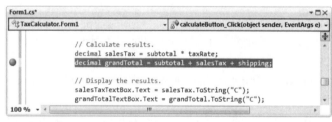

FIGURE 12-1

If you run the program now, execution stops when it reaches that line. You can then study the code as described in the following sections.

The debugger provides an *edit-and-continue* feature that lets you modify a stopped program's code. You can add new statements, remove existing statements, declare new variables, and so forth. Unfortunately, the debugger gets confused if you make certain changes, and you'll have to restart your program. But sometimes you can make small changes without restarting.

 Note that edit-and-continue isn't supported when you're building a 64-bit program, but you can test on a 32-bit program built on a 64-bit system. In Solution Explorer, right-click on the solution and select Properties. Expand the Configuration Properties folder, select the Configuration tab, and set Platform to "x86." After you finish testing, you can switch the program back to 64 bits.

To remove a breakpoint, click the red breakpoint circle or press F9 again.

SPONTANEOUS STOP

If you need to stop a program while it is running and you haven't set any breakpoints, you can select the Debug menu's Break All command or press [Ctrl]+[Alt]+[Break]. The debugger will halt the program in the middle of whatever it is doing and enter break mode.

If the Break All command isn't in the Debug menu (it may not be for some versions of Visual Studio), you can still use the shortcut [Ctrl]+[Alt]+[Break].

This technique is particularly useful for interrupting long tasks or infinite loops.

READING VARIABLES

It's easy to read a variable's value while execution is stopped. Simply hover the mouse over a variable and its value appears in a popup window.

For example, consider the order summary program shown in Figure 12-2. The program is supposed to add a subtotal, 9% sales tax, and shipping costs to get a grand total. It doesn't take Stephen Hawking to realize that something's wrong. If you're really paying $204.50 for a $19.95 purchase, you need to find a new place to shop.

FIGURE 12-2

To debug this program, you could place a breakpoint on a line of code near where you know the bug occurs. For example, the line of code containing the breakpoint in Figure 12-1 calculates the grand total. Because the total displayed in Figure 12-2 is wrong, this seems like a good place to begin the bug hunt. (You can download the TaxCalculator program from the book's web site and follow along if you like.)

When the code is stopped, you can hover the mouse over a variable to learn its value. If you hover the mouse over the variables in that line of code, you'll find that subTotal is 19.95 (correct), shipping is 5 (correct), and salesTax is 179.55 (very much incorrect). Figure 12-3 shows the mouse hovering over the salesTax variable to display its value.

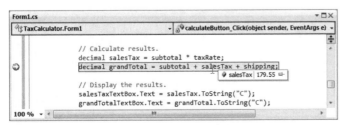

FIGURE 12-3

Now that you know the bug is lurking in the variable `salesTax`, you can hover the mouse over other variables to see how that value was calculated. If you hover the mouse over the variables in the previous line of code, you'll find that `subTotal` is `19.95` (still correct), and `taxRate` is `9`.

You may need to think about that for a bit to realize what's going wrong. To apply a tax rate such as 9 percent, you divide by 100 and then multiply. In this case, `taxRate` should 0.09 not 9.

Having figured out the problem, you can stop the program by opening the Debug menu and selecting the Stop Debugging command or by clicking the Stop Debugging button on the toolbar (see Figure 12-4).

Now you can fix the code and run the program again to see if it works. The following line shows the incorrect line of code (I scrolled it out of view in Figure 12-3 so it wouldn't be a complete giveaway):

```
const decimal taxRate = 9M;
```

When you run the program again, you should get the correct a sales tax $1.80 and grand total $26.75. In a more complicated program, you would need to perform a lot more tests to make sure the program behaved properly for different inputs including weird ones such as when the user enters "ten dollars" for the subtotal or leaves this shipping cost blank. This example isn't robust enough to handle those problems.

STEPPING THROUGH CODE

Once you've stopped the code at a breakpoint, you can step through the execution one statement at a time to see what happens. The Debug menu provides four commands that control execution:

➤ **Continue (F5)** — Makes the program continue running until it finishes or reaches another breakpoint. Use this to run the program normally after you're done looking at the code.

➤ **Step Into (F11)** — Makes the program execute the current statement. If that statement contains a call to a method, function, or other executable piece of code (these are covered in Lesson 20), execution stops inside that code so you can see how it works.

➤ **Step Over (F10)** — Makes the program execute the current statement. If that statement contains a call to another piece of executable code, the program runs that code and returns without stopping inside that code (unless there's a breakpoint somewhere inside that code).

➤ **Step Out ([Shift]+F11)** — Makes the program run the current routine until it finishes and returns to the calling routine (unless it hits another breakpoint first).

 When it is stopped, the debugger highlights the next line of code that it will execute in yellow.

In addition to using the Debug menu or shortcut keys, you can invoke these commands from the toolbar.

Figure 12-4 shows the toolbar buttons for the Debug menu's execution commands.

Normally the program steps through its statements in order, but there is a way to change the order if you feel the need. Right-click the line that you want the code to execute next and select Set Next Statement from the context menu. Alternatively you can place the cursor on the line and press [Ctrl]+[Shift]+F10. When you let the program continue, it starts executing from this line.

Setting the next statement to execute is useful for replaying history to see where an error occurred, re-executing a line after you change a variable's value (described in the "Using the Immediate Window" section later in this lesson), or to jump forward to skip some code.

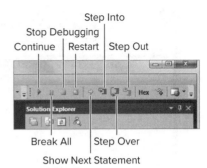

FIGURE 12-4

Note that you can only jump to certain lines of code. For example, you can't jump to a comment or other line of code that doesn't actually do anything (you can't set a breakpoint there either), you can't jump to a different method, you can't jump at all if an error has just occurred, you can't jump to a variable declaration unless it also initializes the variable, and so forth. C# does its best, but it has its limits.

USING WATCHES

Sometimes you may want to check a variable's value frequently as you step through the code one line at a time. In that case, pausing between steps to hover over a variable could slow you down, particularly if you have a lot of code to step through.

To make monitoring a variable easier, the debugger provides watches. A *watch* displays a variable's value whenever the program stops.

To create a watch, break execution, right-click a variable, and select Add Watch from the context menu. Figure 12-5 shows a watch set on the variable `subtotal`. Each time the program executes a line of code and stops, the watch updates to display the variable's current value.

The watch window also highlights variables that have just changed in red. If you're tracking a lot of watches, this makes it easy to find the values that have changed.

> *The Locals window is similar to the Watch window except it shows the values of all of the local variables (and constants). This window is handy if you want to view many of the variables all at once. It also highlights recently changed values in red so you can see what's changing.*

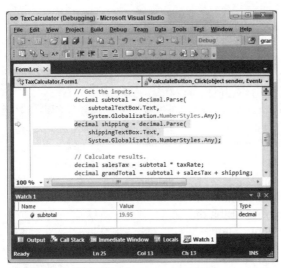

FIGURE 12-5

USING THE IMMEDIATE WINDOW

While the program is stopped, the Immediate window lets you execute simple commands. The four most useful commands that this window supports let you view variable values, evaluate expressions, set variable values, and call methods.

> *If you can't find the Immediate window, open the Debug menu, expand the Windows submenu, and select Immediate.*

To view a variable's value, simply type the variable's name and press [Enter]. (Optionally you can type a question mark in front if it makes you feel more like you're asking a question.)

The following text shows the Immediate window after I typed in the name of the variable `subtotal` (actually I typed "sub" and pressed [Ctrl]+[Space] to let IntelliSense help me type the rest) and pressed [Enter]:

```
subtotal
19.95
```

To evaluate an expression, simply type in the expression and press [Enter]. You can include literal values, variables, properties, constants, and just about anything else that you can normally include inside an expression in the code.

The following text shows the Immediate window after I typed an expression and pressed [Enter]:

```
taxRate * subtotal
179.55
```

To set a variable's value, simply type the variable's name, an equals sign, and the value that you want to give it. The new value can be a literal value or it can be the result of an expression. After you press [Enter], the Immediate window evaluates whatever is on the right of the equals sign, saves it in the variable, and then displays the variable's new value.

> *The same technique lets you set new values for properties. For example, you can change a control's* Location, Text, Visible, BackColor, *and other properties on the fly.*

The following text shows the Immediate window after I typed a statement to give the `grandTotal` variable a new value and pressed [Enter]:

```
grandTotal = subtotal + salesTax
199.5
```

Finally, to call a method, simply type the method call into the Immediate window and press [Enter]. Don't forget to add parentheses to the method call even if the method takes no parameters. The Immediate window calls the method and displays any returned result. If the method has no return value, the Immediate window displays "Expression has been evaluated and has no value."

The following text shows the Immediate window after I executed the `grandTotalTextBox`'s `Clear` method:

```
grandTotalTextBox.Clear()
Expression has been evaluated and has no value
```

> *You must type commands in the Immediate window just as you would in the Code Editor. In particular, you must use the correct capitalization or the window will complain.*

TRY IT

If you look closely at Figure 12-6, you'll see that this program has a serious problem. One tofu dinner at $13.95 each probably shouldn't add up to $142.65. If you look a little more closely, you'll also see that the grand total doesn't add up properly.

In this Try It, you debug this program. You set breakpoints and use the debugger to evaluate variable values to figure out where the code is going wrong.

FIGURE 12-6

You can download the code and resources for this Try It from the book's web page at www.wrox.com *or* www.CSharpHelper.com/24hour.html. *You can find them in the Lesson12 folder in the download. Note that the download contains both the version of the program that isn't working right and the corrected version (named "TryIt12" and "TryIt12Solution", respectively).*

Lesson Requirements

In this lesson, you:

➤ Use the debugger to fix this program. To follow along in the debugger, download this lesson's material from the book's web site and open the TryIt12 solution.

➤ Run the program and experiment with it for a bit to see what seems to work and what seems to be broken. This should give you an idea of where the problem may lie.

➤ Set a breakpoint in the code near where you think there might be a problem. In this case, the tofu dinner cost calculation is wrong so you might set a breakpoint on this line:

```
decimal priceTofu = tofuCost * numTofu;
```

➤ Run the program so it stops at that breakpoint. Hover the mouse over different variables to see whether they look like they make sense.

➤ Step through the code watching each line closely to see what's wrong.

➤ Fix the error.

➤ Run the program again and test it to make sure the change you made works. Try setting two of the quantities to 0 and the third to 1 to see if the program can correctly calculate the non-zero value.

➤ If the program still has problems, run through these steps again.

Step-by-Step

The first two lesson requirements for this Try It are fairly straightforward so they aren't repeated here. The following paragraphs discuss the solution to the mystery so, if you want to try to debug the program yourself, do so before you read any further.

Ready? Let's go.

The following code shows how the program works. The bold line is where I set my breakpoint. If you stare at the code long enough, you'll probably find the bug so don't look too closely. Remember, the point is to practice using the debugger (which will be your only hope in more complicated programs), not to simply fix the program.

```
// Calculate the prices for each entree and the total price.
private void calculateButton_Click(object sender, EventArgs e)
```

```
{
    const decimal chickenCost = 15.85M;
    const decimal steakCost = 18.95M;
    const decimal tofuCost = 13.95M;

    // Get inputs.
    int numChicken = int.Parse(chickenQuantityTextBox.Text);
    int numSteak = int.Parse(steakQuantityTextBox.Text);
    int numTofu = int.Parse(tofuQuantityTextBox.Text);

    // Calculate results.
    decimal total = 0;

    decimal priceChicken = chickenCost * numChicken;
    total += priceChicken;

    decimal priceSteak = steakCost * numSteak;
    total += priceSteak;

    decimal priceTofu = tofuCost * numTofu;
    total += priceTofu;

    // Display results.
    chickenPriceTextBox.Text = priceChicken.ToString("C");
    steakPriceTextBox.Text = priceSteak.ToString("C");
    tofuPriceTextBox.Text = priceChicken.ToString("C");
    totalTextBox.Text = total.ToString("C");
}
```

➤ Run the program so it stops at that breakpoint. Hover the mouse over different variables to see whether they look like they make sense.

> **1.** If you run to the breakpoint and hover the mouse over the variables, you'll find that most of them make sense; the values numChicken = 9, priceChicken = 142.65, and so forth.

➤ Step through the code watching each line closely to see what's wrong.

> **1.** While the program is stopped on the breakpoint, the variable priceTofu has value 0 because the code hasn't yet executed the line that sets its value. Press [F10] to step over that line and you'll see that priceTofu is 13.95 as it should be. So far, you haven't found the bug.
>
> If you continue stepping through the code, watching each line carefully, you'll eventually see the problem in this line:
>
> ```
> tofuPriceTextBox.Text = priceChicken.ToString("C");
> ```
>
> Here the code is making the tofu price TextBox display the value priceChicken!

This is a fairly typical copy-and-paste error. The programmer wrote one line of code, copied and pasted it several times to perform similar tasks (displaying the values in the TextBoxes), but then didn't update each pasted line correctly.

➤ Fix the error.

1. This bug is easy to fix. Simply change the offending line to this:

```
tofuPriceTextBox.Text = priceTofu.ToString("C");
```

➤ Run the program again and test it to make sure the change you made works. Try setting two of the quantities to 0 and the third to 1 to see if the program can correctly calculate the non-zero value.

1. If you run the program again, all should initially look okay. If you reproduce some calculations by hand, however, you may find a small discrepancy in the chicken prices.

2. You can see the problem more easily if you set the quantities of steak and tofu to 0 and the quantity of chicken to 1. Then the program calculates that the price of one chicken dinner (at $15.95 each) is $15.85.

➤ If the program still has problems, run through these steps again.

1. Having found another bug, run through the debugging process again. Set a breakpoint on the line that calculates `priceChicken` and hover over the variables to see if their values make sense.

If you're paying attention, you'll see that the value of the constant `costChicken` is `15.85`, not `15.95` as it should be.

2. Fix the constant declaration and test the program again.

It's extremely common for a program to contain more than one bug. In fact, it's an axiom of software development that any nontrivial program contains at least one bug.

A consequence of that axiom is that, even after you fix the program's "last" bug, it still contains another bug. Sometimes fixing the bug introduces a new bug. (That's not as uncommon as you might think in a complex program.) Other times more bugs are hiding; you just haven't found them yet.

In complex projects, the goal is still to eradicate every single bug but the reality is that often the best you can do is fix as many as you can find until the odds of the user finding one in everyday use are extremely small.

Please select Lesson 12 on the DVD to view the video that accompanies this lesson.

EXERCISES

Putting debugging exercises in a book can be a bit strange. If the book includes the code, you can stare at it until you see the bugs without using the debugger, and that would defeat the purpose.

For that reason, this section only describes the programs containing the bugs and you'll have to download the broken programs from the book's web site at www.wrox.com *or* www.CSharpHelper.com/24hour.html. *You can find the programs and corrected versions in the Lesson12 folder. The corrected versions are named after their exercises, for example, Ex12-1Solution. Modified lines are marked with comments.*

1. Debug the CelsiusToFahrenheit program shown in Figure 12-7. (Hint: 0 Celsius = 32 Fahrenheit and 100 Celsius = 212 Fahrenheit.)

FIGURE 12-7

2. Debug the FeetToMiles program shown in Figure 12-8. (After you fix this one, notice that using constants instead of magic numbers and the approach taken by Exercises 5 and 6 in Lesson 11 would make fixing these bugs easier and might have avoided them from the start. Also note again that the duplicated code is a bad thing that you'll learn how to fix in Lesson 20.)

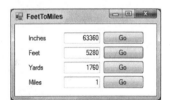

FIGURE 12-8

3. The ResizePicture program is supposed to zoom in on a picture when you adjust its `TrackBar`. Unfortunately when you move the `TrackBar`, the picture seems to shrink and move to a new location. Debug the program.

4. Debug the TaxForm program, which performs a fictitious tax calculation based on a real one. It's an ugly little program, but it's probably the most realistic one in this lesson. (Hint: For the program's initial inputs, the tax due should be $290.00.)

13

Understanding Scope

A variable's *scope* is the code that can "see" or access that variable. It determines whether a piece of code can read the variable's value and give it a new value.

In this lesson you learn what scope is. You learn why restricting scope is a good thing and how to determine a variable's scope.

SCOPE WITHIN A CLASS

A C# class (and note that Form types are classes, too) contains three main kinds of scope: class scope, method scope, and block scope. (If you have trouble remembering what a class is, review Lesson 9's section "Understanding Classes and Instances.")

Variables with *class scope* are declared inside the class but outside of any of its methods. These variables are visible to all of the code throughout the instance of the class and are known as *fields*.

Variables with *method scope* are declared within a method. They are usable by all of the code that follows the declaration within that method.

Variables with *block scope* are declared inside a block defined by curly braces {} nested inside a method. The section "Block Scope" later in this lesson says more about this.

For example, consider the following code that defines the form's constructor (Form1), a field, and some variables inside event handlers:

```
namespace VariableScope
{
    public partial class Form1 : Form
    {
        public Form1()
        {
            InitializeComponent();
        }
```

```
        // A field.
        int a = 1;

        private void clickMeButton_Click(object sender, EventArgs e)
        {
            // A method variable.
            int b = 2;
            MessageBox.Show("a = " + a.ToString() +
                "\nb = " + b.ToString());
        }

        private void clickMeTooButton_Click(object sender, EventArgs e)
        {
            // A method variable.
            int c = 3;
            MessageBox.Show("a = " + a.ToString() +
                "\nc = " + c.ToString());
        }
    }
}
```

The field a is declared outside of the three methods (Form1, clickMeButton_Click, and clickMeTooButton_Click) so it has class scope. That means the code in any of the methods can see and use this variable. In this example, the two Click event handlers each display the value.

The variable b is declared within clickMeButton_Click so it has method scope. Only the code within this method that comes after the declaration can use this variable. In particular, the code in the other methods cannot see it.

Similarly, the code in the clickMeTooButton_Click event handler that comes after the c declaration can see that variable.

Two variables with the same name cannot have the same scope. For example, you cannot create two variables named a at the class level nor can you create two variables named b inside the same method.

Same Named Variables

Although you cannot give two variables the same name within the same scope, you can give them the same name if they are in different methods or one is a field and the other is declared inside a method. For example, the following code defines three variables all named count:

```
// A field.
int count = 0;

private void clickMeButton_Click(object sender, EventArgs e)
{
    // A method variable.
    int count = 1;
    MessageBox.Show(count.ToString());
}
```

```
private void clickMeTooButton_Click(object sender, EventArgs e)
{
    // A method variable.
    int count = 2;
    MessageBox.Show(count.ToString());
}
```

In this example, the method-level variable hides the class-level variable with the same name. For example, within the clickMeButton_Click event handler, its local version of count is visible and has the value 1. The class-level field with value 0 is hidden.

 You can still get the class-level value if you prefix the variable with the executing object. Recall that the special keyword this *means "the object that is currently executing this code." That means you could access the class-level field while inside the* clickMeButton_Click *event handler like this:*

```
private void clickMeButton_Click(object sender, EventArgs e)
{
    // A method variable.
    int count = 1;
    MessageBox.Show(count.ToString());
    MessageBox.Show(this.count.ToString());
}
```

Usually it's better to avoid potential confusion by giving the variables different names in the first place.

Method Variable Lifetime

A variable with method scope is created when its method is executed. Each time the method is called, a new version of the variable is created. When the method exits, the variable is destroyed. If its value is referenced by some other variable, it might still exist, but this variable is no longer available to manipulate it.

One consequence of this is that the variable's value resets each time the method executes. For example, consider the following code:

```
private void clickMeButton_Click(object sender, EventArgs e)
{
    // A method variable.
    int count = 0;
    count++;
    MessageBox.Show(count.ToString());
}
```

Each time this code executes, it creates a variable named count, adds 1 to it, and displays its value. The intent may be to have the message box display an incrementing counter but the result is actually the value 1 each time the user clicks the button.

To save a value between method calls, you can change the variable into a field declared outside of any method. The following version of the preceding code displays the values 1, 2, 3, and so on when the user clicks the button multiple times:

```
// A field.
int count = 0;

private void clickMeButton_Click(object sender, EventArgs e)
{
    count++;
    MessageBox.Show(count.ToString());
}
```

Note that a parameter declared in a method's declaration counts as having method scope. For example, the preceding event handler has two parameters named sender and e. That means you cannot declare new variables within the method with those names.

Block Scope

A method can also contain nested blocks of code that define other variables that have scope limited to the nested code. This kind of variable cannot have the same name as a variable declared at a higher level of nesting within the same method.

Later lessons explain some of these kinds of nesting used to make decisions (Lesson 18), loops (Lesson 19), and error handlers (Lesson 21).

A simple type of nested block of code that is described here simply uses braces to enclose code. The scope of a variable declared within this kind of block includes only the block, and the variable is usable only later in the block.

For example, consider the following code:

```
private void clickMeTooButton_Click(object sender, EventArgs e)
{
    // A method variable.
    int count = 1;
    MessageBox.Show(count.ToString());

    // A nested block of code.
    {
        int i = 2;
        MessageBox.Show(i.ToString());
    }

    // A second nested block of code.
    {
        int i = 3;
        MessageBox.Show(i.ToString());
    }
}
```

This method declares the variable count at the method level and displays its value.

The code then makes a block of code surrounded by braces. It declares the variable i and displays its value. Note that the code could not create a second variable named count inside this block because the higher-level method code contains a variable with that name.

After the first block ends, the code creates a second block. It makes a new variable i within that block and displays its value. Because the two inner blocks are not nested (neither contains the other), it's okay for both blocks to define variables named i.

ACCESSIBILITY

A field's scope determines what parts of the code can see the variable. So far I've focused on the fact that all of the code in a class can see a field declared at the class level, outside of any methods. In fact, a field may also be visible to code running in other classes depending on its accessibility.

A field's *accessibility* determines which code is allowed to access the field. For example, a class might contain a public field that is visible to the code in any other class. It may also define a private field that is visible only to code within the class that defines it.

Accessibility is not the same as scope, but the two work closely together to determine what code can access a field.

Table 13-1 summarizes the field accessibility values. Later when you learn how to build properties and methods, you'll be able to use the same accessibility values to determine what code can access them.

TABLE 13-1

ACCESSIBILITY VALUE	MEANING
public	Any code can see the variable.
private	Only code in the same class can see the variable.
protected	Only code in the same class or a derived class can see the variable. For example, if the Manager class is derived from the Person class, a Manager object can see a Person object's protected variables. (You'll learn more about deriving one class from another in Lesson 23.)
internal	Only code in the same assembly can see the variable. For example, if the variable's class is contained in a library (which is its own assembly), a main program that uses the library cannot see the variable.
protected internal	The variable is visible to any code in the same assembly or any derived class in another assembly.

If you omit the accessibility value for a field, it defaults to private. You can still include the private keyword, however, to make the field's accessibility obvious.

The private keyword sometimes causes confusion. A private field is visible to any code in *any instance* of the same class, not just to the *same instance* of the class.

For example, suppose you build a `Person` class with a private field named `Salary`. Not only can all of the code in an instance see its own `Salary` value, but *any* `Person` object can see any other `Person` object's `Salary` value (assuming it has a reference to another `Person` object).

 In fact, declaring fields to be public is bad programming style. It's better to make a public property instead. Lesson 23 explains why and tells how to make properties. Public fields do work, however, and are good enough for this discussion of accessibility.

RESTRICTING SCOPE AND ACCESSIBILITY

It's a good programming practice to restrict a field's or variable's scope and accessibility as much as possible to limit the code that can access it. For example, if a piece of code has no business using a form's field, there's no reason to give it the opportunity. This not only reduces the chances that you will use the variable incorrectly, but it also removes the variable from IntelliSense so it's not there to clutter up your choices and confuse things.

If you can use a variable declared locally inside an event handler or other method, do so. In fact, if you can declare a variable within a block of code inside a method, such as in a loop, do so. That gives the variable very limited scope so it won't get in the way when you're working with unrelated code.

If you need multiple methods to share the same value or you need it to keep the value between method calls, make it a private field. Only make a variable public if code in another form (or other class) needs to use it.

 ## TRY IT

In this Try It, you build the program shown in Figure 13-1. You use fields to allow two forms to communicate and to perform simple calculations. You also get to try out a new control: `ListView`.

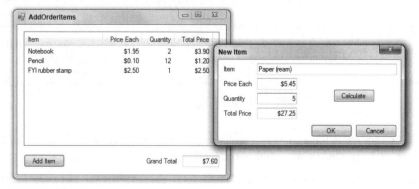

FIGURE 13-1

You can download the code and resources for this Try It from the book's web page at www.wrox.com *or* www.CSharpHelper.com/24hour.html. *You can find them in the Lesson13 folder in the download.*

Lesson Requirements

In this lesson, you:

➤ Create the NewItemForm shown on the top in Figure 13-1.

    ➤ Make the OK button initially start disabled.

    ➤ Provide public fields to let the main form get the data entered by the user.

    ➤ When the user clicks the Calculate button, calculate and display Total Price, and enable the OK button.

➤ Create the main form shown on the bottom in Figure 13-1.

➤ When the user clicks the main form's Add Item button, make the program display the NewItemForm. If the user enters data and clicks the OK button, display the entered values in the main form's ListView control and update the grand total.

Hints

➤ Remember to set the NewItemForm's AcceptButton and CancelButton properties appropriately.

➤ Because the main form's grand total must retain its value as the user adds items, it must be a field.

➤ To allow the main form to see the values entered by the user on the NewItemForm, use public fields.

Step-by-Step

➤ Create the NewItemForm shown on the top in Figure 13-1.

    1. Arrange the controls as shown in Figure 13-1.

    2. Set the form's AcceptButton property to the OK button and its CancelButton property to the Cancel button. The OK button will always close the form so set its DialogResult property to OK.

        ➤ Make the OK button initially start disabled.

        1. Set the OK button's Enabled property to False.

    ➤ Provide public fields to let the main form get the data entered by the user.

1. Declare public fields for the program to use in its calculations. Use code similar to the following placed outside of any methods:

```
// Public fields. (They should really be properties.)
public string ItemName;
public decimal PriceEach, Quantity, TotalPrice;
```

➤ When the user clicks the Calculate button, calculate and display Total Price, and enable the OK button.

1. Use the techniques described in Lesson 11 to get the values entered by the user and calculate the item's total price. Use the fields you created in the previous step.

2. Set the OK button's `Enabled` property to `True`.

➤ Create the main form shown on the bottom in Figure 13-1.

1. Create the `ListView`, `Button`, `Label`, and `TextBox`. Set their `Anchor` properties and make the `TextBox` read-only.

2. To make the `ListView` display its items in a list as shown:

   a. Set its `View` property to `Details`.

   b. Select its `Columns` property and click the ellipsis to the right to open the ColumnHeader Collection Editor shown in Figure 13-2. Click the Add button four times to make the four columns. Use the property editor on the right to set each column's `Name` and `Text` properties, and to set `TextAlign` to `Right` for the numeric columns.

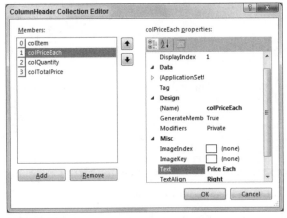

FIGURE 13-2

➤ When the user clicks the main form's Add Item button, make the program display the `NewItemForm`. If the user enters data and clicks the OK button, display the entered values in the main form's `ListView` control and update the grand total.

1. The button's `Click` event handler should use code similar to the following.

```
// Let the user add a new item to the list.
private void addItemButton_Click(object sender, EventArgs e)
{
    NewItemForm frm = new NewItemForm();
    if (frm.ShowDialog() == DialogResult.OK)
    {
        // Get the new values.
        ListViewItem lvi = itemsListView.Items.Add(frm.ItemName);
        lvi.SubItems.Add(frm.PriceEach.ToString("C"));
        lvi.SubItems.Add(frm.Quantity.ToString());
        lvi.SubItems.Add(frm.TotalPrice.ToString("C"));

        // Add to the grand total and display the new result.
        GrandTotal += frm.TotalPrice;
        grandTotalTextBox.Text = GrandTotal.ToString("C");
    }
}
```

 Please select Lesson 13 on the DVD to view the video that accompanies this lesson.

EXERCISES

1. Use a design similar to the one used in the Try It to let the user fill out an appointment calendar. The main form should contain a `ListView` with columns labeled Subject, Date, Time, and Notes. The `NewAppointmentForm` should provide textboxes for the user to enter these values and should have public fields `AppointmentSubject`, `AppointmentDate`, `AppointmentTime`, and `AppointmentNotes` to let the main form get the entered values. Instead of a grand total, the main form should display the number of appointments.

2. Build a form that contains a `ListBox`, `TextBox`, and `Button`. When the user clicks the `Button`, display a dialog that lets the user enter a number. Give the dialog a public field to return the value to the main form.

If the user enters a value and clicks OK, the main form should add the number to its `ListBox`. It should then display the average of its numbers. To do that, use a private field containing the numbers' total. Add the new number to the total and divide by the number of values.

3. Build the conference schedule designer shown in Figure 13-3. Give the main form (on the bottom in Figure 13-3) the following features:

➤ Create private fields named `SessionIndex1`, `SessionIndex2`, and so forth to hold the indexes of the user's choices.

➤ When the user clicks an ellipsis button, display the session selection dialog shown on the top in Figure 13-3.

➤ After creating the dialog but before displaying it, set its `Text` property to indicate the session time as shown in the figure.

➤ Also before displaying the dialog, use code similar to the following to tell the dialog about the user's previous selection for this session. (The `SessionIndex` and `SessionTitle` variables are public fields defined by the dialog and discussed shortly.)

```
frm.SessionIndex = SessionIndex1;
```

➤ If the user clicks OK, use code similar to the following to save the index of the user's choice and to display the session's title.

```
// Save the new selection.
sessionIndex1 = frm.SessionIndex;
choice1TextBox.Text = frm.SessionTitle;
```

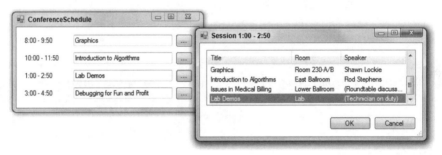

FIGURE 13-3

Give the dialog the following features:

➤ Set the `ListView`'s `FullRowSelect` property to `True` and set its `MultiSelect` property to `False`.

➤ Use the Properties window to define the `ListView`'s column headers. Select the `ListView`, click its `Columns` property, click the ellipsis to the right, and use the editor to define the headers.

➤ Use the Properties window's editors to define the `ListView`'s items. Select the `ListView`, click its `Items` property, click the ellipsis to the right, and use the editor to define the items. Set the `Text` property to determine an item's text. Click the `SubItems` property and then click the ellipsis to the right to define the sub-items (Room and Speaker).

➤ Use the following code to create public fields to communicate with the main form:

```
// Public fields to communicate with the main form.
public int SessionIndex;
public string SessionTitle;
```

➤ Create a `Load` event handler that uses the following code to initialize the dialog. This code selects the proper session in the `ListView` control and then makes the control scroll if necessary so that session is visible.

```
// Initialize the selection.
private void PickSessionForm_Load(object sender, EventArgs e)
{
    sessionsListView.SelectedIndices.Add(SessionIndex);

    // Ensure that the selection is visible.
    sessionsListView.SelectedItems[0].EnsureVisible();
}
```

➤ In the OK button's `Click` event handler, use the following code to save the selected item's index and title for the main form to use:

```
// Save the user's selection.
private void okButton_Click(object sender, EventArgs e)
{
    SessionIndex = sessionsListView.SelectedIndices[0];
    SessionTitle = sessionsListView.SelectedItems[0].Text;
}
```

 You can download the solutions to these exercises from the book's web page at www.wrox.com *or* www.CSharpHelper.com/24hour.html. *They can be found in the Lesson13 folder in the download.*

14

Working with Strings

Previous lessons provided a sneak peek at some of the things that a C# program can do with strings. Lesson 11 explained how you can use the + operator to concatenate two strings. Several lessons show how to use the ToString method to convert numeric values into strings that you can then display to the user.

In this lesson, you learn a lot more about strings. You learn about string class methods that let you search strings, replace parts of strings, and extract pieces of strings. You also learn new ways to format numeric and other kinds of data to produce strings.

STRING METHODS

The string class provides a lot of useful methods for manipulating strings. For example, the EndsWith method returns true if a string ends with a particular substring. The following code determines whether a string ends with the substring dog:

```
string str = "The quick brown fox jumps over the lazy dog.";
MessageBox.Show("Ends with \"dog.\": " + str.EndsWith("dog."));
```

Table 14-1 summarizes the string class's most useful methods.

TABLE 14-1

METHOD	PURPOSE
Contains	Returns true if the string contains a target string.
EndsWith	Returns true if the string ends with a target string.
IndexOf	Returns the index of a target character or string within the string.
IndexOfAny	Returns the index of the first occurrence of any of a set of characters in the string.
Insert	Inserts text in the middle of the string.

continues

TABLE 14-1 *(continued)*

METHOD	PURPOSE
LastIndexOf	Returns the index of the last occurrence of a target character or string within the string.
LastIndexOfAny	Returns the index of the last occurrence of any of a set of characters in the string.
PadLeft	Pads the string to a given length by adding characters on the left if necessary.
PadRight	Pads the string to a given length by adding characters on the right if necessary.
Remove	Removes a piece of the string.
Replace	Replaces occurrences of a string or character with new values within the string.
Split	Splits the string apart at a delimiter (for example, commas) and returns an array containing the pieces.
StartsWith	Returns true if the string starts with a target string.
Substring	Returns a substring.
ToLower	Returns the string converted to lowercase.
ToUpper	Returns the string converted to uppercase.
Trim	Removes leading and trailing characters from the string. An overloaded version that takes no parameters removes whitespace characters (space, tab, newline, and so on).
TrimEnd	Removes trailing characters from the string.
TrimStart	Removes leading characters from the string.

 Remember that string indexing starts with 0 so the first letter has index 0, the second has index 1, and so forth.

In addition to all of these methods, the string class provides a very useful Length property. As you can probably guess, Length returns the number of characters in the string.

The string class also provides the useful static (shared) methods Format and Join. A static method is one that is provided by the class itself rather than an instance of the class. You invoke a static method using the class's name instead of a variable's name.

The `Format` method formats a series of parameters according to a format string and returns a new string. For example, the following code uses the `string` class's `Format` method to display the values in the variables x and y surrounded by parentheses and separated by a comma:

```
int x = 10, y = 20;
string txt = string.Format("({0}, {1})", x, y);
```

The following text shows the result:

```
(10, 20)
```

The next section says more about the `Format` method.

The `Join` method does the opposite of the `Split` method: it joins a series of strings, separating them with a delimiter. Lesson 16 says more about arrays and provides some examples that use `Split` and `Join`.

FORMAT AND TOSTRING

The `string` class's `Format` method builds a formatted `string`. Its first parameter is a format string that tells how the method should display its other parameters. The format string can contain literal characters that are displayed as they appear, plus formatting fields.

Each field has the following syntax:

```
{index[,alignment][:formatString]}
```

The curly braces are required. The square brackets indicate optional pieces.

The key pieces of the field are:

➤   `index` — The zero-based index of the `Format` method's parameters that should be displayed by this field.

➤   `alignment` — The minimum number of characters that the field should use. If this is negative, the field is left-justified.

➤   `formatString` — The format string that indicates how the field's value should be formatted. The following format sections describe some of the many values that you can use here in addition to literal characters.

For example, the following code defines a `string` and two `decimal` values. It then uses `Console.WriteLine` to display a string built by `string.Format` in the Output window.

```
string itemName = "Fiendishly Difficult Puzzles";
decimal quantity = 2M;
decimal price_each = 9.99M;

Console.WriteLine(
    string.Format("You just bought {1} {0} at {2:C} each.",
    itemName, quantity, price_each));
```

The format string is `"You just bought {1} {0} at {2:C} each."`

The first field is {1}. This displays parameter number 1 (the second parameter — remember they're zero-based).

The second field is {0}. This displays the first parameter.

The third field is {2:C}. This displays the third parameter with the format string C, which formats the value as currency.

The result is:

```
You just bought 2 Fiendishly Difficult Puzzles at $9.99 each.
```

The following code shows an example that uses field widths to make values line up in columns. Before the code executes, assume that itemName1, quantity1, and the other variables have already been initialized.

```
Console.WriteLine(
    string.Format("{0,-20}{1,5}{2,10}{3,10}",
    "Item", "Qty", "Each", "Total")
);
Console.WriteLine(
    string.Format("{0,-20}{1,5}{2,10:C}{3,10:C}",
    itemName1, quantity1, priceEach1, quantity1 * priceEach1)
);
Console.WriteLine(
    string.Format("{0,-20}{1,5}{2,10:C}{3,10:C}",
    itemName2, quantity2, priceEach2, quantity2 * priceEach2)
);
Console.WriteLine(
    string.Format("{0,-20}{1,5}{2,10:C}{3,10:C}",
    itemName3, quantity3, priceEach3, quantity3 * priceEach3)
);
```

Notice that the code begins with a line that defines the column headers. Its formatting string uses the same indexes and alignment values as the other formatting strings so the headers line up with the values below.

The following shows the result:

```
Item                  Qty      Each     Total
Pretzels (dozen)        4     $5.95    $23.80
Blue laser pointer      1   $149.99   $149.99
Titanium spork          2     $8.99    $17.98
```

Because the format string is just a string, you could define it in a constant or variable and then use that variable as the first argument to the Format method. That way you are certain that all of the Format statements use the same string. This also makes it easier to change the format later if necessary.

Every object provides a ToString method that converts the object into a string. For simple data types such as numbers and dates, the result is the value in an easy-to-read string.

The `ToString` method for some objects can take a format parameter that tells how you want the item formatted. For example, the following statement displays the variable `cost` formatted as a currency value in the Output window:

```
Console.WriteLine(cost.ToString("C"));
```

The following sections describe standard and custom format strings for numbers, dates, and times. You can use these as arguments to the `ToString` method or as the `formatString` part of the `string.Format` method's format strings.

Standard Numeric Formats

Formatting characters tell `string.Format` and `ToString` how to format a value. For the characters discussed in this section, you can use either an uppercase or lowercase letter. For example, you can use C or c for the currency format.

Table 14-2 summarizes the standard numeric formatting characters.

TABLE 14-2

CHARACTER	MEANING	EXAMPLE
C	Currency with a currency symbol, thousands separators, and a decimal point.	$12,345.67
D	Decimal. Integer types only.	12345
E	Scientific notation.	1.234567E+004
F	Fixed-point.	12345.670
G	General. Either fixed-point or scientific notation, whichever is shorter.	12345.67
N	Similar to currency except without the currency symbol.	12,345.67
P	Percent. The number is multiplied by 100 and a percent sign is added appropriately for the computer's locale. Includes thousands separators and a decimal point.	123.45 %
R	Round trip. The number (double or float only) is formatted in a way that guarantees it can be parsed back into its original value.	1234.567
X	Hexadecimal.	3A7

You can follow several of these characters with a *precision specifier* that affects how the value is formatted. How this value works depends on the format character that it follows.

For the D and X formats, the result is padded on the left with zeros to have the length given by the precision specifier. For example, the format D10 produces a decimal value padded with zeros to 10 characters.

For the C, E, F, N, and P formats, the precision specifier indicates the number of digits after the decimal point.

Custom Numeric Formats

If the standard numeric formatting characters don't do what you want, you can use a custom numeric format. Table 14-3 summarizes the custom numeric formatting characters.

TABLE 14-3

CHARACTER	MEANING
0	Digit or zero. A digit is displayed here or a zero if there is no corresponding digit in the value being formatted.
#	Digit or nothing. A digit is displayed here or nothing if there is no corresponding digit in the value being formatted.
.	Decimal separator. The decimal separator goes here. Note that the actual separator character may not be a period depending on the computer's regional settings, although you still use the period in the format string.
,	Thousands separator. The thousands separator goes here. The actual separator character may not be a comma depending on the computer's regional settings, although you still use the comma in the format string.
%	Percent. The number is multiplied by 100 and the percent sign is added at this point. For example, %0 puts the percent sign before the number and 0% puts it after.
E+0	Scientific notation. The number of 0s indicates the number of digits in the exponent. If + is included, the exponent always includes a + or − sign. If + is omitted, the exponent only includes a sign if the exponent is negative. For example, the format string #.##E+000 used with the value 1234.56 produces the result 1.23E+003.
\	Escape character. Whatever follows the \ is displayed without any conversion. For example, the format 0.00\% would add a percent sign to a number without scaling it by 100 as the format 0.00% does. Note that you must escape the escape character itself in a normal (non-verbatim) string. For example, a format string might look like {0:0.00\\%} in the code.
'ABC'	Literal string. Characters enclosed in single or double quotes are displayed without any conversion.
;	Section separator. See the following text.

You can use a section separator to divide a formatting string into two or three sections. If you use two sections, the first applies to values greater than or equal to zero, and the second section applies to values less than zero. If you use three sections, they apply to values that are greater than, less than, and equal to zero, respectively.

For example, Table 14-4 shows the result produced by the three-section custom formatting string `"{0:$#,##0.00;($#,##0.00);-- zero --}"` for different values.

TABLE 14-4

VALUE	FORMATTED RESULT
12345.678	$12,345.68
-12345.678	($12,345.68)
0.000	-- zero --

Standard Date and Time Formats

Just as numeric values have standard and custom formatting strings, so too do dates and times.

Table 14-5 summarizes the standard date and time formatting patterns. The examples are those produced for 1:23 PM August 20, 2010 on my computer set up for US English. Your results will depend on how your computer is configured. Note that for many of the characters in this table, the uppercase and lowercase versions have different meanings.

TABLE 14-5

CHARACTER	MEANING	EXAMPLE
d	Short date	8/20/2010
D	Long date	Friday, August 20, 2010
f	Full date, short time	Friday, August 20, 2010 1:23 PM
F	Full date, long time	Friday, August 20, 2010 1:23:00 PM
g	General date/time, short time	8/20/2010 1:23 PM
G	General date/time, long time	8/20/2010 1:23:00 PM
M or m	Month day	August 20
O	Round trip	2010-08-20T13:23:00.0000000
R or r	RFC1123	Fri, 20 Aug 2010 13:23:00 GMT
s	Sortable date/time	2010-08-20T13:23:00
t	Short time	1:23 PM
T	Long time	1:23:00 PM
u	Universal sortable short date/time	2010-08-20 13:23:00Z

continues

TABLE 14-5 *(continued)*

CHARACTER	MEANING	EXAMPLE
U	Universal sortable full date/time	Friday, August 20, 2010 1:23:00 PM
Y or y	Year month	August, 2010

The `DateTime` class also provides several methods that return the date's value as a string formatted in the most common date and time formats. Table 14-6 summarizes the most useful of these methods and shows the results on my computer set up for US English. Your results will depend on how your computer is configured.

TABLE 14-6

METHOD	FORMAT	EXAMPLE
ToLongDateString	Long date (D)	Friday, August 20, 2010
ToLongTimeString	Long time (T)	1:23:00 PM
ToShortDateString	Short date (d)	8/20/2010
ToShortTimeString	Short time (t)	1:23 PM
ToString	General date and time (G)	8/20/2010 1:23:00 PM

Custom Date and Time Formats

If the standard date and time formatting characters don't do the trick, you can use a custom format. Table 14-7 summarizes the custom date and time formatting strings. Note that for many of the characters in this table, the uppercase and lowercase versions have different meanings.

TABLE 14-7

CHARACTER	MEANING
d	Day of month between 1 and 31.
dd	Day of month between 01 and 31.
ddd	Abbreviated day of week (Mon, Tue, and so on).
dddd	Full day of week (Monday, Tuesday, and so on).
f	Digits after the decimal for seconds. For example, ffff means use four digits.
F	Similar to f but trailing zeros are not displayed.
g	Era specifier. For example, A.D.

CHARACTER	MEANING
h	Hours between 1 and 12.
hh	Hours between 01 and 12.
H	Hours between 0 and 23.
HH	Hours between 00 and 23.
m	Minutes between 1 and 59.
mm	Minutes between 01 and 59.
M	Month between 1 and 12.
MM	Month between 01 and 12.
MMM	Month abbreviation (Jan, Feb, and so on).
MMMM	Month name (January, February, and so on).
s	Seconds between 1 and 59.
ss	Seconds between 01 and 59.
t	First character of AM/PM designator.
tt	AM/PM designator.
y	One- or two-digit year. If the year has fewer than two digits, is it not zero padded.
yy	Two-digit year, zero padded if necessary.
yyy	Three-digit year, zero padded if necessary.
yyyy	Four-digit year, zero padded if necessary.
yyyyy	Five-digit year, zero padded if necessary.
z	Signed time zone offset from GMT. For example, Pacific Standard Time is −8.
zz	Signed time zone offset from GMT in two digits. For example, Pacific Standard Time is −08.
zzz	Signed time zone offset from GMT in hours and minutes. For example, Pacific Standard Time is −08:00.
:	Hours, minutes, and seconds separator.
/	Date separator.
'ABC'	Literal string. Characters enclosed in single or double quotes are displayed without any conversion.

Table 14-8 shows some example formats and their results. The date used was 1:23:45.678 PM August 20, 2010 on my computer set up for US English. Your results will depend on how your computer is configured.

TABLE 14-8

FORMAT	RESULT
M/d/yy	8/20/10
d MMM yy	20 Aug 10
HH:mm 'hours'	13:23 hours
h:mm:ss.ff, M/d/y	1:23:45.67, 8/20/10
dddd 'at' h:mmt	Friday at 1:23P
ddd 'at' h:mmt	Fri at 1:23PM

TRY IT

In this Try It, you build a program that displays the current date and time in a `Label` when it starts as shown in Figure 14-1.

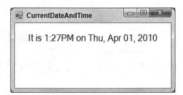

FIGURE 14-1

Lesson Requirements

In this Try It:

➤ Start a new project and add a `Label` to its form.

➤ Give the form a `Load` event handler that sets the `Label`'s text as shown in Figure 14-1.

> *You can download the code and resources for this Try It from the book's web page at* www.wrox.com *or* www.CSharpHelper.com/24hour.html. *The programs can be found within the Lesson14 folder.*

Hints

➤ The `DateTime.Now` property returns the current date and time.

➤ Either use `string.Format` or the value's `ToString` method to format the result.

Step-by-Step

➤ Start a new project and add a `Label` to its form.

   1. Create the new project and its `Label`.

   2. Set the `Label`'s `AutoSize` property to `False` and set its font size to 12. Then position and anchor it on the form.

   3. Set the `Label`'s `TextAlign` property to `MiddleCenter`.

➤ Give the form a `Load` event handler that sets the `Label`'s text as shown in Figure 14-1.

   1. Use code similar to the following:

```
// Display the current date and time.
private void Form1_Load(object sender, EventArgs e)
{
    greetingLabel.Text = DateTime.Now.ToString(
        "'It is' h:mmtt 'on' ddd, MMM dd yyyy");
}
```

 Please select Lesson 14 on the DVD to view the video that accompanies this lesson.

EXERCISES

1. Lesson 13's Try It reads and displays currency values, but it displays quantities without thousands separators. If you ordered 1,200 pencils, the program would display 1200.

Copy that program (or download the Lesson 13 Try It from the book's web site) and modify it so quantities are displayed with thousands separators.

2. Make a program that displays the time every second. Hint: Use a `Timer` control with `Enabled` set to `True`, and `Interval` set to `1000`. Update a `Label`'s `Text` property in the `Timer`'s `Tick` event.

3. Copy the program that you built for Exercise 1 and modify it so the main form displays items in a `ListBox` instead of a `ListView`. Make the program use `string.Format` to add items to the `ListBox` in a format similar to the following:

```
1,200 Gummy slugs at $0.02 each = $24.00
```

4. Make a program that replaces all occurrences of the letter e in a string entered by the user with the character -.

 You can download the solutions to these exercises from the book's web page at www.wrox.com *or* www.CSharpHelper.com/24hour.html. *They can be found in the* Lesson14 *folder.*

15

Working with Dates and Times

One of C#'s more confusing data types is DateTime. A DateTime represents a date, a time, or both. For example, a DateTime variable might represent Thursday April 1, 2010 at 9:15 AM.

In this lesson, you learn how to work with dates and times. You learn how to create DateTime variables, find the current date and time, and calculate elapsed time.

CREATING DATETIME VARIABLES

C# doesn't have DateTime literal values so you cannot simply set a DateTime variable equal to a value as you can with some other data types. Instead you can use the new keyword to initialize a new DateTime variable, supplying arguments to define the date and time.

For example, the following code creates a DateTime variable named aprilFools and initializes it to the date April 1, 2010. It then displays the date using the short date format described in Lesson 14 and by calling the variable's ToShortDateString method.

```
DateTime aprilFools = new DateTime(2010, 4, 1);
MessageBox.Show(aprilFools.ToString("d"));
MessageBox.Show(aprilFools.ToShortDateString());
```

The preceding code uses a year, month, and day to initialize its DateTime variable, but the DateTime type lets you use many different kinds of values. The three most useful combinations of arguments specify (all as integers):

➤ Year, month, day

➤ Year, month, day, hour, minute, second

➤ Year, month, day, hour, minute, second, milliseconds

You can also add a kind parameter to the end of the second and third of these combinations to indicate whether the value represents local time or UTC time. (Local and UTC times are explained in the next section.) For example, the following code creates a `DateTime` representing 12 noon on March 15, 2010 in the local time zone:

```
DateTime idesOfMarch =
    new DateTime(2010, 3, 15, 12, 0, 0, DateTimeKind.Local);
```

LOCAL AND UTC TIME

Windows has several different notions of dates and times. Two of the most important of these are local time and Coordinated Universal Time (UTC).

Local time is the time on your computer as it is configured for a particular locale. It's what you and a program's user typically think of as time.

UTC time is basically the same as Greenwich Mean Time (GMT), the time at the Royal Academy in Greenwich, London.

For most everyday tasks, local time is fine. If you need to compare data on computers running in different time zones, however, UTC time can make coordination easier. For example, if you want to know whether a customer in New York created an order before another customer created an order in San Salvador, UTC lets you compare the times without worrying about the customers' time zones.

A `DateTime` object has a `Kind` property that indicates whether the object represents local time, UTC time, or an unspecified time. When you create a `DateTime`, you can indicate whether you are creating a local or UTC time. If you do not specify the kind of time, C# assumes you are making an unspecified time.

After you create a `DateTime`, the type provides a couple of methods for converting it between local and UTC values. The `ToLocalTime` method converts a `DateTime` object to local time. Conversely, the `ToUniversalTime` method converts a time to UTC time.

 The `ToLocalTime` *and* `ToUniversalTime` *methods don't affect a* `DateTime` *if it is already in the desired format. For example, if you call* `ToLocalTime` *on a variable that already uses local time, the result is the same as the original variable.*

DATETIME PROPERTIES AND METHODS

The `DateTime` type provides many useful properties and methods for manipulating dates and times. The following table summarizes some of `DateTime`'s most useful methods. Table 15-1 indicates which methods are static, meaning you invoke them using the type name rather than a variable name, as in `DateTime.IsLeapYear(2010)`.

TABLE 15-1

METHOD	PURPOSE
Add	Adds a `TimeSpan` to the `DateTime`. The following section describes `TimeSpan`.
AddDays	Adds a specified number of days to the `DateTime`.
AddHours	Adds a specified number of hours to the `DateTime`.
AddMinutes	Adds a specified number of minutes to the `DateTime`.
AddMonths	Adds a specified number of months to the `DateTime`.
AddSeconds	Adds a specified number of seconds to the `DateTime`.
AddYears	Adds a specified number of years to the `DateTime`.
IsDaylightSavingsTime	Returns `true` if the date and time is within the Daylight Savings Time period for the local time zone.
IsLeapYear	(static) Returns `true` if the indicated year is a leap year.
Parse	(static) Parses a string and returns the corresponding `DateTime`.
Subtract	Subtracts another `DateTime` from this one and returns a `TimeSpan`. The following section says more about `TimeSpan`.
ToLocalTime	Converts the `DateTime` to a local value.
ToLongDateString	Returns the `DateTime` in long date format.
ToLongTimeString	Returns the `DateTime` in long time format.
ToShortDateString	Returns the `DateTime` in short date format.
ToShortTimeString	Returns the `DateTime` in short time format.
ToString	Returns the `DateTime` in general format.
ToUniversalTime	Converts the `DateTime` to a UTC value.

Table 15-2 summarizes the `DateTime`'s most useful properties.

TABLE 15-2

PROPERTY	PURPOSE
Date	Gets the `DateTime`'s date without the time.
Day	Gets the `DateTime`'s day of the month between 1 and 31.
DayOfWeek	Gets the `DateTime`'s day of the week as in Monday.

continues

TABLE 15-2 *(continued)*

PROPERTY	PURPOSE
DayOfYear	Gets the `DateTime`'s day of the year between 1 and 366 (leap years have 366 days).
Hour	Gets the `DateTime`'s hour between 0 and 23.
Kind	Returns the `DateTime`'s kind: `Local`, `Utc`, or `Unspecified`.
Millisecond	Gets the `DateTime`'s time's millisecond.
Minute	Gets the `DateTime`'s minute between 0 and 59.
Month	Gets the `DateTime`'s month between 1 and 12.
Now	(static) Gets the current date and time.
Second	Gets the `DateTime`'s second between 0 and 59.
TimeOfDay	Gets the `DateTime`'s time without the date.
Today	(static) Gets the current date without a time.
UtcNow	(static) Gets the current UTC date and time.
Year	Gets the `DateTime`'s year.

TIMESPANS

A `DateTime` represents a point in time (July 20, 1969 at 20:17:40). A `TimeSpan` represents an elapsed period of time (1 day, 17 hours, 27 minutes, and 12 seconds).

One of the more useful ways to make a `TimeSpan` is to subtract one `DateTime` from another to find the amount of time between them. For example, the following code calculates the time that elapsed between the first and last manned moon landings:

```
DateTime firstLanding = new DateTime(1969, 7, 20, 20, 17, 40);
DateTime lastLanding = new DateTime(1972, 12, 11, 19, 54, 57);
TimeSpan elapsed = lastLanding - firstLanding;
Console.WriteLine(elapsed.ToString());
```

The code creates `DateTime` values to represent the times of the two landings. It then subtracts the first date from the second to get the elapsed time and uses the resulting `TimeSpan`'s `ToString` method to display the duration. The following text shows the code's output in the format `days.hours:minutes:seconds`:

```
1239.23:37:17
```

Table 15-3 summarizes the TimeSpan's most useful properties and methods.

TABLE 15-3

PROPERTY	MEANING
Days	The number of days.
Hours	The number of hours.
Milliseconds	The number of milliseconds.
Minutes	The number of minutes.
Seconds	The number of seconds.
ToString	Converts the TimeSpan into a string in the format days.hours:minutes:seconds.fractionalSeconds.
TotalDays	The entire TimeSpan represented as days. For a 36-hour duration, this would be 1.5.
TotalHours	The entire TimeSpan represented as hours. For a 45-minute duration, this would be 0.75.
TotalMilliseconds	The entire TimeSpan represented as milliseconds. For a 1-second duration, this would be 1,000.
TotalMinutes	The entire TimeSpan represented as minutes. For a 1-hour duration, this would be 60.
TotalSeconds	The entire TimeSpan represented as seconds. For a 1-minute TimeSpan, this would be 60.

Note that you can use the + and – operators to add and subtract TimeSpans, getting a new TimeSpan as a result. This works in a fairly obvious way. For example, a 90-minute TimeSpan minus a 30-minute TimeSpan gives a 60-minute TimeSpan.

TRY IT

In this Try It, you use the DateTime and TimeSpan variables to build the stopwatch application shown in Figure 15-1. When the user clicks the Start Button, the program starts its counter. When the user clicks the Stop Button, the program stops the counter.

FIGURE 15-1

Normally the `TimeSpan`'s `ToString` method displays a value in the format `d.hh:mm:ss.fffffff`. In this example, you use `string.Format` to display the elapsed time in the format `hh:mm:ss.ff`.

 You can download the code and resources for this Try It from the book's web page at www.wrox.com *or* www.CSharpHelper.com/24hour.html. *You can find them within the Lesson15 folder.*

Lesson Requirements

➤ Create the form shown in Figure 15-1. In addition to the controls that are visible, give the form a `Timer` with `Interval = 1`. Initially disable the Stop button.

➤ When the user clicks the Start button, start the `Timer`, disable the Start button, and enable the Stop button.

➤ When the user clicks the Stop button, stop the `Timer`, enable the Start button, and disable the Stop button.

➤ When the `Timer`'s `Tick` event fires, display the elapsed time in the format `hh:mm:ss.ff`.

Hints

➤ `TimeSpan` doesn't use the same formatting characters as a `DateTime`, so for example, you can't simply use a format string such as `hh:mm:ss.ff`. Instead use the `TimeSpan` properties to get the elapsed hours, minutes, seconds, and milliseconds and then format those values.

Step-by-Step

➤ Create the form shown in Figure 15-1. In addition to the controls that are visible, give the form a `Timer` with `Interval = 1`. Initially disable the Stop button.

1. Add the Start and Stop buttons and a `Label` to the form as shown in Figure 15-1. Set the Stop button's `Enabled` property to `False`.

2. Add a `Timer` and set its `Interval` property to 1 millisecond. (This is much faster than your computer can actually fire the `Timer`'s `Click` event, so the `Timer` will run as quickly as it can.)

➤ When the user clicks the Start button, start the `Timer`, disable the Start button, and enable the Stop button.

1. To remember the time when the user clicked the Start button, create a `DateTime` field named `StartTime`.

```
// The time when the user clicked Start.
private DateTime StartTime;
```

2. Add the following code to the Start button's Click event handler:

```
// Start the Timer.
private void startButton_Click(object sender, EventArgs e)
{
    StartTime = DateTime.Now;
    startButton.Enabled = false;
    stopButton.Enabled = true;
    updateLabelTimer.Enabled = true;
}
```

➤ When the user clicks the Stop button, stop the Timer, enable the Start button, and disable the Stop button.

1. Add the following code to the Stop button's Click event handler:

```
// Stop the Timer.
private void stopButton_Click(object sender, EventArgs e)
{
    startButton.Enabled = true;
    stopButton.Enabled = false;
    updateLabelTimer.Enabled = false;
}
```

➤ When the Timer's Tick event fires, display the elapsed time in the format hh:mm:ss.ff.

1. Use code similar to the following. Notice that the code divides the number of milliseconds by 10 to convert it into hundredths of seconds.

```
// Display the elapsed time.
private void updateLabelTimer_Tick(object sender, EventArgs e)
{
    // Subtract the start time from the current time
    // to get elapsed time.
    TimeSpan elapsed = DateTime.Now - StartTime;

    // Display the result.
    elapsedTimeLabel.Text = string.Format(
        "{0:00}:{1:00}:{2:00}.{3:00}",
        elapsed.Hours,
        elapsed.Minutes,
        elapsed.Seconds,
        elapsed.Milliseconds / 10);
}
```

 Please select Lesson 15 on the DVD to view the video that accompanies this lesson.

EXERCISES

1. Make a program with a Birth Date TextBox and a Calculate Button. When the user enters a birth date and clicks the Button, calculate the person's current age and add items to a ListBox that display the age converted into each of days, hours, minutes, and seconds.

2. Make a program that displays the days of the week for your next 10 birthdays in a ListBox.

3. Make a program with two TextBoxes for dates and a Button. When the user clicks the Button, the program should calculate the time between the dates and display it in a message box.

4. Modify the program you built for Exercise 3 to use DateTimePicker controls instead of TextBoxes. To keep things simple, just display the total number of days between the dates. Use the controls' Value properties to get the selected dates. (This control prevents the user from entering invalid dates. Preventing the user from making mistakes is generally a good idea.)

You can download the solutions to these exercises from the book's web page at www.wrox.com *or* www.CSharpHelper.com/24hour.html. *You can find them in the Lesson15 folder.*

16

Using Arrays and Collections

The data types described in previous lessons each hold a single piece of data. A variable might hold an integer, string, or point in time.

Sometimes it's convenient to work with a group of related values all at once. For example, suppose you're the CEO of a huge company that just posted huge losses. In that case, you might want to give each hourly employee a 10 percent pay cut and give each executive a 15 percent bonus.

In cases like this, it would be handy to be able to store all of the hourly employee data in one variable so you could easily work with it. Similarly you might like to store the executives' data in a second variable so it's easy to manage.

In this lesson, you learn how to make variables that can hold more than one piece of data. You learn how to make arrays and different kinds of collections such as Lists, Dictionaries, Stacks, and Queues.

This lesson explains how to build these objects and add and remove items from them. Lesson 19 explains how to get the full benefit of them by looping through them to perform some action on each of the items they contain.

ARRAYS

An *array* is a group of values that all have the same data type and that all share the same name. Your code uses an *index*, which is an integer greater than or equal to 0, to pick a particular item in the array.

An array is similar to the mailboxes in an apartment building. The building has a single bank of mailboxes that all have the same street address (the array's name). You use the apartment numbers to pick a particular cubbyhole in the bank of mailboxes.

Figure 16-1 shows an array graphically. This array is named values. It contains eight entries with indexes 0 through 7.

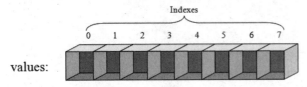

FIGURE 16-1

 An array's smallest and largest indexes are called its lower bound and upper bound. In C#, the lower bound is always 0, and the upper bound is always one less than the length of the array.

Creating Arrays

The following code shows how you might declare an array of integers. The square brackets indicate an array so the first part of the statement `int[]` means the variable's data type is an array of integers.

```
int[] values;
```

After you declare an array variable, you can assign it to a new uninitialized array. The following code initializes the variable `values` to a new integer array that can hold eight elements:

```
values = new int[8];
```

Remember that an array's lower bound is always 0 in C# so this array has indexes 0 through 7.

As is the case with other variables, you can declare and initialize an array in a single step. The following code declares and creates the `values` array in a single statement:

```
int[] values = new int[8];
```

After you have created an array, you can access its members by using the array's name followed by an index inside square brackets. For example, the following code initializes the `values` array by setting the Nth entry equal to N squared:

```
values[0] = 0 * 0;
values[1] = 1 * 1;
values[2] = 2 * 2;
values[3] = 3 * 3;
values[4] = 4 * 4;
values[5] = 5 * 5;
values[6] = 6 * 6;
values[7] = 7 * 7;
```

 Most programmers pronounce `values[5]` *as "values of 5," "values sub 5," or "the 5th element of values."*

After you have placed values in an array, you can read the values using the same square bracket syntax. The following code displays a message box that uses one of the array's values:

```
MessageBox.Show("7 * 7 is " + values[7].ToString());
```

To make initializing arrays easier, C# provides an abbreviated syntax that lets you declare an array and set its values all in one statement. Simply set the variable equal to the values you want separated by commas and surrounded by braces as shown in the following code:

```
int[] values = { 0, 1, 1, 2, 3, 5, 8, 13, 21, 34 };
```

A FIBONACCI ARRAY

The Fibonacci program shown in Figure 16-2 (and available as part of this lesson's code download) uses an array to display Fibonacci numbers. Use the `NumericUpDown` control to select a number and click Calculate to see the corresponding Fibonacci number.

FIGURE 16-2

When the user clicks Calculate, the program executes the following code:

```
private void calculateButton_Click(object sender, EventArgs e)
{
    int[] values = new int[21];
    values[0] = 0;
    values[1] = 1;
    values[2] = values[0] + values[1];
    values[3] = values[1] + values[2];
    values[4] = values[2] + values[3];
    ...
    values[20] = values[18] + values[19];

    int index = (int)numberNumericUpDown.Value;
    resultsTextBox.Text = values[index].ToString();
}
```

The code starts by initializing the `values` array to hold the first 21 Fibonacci numbers. It uses the following definition of the numbers to calculate the values:

```
Fibonacci(i) = Fibonacci(i - 1) + Fibonacci(i - 2)
```

After initializing the array, the program gets the value selected by the `NumericUpDown` control, converts it from a `decimal` to an `int`, uses it as an index into the `values` array, and displays the result in `resultTextBox`.

When you use this syntax, C# uses the number of values you supply to define the array's size. In the preceding code, C# would give the `values` array 10 entries because that's how many values the code supplies.

Multi-Dimensional Arrays

The arrays described in the previous section hold a single row of items but C# also lets you define multi-dimensional arrays. You can think of these as higher dimensional sequences of apartment mailboxes.

Figure 16-3 shows a graphic representation of a two-dimensional array with four rows and eight columns.

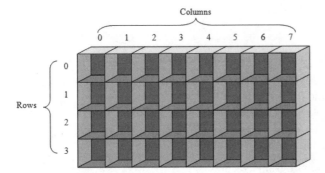

FIGURE 16-3

The following code shows how you could declare, allocate, and initialize this array to hold a multiplication table with values up to 4 times 7:

```
int[,] values = new int[5, 7];
values[0, 0] = 0 * 0;
values[0, 1] = 0 * 1;
values[0, 2] = 0 * 2;
...
values[1, 1] = 1 * 1;
values[1, 2] = 1 * 2;
...
values[4, 7] = 4 * 7;
```

The following code shows the C# syntax for quickly defining and initializing a two-dimensional array:

```
int[,] cell =
{
    {0, 1, 2},
    {3, 4, 5},
    {6, 7, 8},
};
```

You can use similar syntax to make and initialize higher-dimensional arrays. For example, the following code makes a four-dimensional array of strings:

```
string[, , ,] employeeData = new string[10, 20, 30, 40];
```

Notice that the definition of the array's final row ends with a comma. You don't need this comma because nothing follows this last row but C# allows you to include it to give the rows a more uniform format. The commas after the other rows are required because more rows follow them.

Array Properties and Methods

All arrays have a `Length` property that your code can use to determine the number of items in the array. Arrays all have lower bound 0, and for one-dimensional arrays, `Length - 1` gives an array's upper bound.

Arrays also have `GetLowerBound` and `GetUpperBound` methods that return the lower and upper bounds for a particular dimension in an array.

For example, the following code creates a 5-by-10 array. It then displays the lower and upper bounds for the first dimension. (The dimension numbers start at 0.)

```
int[,] x = new int[5, 10];
MessageBox.Show("The first dimension runs from " +
    x.GetLowerBound(0) + " to " + x.GetUpperBound(0));
```

The `Array` class also provides several useful static methods that you can use to manipulate arrays. For example, the following code sorts the array named `salaries`:

```
Array.Sort(salaries);
```

To sort an array, the array must contain things that can be compared in a meaningful way. For example, `int` and `string` data have a natural order, so it's easy to say that the string "Jackson" should come before the string "Utah."

If an array holds `Employee` objects, however, it's unclear how you would want to compare two items. In fact, it's likely that you couldn't define an order that would always work because sometimes you might want to sort employees by name and other times you might want to sort them by employee ID or even salary.

You can solve this problem in a couple of ways including the `IComparer` interface (mentioned briefly in Lesson 27's Exercise 2) and making the `Employee` class implement `IComparable` (mentioned in Lesson 28). These are slightly more advanced topics, so they aren't covered in great depth here.

The `Sort` method has many overloaded versions that perform different kinds of sorting. For example, instead of passing it a single array you can pass it an array of keys and an array of items. In that case the method sorts the keys, moving the items so they remain matched up with their corresponding keys.

The Table 16-1 summarizes the most useful methods provided by the `Array` class.

TABLE 16-1

METHOD	PURPOSE
BinarySearch	Uses binary search to find an item in a sorted array.
Clear	Resets a range of items in the array to the default value for the array's data type (0, false, or null).
Copy	Copies a range of items from one array to another.
IndexOf	Returns the index of a particular item in the array.
LastIndexOf	Returns the index of the last occurrence of a particular item in the array.
Resize	Resizes the array, preserving any items that fit in the new size.
Reverse	Reverses the order of the items in the array.
Sort	Sorts the array's items.

COLLECTION CLASSES

An array holds a group of items and lets you refer to them by index. The .NET Framework used by C# also provides an assortment of *collection classes* that you can use to store and manipulate items in other ways. For example, a Dictionary stores items with keys and lets you very quickly locate an item from its key. You could use a Dictionary to make an employee phone book and very quickly look up a phone number given someone's name.

Generic Classes

The following sections describe some particular kinds of classes that come pre-built by the .NET Framework. These are generic classes so before you learn about them you should know a little about what a generic class is.

A *generic class* is one that is not tied to a particular data type. For example, suppose you built a StringList class that can store a list if strings. Now suppose you decided you wanted an IntegerList class to store lists of integers. The two classes would be practically identical, just for different data types.

I've mentioned several times that duplicated code is a bad thing. Having two nearly identical classes means debugging and maintaining two different sets of code that are practically the same.

One solution to this situation is to make a more general AnythingList class that uses the general object data type to store items. An object can hold any kind of data, so this class could hold lists of integers, strings, or Customer objects. Unfortunately that has two big problems.

First, you would also do a lot of work converting the items with the general object data type stored in the list into the int, string, or Customer type of the items that you put in there. This is annoying because it gives you more work to do and makes your code more complicated and harder to read.

A bigger problem is that a list that can hold anything can hold *anything*. If you make a list to hold customer data, it could still hold `ints`, `strings`, and `PurchaseOrder` objects. Your code would need to do a lot of work guarding against accidentally putting the wrong kind of item in the list.

A much better approach is to use generic classes. These classes take data types in their declarations so they know what kind of data they will manipulate. Using this kind of class, you can build a list of integers, strings, or what have you.

The following code declares and initializes a generic `List` class.

```
List<string> names = new List<string>();
```

The `<string>` part of the declaration indicates that the class will work with strings. You can put strings into the list and take strings out of it. You cannot add an integer to the list, just as you can't set a string variable equal to an integer. Visual Studio knows that the list works with strings and won't let you use anything else.

Note that IntelliSense knows about generic classes and provides help. If you begin a declaration with `List`, IntelliSense displays `List<>` to let you know that it is a generic class.

Now if you type the opening pointy bracket, IntelliSense displays a list of the class's type parameters and even describes them as you type. (The `List` class has only one type parameter but some such as `Dictionary` have more.) After you finish the declaration, the class knows what data types it will manipulate, and it can behave as if it were designed with that data type in mind.

Now, with some understanding of generic classes, you're ready to look at some generic collection classes.

Lists

A `List` is a simple ordered list of items. You can declare and initialize a `List` as in the following code.

```
List<string> names = new List<string>();
```

The `List` class provides several methods for manipulating the items it contains. The three most important are `Add`, `Remove`, and `RemoveAt`.

➤ The `Add` method adds a new item to the end of the list, automatically resizing the `List` if necessary. This is easier than adding an item to an array, which requires you to resize the array first.

➤ The `Remove` method removes a particular item from the list. Note that you pass the target item to `Remove`, not the index of the item that you want to remove. If you know that the string `"Zaphod"` is in the list `names`, the following code removes the first instance of that name from the list:

```
names.Remove("Zaphod");
```

 The `Remove` *method removes only the first occurrence of an item from the* `List`.

➤ The `RemoveAt` method removes an item from a particular position in the list. It then compacts the list to remove the hole where the item was. This is much easier than removing an item from an array, which requires you to shuffle items from one part of the array to another and then resize the array to reduce its size.

In addition to these methods, you can use square brackets to get and set a `List`'s entries much as you can with an array. For example, the following code sets and then displays the value of the first entry in a list:

```
names[0] = "Mickey";
MessageBox.Show("The first name is " + names[0]);
```

Note that this works only if the index you use exists in the list. If the list holds 10 names and you try to set the 14th, the program crashes.

SortedLists

A `SortedList` stores a list of key/value pairs, keeping the list sorted by the keys. The types of the keys and values are generic parameters, so for example, you could make a list that uses numbers (such as employee IDs) for keys and strings (such as names) for values.

Note that the list will not allow you to add two items with the same key. Multiple items can have the same value, but if you try to add two with the same key, the program crashes.

Table 16-2 summarizes useful methods provided by the `SortedList` class.

TABLE 16-2

METHOD	PURPOSE
Add	Adds a key and value to the list.
Clear	Empties the list.
Contains	Returns true if the list contains a given value.
ContainsKey	Returns true if the list contains a given key.
ContainsValue	Returns true if the list contains a given value.
GetKeyList	Returns a list holding the keys.
GetValueList	Returns a list holding the values.
Remove	Removes the item with a specific key from the list.

In addition to these methods, you can use square brackets to index into the list, using the items' keys as indexes.

The following code demonstrates a `SortedList`:

```
SortedList<string, string> addresses =
    new SortedList<string, string>();
```

```
addresses.Add("Dan", "4 Deer Dr, Bugville VT, 01929");
addresses.Add("Bob", "8273 Birch Blvd, Bugville VT, 01928");

addresses["Cindy"] = "32878 Carpet Ct, Bugville VT, 01929";
addresses["Alice"] = "162 Ash Ave, Bugville VT, 01928";
addresses["Bob"] = "8273 Bash Blvd, Bugville VT, 01928";

MessageBox.Show("Bob's address is " + addresses["Bob"]);
```

The code starts by declaring and initializing the list. It uses the `Add` method to add some entries and then uses square brackets to add some more.

Next the code uses the square bracket syntax to update Bob's address. Finally the code displays Bob's new address.

You can't see it from this example, but unlike the `List` class, `SortedList` actually stores its items ordered by key. For example, you could use the `GetKeyList` and `GetValueList` methods to get the list's keys and values in that order.

Dictionaries

The `Dictionary` and `SortedDictionary` classes provide features similar to the `SortedList` class, manipulating key/value pairs. The difference is in the data structures the three classes use to store their items.

Without getting into technical details, the results are that the three classes use different amounts of memory and work at different speeds. In general, `SortedList` is the slowest but takes the least memory, while `Dictionary` is the fastest but takes the most memory.

For small programs, the difference is insignificant. For big programs that work with thousands of entries, you might need to be more careful about picking a class. (Personally I like `Dictionary` for most purposes because speed is nice, memory is relatively cheap, and the name is suggestive of the way you use the class: to look up something by key.)

Queues

A `Queue` is a collection that lets you add items at one end and remove them from the other. It's like the line at a bank where you stand at the back of the line and the teller helps the person at the front of the line until eventually it's your turn.

Because a queue retrieves items in first-in-first-out order, queues are sometimes called FIFO lists or FIFOs. ("FIFO" is pronounced fife-o.)

Table 16-3 summarizes the `Queue`'s most important methods.

TABLE 16-3

METHOD	PURPOSE
Clear	Removes all items from the `Queue`.
Dequeue	Returns the item at the front of the `Queue` and removes it.
Enqueue	Adds an item to the back of the `Queue`.
Peek	Returns the item at the front of the `Queue` without removing it.

Stacks

A `Stack` is a collection that lets you add items at one end and remove them from the same end. It's like a stack of books on the floor: you can add a book to the top of the stack and remove a book from the top, but you can't pull one out of the middle or bottom without risking a collapse.

> *Because a stack retrieves items in last-in-first-out order, stacks are sometimes called LIFO lists or LIFOs. ("LIFO" is pronounced life-o.)*
>
> *The top of a stack is also sometimes called its head. The bottom is sometimes called its tail.*

Table 16-4 summarizes the `Stack`'s most important methods.

TABLE 16-4

METHOD	PURPOSE
Clear	Removes all items from the `Stack`.
Peek	Returns the item at the top of the `Stack` without removing it.
Pop	Returns the item at the top of the `Stack` and removes it.
Push	Adds an item to the top of the `Stack`.

TRY IT

In this Try It, you use a `Dictionary` to build the order lookup system shown in Figure 16-4. When the user clicks the Add button, the program adds a new item with the given order ID and items. If the user enters an order ID and clicks Find, the program

FIGURE 16-4

retrieves the corresponding items. If the user enters an order ID and some items and then clicks Update, the program updates the order's items.

 You can download the code and resources for this Try It from the book's web page at www.wrox.com *or* www.CSharpHelper.com/24hour.html. *You can find them in the Lesson16 folder in the download.*

Lesson Requirements

➤ Create the form shown in Figure 16-4.

➤ Add code that creates a `Dictionary` field named `Orders`. Set its generic type parameters to `int` (for order ID) and `string` (for items).

➤ Add code to the Add button that creates the new entry in the dictionary.

➤ Add code to the Find button that retrieves the appropriate entry from the dictionary.

➤ Add code to the Update button to update the indicated entry.

 This program will be fairly fragile and will crash if you don't enter an order ID, enter an ID that is not an integer, try to enter the same ID twice, try to find a nonexistent ID, and so on. Don't worry about these problems. You learn how to handle them later, notably in Lessons 18 and 21.

Step-by-Step

➤ Create the form shown in Figure 16-4.

   1. This is relatively straightforward. The only tricks are to set the `Items` TextBox's `MultiLine` and `AcceptsReturn` properties to `True`.

➤ Add code that creates a `Dictionary` named `orders`. Set its generic type parameters to `int` (for order ID) and `string` (for items).

   1. Use code similar to the following to make the `Orders` field:

```
// The dictionary to hold orders.
private Dictionary<int, string> Orders =
    new Dictionary<int, string>();
```

➤ Add code to the Add button that creates the new entry in the dictionary.

   1. This code should call the `Dictionary`'s `Add` method passing it the order ID and items entered by the user. The `Dictionary`'s order ID must be an integer so use `int.Parse` to convert the value entered by the user into an `int`.

Optionally you can add code to clear the textboxes to get ready for the next entry.

The code could be similar to the following:

```
// Add an order.
private void addButton_Click(object sender, EventArgs e)
{
    // Add the oredr data.
    Orders.Add(int.Parse(orderIdTextBox.Text), itemsTextBox.Text);

    // Get ready for the next one.
    orderIdTextBox.Clear();
    itemsTextBox.Clear();
    orderIdTextBox.Focus();
}
```

➤ Add code to the Find button that retrieves the new appropriate entry from the dictionary.

   1. Use code similar to the following:

```
// Look up an order.
private void findButton_Click(object sender, EventArgs e)
{
    itemsTextBox.Text = Orders[int.Parse(orderIdTextBox.Text)];
}
```

➤ Add code to the Update button to update the indicated entry.

   1. Use code similar to the following:

```
// Update an order.
private void updateButton_Click(object sender, EventArgs e)
{
    Orders[int.Parse(orderIdTextBox.Text)] = itemsTextBox.Text;
}
```

 Please select Lesson 16 on the DVD to view the video that accompanies this lesson.

EXERCISES

1. Make a program similar to the Fibonacci program that looks up factorials in an array. When the program starts, make it create the array to hold the first 20 factorials. Use the following definition for the factorial (where N! means the factorial of N):

```
0! = 1
N! = N * (N - 1)!
```

2. Make a program that demonstrates a stack of strings. The program should display a textbox and two buttons labeled Push and Pop. When the user clicks Push, add the current text to the stack. When the user clicks Pop, remove the next item from the stack and display it in the textbox.

3. Make a program that demonstrates a queue of strings. The program should display a textbox and two buttons labeled Enqueue and Dequeue. When the user clicks Enqueue, add the current text to the queue. When the user clicks Dequeue, remove the next item from the queue and display it in the textbox.

4. Make a program similar to the one you built for this lesson's Try It except make it store appointment information. The `Dictionary` should use the `DateTime` type for keys and the `string` type for values. Let the user pick dates from a `DateTimePicker`.

Hint: When the `DateTimePicker` first starts, it defaults to the current time, which may include fractional seconds. After the user changes the control's selection, however, the value no longer includes fractional seconds. That makes it hard to search for the exact same date and time later, at least if the user enters a value before changing the control's initial value.

To avoid this problem, when the form loads, initialize the `DateTimePicker` to a value that doesn't include fractional seconds. Use the properties provided by `DateTime.Now` to create a new `DateTime` and set the `DateTimePicker`'s value to that.

5. Make a day planner application. The code should make an array of 31 strings to hold each day's plan. Initialize the array to show fake plans such as "Day 1."

Use a `ComboBox` to let the user select a day of the month. When the `ComboBox`'s value changes, display the corresponding day's plan in a large `TextBox` on the form. (Hint: Use the `ComboBox`'s `SelectedIndex` property as an index into the array. Note that this program doesn't let the user enter or modify the plan, it just displays hardcoded values. To let the user modify the plan, you would need Find and Update buttons similar to those used in other exercises.)

You can download the solutions to these exercises from the book's web page at www.wrox.com *or* www.CSharpHelper.com/24hour.html. *You can find them in the Lesson16 folder.*

17

Using Enumerations and Structures

The data types you've learned about so far hold strings, integers, dates, and other predefined kinds of information, but sometimes it would be nice to define your own data types. Enumerations let you define a data type that can hold only certain values. For example, a menu program might define a `MealType` data type that can hold the values `Breakfast`, `Lunch`, and `Dinner`.

The data types described in previous lessons also can hold only a single piece of data: a name, address, date, or whatever. Sometimes it would be nice to keep related pieces of data together. Instead of storing a name, address, and phone number in separate strings, you might like to store them as a single unit.

Enumerations and structures let you do these things. An *enumeration* (or *enumerated type*) lets you define a new data type that can take only one of an allowed list of values. A *structure* lets you define a group of related pieces of data that should be kept together.

In this lesson, you learn how to define and use enumerations and structures to make your code easier to understand and debug.

ENUMERATIONS

An enumeration is simply a data type that allows only specific values. The following code defines a `ContactMethod` enumeration that can hold the values `None`, `Email`, `Phone`, or `SnailMail`:

```
// Define possible contact methods.
enum ContactMethod
{
    None = 0,
    Email,
    Phone,
    SnailMail,
}
```

The final comma in this example is optional. You don't need it because there is no value after SnailMail, *but C# allows it to make the lines of code more consistent.*

Internally an enumeration is stored as an integral data type, by default an int. A number after a value tells C# explicitly which integer to assign to that value. In the preceding code, None is explicitly assigned the value 0.

If you don't specify a value for an enumeration's item (and often you don't care what these values are), its value is one greater than the previous item's value (the first item gets value 0). In this example, None is 0, Email is 1, Phone is 2, and SnailMail is 3.

You create an instance of an enumerated type just as you make an instance of a primitive type such as int, decimal, or string. The following code declares a variable of type ContactMethod, assigns it the value ContactMethod.Email, and then displays its value in the Output window:

```
ContactMethod contactMethod = ContactMethod.Email;
Console.WriteLine(contactMethod.ToString());
```

An enumeration's ToString method returns the value's name, in this case "Email."

STRUCTURES

Defining a structure is easy. The following code defines a simple structure named Address that holds name and address information:

```
// Define a structure to hold addresses.
struct Address
{
    public string Name;
    public string Street;
    public string City;
    public string State;
    public string Zip;
    public string Email;
    public string Phone;
    public ContactMethod PreferredMethod;
}
```

Inside the braces, the structure defines the bits of data that it holds together. The public keywords in this example mean that the fields inside the structure (Name, Street, and so on) are visible to any code that can see an Address.

Notice that the structure can use an enumeration. In this example, the Address structure's PreferredMethod field has type ContactMethod.

In many ways structures behave like simple built-in types such as int and float. In particular, when you declare a variable with a structure type, the code not only declares it but also creates it. That means you don't need to use the new keyword to create a structure.

After defining the variable, you can access its fields using syntax similar to the way you access a control's properties. Start with the variable's name, follow it with a dot, and then add the field's name.

The following code creates and initializes a new `Address` structure named `homeAddress`:

```
Address homeAddress;

homeAddress.Name = nameTextBox.Text;
homeAddress.Street = streetTextBox.Text;
homeAddress.City = cityTextBox.Text;
homeAddress.State = stateTextBox.Text;
homeAddress.Zip = zipTextBox.Text;
homeAddress.Email = emailTextBox.Text;
homeAddress.Phone = phoneTextBox.Text;
homeAddress.PreferredMethod =
    (ContactMethod)preferredMethodComboBox.SelectedIndex;
```

This code fills in the text fields using values entered by the user in textboxes.

The final field is a `ContactMethod` enumeration. The user selects a value for this field from the `preferredMethodComboBox`. The code takes the index of the `ComboBox`'s selected item, converts it from an integer into a `ContactMethod`, and saves the result in the structure's `PreferredMethod` field.

 To correctly convert a `ComboBox` *selection into an enumeration value, the* `ComboBox` *must display the choices in the same order in which they are defined by the enumeration. In this example, the* `ComboBox` *must contain the items None, Email, Phone, and SnailMail in that order to match up with the enumeration's items.*

STRUCTURES VERSUS CLASSES

In many ways structures are very similar to classes. Lesson 23 says a lot more about classes and the sorts of things you can do with them, and many of the same techniques apply to structures.

For example, both can contain properties, methods, and events. Both can also have constructors, special methods that are executed when you use `new` to create a new one. These are described in greater detail in Lesson 23.

While structures and classes have many things in common, they also have many differences. A lot of these differences are outside the scope of this book, so I won't cover them here, but one very important difference that you should understand is that structures are value types while classes are reference types.

➤ A **reference type** doesn't actually hold an instance of a class. Instead it holds a reference to an instance. For example, the following code creates a reference to an object of type `NewUserForm`. The second statement actually creates that instance and then the third statement displays it. If you tried to display the form without the second statement, the program would crash because the variable wouldn't be referring to an instance yet.

```
NewUserForm userForm;
userForm = new NewUserForm();
userForm.ShowDialog();
```

➤ In contrast, a **value type** actually contains its data instead of referring to it. For example, the following code declares an `Address` variable. When execution passes that statement, the variable already contains an Address structure, its fields have default values, and it is ready for use.

```
Address homeAddress;
homeAddress.Name = "Benjamin";
```

One other important difference between value and reference types is that when you set a variable with a value type equal to another, the first variable receives a copy of the second variable's value. For example, if x and y are integers, then the statement x = y makes x hold the same value as y.

Similarly if ann and ben are variables of the structure type Person, then ben = ann makes all of the fields in ben have the same values as all of the fields in ann, but they are still two separate Person structures.

In contrast, if you set a variable with a reference type equal to another, the first variable now refers to the same object as the other not just a copy of that object. For example, suppose cindy and dan are two variables that hold references to Student objects. The statement dan = cindy makes the variable dan refer to the same object to which cindy refers. If you change one of dan's properties, cindy also sees the change because they point to the same object.

The StructureVersusClass example program that is available in the Lesson 17 download demonstrates this difference.

So which should you use, a structure or a class? In many programs the difference doesn't matter much. As long as you are aware of the relevant differences, you can often use either.

Microsoft's "Classes and Structs (C# Programming Guide)" web page at msdn.microsoft.com/ library/ms173109.aspx gives this advice:

> *In general, classes are used to model more complex behavior, or data that is intended to be modified after a class object is created. Structs are best suited for small data structures that contain primarily data that is not intended to be modified after the struct is created.*

TRY IT

In this Try It, you use an enumeration and a structure to make the address book shown in Figure 17-1. When the user clicks the Add button, the program saves the entered address values. If the user enters a name and clicks Find, the program retrieves the corresponding address data.

FIGURE 17-1

You can download the code and resources for this Try It from the book's web page at www.wrox.com *or* www.CSharpHelper.com/24hour.html. *You can find them in the Lesson17 folder in the download.*

Lesson Requirements

➤ Create the form shown in Figure 17-1.

➤ Define the `ContactMethod` enumeration with values `None`, `Email`, `Phone`, and `SnailMail`.

➤ Define an `Address` structure to hold the entered address information.

➤ Create a `Dictionary<string, Address>` field to hold the address data.

➤ Add code to initially select the `ComboBox`'s `None` entry when the form loads (just so something is selected).

➤ Add code to the Add button that creates the new entry in the `Dictionary`.

➤ Add code to the Find button that retrieves the appropriate entry from the `Dictionary` and displays it.

Step-by-Step

➤ Create the form shown in Figure 17-1.

1. This is relatively straightforward.

➤ Define the `ContactMethod` enumeration with values `None`, `Email`, `Phone`, and `SnailMail`.

1. Use code similar to the following at the form's class level (not inside any event handler):

```
// Define contact methods.
private enum ContactMethod
{
    None = -1,
    Email = 0,
    Phone = 1,
    SnailMail = 2,
}
```

➤ Define an `Address` structure to hold the entered address information.

1. Use code similar to the following at the form's class level (not inside any event handler):

```
// Define an address structure.
private struct Address
{
    public string Name;
    public string Street;
    public string City;
    public string State;
    public string Zip;
```

```
        public string Email;
        public string Phone;
        public ContactMethod PreferredMethod;
    }
```

➤ Create a `Dictionary<string, Address>` field to hold the address data.

1. Use code similar to the following code at the form's class level (not inside any event handler):

```
// Make a Dictionary to hold addresses.
private Dictionary<string, Address> Addresses =
    new Dictionary<string, Address>();
```

➤ Add code to initially select the `ComboBox`'s `None` entry when the form loads.

1. Use code similar to the following:

```
// Make sure the ComboBox starts with an item selected.
private void Form1_Load(object sender, EventArgs e)
{
    preferredMethodComboBox.SelectedIndex = 0;
}
```

➤ Add code to the Add button that creates the new entry in the `Dictionary`.

1. Use code similar to the following. Optionally you can clear the TextBoxes to get ready for the next address.

```
// Add a new address.
private void addButton_Click(object sender, EventArgs e)
{
    // Fill in a new Address structure.
    Address newAddress;
    newAddress.Name = nameTextBox.Text;
    newAddress.Street = streetTextBox.Text;
    newAddress.City = cityTextBox.Text;
    newAddress.State = stateTextBox.Text;
    newAddress.Zip = zipTextBox.Text;
    newAddress.Email = emailTextBox.Text;
    newAddress.Phone = phoneTextBox.Text;
    newAddress.PreferredMethod =
        (ContactMethod)preferredMethodComboBox.SelectedIndex;

    // Add the name and address to the dictionary.
    Addresses.Add(nameTextBox.Text, newAddress);

    // Get ready for the next one.
    nameTextBox.Clear();
    streetTextBox.Clear();
    cityTextBox.Clear();
    stateTextBox.Clear();
    zipTextBox.Clear();
    emailTextBox.Clear();
    phoneTextBox.Clear();
    preferredMethodComboBox.SelectedIndex = 0;
```

```
        nameTextBox.Focus();
    }
```

➤ Add code to the Find button that retrieves the appropriate entry from the Dictionary and displays it.

1. Use code similar to the following:

```
// Look up an address.
private void findButton_Click(object sender, EventArgs e)
{
    // Get the Address.
    Address selectedAddress = Addresses[nameTextBox.Text];

    // Display the Address's values.
    nameTextBox.Text = selectedAddress.Name;
    streetTextBox.Text = selectedAddress.Street;
    cityTextBox.Text = selectedAddress.City;
    stateTextBox.Text = selectedAddress.State;
    zipTextBox.Text = selectedAddress.Zip;
    emailTextBox.Text = selectedAddress.Email;
    phoneTextBox.Text = selectedAddress.Phone;
    preferredMethodComboBox.SelectedIndex =
        (int)selectedAddress.PreferredMethod;
}
```

 Please select Lesson 17 on the DVD to view the video that accompanies this lesson.

EXERCISES

1. Copy the program you built for this lesson's Try It. Add a Delete button that removes an item by calling the Dictionary's Remove method.

2. Copy the program you built for Exercise 1. Modify it by adding a new integer Id field to the structure. Then create a second Dictionary that uses Id as its key. Allow the user to click Find by Name or Find by ID buttons to locate an item using either the customer's name or ID. Also provide Delete buttons that delete by name or ID. (Hint: When the user clicks a Delete button, be sure to remove the item from both Dictionaries.)

3. Copy the program you built for Exercise 1 and modify it to store appointment data. Use a structure with the following fields: Time, Attendees, Type, Topic, and Notes. Make Type come from the AppointmentType enumeration that includes the values None, Work, Home, and Other. (Hint: See Lesson 16's Exercise 4 for tips on how to use a DateTimePicker control's values as keys.)

 You can download the solutions to these exercises from the book's web page at www.wrox.com or www.CSharpHelper.com/24hour.html. You can find them in the Lesson17 folder in the download.

SECTION III
Program Statements

The lessons in Section II focused on working with variables. They explained how to declare variables, set their values, and perform calculations.

Those techniques let you do some fairly complex things, but they're still relatively straightforward things that you could do yourself by hand if you really had to. For example, you could easily calculate line item totals, sales tax, shipping, and a grand total for a purchase order.

With what you know so far, you really can't write a program that takes full advantage of the computer's power. You can't make the program add up an unknown number of values stored in a ListBox, perform the same task (such as calculating an account balance) for thousands of customers, or take different actions depending on the user's inputs. You can't even write a program that can tell if the user entered "seventy-eight" in a TextBox that should contain a number.

The lessons in this section explain how to perform these kinds of tasks. They explain ways you can make a program take different courses of action depending on circumstances, repeat a set of actions many times, break code into manageable pieces to make it easier to write and debug, and handle unexpected errors. After you finish reading these chapters, you'll be able to write applications that are much more powerful than those you can write now.

▶ **LESSON 18:** Making Choices

▶ **LESSON 19:** Repeating Program Steps

▶ **LESSON 20:** Reusing Code with Methods

▶ **LESSON 21:** Handling Errors

▶ **LESSON 22:** Preventing Bugs

18

Making Choices

All of the code used in the lessons so far has been completely linear. The program follows a series of steps in order with no deviation.

For example, a sales program could multiply a unit price by quantity desired, add several items' values, multiply to get sales tax and shipping costs, and calculate a grand total.

So far there's been no way to perform different steps under different circumstances. For example, the sales program couldn't charge different prices for different quantities purchased or waive shipping charges for orders over $100. It couldn't even check quantities to see if they make sense. So far a clever customer could order –1,000 items to get a huge credit!

In this lesson you learn how a program can make decisions. You learn how the program can take different actions based on user inputs and other circumstances.

DECISION STATEMENTS

Programs often need to decide between two or more courses of action. For example:

➤ If it's before 4:00 PM, ship today. Otherwise ship tomorrow.

➤ If the user enters an order quantity less than zero, make the user fix it.

➤ If a word processor has unsaved changes, refuse to exit.

➤ Calculate shipping based on order total: $5 if total < $20, $7.50 if total < $50, $10 if total < $75, and free if total ≥ $75.

The basic idea is the same in all of these cases. The program examines a value and takes one of several different actions depending on the value.

The following sections describe the different statements that C# provides for making this sort of decision.

IF STATEMENTS

The `if` statement examines a condition and takes action only if the condition is true. The basic syntax for the `if` statement is:

```
if (condition) statement;
```

Here `condition` is some Boolean expression that evaluates to either true or false, and `statement` is a statement that should be executed if `condition` is true.

Suppose you are writing an order entry program and shipping should be $5 for orders under $100 and free for orders of at least $100. Suppose also that the program has already calculated the variable `total`. The following code shows how the program might handle this:

```
decimal shipping = 5.00M;          // Default shipping cost.
if (total >= 100) shipping = 0;    // Shipping is free if total >= 100.
```

The code starts by setting the variable `shipping` to $5. Then if the `total` (which is calculated in code not shown here) is at least $100, the program sets `shipping` to $0.

If `total` is less than $100, the code inside the `if` block is not executed and `shipping` keeps its original value of $5.

If you want to execute more than one statement when `condition` is true, place them inside braces as in the following code:

```
decimal shipping = 5.00M;      // Default shipping cost.
if (total >= 100)
{
    shipping = 0;              // Shipping is free if total >= 100.
    giveFreeGift = true;       // Give a free gift if total >= 100.
}
```

You can place as many statements as you like in the braces, and they are all executed if `condition` is true.

To make the code more consistent and easier to read, some programmers always use braces even if the program should execute only one statement. The following code shows an example:

```
if (total >= 100)
{
    shipping = 0;
}
```

IF-ELSE

The previous example set `shipping` to a default value and then changed it if `total` was at least $100.

Another way to think about this problem is to imagine taking one of two actions depending on total's value. If total is less than $100, the program should set shipping to $5. Otherwise the program should set shipping to $0.

The if-else construct lets a program follow this approach, taking one of two actions depending on some condition.

The syntax for if-else is:

```
if (condition)
{
    statementsIfTrue;
}
else
{
    statementsIfFalse;
}
```

If condition is true, the first block statementsIfTrue is executed. Otherwise, if condition is false, the second block statementsIfFalse is executed.

Using the else keyword, the preceding code could be rewritten like this:

```
decimal shipping;
if (total < 100)
{
    shipping = 5M;      // Shipping is $5 if total < 100.
}
else
{
    shipping = 0M;      // Shipping is free if total >= 100.
}
```

CASCADING IF STATEMENTS

The if-else construct performs one of two actions depending on whether the condition is true or false. One action that programs commonly take when the condition is false is to perform another if test.

For example, suppose an order entry program calculates shipping charges depending on the total purchase amount according to this schedule:

➤   If total < $20, shipping is $5.00.

➤   Otherwise, if total < $50, shipping is $7.50.

➤   Otherwise, if total < $75, shipping is $10.00.

➤   Otherwise, shipping is free.

You can make a program make each of these tests one after another by making a second `if` statement be the `else` part of a first `if` statement. The following code shows how you can calculate shipping according to the preceding schedule:

```
decimal shipping;
if (total < 20)
{
    shipping = 5M;
}
else if (total < 50)
{
    shipping = 7.5M;
}
else if (total < 75)
{
    shipping = 10M;
}
else
{
    shipping = 0M;
}
```

When the program encounters a cascading series of `if` statements, it executes each in turn until it finds one with a true condition.

For example, consider the previous code and suppose `total` is $60. The code evaluates the first condition and decides that `(total < 20)` is false, so it does not execute the first code block.

The program skips to the `else` statement and executes the next `if` test. The program decides that `(total < 50)` is also not true, so it skips to this `if` statement's `else` block.

The program executes the third `if` test and finds that `(total < 75)` is true so it executes the statement `shipping = 10M`.

Because the program found an `if` statement with a true condition, it skips the following `else` statement, so it passes over any `if` statements that follow without evaluating their conditions.

NESTED IF STATEMENTS

Another common arrangement of `if` statements nests one `if` statement within another. The inner `if` statement is executed only if the first statement's condition allows the program to reach it.

For example, suppose you charge customers 5 percent state sales tax. If a customer lives within your county, you also charge a county transportation tax. Finally, if the customer also lives within city limits, you charge a city sales tax. (Taxes where I live are at least this confusing.)

The following code performs these checks, where the variables `inCounty` and `inCity` indicate whether the customer lives within the county and city:

```
if (inCounty)
{
    if (inCity)
```

```
    {
        salesTaxRate = 0.09M;
    }
    else
    {
        salesTaxRate = 0.07M;
    }
}
else
{
    salesTaxRate = 0.05M;
}
```

You can nest `if` statements as deeply as you like, although at some point the code gets hard to read.

*There are always ways to rearrange code by using the && (logical and) and ||
(logical or) operators to remove nested `if` statements. For example, the following
code does the same thing as the previous version without nesting:*

```
if (inCounty && inCity)
{
    salesTaxRate = 0.09M;
}
else if (inCounty)
{
    salesTaxRate = 0.07M;
}
else
{
    salesTaxRate = 0.05M;
}
```

*In fact, if you know that the city lies completely within the county, you could
rewrite the first test as* `if (inCity)`.

SWITCH STATEMENTS

The `switch` statement provides an easy-to-read equivalent to a series of cascading `if` statements that compare one value to a series of other values.

The syntax of the `switch` statement is:

```
switch (testValue)
{
    case (value1):
        statements1;
        break;

    case (value2):
```

```
        statements2;
        break;

    ...

    default:
        statementsDefault;
        break;
}
```

Here *testValue* is the value that you are testing; *value1*, *value2*, and so on, are the values to which you are comparing *testValue*; and *statements1*, *statements2*, and so on, are statements that you want to execute for each case. The other pieces (switch, case, break, and default) are keywords that you must type as they appear here.

If you include the optional default section, its statements execute if no other case applies. (Actually you don't need to include any case statements, either, although that would be unusual.)

Note that a case's code block doesn't need to include any statements other than break. You can use that to make the code take no action when a particular case occurs.

For example, suppose you build a form where the user selects a hotel from a combobox. The program uses that selection to initialize an enumerated variable named hotelChoice. The following code sets the lodgingPrice variable depending on which hotel the user selected:

```
decimal lodgingPrice;
switch (hotelChoice)
{
    case HotelChoice.LuxuryLodge:
        lodgingPrice = 45;
        break;

    case HotelChoice.HamiltonArms:
        lodgingPrice = 80;
        break;

    case HotelChoice.InvernessInn:
        lodgingPrice = 165;
        break;

    default:
        MessageBox.Show("Please select a hotel");
        lodgingPrice = 0;
        break;
}
```

The case statements check for the three expected choices and set lodgingPrice to the appropriate value. If the user doesn't select any hotel, the default section's code displays a message box and sets lodgingPrice to 0 to indicate a problem.

A switch statement is most robust (less prone to bugs and crashes) if its cases can handle every possible value. That makes them work very well with enumerated types because you can list every possible value.

Even then, it's good practice to include a `default` section just in case another value sneaks into the code. For example, a bug in the code could convert an integer into an enumeration value that doesn't exist, or you could later add a new value to the enumeration and forget to add a corresponding `case` statement. In those cases, the default statement can catch the bug or change, take some default action, and possibly warn you that something is wrong.

When you use other data types for the switch's value, be sure to consider unexpected values, particularly if the user entered the value. For example, don't assume the user will always enter a valid string. Allowing the user to select a string from a combobox is safer, but you should still include a `default` statement.

FIGURE 18-1

TRY IT

In this Try It, you build the OrderForm program shown in Figure 18-1. The program uses a cascading series of `if` statements to calculate shipping cost based on the subtotal.

 You can download the code and resources for this Try It from the book's web page at www.wrox.com *or* www.CSharpHelper.com/24hour.html. *You can find them in the Lesson18 folder in the download.*

Lesson Requirements

➤ Build the form shown in Figure 18-1.

➤ Write the code for the Calculate button so it calculates the subtotal, sales tax, shipping, and grand total. The sales tax should be 7 percent of the subtotal and shipping should be as follows: $5 if subtotal < $20, $7.50 if subtotal < $50, $10 if subtotal < $75, and free if subtotal ≥ $75.

Hints

➤ Make the sales tax rate a constant, giving it the most limited scope you can.

Step-by-Step

➤ Build the form shown in Figure 18-1.

1. This is relatively straightforward.

➤ Write the code for the Calculate button so it calculates the subtotal, sales tax, shipping, and grand total. The sales tax should be 7 percent of the subtotal and shipping should be as follows: $5 if subtotal < $20, $7.50 if subtotal < $50, $10 if subtotal < $75, and free if subtotal ≥ $75.

1. Calculate the total costs for each of the four items. Add them together to get the subtotal.

2. Calculate sales tax by multiplying the tax rate by the subtotal.

3. Use a series of cascading `if-else` statements to calculate the shipping cost based on the subtotal as in the following code:

```
// Calculate shipping cost.
decimal shipping;
if (subtotal < 20)
{
    shipping = 5;
}
else if (subtotal < 50)
{
    shipping = 7.5m;
}
else if (subtotal < 75)
{
    shipping = 10;
}
else
{
    shipping = 0;
}
```

4. Add the subtotal, tax, and shipping cost to get the grand total.

 Please select Lesson 18 on the DVD to view the video that accompanies this lesson.

EXERCISES

1. Build the ConferenceCoster program shown in Figure 18-2.

FIGURE 18-2

When the user clicks the Calculate button, first check each `ListBox`'s `SelectedIndex` property. If any `SelectedIndex` is less than zero (indicating the user didn't make a choice), display an error message.

If the user made a choice for all of the ListBoxes, create a variable total to hold the total cost. Use three switch statements to add the appropriate amounts to total and display the result. (Tip: Add a default statement to each switch statement to catch unexpected selections, even though none should occur in this program. Try adding a new hotel and see what happens if you select it.)

2. (SimpleEdit) Copy the SimpleEdit program you built in Lesson 8, Exercise 3 (or download Lesson 8's version from the book's web site) and add code to protect the user from losing unsaved changes.

The basic idea is to check whether the document has been modified before doing anything that will lose the changes, such as starting a new document, opening another file, or exiting the program.

a. In the File menu's New, Open, and Exit event handlers, check the RichTextBox's Modified property to see if the document has unsaved changes.

b. If there are unsaved changes, ask if the user wants to save them. Display a message box with the buttons Yes, No, and Cancel.

c. If the user clicks Yes, save the changes and continue the operation.

d. If the user clicks No, don't save the changes (do nothing special) and let the operation continue.

e. If the user clicks Cancel, don't perform the operation. For example, don't open a new file.

f. After starting a new document or saving an old one, set the RichTextBox control's Modified property to false to indicate that there are no unsaved changes any more.

3. (SimpleEdit) Copy the SimpleEdit program you built for Exercise 2. That program protects against lost changes if the user opens the File menu and selects Exit, but there are several other ways the user can close the program such as pressing [Alt]+F4, clicking the "X" button in the program's title bar, and opening the system menu in the form's upper left corner and selecting Close. Currently the program doesn't guard unsaved changes for any of those.

To fix this, give the form a FormClosing event handler. When the form is about to close, it raises this event. If you set the event's e.Cancel parameter to true, the form cancels the close and remains open. Add code to this event handler to protect unsaved changes.

Now that the FormClosing event handler is protecting against lost changes, you don't need to perform the same checks in the Exit menu item's event handler. Make that event handler simply call this.Close and FormClosing will do the rest.

You can download the solutions to these exercises from the book's web page at www.wrox.com *or* www.CSharpHelper.com/24hour.html. *You can find them in the Lesson18 folder.*

19

Repeating Program Steps

One of the computer's greatest strengths is its ability to perform the exact same calculation again and again without getting bored or making careless mistakes. It can calculate the average test scores for a dozen students, print a hundred advertisements, or compute the monthly bills for a million customers with no trouble or complaining.

The lessons you've read so far, however, don't tell you how to do these things. So far every step the computer takes requires a separate line of code. To add up 10 numbers, you would need to write 10 lines of code.

In this lesson you learn how to make the computer execute the same lines of code many times. You learn how to loop through arrays and collections of items to take action or perform calculations on them.

The following sections describe the kinds of loops provided by C#. The final section describes two statements you can use to change the way a loop works: break and continue.

FOR LOOPS

A for loop uses a variable to control the number of times it executes a series of statements. The for loop's syntax is as follows:

```
for (initialization; doneTest; next)
{
    statements...
}
```

Where:

> *initialization* — This statement gets the loop ready to start. Often this part declares and initializes the looping variable.

> *doneTest* — This is a Boolean expression that determines when the loop stops. The loop continues running as long as this expression is true.

➤ *next* — This statement prepares the loop for its next iteration. Often this increments the looping variable declared in the *initialization*.

➤ *statements* — These are the statements that you want the loop to execute.

Note that none of the `initialization`, `doneTest`, or `next` statements are required, although they are all used by the simplest kinds of `for` loops.

For example, the following code displays the numbers 0 through 9 followed by their squares in the Console window:

```
for (int i = 0; i < 10; i++)
{
    int iSquared = i * i;
    Console.WriteLine(string.Format("{0}: {1}", i, iSquared));
}
```

In this code the *initialization* statement declares the variable `i` and sets it to 0, the *next* statement adds 1 to `i`, and the *doneTest* keeps the loop running as long as `i < 10`.

Here's a slightly more complicated example that calculates factorials. The program converts the value selected in the `NumericUpDown` named `numberNumericUpDown` into a long integer and saves it in variable n. It initializes the variable `factorial` to 1 and then uses a loop to multiply `factorial` by each of the numbers between 2 and n. The result is 1 * 2 * 3 * ... * n, which is n!.

```
// Get the input value N.
long n = (long)numberNumericUpDown.Value;

// Calculate N!.
long factorial = 1;
for (int i = 2; i <= n; i++)
{
    checked
    {
        factorial *= i;
    }
}

// Display the result.
resultTextBox.Text = factorial.ToString();
```

You may recall that Lesson 16 used code to calculate Fibonacci numbers, and in that lesson's Exercise 1 you calculated factorials. Those programs used 20 lines of code to calculate and store 20 values that the program then used as a kind of lookup table.

The factorial calculation code shown here is more efficient. It doesn't require a large array to hold values. It also doesn't require that you know ahead of time how many values you might need to calculate (20 for the earlier programs), although the factorial function grows so quickly that this program can only calculate values up to 20! before the result won't fit in a `long`.

The `for` loop is often the best choice if you know exactly how many times you need the loop to execute.

FOREACH LOOPS

A `foreach` loop executes a block of code once for each item in an array or list. The syntax of the `foreach` loop is as follows:

```
foreach (variableDeclaration in items)
{
    statements...
}
```

Where:

➤ `variableDeclaration` — This piece declares the looping variable. Its type must be the same as the items in the array or list.

➤ `items` — This is the array or list of items over which you want to loop.

➤ `statements` — These are the statements that you want the loop to execute.

For example, the following code calculates the average of the test scores stored in the `ListBox` named `scoresListBox`. Note that the ListBox must contain integers or something the program can implicitly convert into an integer or else the program will crash.

```
// Make sure the list isn't empty.
if (valuesListBox.Items.Count < 1)
{
    MessageBox.Show("There are no items to average.");
}
else
{
    // Add up the values.
    int total = 0;
    foreach (int value in valuesListBox.Items)
    {
        total += value;
    }

    // Calculate the average.
    float average = (float)total / valuesListBox.Items.Count;

    // Display the result.
    MessageBox.Show("Average: " + average.ToString("0.00"));
}
```

The code creates a variable named `total` and sets it equal to 0. It then loops through the items in the `ListBox`, adding each value to `total`.

 This code loops over the items in a `ListBox` treating those items as integers. If the `ListBox` contains something other than integers, the program will crash.

The code finishes by dividing the total by the number of items in the `ListBox`.

 If you need to perform some operation on all of the items in an array or list, a foreach *loop is often your best choice.*

WHILE LOOPS

A `while` loop executes as long as some condition is true. The syntax for a `while` loop is as follows:

```
while (condition)
{
    statements...
}
```

Where:

➤ `condition` — The loop executes as long as this Boolean expression is true.

➤ `statements` — These are the statements that you want the loop to execute.

For example, the following code calculates a number's prime factors:

```
// Find the number's prime factors.
private void factorButton_Click(object sender, EventArgs e)
{
    // Get the input number.
    long number = long.Parse(numberTextBox.Text);

    // Find the factors.
    string result = "1";

    // Consider factors between 2 and the number.
    for (long factor = 2; factor <= number; factor++)
    {
        // Pull out as many copies of this factor as possible.
        while (number % factor == 0)
        {
            result += " x " + factor.ToString();
            number = number / factor;
        }
    }

    // Display the result.
    resultTextBox.Text = result;
}
```

The code starts by getting the user's input number. It builds a result string and initializes it to 1.

Next the code users a `for` loop to consider the numbers between 2 and the user's number as possible factors.

For each of the possible factors, it uses a `while` loop to remove that factor from the number. As long as the factor divides evenly into the remaining number, the program adds the factor to the result and divides the user's number by the factor.

The code finishes by displaying its result.

Loops that use incrementing integers to decide when to stop are often easier to write using `for` *loops instead of* `while` *loops. A* `while` *loop is particularly useful when the stopping condition occurs at a less predictable time, as in the factoring example.*

DO LOOPS

A `do` loop is similar to a `while` loop except it checks its stopping condition at the end of the loop instead of at the beginning. The syntax of a `do` loop is as follows:

```
do
{
    statements...
} while (condition);
```

Where:

➤ `statements` — These are the statements that you want the loop to execute.

➤ `condition` — The loop continues to execute as long as this Boolean expression is true.

The following code uses a `do` loop to calculate the greatest common divisor (GCD) of two numbers, the largest number that divides them both evenly:

```
// Calculate GCD(A, B).
private void calculateButton_Click(object sender, EventArgs e)
{
    // Get the input values.
    long a = long.Parse(aTextBox.Text);
    long b = long.Parse(bTextBox.Text);

    // Calculate the GCD.
    long remainder;
    do
    {
        remainder = a % b;
        if (remainder != 0)
```

```
        {
            a = b;
            b = remainder;
        }
    } while (remainder > 0);

    resultTextBox.Text = b.ToString();
}
```

 Notice that the variable remainder *used to end the loop is declared outside of the loop even though it doesn't really do anything outside of the loop. Normally to restrict scope as much as possible, you would want to declare this variable inside the loop if you could.*

However, the end test executes in a scope that lies outside of the loop, so any variables declared inside the loop are hidden from it.

It's important that any loop eventually ends, and in this code it's not completely obvious why that happens. It turns out that each time through the loop (with the possible exception of the first time), a and b get smaller. If you run through a few examples, you'll be able to convince yourself.

If the loop runs long enough, b eventually reaches 1. At that point b must evenly divide a no matter what a is so the loop ends. If b does reach 1, then 1 is the greatest common divisor of the user's original numbers and those numbers are called *relatively prime*.

EUCLID'S ALGORITHM

This algorithm was described by the Greek mathematician Euclid (circa 300 BC), so it's called the *Euclidean algorithm* or *Euclid's algorithm*. I don't want to explain why the algorithm works because it's nontrivial and irrelevant to this discussion of loops (you can find a good discussion at primes.utm.edu/glossary/xpage/ EuclideanAlgorithm.html), but I do want to explain what the code does.

The code starts by storing the user's input numbers in variables a and b. It then declares variable remainder and enters a do loop.

Inside the loop, the program calculates the remainder when you divide a by b. If that value is not 0 (that is, b does not divide a evenly), then the program sets a = b and b = remainder.

Now the code reaches the end of the loop. The while statement makes the loop end if remainder is 0. At that point, b holds the greatest common divisor.

You may want to step through the code in the debugger to see how the values change.

A do *loop always executes its code at least once because it doesn't check its condition until the end. Often that feature is why you should pick a* do *loop over a* while *loop or vice versa. If you might not want the loop to execute even once, use a* while *loop. If you need to run the loop once before you can tell whether to stop, use a* do *loop.*

BREAK AND CONTINUE

The break and continue statements change the way a loop works.

The break statement makes the code exit the loop immediately without executing any more statements inside the loop.

For example, the following code searches the selected items in a ListBox for the value Carter. If it finds that value, it sets the Boolean variable carterSelected to true and breaks out of the loop. If the ListBox has many selected items, breaking out of the loop early may let the program skip many loop iterations and save some time.

```
// See if Carter is one of the selected names.
bool carterSelected = false;
foreach (string name in namesListBox.SelectedItems)
{
    if (name == "Carter")
    {
        carterSelected = true;
        break;
    }
}
MessageBox.Show(carterSelected.ToString());
```

The continue statement makes a loop jump to its looping statement early, skipping any remaining statements inside the loop after the continue statement.

For example, the following code uses a foreach loop to display the square roots of the numbers in an array. The Math.Sqrt function cannot calculate the square root of a negative number so, to avoid trouble, the code checks each value. If it finds a value less than zero, it uses the continue statement to skip the rest of that trip through the loop so it doesn't try to take the number's square root. It then continues with the next number in the array.

```
// Display square roots.
float[] values = { 4, 16, -1, 60, 100 };
foreach (float value in values)
{
    if (value < 0) continue;
    Console.WriteLine(string.Format("The square root of {0} is {1:0.00}",
        value, Math.Sqrt(value)));
}
```

The following text shows this program's results:

```
The square root of 4 is 2.00
The square root of 16 is 4.00
The square root of 60 is 7.75
The square root of 100 is 10.00
```

The break *and* continue *statements make loops work in nonstandard ways and sometimes that can make the code harder to read, debug, and maintain. Use them if it makes the code easier to read, but ask yourself whether there's another simple way to write the loop that avoids these statements. For example, the following code does the same things as the previous code but without a* continue *statement:*

```
// Display square roots.
float[] values = { 4, 16, -1, 60, 100 };
foreach (float value in values)
{
    if (value >= 0)
    {
        Console.WriteLine(string.Format("The square root of {0} is
            {1:0.00}",
            value, Math.Sqrt(value)));
    }
}
```

TRY IT

In this Try It, you make the simple login form shown in Figure 19-1. When the program's startup form loads, it enters a loop that makes it display this form until the user enters the correct username and password or clicks the Cancel button.

FIGURE 19-1

You can download the code and resources for this Try It from the book's web page at www.wrox.com *or* www.CSharpHelper.com/24hour.html. *You can find them in the Lesson19 folder in the download.*

Lesson Requirements

➤ Build a main form that displays a success message.

➤ Build the login dialog shown in Figure 19-1.

➤ In the main form's Load event handler, create an instance of the login dialog. Then enter a while loop that displays the dialog and doesn't stop until the user enters a username and password that match values in the code. If the user clicks Cancel, close the main form.

Hints

➤ Use a Boolean variable named `tryingToLogin` to control the loop. Initialize it to true before the loop and set it to false when the user either cancels or enters the right username and password.

➤ To decide whether the user entered a valid username and password, compare them to the strings "User" and "Secret." (A real application would validate these values with a database or by using some other authentication method.)

Step-by-Step

➤ Build a main form that displays a success message.

1. Place labels on the form to display the message.

➤ Build the login dialog shown in Figure 19-1.

1. Create the controls shown in Figure 19-1.

2. Set the password `TextBox`'s `PasswordChar` property to `X`.

➤ In the main form's `Load` event handler, create an instance of the login dialog. Then enter a `while` loop that displays the dialog and doesn't stop until the user enters a username and password that match values in the code. If the user clicks Cancel, close the main form and break out of the loop.

1. The following code shows one possible solution:

```
// Make the user log in.
private void Form1_Load(object sender, EventArgs e)
{
    // Create a LoginForm.
    LoginForm frm = new LoginForm();

    // Repeat until the user successfully logs in.
    bool tryingToLogin = true;
    while (tryingToLogin)
    {
        // Display the login dialog and check the result.
        if (frm.ShowDialog() == DialogResult.Cancel)
        {
            // The user gives up. Close and exit the loop.
            this.Close();
            tryingToLogin = false;
        }
        else
        {
            // See if the user entered valid values.
            if ((frm.usernameTextBox.Text == "User") &&
                (frm.passwordTextBox.Text == "Secret"))
            {
                // Login succeeded. Stop trying to log in.
                tryingToLogin = false;
            }
```

```
            else
            {
                // Login failed. Display a message and let the loop continue.
                MessageBox.Show("Invalid username and password.");
            }
        }
    }

    // If we get here, we're done trying to log in.
}
```

 Please select Lesson 19 on the DVD to view the video that accompanies this lesson.

EXERCISES

1. Make a program that calculates the sum 1 + 2 + 3 + ... + N for a number N entered by the user.

2. Make a program that calculates the Nth Fibonacci number for a number N entered by the user. The Fibonacci sequence is defined by:

```
Fibonacci(0) = 0
Fibonacci(1) = 1
Fibonacci(N) = Fibonacci(N - 1) + Fibonacci(N - 2)
```

Hint: Use a loop. Define variables `fibo1`, `fibo2`, and `fiboN` outside the loop. Inside the loop, make the variables hold Fibonacci(N - 1), Fibonacci(N - 2), and Fibonacci(N). (To test your code, Fibonacci(10) = 55 and Fibonacci(20) = 6,765.)

3. Make a program that lets the user enter test scores into a `ListBox`. After adding each score, display the minimum, maximum, and average values. (Hint: Before you start the loop, initialize `minimum` and `maximum` variables to the value of the first score. Then loop through the list revising the variables as needed.)

4. Copy the program you built for Lesson 14's Exercise 1 (or download Lesson 14's version from the book's web site) and add the List Items button shown in Figure 19-2. When the user clicks the button, display the items and their values in the Console window as a semicolon-separated list similar to the following:

FIGURE 19-2

```
**********
Pencil;$0.10;12;$1.20;
Pen;$0.25;12;$3.00;
Notebook;$1.19;3;$3.57;
**********
```

Hint: The `ListView` control's `Items` property is a collection of `ListViewItem` objects. Loop through that collection to get information about each row.

Hint: Each `ListViewItem` has a `SubItems` property that is a collection of `ListViewItem.ListViewSubItem` objects. For each row, loop through the item's subitem collection to get the values for that row. Use `Console.Write` to add data to the `Console` window without adding a carriage return.

5. Make a program similar to the one shown in Figure 19-3 that generates all possible four-letter words using the letters A, B, C, and D. (Hint: Make an array containing the letters A, B, C, and D. Use a `foreach` loop to loop through the letters. Inside that loop, use another loop to loop through the letters again. After four depths of nested loops, concatenate the looping variables to get the word.)

FIGURE 19-3

 You can download the solutions to these exercises from the book's web page at www.wrox.com *or* www.CSharpHelper.com/24hour.html. *You can find them in the Lesson19 folder.*

20

Reusing Code with Methods

Sometimes a program needs to perform the same action in several places. For example, suppose you're using a simple editor such as WordPad, you make some changes, and then you select the File menu's New command. The program realizes that you have unsaved changes and asks if you want to save them. Depending on whether you click Yes, No, or Cancel, the program saves the changes, discards the changes, or cancels the attempt to create a new file.

Now think about what happens when you try to open a file while you have unsaved changes. The program goes through basically the same steps, asking if you want to save the changes. It does practically the same thing if you select the File menu's Exit command, or click the X in the program's upper-right corner, or open the window's system menu and select Close, or press [Alt]+F4. In all of these cases, the program performs basically the same checks.

Instead of repeating code to handle unsaved changes everywhere it might be needed, it would be nice if you could centralize the code in a single location and then invoke that code when you need it. In fact, you can do exactly that by using methods.

A *method* is a group of programming statements wrapped in a neat package so you can invoke it as needed. A method can take parameters that the calling code can use to give it information, it can perform some actions, and then it can return a single value to pass information back to the calling code.

In this lesson, you learn how to use methods. You learn why they are useful, how to write them, and how to call them from other pieces of code.

METHOD ADVANTAGES

The file editing scenario described in the previous section illustrates one of the key advantages to methods: code reuse. By placing commonly needed code in a single method, you can reuse that code in many places. Clearly that saves you the effort of writing the code several times.

Much more importantly, it also saves you the trouble of debugging the code several times. Often debugging a piece of complex code takes much longer than typing in the code in the first place, so being able to debug the code in only one place can save you a lot of time.

Reusing code also greatly simplifies maintenance. If you later find a bug in the code, you only need to fix it in one place. If you had several copies of the code scattered around, you'd need to fix each one individually and make sure all of the fixes were the same. That may sound easy enough, but making synchronized changes is actually pretty hard, particularly for larger projects. It's just too easy to miss one change or to make slightly different changes that later cause big problems.

Methods can sometimes make finding and fixing bugs much easier. For example, suppose you're working on an inventory program that can remove items from inventory for one of many reasons: external sales, internal sales, ownership transfer, spoilage, and so forth. Unfortunately the program occasionally "removes" items that don't exist, leaving you with negative inventory. If the program has code in many places that can remove items from inventory, figuring out which place is causing the problem can be tricky. If all of the code uses the same method to remove items, you can set breakpoints inside that single method to see what's going wrong. When you see the problem occurring, you can trace the program's flow to see where the problem originated.

A final set of advantages to using methods makes the pieces of the program easier to understand and use. Breaking a complex calculation into a series of simpler method calls can make the code easier to understand. No one can keep all of the details of a large program in mind all at once. Breaking the program into methods makes it possible to understand the pieces separately.

A well-designed method also encapsulates an activity at an abstract level so other developers don't need to know the details. For example, you could write a `FindItemForPurchase` method that searches through a database of vendors to find the best possible deal on a particular item. Now developers writing other parts of the program can call that method without needing to understand exactly how the search works. The method might perform an amazingly complex search to minimize price and long-term expected maintenance costs but the programmer calling the method doesn't need to know or care how it works.

In summary, some of the key benefits to using methods are:

- ➤ **Code reuse** — You write the code once and use it many times.
- ➤ **Centralized debugging** — You only need to debug the shared code once.
- ➤ **Centralized maintenance** — If you need to fix the code, you only need to do so in the method, not everywhere it is used.
- ➤ **Problem decomposition** — Methods can break complex problems into simple pieces.
- ➤ **Encapsulation** — The method can hide complex details from developers.

METHOD SYNTAX

In C#, all methods must be part of some class. In many simple programs, the main form contains all of the program's code, including all of its methods.

The syntax for defining a method is:

```
accessibility returnType methodName(parameters)
{
    ...statements...
    return returnValue;
}
```

Where:

> ➤ *accessibility* — This is an accessibility keyword such as `public` or `private`. This keyword determines what other code in the project can invoke the method.

> ➤ *returnType* — This is the data type that the method returns. It can take normal values such as `int`, `bool`, or `string`. It can also take the special value `void` to indicate that the method won't return a result to the calling code.

> ➤ *methodName* — This is the name that you want to give the method. You can give the method any valid name. Valid names must start with a letter or underscore and include letters, underscores, and numbers. A valid name also cannot be a keyword such as `if` or `while`.

> ➤ *parameters* — This is an optional parameter list that you can pass to the method. I'll say more about this shortly.

> ➤ *statements* — These are the statements that the method should execute.

> ➤ *returnValue* — To return a value to the calling code, the method should execute a `return` statement, passing it whatever value the method should return. Use `return` without a parameter to return from a `void` method.

 You can use the `return` *statement as many times as you like in a method (for example, after different branches in an* `if-else` *structure). The C# compiler tries to guarantee that all paths through the code end at a* `return` *statement and will warn you if the code might not return a value.*

The method's parameters allow calling code to pass information into the method. The parameters in the method's declaration give names to the parameters while they are in use inside the method.

For example, recall the definition of the factorial function. The factorial of a number N is written N! and pronounced *N factorial*. The definition of N! is 1 * 2 * 3 * ... * N.

The following C# code implements the factorial method:

```
// Return value!
private long Factorial(long value)
{
    long result = 1;
    for (long i = 2; i <= value; i++)
    {
        result *= i;
    }
```

```
        return result;
    }
```

The method is declared `private` so only code within this class can use it. For simple programs, that's all of the code anyway so this isn't an issue.

The method's data type is `long` so it must return a value of type `long`.

The method's name is `Factorial`. You should try to give your methods names that are simple and that convey the methods' purposes so it's easy to remember what they do.

The method takes a single parameter of type `long` named `value`.

The method creates a variable `result` and multiplies it by the values 2, 3, ..., `value`.

The method finishes by executing the `return` statement, passing it the final value of `result`.

The following code shows how a program might call the `Factorial` method:

```
long number = long.Parse(numberTextBox.Text);
long answer = Factorial(number);
resultTextBox.Text = answer.ToString();
```

This code starts by creating a `long` variable named `number` and initializing it to whatever value is in `numberTextBox`.

The code then calls the `Factorial` method, passing it the value `number` and saving the returned result in the new `long` variable named `answer`.

Notice that the names of the variables in the calling code (`number` and `answer`) have no relation to the names of the parameters and variables used inside the method (`value` and `result`). The method's parameter declaration determines the names those values have while inside the method.

The code finishes by displaying the result.

A method's parameter list can include zero, one, or more parameters separated by commas. For example, the following code defines the method `Gcd`, which returns the greatest common divisor (GCD) of two integers. (The GCD of two integers is the largest integer that evenly divides them both.)

```
// Calculate GCD(a, b).
private long Gcd(long a, long b)
{
    long remainder;
    do
    {
        remainder = a % b;
        if (remainder != 0)
        {
            a = b;
            b = remainder;
        }
    } while (remainder > 0);

    return b;
}
```

The following code shows how you might call the Gcd method. The code initializes two integers and then passes them to the Gcd method, saving the result. It then displays the two integers and their GCD.

```
// Get the input values.
long a = long.Parse(aTextBox.Text);
long b = long.Parse(bTextBox.Text);

// Calculate the GCD.
long result = Gcd(a, b);

// Display the result.
resultTextBox.Text = b.ToString();
```

PARAMETERS BY REFERENCE

Parameter lists have one more feature that's confusing enough to deserve its own section. Parameters can be passed to a method by value or by reference.

When you pass a parameter *by value*, C# makes a copy of the value and passes the copy to the method. The method can then mess up its copy without damaging the value used by the calling code.

In contrast, when you pass a value *by reference*, C# passes the location of the value's memory into the method. If the method modifies the parameter, the value is changed in the calling code as well.

Normally values are passed by value. That's less confusing because changes that are hidden inside the method cannot confuse the calling code.

Sometimes, however, you may want to pass a parameter by reference. To do that, add the keyword ref before the parameter's declaration.

To tell C# that you understand that a parameter is being passed by reference and that it's not just a terrible mistake, you must also add the keyword ref before the value you are passing into the method.

For example, suppose you want to write a method named GetMatchup that selects two chess players to play against each other. The method should return true if it can find a match and false if no other matches are possible (because you've played them all). The method can only return one value (true or false) so it must find another way to return the two players.

The following code shows how the method might be structured:

```
private bool GetMatchup(ref string player1, ref string player2)
{
    // Do complicated stuff to pick an even match.
    ...
    // Somewhere in here the code should set player1
    // and player2.
    ...

    // We found a match.
    return true;
}
```

The method takes two parameters, `player1` and `player2`, that are passed by reference. The method performs some complex calculations not shown here to assign the variables `player1` and `player2`. It then returns `true` to indicate that it found a match.

The following code shows how a program might call this method:

```
string playerA = null, playerB = null;

if (GetMatchup(ref playerA, ref playerB))
{
    // Announce this match.
    ...
}
else
{
    // No match is possible. We're done.
    ...
}
```

This code declares variables `playerA` and `playerB` to hold the selected players' names. It calls the method, passing it the two player name variables preceded with the `ref` keyword. Depending on whether the method returns `true` or `false`, the program announces the match or does whatever it should when all of the matches have been played.

The `out` keyword works similarly to the `ref` keyword except it doesn't require that the input variables be initialized. For example, in the preceding example if you don't initialize `playerA` and `playerB` to some value, Visual Studio will warn you that the variables are not initialized and won't let you run the program.

In contrast, if you use the `out` keyword instead of `ref`, the values are assumed to be output parameters from the method, and you are not required to initialize them.

If you use the `out` keyword for a parameter, be sure that the method does not try to use the value passed in for that parameter because it may not be initialized.

> *In general it's considered bad practice to return results from a method through parameters passed by reference because it can be confusing.*
>
> *A better approach is to pass the method inputs through parameters and make the method return all of its return values with the* return *statement. For instance, the chess matchup example could return a structure or instance of a class that contains the names of the two players.*

TRY IT

In this Try It, you make a method that calculates the minimum, maximum, and average values for an array of `doubles`. You build the program shown in Figure 20-1 to test the method.

You can download the code and resources for this Try It from the book's web page at www.wrox.com *or* www.CSharpHelper.com/24hour.html. *You can find the code in the Lesson20 folder.*

Lesson Requirements

➤ Build the program shown in Figure 20-1.

➤ Build a method that takes four parameters: an array of `doubles`, and three more `doubles` passed by reference. It should loop through the array to find the minimum and maximum, and to calculate the average.

➤ Build a form to let the user enter a series of values and execute the method.

FIGURE 20-1

Hints

➤ Think about how the method needs to use the parameters passed by reference. Should it use `ref` or `out`?

Step-by-Step

➤ Build the program shown in Figure 20-1.

1. This is reasonably straightforward.

➤ Build a method that takes four parameters: an array of `doubles`, and three more `doubles` passed by reference. It should loop through the array to find the minimum and maximum, and to calculate the average.

1. This method calculates its results purely by examining the values in the input array so it doesn't need to use whatever values are passed in through its other parameters. That means the minimum, maximum, and average parameters should use the `out` keyword instead of the `ref` keyword.

2. Initialize minimum and maximum variables to the first entry in the array.

3. Initialize a total variable to the first entry in the array.

4. Loop through the rest of the array (skipping the first entry) updating the minimum and maximum variables as needed, and adding the values in the array to the total.

5. After finishing the loop, divide the total by the number of values to get the average.

The following code shows how you might build this method:

```
// Calculate the minimum, maximum, and average values for the array.
private void FindMinimumMaximumAverage(double[] values,
```

```
        out double minimum, out double maximum, out double average)
    {
        // Initialize the minimum, maxiumum, and total values.
        minimum = values[0];
        maximum = values[0];
        double total = values[0];

        // Loop through the rest of the array.
        for (int i = 1; i < values.Length; i++)
        {
            if (values[i] < minimum) minimum = values[i];
            if (values[i] > maximum) maximum = values[i];
            total += values[i];
        }

        // Calculate the average.
        average = total / values.Length;
    }
```

➤ Build a form to let the user enter a series of values and execute the method.

1. Build a form as shown in Figure 20-1.

2. When the user clicks the button, take the textbox's text and use its `Split` method to break the user's values into an array of strings.

3. Make a `double` array and parse the text values into it.

4. Call the method to calculate the necessary results.

5. Display the results.

The following code shows how you might build the button's event handler:

```
// Find and display the minimum, maximum, and average of the values.
private void calculateButton_Click(object sender, EventArgs e)
{
    // Get the values.
    string[] textValues = valuesTextBox.Text.Split();
    double[] values = new double[textValues.Length];
    for (int i = 0; i < textValues.Length; i++)
    {
        values[i] = double.Parse(textValues[i]);
    }

    // Calculate.
    double smallest = 0, largest = 0, average = 0;
    FindMinimumMaximumAverage(values,
        out smallest, out largest, out average);

    // Display the results.
    minimumTextBox.Text = smallest.ToString();
    maximumTextBox.Text = largest.ToString();
    averageTextBox.Text = average.ToString("0.00");
}
```

This lesson mentions that returning values through parameters passed by reference isn't a good practice. So how could you modify this example to avoid that?

You could break the FindMinimumMaximumAverage *method into three separate methods,* FindMinimum, FindMaximum, *and* FindAverage, *and have each return its result by using a* return *statement. In addition to avoiding parameters passed by reference, that makes each routine perform a single well-focused task so it makes them easier to understand and use. It also makes them easier to use separately in case you only wanted to find the array's minimum and not the maximum or average.*

(Also note that the array class provides methods that can find these values for you, so you really don't need to write these functions anyway. They're here purely to demonstrate parameters passed by reference.)

Please select Lesson 20 on the DVD to view the video that accompanies this lesson.

EXERCISES

1. Make a program that calculates the least common multiple (LCM) of two integers. (The LCM of two integers is the smallest integer that the two numbers divide into evenly.) Hints: LCM(a, b) = a * b / GCD(a, b). Also don't write the LCM method from scratch. Instead make it call the GCD method described earlier in this lesson.

2. A *recursive method* is one that calls itself. Write a recursive factorial method by using the definition:

   ```
   0! = 1
   N! = N * (N-1)!
   ```

   Hint: Be sure to check the stopping condition N = 0 so the method doesn't call itself forever. (Also note that recursive methods can be very confusing to understand and debug so often it's better to write the method without recursion. Some problems have natural recursive definitions but usually a non-recursive method is better.)

3. Write a program that recursively calculates the Nth Fibonacci number using the definition:

   ```
   Fibonacci(0) = 0
   Fibonacci(1) = 1
   Fibonacci(N) = Fibonacci(N - 1) + Fibonacci(N - 2)
   ```

   Compare the performance of the recursive factorial and Fibonacci methods when N is around 30 or 40.

4. (SimpleEdit) Copy the SimpleEdit program you built in Lesson 18, Exercise 3 (or download Lesson 18's version from the book's web site) and move the code that checks for unsaved changes into a method named `IsDataSafe`. The `IsDataSafe` method should perform the same checks as before and return `true` if it is safe to continue with whatever operation the user is about to perform (new file, open file, or exit).

Other code that needs to decide whether to continue should call `IsDataSafe`. For example, the `fileNewMenuItem_Click` event handler can now look like this:

```
private void fileNewMenuItem_Click(object sender, EventArgs e)
{
    // See if it's safe to continue.
    if (IsDataSafe())
    {
        // Make the new document.
        contentRichTextBox.Clear();

        // There are no unsaved changes now.
        contentRichTextBox.Modified = false;
    }
}
```

Many of the examples and exercises in earlier lessons use duplicated code. For further practice, rewrite some of them to move the duplicated code into methods.

You can download the solutions to these exercises from the book's web page at `www.wrox.com` *or* `www.CSharpHelper.com/24hour.html`. *The solutions can be found in the Lesson20 folder.*

21

Handling Errors

The best way to handle errors is to not give the user the ability to make them in the first place. For example, suppose a program can take purchase orders for between 1 and 100 reams of paper. If the program lets you specify the quantity by using a `NumericUpDown` control with `Minimum = 1` and `Maximum = 100`, you cannot accidentally enter invalid values like –5 or 10,000.

Sometimes, however, it's hard to build an interface that protects against all possible errors. For example, if the user needs to type in a numeric value, you need to worry about invalid inputs such as 1.2.3 and ten. If you write a program that works with files, you can't always be sure the file will be available when you need it. For example, it might be on a CD or floppy disk that has been removed, or it might be locked by another program.

In this lesson, you learn how to deal with these kinds of unexpected errors. You learn how to protect against invalid values, unavailable files, and other problems that are difficult or impossible to predict in advance.

ERRORS AND EXCEPTIONS

An *error* is a mistake. It occurs when the program does something incorrect. Sometimes an error is a bug, for example, if the code just doesn't do the right thing.

Sometimes an error is caused by circumstances outside of the program's control. If the program expects the user to enter a numeric value in a textbox but the user types 1.2.3, the program won't be able to continue its work until the user fixes the problem.

Sometimes you can predict when an error may occur. For example, if a program needs to open a file, there's a chance that the file won't exist. In predictable cases such as this one, the program should try to anticipate the error and protect itself. In this case, it should check to see if the file exists before it tries to open it. It can then display a message to the user and ask for help.

Other errors are hard or impossible to predict. Even if the file exists, it may be locked by another program. The user entering invalid data is another example. In those cases, the program may need to just try to do its job. If the program tries to do something seriously invalid, it will receive an exception.

An *exception* tells the program that something generally very bad occurred such as trying to divide by zero, trying to access an entry in an array that doesn't exist (for example, setting `values[100] = 100` when `values` only holds 10 items), or trying to convert "ten" into an integer.

In cases like these, the program must *catch* the exception and deal with it. Sometimes it can figure out what went wrong and fix the problem. Other times it might only be able to tell the user about the problem and hope the user can fix it.

> *In C# terms, the code that has the problem throws the exception. Code higher up in the chain can catch the exception and try to handle it.*

To catch an exception, a program uses a `try-catch` block.

TRY-CATCH BLOCKS

In C#, you can use a `try-catch` block to catch exceptions. One common form of this statement has the following syntax:

```
try
{
    ...codeToProtect...
}
catch (ExceptionType1 ex)
{
    ...exceptionCode1...
}
catch (ExceptionType2 ex)
{
    ...exceptionCode2...
}
finally
{
    ...finallyCode...
}
```

Where:

➤ *codeToProtect* — The code that might throw the exception.

➤ *ExceptionType1, ExceptionType2* — These are exception types such as `FormatException` or `DivideByZeroException`. If this particular exception type occurs in the *codeToProtect*, the corresponding `catch` block executes.

➤ *ex* — A variable that has the type *ExceptionType*. You pick the name for this variable. If an error occurs, you can use this variable to learn more about what happened.

➤ *exceptionCode* — The code that the program should execute if the corresponding exception occurs.

➤ *finallyCode* — This code always executes whether or not an error occurs.

A `try-catch-finally` block can include any number of `catch` blocks with different exception types. If an error occurs, the program looks through the `catch` blocks until it finds one that matches the error. It then executes that block's code and jumps to the `finally` statement if there is one.

If you use a `catch` statement without an exception type and variable, that block catches all exceptions.

If you omit the `catch` *statement's exception type and variable, the code cannot learn anything about the exception that occurred. Sometimes that's okay if you don't really care what went wrong as long as you know that something* went wrong. *An alternative strategy is to catch a generic* Exception *object, which matches any kind of exception and provides more information. Then you can at least display an error message as shown in the following code, which tries to calculate a student's test score average assuming the variables* totalScore *and* numTests *are already initialized. If the code throws an exception, the* catch *block displays the exception's default description.*

```
try
{
    // Try to divide by zero.
    int averageScore = totalScore / numTests;

    // Display the student's average score.
    MessageBox.Show("Average Score: " + averageScore.ToString
        ("0.00"));
}
catch (Exception ex)
{
    // Display a message describing the exception.
    MessageBox.Show("Error calculating average.\n" + ex.Message);
}
```

In this example the error that this code is most likely to encounter is a DivideByZeroException *thrown if* numTests *is 0. Because that kind of error is predictable, the code should probably specifically look for it. Better still, it should check* numTests *and not perform the calculation if* numTests *is 0. Then it can avoid the exception completely. The best strategy is to catch the most specific type of exception possible to get the most information. Then catch more generic exceptions just in case.*

A `try-catch-finally` block must include at least one `catch` block or the `finally` block, although none of them needs to contain any code. For example, the following code catches and ignores all exceptions:

```
try
{
    ...codeToProtect...
}
```

```
catch
{
}
```

The code in the `finally` block executes whether or not an exception occurs. If an error occurs, the program executes a `catch` block (if one matches the exception) and then executes the `finally` block. If no error occurs, the program executes the `finally` block after it finishes the `codeToProtect` code.

In fact, if the code inside the `try` or `catch` section executes a `return` statement, the `finally` block still executes before the program actually leaves the method!

THROWING ERRORS

Occasionally it's useful to be able to throw your own errors. For example, consider the factorial function you wrote in Lesson 20 and suppose the program invokes the function passing it the value –10 for its parameter. The value –10! is not defined, so what should the function do? It could just declare that –10! is 1 and return that, but that approach could hide a potential error in the rest of the program.

A better solution is to throw an exception telling the program what's wrong. The calling code can then use a `try-catch-finally` block to catch the error and tell the user what's wrong.

The following code shows an improved version of the factorial function described in Lesson 20. Before calculating the factorial, the code checks its parameter and, if the parameter is less than zero, it throws a new `ArgumentOutOfRangeException`. The exception's constructor has several overloaded versions. The one used here takes as parameters the name of the parameter that caused the problem and a description of the error.

```
// Return value!
private long Factorial(long value)
{
    // Check the parameter.
    if (value < 0)
    {
        // This is invalid. Throw an exception.
        throw new ArgumentOutOfRangeException(
            "value",
            "The Factorial parameter must be at least 0.");
    }

    // Calculate the factorial.
    long result = 1;
    for (long i = 2; i <= value; i++)
    {
        result *= i;
    }
    return result;
}
```

The following code shows how the program might invoke the new version of the Factorial function. It uses a try-catch block to protect itself in case the Factorial function throws an error. The block also protects against other errors such as the user entering garbage in the textbox.

```csharp
// Calculate the factorial.
private void calculateButton_Click(object sender, EventArgs e)
{
    try
    {
        // Get the input value.
        long number = long.Parse(numberTextBox.Text);

        // Calculate the factorial.
        long answer = Factorial(number);

        // Display the factorial.
        resultTextBox.Text = answer.ToString();
    }
    catch (Exception ex)
    {
        // Display an error message.
        MessageBox.Show(ex.Message);
        resultTextBox.Clear();
    }
}
```

Exceptions take additional overhead and disrupt the natural flow of code making it harder to read, so only throw exceptions to signal exceptional conditions.

If a method needs to tell the calling code whether it succeeded or failed, that isn't an exceptional condition so use a return value. If a method has an invalid input parameter (such as a 0 in a parameter that cannot be 0), that's an error, so throw an exception.

TRY IT

In this Try It, you add validation and error handling code to the program you built for Lesson 19's Exercise 4. When the user clicks the NewItemForm's Calculate and OK buttons, the program should verify that the values make sense and protect itself against garbage such as the user entering the quantity "one," as shown in Figure 21-1.

You can download the code and resources for this Try It from the book's web page at www.wrox.com or www.CSharpHelper.com/24hour.html. You can find the code in the Lesson21 folder.

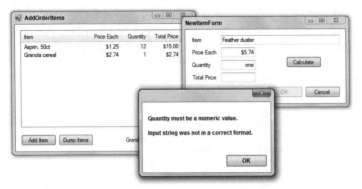

FIGURE 21-1

Lesson Requirements

➤ Copy the program you built in Lesson 19, Exercise 4 (or download Lesson 19's version from the book's web site).

➤ The previous version of this program uses repeated code to perform calculations when the user clicks either Calculate or OK. Move that code into a new `ValuesAreOk` method that validates the user's inputs. In addition to protecting the form from format errors, the function should verify that:

   ➤ Item name is not blank.

   ➤ Price Each > 0.

   ➤ Quantity > 0.

➤ If `ValuesAreOk` finds a problem, it should:

   ➤ Tell the user.

   ➤ Set focus to the textbox that caused the problem.

   ➤ Return `false`.

➤ If `ValuesAreOk` finds that all of the values are okay, it should return `true`.

Hints

➤ If the user clicks the OK button, the form should close only if the user's inputs are valid. Be sure the OK button's `DialogResult` property doesn't automatically close the form.

➤ Use `try-catch` blocks to protect against format errors.

Step-by-Step

➤ Copy the program you built in Lesson 19, Exercise 4 (or download Lesson 19's version from the book's web site).

   1. This is straightforward.

➤ The previous version of this program uses repeated code to perform calculations when the user clicks either Calculate or OK. Move that code into a new `ValuesAreOk` method that validates the user's inputs. In addition to protecting the form from format errors, the function should verify that:

➤ Item name is not blank.

➤ Price Each > 0.

➤ Quantity > 0.

1. Copy the item name into a `string` variable and verify that its length is at least 1.

2. Parse the Price Each and verify that it is greater than zero.

3. Parse the Quantity and verify that it is greater than zero.

➤ If `ValuesAreOk` finds a problem, it should:

➤ Tell the user.

➤ Set focus to the textbox that caused the problem.

➤ Return `false`.

1. Whenever the function finds a problem, it should display a message box, set focus to the textbox containing the error, and return `false`. For example, the following code shows how you might verify the price each:

```
// Validate price each.
try
{
    PriceEach = decimal.Parse(priceEachTextBox.Text, NumberStyles.Any);

    if (PriceEach <= 0)
    {
        MessageBox.Show("Price Each must be greater than 0.");
        priceEachTextBox.Focus();
        return false;
    }
}
catch (Exception ex)
{
    MessageBox.Show("Price Each must be a dollar amount.\n\n" +
        ex.Message);
    priceEachTextBox.Focus();
    return false;
}
```

➤ If `ValuesAreOk` finds that all of the values are okay, it should return `true`.

1. Each of the method's tests returns if there is a problem so, if the code reaches the end of the routine, all of the tests passed. At that point, simply return `true`.

 Please select Lesson 21 on the DVD to view the video that accompanies this lesson.

EXERCISES

1. Copy the LCM program you built in Lesson 20, Exercise 1 (or download Lesson 20's version from the book's web site) and add error handling to it. If a value causes an error, display a message and set focus to its textbox. Hints: Validate both the GCD and LCM methods so they only allow inputs greater than 0. That way they're both covered if a different program uses GCD directly. Also use a `try-catch` block in the Calculate button's Click event handler to protect against format errors.

2. Copy the Fibonacci program you built in Lesson 19, Exercise 2 (or download Lesson 19's version from the book's web site) and add error handling and validation to it. Protect the program against format errors. Also move the calculation itself into a new method. Make the method throw an error if its input is less than 0.

3. (SimpleEdit) Copy the SimpleEdit program you built in Lesson 20, Exercise 4 (or download Lesson 20's version from the book's web site) and add error handling to the functions that open and save files. To test the program, open the file Test.rtf in Microsoft Word. Then make changes in the SimpleEdit program and try to save them into that file.

4. The quadratic equation finds solutions to equations with the form where a, b, and c are constants.

$$a * x^2 + b * x + c = 0$$

The solutions to this equation (the values of x that make it true) are given by the quadratic formula:

$$x = \frac{-b \pm \sqrt{b^2 - 4ac}}{2a}$$

Build a program similar to the one shown in Figure 21-2 that calculates solutions to quadratic equations. Use a `try-catch` block to protect against format errors. Hints: Use `Math.Sqrt` to take square roots. The equation has zero, one, or two real solutions depending on whether the *discriminant $b^2 - 4ac$* is less than, equal to, or greater than zero. Use `if` statements to avoid trying to take the square root of a negative number.

FIGURE 21-2

 You can download the solutions to these exercises from the book's web page at www.wrox.com *or* www.CSharpHelper.com/24hour.html. *You can find them in the Lesson21 folder.*

22

Preventing Bugs

Many programmers believe that the way to make a program robust is to make it able to continue running even if it encounters errors. For example, consider the following version of the `Factorial` method:

```
// Recursively calculate n!
private long Factorial(long n)
{
    if (n <= 1) return 1;
    return n * Factorial(n - 1);
}
```

This method is robust in the sense that it can handle nonsensical inputs such as –10. The function cannot calculate –10!, but at least it doesn't crash so you might think this is a safe method.

Unfortunately while the function doesn't crash on this input, it also doesn't return a correct result because –10! is not defined. That makes the program continue running even though it has produced an incorrect result.

The method also has a problem if its input is greater than 20. In that case, the result is too big to fit in the `long` data type so the calculations cause an integer overflow. By default, the program silently ignores the error, and the result you get uses whatever bits are left after the overflow. In this case, the result looks like a large negative number. Again the method doesn't crash but it doesn't return a useful result, either.

In general, bugs that cause a program to crash are a lot easier to find and fix than bugs like this one that produce incorrect results but continue running.

In this lesson, you learn techniques for detecting and correcting bugs. You learn how to make bugs jump out so they're easy to fix instead of remaining hidden.

INPUT ASSERTIONS

In C# programming, an *assertion* is a statement that the code claims is true. If the statement is false, the program stops running so you can decide whether a bug occurred.

One way to make an assertion is to evaluate the statement and, if it is false, throw an error. That guarantees that the program cannot continue running if the assertion is false.

The following code shows a `Factorial` method with assertions. If the method's parameter is less than 0 or greater than 20, the code throws an exception.

```
// Recursively calculate n!
private long Factorial(long n)
{
    // Validate the input.
    if ((n < 0) || (n > 20))
        throw new ArgumentOutOfRangeException(
            "n", "Factorial parameter must be between 0 and 20.");

    if (n <= 1) return 1;
    return n * Factorial(n - 1);
}
```

To make this kind of assertion easier, the .NET Framework provides a `Debug` class. The `Debug` class's static `Assert` method takes as a parameter a Boolean value. If the value is `false`, `Assert` displays an error message showing the program's stack dump at the time so you can figure out where the error occurred.

The following code shows a new version of the factorial method that uses `Debug.Assert`. The optional second parameter to `Debug.Assert` gives a message that should be displayed if the assertion fails.

```
// Recursively calculate n!
private long Factorial(long n)
{
    // Validate the input.
    Debug.Assert((n >= 0) && (n <= 20),
        "Factorial parameter must be between 0 and 20.");

    if (n <= 1) return 1;
    return n * Factorial(n - 1);
}
```

The `Debug` *class is in the* `System.Diagnostics` *namespace. If you want to use it without including the namespace, as in the preceding code, you can include the following* using *directive at the top of the file:*

```
using System.Diagnostics;
```

Normally when you develop a program you make debug builds. These include extra debugging symbols so you can step through the code in the debugger. If you switch to a release build, those symbols are omitted, making the compiled program a bit smaller. The `Debug.Assert` method also has no effect in release builds.

The idea is that you can use `Debug.Assert` to test the program but then skip the assertions after the program is debugged and ready for release to the user. Of course this only works if the code is robust enough to behave correctly even if a bug does slip past the testing process and appears in the release build. In the case of the `Factorial` method, this code must always protect itself against input errors so it should throw an exception rather than using `Debug.Assert`.

To switch from a debug to a release build or vice versa, open the Build menu and select the Configuration Manager command to display the dialog shown in Figure 22-1. Select Debug or Release from the dropdown menu and click Close.

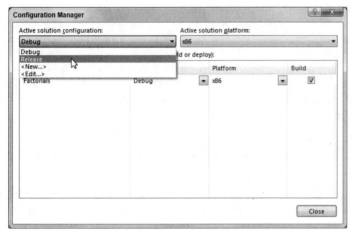

FIGURE 22-1

When you build the program, Visual Studio places the compiled executable in the project's `bin\Debug` or `bin\Release` subdirectory. Be sure you use the correct version or you may find `Debug.Assert` statements displaying errors in what you thought was a release build.

The `Debug` class provides some other handy methods in addition to `Assert`. The `WriteLine` method displays a message in the Output window. You can use it to display messages showing you what methods are executing, to display parameter values, and to give you other information that you might otherwise need to learn by stepping through the code in the debugger.

The `Debug` class's `Indent` method lets you change the indentation of output produced by `Debug.WriteLine` so, for example, you can indicate nesting of method calls.

Like the other `Debug` methods, these do nothing in release builds so the end user never sees these messages.

OTHER ASSERTIONS

In addition to input assertions, a method can make other assertions as it performs calculations. A method can use assertions to check intermediate results and to validate final results before returning them. A program can even use assertions to validate the value it receives from another method.

Often these assertions cannot be as exact as those you can perform on inputs but you may still be able to catch some really ludicrous values.

For example, suppose an order processing form lets the user enter items for purchase and then calculates the total cost. You could use assertions to verify that the total cost is between $0.01 and $1 million. This is a pretty wide range so you are unlikely to catch any but the most egregious errors, but you may catch a few.

Note that you should not test user input errors with assertions. An assertion interrupts the program so you can try to find a bug. Your code should check for user input errors and handle them without interrupting the program. Remember, when you make a release build, `Debug.Assert` calls go away so you cannot rely on them to help the user enter valid values.

One drawback to assertions is that it's hard to make programmers use them. When you're writing code, it's hard to convince yourself that the code could be wrong. After all, if you knew there was a bug in the code, you'd fix it.

Assertions are like seat belts, airbags, and bicycle helmets. You don't use them because you expect to need them today; you use them just on the off chance that you'll need them some day. Usually your assertions will just sit there doing nothing but if a bug does rear its ugly head a good set of assertions can make the difference between finding the bug in seconds, hours, or days.

TRY IT

In this Try It, you write a method to calculate a department's average salary. The interesting part is adding assertions to make sure the method is being called correctly.

To test the method, you'll build the program shown in Figure 22-2.

The focus of this Try It is on the method that calculates the average, not on the user interface. The assumption is that some other part of a larger program would call this method, so the user interface shown in Figure 22-2 is purely for testing purposes. A real program would not allow the user to enter invalid values.

FIGURE 22-2

You can download the code and resources for this Try It from the book's web page at www.wrox.com *or* www.CSharpHelper.com/24hour.html. *You can find them in the Lesson22 folder in the download.*

Lesson Requirements

➤ Build a program similar to the one shown in Figure 22-2.

➤ When the user clicks Calculate, make the program split the values entered in the textbox apart, copy them into an array of decimals, pass them to the AverageSalary method, and display the result.

➤ Make the AverageSalary method validate its inputs by asserting that the array has a reasonable number of elements and that the salaries are reasonable. (Assume you're not working on Wall Street so salaries are at least $10,000 and less than $1 million.) Also validate the average.

Hints

➤ Think about how the program should react in a final release build for each of the input conditions.

For example, if the values array contains a salary of $1,600, what should the method do? In this case, that value is unusual but it could be valid (perhaps the company hired an intern for a week) so the method can calculate a meaningful (although unusual) result. The method should check this condition with Debug.Assert so it can calculate a result in the release version.

For another example, suppose the values array is empty. In this case the method cannot calculate a meaningful value so it should throw an exception so the code calling it can deal with the problem.

Step-by-Step

➤ Build a program similar to the one shown in Figure 22-2.

1. This is reasonably straightforward.

➤ When the user clicks Calculate, make the program split the values entered in the textbox apart, copy them into an array of decimals, pass them to the AverageSalary method, and display the result.

1. You can use code similar to the following:

```
// Calculate and display the average salary.
private void calculateButton_Click(object sender, EventArgs e)
{
    try
    {
        // Copy the salaries into an array.
        string[] string_salaries = salariesTextBox.Text.Split();
        decimal[] salaries = new decimal[string_salaries.Length];
        for (int i = 0; i < string_salaries.Length; i++)
        {
            salaries[i] =
                decimal.Parse(string_salaries[i], NumberStyles.Any);
        }
```

```
        // Calculate the average.
        decimal averageSalary = AverageSalary(salaries);

        // Display the result.
        averageTextBox.Text = averageSalary.ToString("C");
    }
    catch (Exception ex)
    {
        averageTextBox.Clear();
        MessageBox.Show(ex.Message);
    }
}
```

Again a real program shouldn't let the user enter salaries as string like this because the user could enter invalid values.

➤ Make the `AverageSalary` method validate its inputs by asserting that the array has a reasonable number of elements and that the salaries are reasonable. (Assume you're not working on Wall Street so salaries are at least $10,000 and less than $1 million.) Also validate the average.

1. You can use code similar to the following:

```
// Calculate the average of this array of salaries.
private decimal AverageSalary(decimal[] salaries)
{
    // Sanity checks.
    if (salaries.Length < 1)
    {
        throw new ArgumentOutOfRangeException("salaries",
            "AverageSalary method cannot calculate average " +
            "salary for an empty array.");
    }
    Debug.Assert(salaries.Length < 100, "Too many salaries.");
    for (int i = 0; i < salaries.Length; i++)
    {
        Debug.Assert(salaries[i] >= 10000, "Salary is too small.");
        Debug.Assert(salaries[i] < 1000000, "Salary is too big.");
    }

    // Calculate the result.
    decimal total = 0;
    for (int i = 0; i < salaries.Length; i++)
    {
        total += salaries[i];
    }
    decimal result = total / salaries.Length;

    // Validate the result.
    Debug.Assert(result >= 10000, "Average salary is too small.");
    Debug.Assert(result < 1000000, "Average salary is too big.");

    return result;
}
```

Please select Lesson 22 on the DVD to view the video that accompanies this lesson.

EXERCISES

1. Suppose you're writing a routine for sorting orders based on priority. Use the following definition for an `Order` structure:

   ```
   private struct Order
   {
       public int OrderId;
       public int Priority;
   }
   ```

   Write the `SortOrders` method, which takes as a parameter an array of `Orders` and sorts them. Don't actually write the code that sorts the orders, just write assertions to validate the inputs and outputs.

2. Build the program shown in Figure 22-3 to convert temperatures between the Fahrenheit, Celsius, and Kelvin scales. Write methods `FahrenheitToCelsius`, `KelvinToCelsius`, `CelsiusToFahrenheit`, and `CelsiusToKelvin` to perform the conversions using the following formulas:

   $$C = (F - 32) * 5 / 9$$

   $$C = K - 273.15$$

   $$F = C * 9 / 5 + 32$$

   $$K = C + 273.15$$

   FIGURE 22-3

   Use assertions to help the conversion methods ensure that Fahrenheit values are between −130 and 140, Celsius values are between −90 and 60, and Kelvin values are between 183 and 333.

3. Make a program that lets the user input miles and gallons of fuel and calculates miles per gallon using a `MilesPerGallon` method. Make the method protect itself against miles and gallons values that are too big or too small. Make it also validate its result so it doesn't return values that are too large or small.

 You can download the solutions to these exercises from the book's web page at www.wrox.com *or* www.CSharpHelper.com/24hour.html. *You can find those solutions in the Lesson22 folder.*

SECTION IV
Classes

The lessons in Section III focus on C# programming statements. They explain how to make decisions with `if` and `switch` statements, repeat program steps with loops, reuse code with methods, and catch exceptions.

Methods are particularly useful for programming at a higher level because they let you encapsulate complex behaviors in a tightly wrapped package. For example, you might write a `CalculateGrade` method that determines a student's grades. This method can hide all of the details of how grades are calculated. (Are tests graded on a curve? Is the grade a weighted average of tests and homework assignments? How much is attendance worth?) The main program only needs to know how to call the method, not how it works.

Classes provide another even more powerful method for abstracting complex entities into manageable packages. For example, a `Student` class might embody the idea of a student and include basic information (name, address, phone), the courses that the student is taking, grades (test scores, homework grades), and even attendance. It would also include methods such as `CalculateGrade` for manipulating the `Student` data.

The lessons in this section explain classes. They explain how you can build classes, make one class inherit the capabilities of another, and make a class override the features of its parent class.

▶ **LESSON 23:** Defining Classes

▶ **LESSON 24:** Initializing Objects

▶ **LESSON 25:** Fine-Tuning Classes

▶ **LESSON 26:** Overloading Operators

▶ **LESSON 27:** Using Interfaces

▶ **LESSON 28:** Making Generic Classes

23

Defining Classes

This book hasn't emphasized the fact, but you've been working with classes since the very beginning. The very first program you created in Lesson 1 included several classes such as the program's main form and some behind-the-scenes classes that help get the program running. Since then, you've used all kinds of control classes, the MessageBox class, the Array class, collection classes, and more. You can even treat primitive data types such as int and string as classes under some circumstances.

In this lesson you learn how to create your own classes. You learn how to define a class and give it properties, methods, and events to make it useful.

WHAT IS A CLASS?

A *class* defines a type of object. It defines the properties, methods, and events provided by its type of object. After you define a class, you can make as many instances of that class as you like.

For example, the Button class defines the properties and behaviors of a button user interface element. You can create any number of instances of Buttons and place them on your forms.

You can think of a class as a blueprint for making objects. When you create an instance of the class, you use the blueprint to make an object that has the properties and behaviors defined by the class.

You can also think of a class as a cookie cutter. Once you've created the cookie cutter, you can make any number of cookies that all have the same shape.

Classes are very similar to the structures described in Lesson 17 and many of the techniques you learned there apply here as well. For example, you can give a class fields that the instance can use to perform calculations.

There are several important differences between structures and classes, but one of the most important is that structures are value types while classes are reference types. Perhaps the most confusing consequence of this is that when you assign structure variable A equal to structure variable B, A becomes a copy of B. In contrast, if you assign class variable C equal to class variable D, then variable C now points to the same object that variable D does.

For a more detailed discussion of some of these differences, see the section "Structures Versus Classes" in Lesson 17.

The rest of this lesson focuses on classes and doesn't really talk about structures.

Note that the same techniques apply to structures and classes. For example, structures have the same benefits as classes described in the following section. Just because I'm describing them here doesn't mean I'm trying to imply that classes are better because they have these advantages that structures don't.

CLASS BENEFITS

The biggest benefit of classes is encapsulation. A well-designed class hides its internal workings from the rest of the program so the program can use the class without knowing how the class works.

For example, suppose you build a Turtle class to represent a turtle crawling across the screen drawing lines as it moves. The class would need properties such as X, Y, and Direction to define the Turtle's location and direction. It might also provide methods such as Turn to make it change direction and Move to make it move.

The Turtle class needs to know how to draw the Turtle's path as it moves, but the main program doesn't need to know how it works. It doesn't need to know about Graphics objects, Pens, or the trigonometric functions the Turtle uses to figure out where to go. The main program only needs to know how to set the Turtle's properties and call its methods.

You can download the Turtle example program from the book's web site as part of the Lesson23 folder and follow along in its code as you read through this lesson.

Some other benefits of classes (and structures for that matter) include:

➤ **Grouping data and code** — The code that makes a Turtle move is right in the same object as the data that determines the Turtle's position and direction.

➤ **Code reuse** — You only need to write the code for the Turtle class once and then all instances of the class get to use it. You get even more code reuse through inheritance, which is described in the section "Inheritance" later in this lesson.

➤ **Polymorphism** — Polymorphism means you can treat an object as if it were from another class as long as it inherits from that class. For example, a Student is a type of Person so you should be able to treat a Student object as if it were either a Student or a Person. The section "Polymorphism" later in this lesson describes this further.

MAKING A CLASS

Now that you know a bit about what classes are for, it's time to learn how to build one.

Making a class in C# is simple. Open the Project menu and select Add Class. Give the class a good name and click Add.

Initially the class looks something like the following:

```
using System;
using System.Collections.Generic;
using System.Linq;
using System.Text;

namespace MyProgram
{
    class Employee
    {
    }
}
```

Here `MyProgram` is your program's default namespace, which by default is the name of your program. It is used as the namespace for all of the forms and other classes that you add to the program.

`Employee` is the name that I gave the class in this example.

At this point, the class can't do anything. You can write code to create an instance of the class but it will just sit there. To make the class useful, you need to add properties, methods, and events.

➤ **Properties** are values associated with a class. For example, an `Employee` class might define `FirstName`, `LastName`, and `EmployeeId` properties.

➤ **Methods** are actions that an object can perform. For example, an `Employee` class might provide a `CalculateBonus` method that calculates the employee's end-of-year bonus based on performance during the year.

➤ **Events** are raised by the class to tell the rest of the program that something interesting happened, sort of like raising a flag to draw attention to something. For example, the `Employee` class might raise a `TooManyHours` event if the program tried to assign an employee more than 40 hours of work in a week.

Properties, methods, and events allow a program to control and interact with objects. The following sections explain how you can add properties, methods, and events to your classes.

Properties

If you give a class a public field, other pieces of code can get and set that field's values. This kind of variable is called a *field*. A field is similar to a property but it has one big disadvantage: it provides unrestricted access to its value. That means other parts of the program could dump any garbage into the field without the class being able to stop them.

In contrast, a class implements a property by using *accessor methods* that can include code to protect the class from garbage values. You'll learn more about this as you see how to build properties.

The following sections describe the two most common approaches for implementing properties: auto-implemented properties and backing fields.

Auto-Implemented Properties

The easiest way to make a property is to use an auto-implemented property. The syntax for an auto-implemented property is:

```
accessibility dataType Name { get; set; }
```

Here `accessibility` determines what code can use the property. It can be `public`, `private`, and so on. The `dataType` determines the property's data type and `Name` determines its name. The `get` and `set` keywords indicate that other code should be able to get and set the property's value.

 You can omit the `set` *clause to create a read-only property.*

The following code creates a simple property named `X` of type `int`.

```
public int X { get; set; }
```

Creating an auto-implemented property is almost as easy as making a field, but it's a tiny bit more work, so why should you bother?

Making an auto-implemented property sets up the code so it will be easy to upgrade the property to use more complicated code later. For example, suppose you decide that the `Turtle` class's `Direction` method should only allow angles between 0 and 259 degrees. In that case you can convert the auto-implemented property into a property built using a backing field as described in the next section.

Backing Fields

When you make an auto-implemented property, C# automatically generates accessors that let you get and set the property's value. You can use those accessors without needing to know the details of how they work.

When you make a property that is not auto-implemented, you need to write the accessors yourself.

The following shows the basic syntax used to define a property that is not auto-implemented:

```
accessibility dataType Name
{
    get
    {
        ...getCode...
    }
    set
    {
        ...setCode...
    }
}
```

Here `accessibility`, `dataType`, and `Name` are the same as before. The `getCode` and `setCode` are the pieces of code that get and set the property's value.

One common way to implement this kind of property is with a backing field. A *backing field* is a field that stores data to represent the property. The `getCode` and `setCode` use the field to get and set the property's value.

The following C# code shows a version of the `Direction` property stored in the backing field named `direction`:

```
// The Turtle's direction in degrees.
private int direction = 0;      // Backing field.
public int Direction
{
    get { return direction; }
    set { direction = value; }
}
```

The code starts by defining the field `direction` to hold the property's value. The field is private so only the code inside the class can see it.

The property's `get` accessor simply returns the value of `direction`.

The property's `set` accessor saves a new value in the backing field `direction`. The new value that the calling code is trying to assign to the property is stored in a parameter named `value`. This parameter is a bit odd because it isn't declared anywhere. The `set` accessor implicitly defines `value` and can use it.

The preceding code simply copies values in and out of the backing field, so why did you bother? There are several reasons.

First, a property hides its details from the outside world, increasing the class's encapsulation. As far as the outside world is concerned, a description of the `Direction` property tells you *what* is stored (the direction in degrees) but not *how* it is stored (as an integer value in degrees).

This example stores the direction in degrees but suppose you decided that the class would work better if you stored the direction in radians. If `Direction` is a field, then any code that uses it would now break because it is using degrees. If you use accessors, they can translate between degrees and radians as needed so the code outside the class doesn't need to know that anything has changed.

The following code shows a new version of the `Direction` property that stores the value in radians. As far as the code outside the class is concerned, nothing has changed.

```
// The Turtle's direction in radians.
private double direction = 0;      // Backing field.
public int Direction
{
    get { return (int)(direction * 180 / Math.PI); }
    set { direction = value * Math.PI / 180; }
}
```

You can also add validation code to property accessors. For example, suppose the `Direction` property represents an angle in degrees and you only want to allow values between 0 and 359. The following code asserts that the new value is between 0 and 359 degrees. The program can continue correctly if the value is outside of this range so the code uses Debug.Assert instead of throwing an exception.

```
// The Turtle's direction in degrees.
private int direction = 0;        // Backing field.
public int Direction
{
    get { return direction; }
    //set { direction = value; }
    set
    {
        Debug.Assert((value >= 0) && (value <= 359),
            "Direction should be between 0 and 359 degrees");
        direction = value;
    }
}
```

Property accessors also give you a place to set break-points if something is going wrong. For example, if you know that some part of your program is setting a Turtle's Direction to 45 when it should be set-ting it to 60 but you don't know where, you could set a breakpoint in the set accessor to see where the change is taking place.

TRY IT

In this first Try It in the lesson, you cre-ate a simple Person class with FirstName, LastName, City, Street, and Zip properties, some having simple validations. You also build a simple test application shown in Figure 23-1.

FIGURE 23-1

 You can download the code and resources for this Try It from the book's web page at www.wrox.com or www.CSharpHelper.com/24hour.html. You can find them in the TryIt23a folder in the Lesson23 folder of the download.

Lesson Requirements

➤   Build the program shown in Figure 23-1.

➤   Create a Person class.

➤   Make auto-implemented properties for Street, City, State, and Zip.

➤   For this application, assume that setting FirstName or LastName to a blank string is an error and add validation code to their property accessors.

Hints

➤ Also, don't allow first or last to be set to null, which is different from setting them equal to blank strings. If you don't check for these, the other code in the accessors will throw an error anyway, but if you check yourself, then you can provide a more meaningful exception.

Step-by-Step

➤ Build the program shown in Figure 23-1.

1. This is reasonably straightforward.

➤ Create a Person class.

1. Use the Project menu's Add Class item. Name the class Person.

➤ Make auto-implemented properties for Street, City, State, and Zip.

1. You can use code similar to the following:

```
// Auto-implemented properties.
public string Street { get; set; }
public string City { get; set; }
public string State { get; set; }
public string Zip { get; set; }
```

➤ For this application, assume that setting FirstName or LastName to a blank string is an error and add validation code to their property accessors.

1. The following code shows how you might implement the FirstName property. The code for the LastName property is similar.

```
// FirstName property.
private string firstName = "";
public string FirstName
{
    get
    {
        return firstName;
    }
    set
    {
        if (value == null)
            throw new ArgumentOutOfRangeException("FirstName",
                "Person.FirstName cannot be null.");
        if (value.Length < 1)
            throw new ArgumentOutOfRangeException("FirstName",
                "Person.FirstName cannot be blank.");
    }
}
```

METHODS

A method is simply a piece of code in the class that other parts of the program can execute. The following method shows how the `Turtle` class might implement its `Move` method:

```
// Make the Turtle move the indicated distance
// in its current direction.
public void Move(int distance)
{
    // Calculate the new position.
    double radians = Direction * Math.PI / 180;
    int newX = (int)(X + Math.Cos(radians) * distance);
    int newY = (int)(Y + Math.Sin(radians) * distance);

    // Draw to the new position.
    using (Graphics gr = Graphics.FromImage(Canvas))
    {
        gr.DrawLine(Pens.Blue, X, Y, newX, newY);
    }

    // Save the new position.
    X = newX;
    Y = newY;
}
```

The method takes as a parameter the distance it should move. It uses the `Turtle`'s current position and direction to figure out where this move will finish. It uses some graphics code to draw a line from the current position to the new one (don't worry about the details) and finishes by saving the new position.

EVENTS

Events let the class tell the rest of the program that something interesting is happening. For example, if a `BankAccount` object's balance falls below 0, it could raise an `AccountOverdrawn` event to notify the main program.

Declaring an event in C# is a bit tricky because you first need to understand delegates.

Delegates

A *delegate* is a data type that can hold a specific kind of method. For example, you could make a delegate type that represents methods that take no parameters and return a `double`. You could then declare a variable of that type and save a method in it.

Confusing? You bet!

The key to understanding delegates is to remember that a delegate type is a new data type just like a `string` or `int`. The difference is that a variable with a delegate type holds a method, not a simple value like "Hello" or 27.

Example program Delegates, which is part of this lesson's download on the book's web site, provides a simple example. The program uses four steps to demonstrate delegates: declare the delegate type, create variables of that type, initialize the variables, and use the variables' values.

First the program declares a delegate type:

```
// Define a delegate type that takes no parameters and returns nothing.
private delegate void DoSomethingMethod();
```

The declaration begins with the accessibility keyword `private` and then the keyword `delegate` to tell C# that it is defining a delegate type. The rest of the declaration gives the delegate type's name `DoSomethingFunction`. It also indicates that instances of this type must refer to methods that return nothing (`void`) and take no parameters.

Now that it has defined the delegate type, the code declares three fields of that type. Each of the variables can hold a reference to a method that takes no parameters and returns nothing:

```
// Declare three DoSomethingMethod variables.
private DoSomethingMethod method1, method2, method3;
```

Next the program defines two methods that match the delegate's definition:

```
// Define some methods that have the delegate's type.
private void SayHi()
{
    MessageBox.Show("Hi");
}
private void SayClicked()
{
    MessageBox.Show("Clicked");
}
```

When the program starts, it sets the values of the fields `method1`, `method2`, and `method3` so they point to these two methods. Notice that the code makes `method1` and `method3` point to the same method, `SayHi`.

```
// Initialize the delegate variables.
private void Form1_Load(object sender, EventArgs e)
{
    method1 = SayHi;
    method2 = SayClicked;
    method3 = SayHi;
}
```

At this point, the program has defined the delegate type, created three variables of that type, and initialized those variables so they refer to the `SayHi` and `SayClicked` methods. The program is ready to use the variables.

This program displays three buttons. When you click them, the following event handlers execute. Each button simply invokes the method referred to by one of the delegate variables.

```
// Invoke the method stored in the delegates.
private void method1Button_Click(object sender, EventArgs e)
{
    method1();
```

```
    }
    private void method2Button_Click(object sender, EventArgs e)
    {
        method2();
    }

    private void method3Button_Click(object sender, EventArgs e)
    {
        method3();
    }
```

This isn't an extremely practical program, and it's hard to imagine a situation where you would just want buttons to invoke different delegate instances. This example is just much simpler than many that use delegates.

Event Handler Delegates

Now that you know a bit about delegates, you can learn how to use them to make an event.

First, in the class that will raise the event, declare a delegate type to define the event handler. Usually developers end the delegate's name with `EventHandler` to make it obvious what the delegate represents.

By convention, event handlers usually take two parameters named `sender` and `e`. The `sender` parameter is an object that contains a reference to whatever `object` is raising the event. The `e` parameter contains data specific to the event.

The `Turtle` class's `OutOfBounds` event passes its event handlers an object of type `TurtleOutOfBoundsEventArgs` to give them extra information. The following code shows how the `Turtle` class defines this class.

```
// The TurtleOutOfBoundsEventArgs data type.
public class TurtleOutOfBoundsEventArgs
{
    // Where the Turtle would stop if
    // this were not out of bounds.
    public int X { get; set; }
    public int Y { get; set; }
};
```

The following code shows how the `Turtle` class declares its `OutOfBoundsEventHandler` delegate:

```
// Declare the OutOfBound event's delegate.
public delegate void OutOfBoundsEventHandler(
    object sender, TurtleOutOfBoundsEventArgs e);
```

Next the class must declare the actual event to tell C# that the class will provide this event. The declaration should begin with an accessibility keyword (`public`, `private`, and so on) followed by the keyword `event`. Next it should give the event handler's delegate type. It finishes with the event's name.

The following code declares the `OutOfBounds` event, which is handled by event handlers of type `OutOfBoundsEventHandler`:

```
// Declare the OutOfBounds event.
public event OutOfBoundsEventHandler OutOfBounds;
```

The final piece of code that you need to add to the class is the code that raises the event. This code simply invokes the event handler, passing it any parameters that it should receive.

Before it raises the event, however, the code should verify that some other piece of code has registered to receive the event. The code does that by checking whether the event is null.

The following code raises the Turtle class's OutOfBounds event:

```
if (OutOfBounds != null)
{
    TurtleOutOfBoundsEventArgs args = new TurtleOutOfBoundsEventArgs();
    args.X = newX;
    args.Y = newY;
    OutOfBounds(this, args);
}
```

If OutOfBounds is not null, this code creates a new TurtleOutOfBoundsEventArgs object, initializes it, and then calls OutOfBounds, passing it the correct arguments.

A class uses code to decide when to raise the event. The following code shows how the Turtle class raises its event when the Move method tries to move beyond the edge of the Turtle's Bitmap:

```
// Make the Turtle move the indicated distance
// in its current direction.
public void Move(int distance)
{
    // Calculate the new position.
    double radians = Direction * Math.PI / 180;
    int newX = (int)(X + Math.Cos(radians) * distance);
    int newY = (int)(Y + Math.Sin(radians) * distance);

    // See if the new position is off the Bitmap.
    if ((newX < 0) || (newY < 0) ||
        (newX >= Canvas.Width) || (newY >= Canvas.Height))
    {
        // Raise the OutOfBounds event, passing
        // the event handler the new coordinates.
        if (OutOfBounds != null)
        {
            TurtleOutOfBoundsEventArgs args =
                new TurtleOutOfBoundsEventArgs();
            args.X = newX;
            args.Y = newY;
            OutOfBounds(this, args);
        }
        return;
    }

    // Draw to the new position.
    using (Graphics gr = Graphics.FromImage(Canvas))
    {
        gr.DrawLine(Pens.Blue, X, Y, newX, newY);
    }

    // Save the new position.
```

```
    X = newX;
    Y = newY;
}
```

There's still one piece missing to all of this. The main program must register to receive the `OutOfBound` event or it won't know if the `Turtle` has raised it.

When the Turtle program starts, its `Form_Load` event handler executes the following code. This adds the `Turtle_OutOfBounds` method as an event handler for the `MyTurtle` object's `OutOfBounds` event. Now if the `MyTurtle` object raises its event, the program's `Turtle_OutOfBounds` event handler executes.

```
// Register to receive the OutOfBounds event.
MyTurtle.OutOfBounds += Turtle_OutOfBounds;
```

 You can remove an event handler in code like this:

```
    MyTurtle.OutOfBounds -= Turtle_OutOfBounds;
```

The following code shows the Turtle program's `Turtle_OutOfBounds` event handler:

```
// Handle the OutOfBounds event.
private void Turtle_OutOfBounds(object sender, Turtle.TurtleOutOfBoundsEventArgs e)
{
    MessageBox.Show(string.Format("Oops! ({0}, {1}) is out of bounds.",
        e.X, e.Y));
}
```

TRY IT

In this second Try It in the lesson, you create a `BankAccount` class. You give it a `Balance` property and two methods, `Credit` and `Debit`. The `Debit` method raises an `Overdrawn` event if a withdrawal would give the account a negative balance.

You also build the test application shown in Figure 23-2.

FIGURE 23-2

 You can download the code and resources for this Try It from the book's web page at www.wrox.com or www.CSharpHelper.com/24hour.html. You can find them in the TryIt23b folder in the Lesson23 folder of the download.

Lesson Requirements

➤ Build the program shown in Figure 23-2.

➤ Create a BankAccount class. Give it a Balance property.

➤ Add Debit and Credit methods to add and remove money from the account.

➤ Define the AccountOverdrawnArgs class to pass to event handlers.

➤ Define the OverdrawnEventHandler delegate type.

➤ Declare the Overdrawn event itself.

➤ Make the Debit method raise the event when necessary.

➤ In the main program, register to receive the Overdrawn event so it can display a message box.

Hints

➤ This example doesn't do anything special with the Balance property so you can make it auto-implemented.

➤ Make the main form create an instance of the BankAccount class to manipulate.

Step-by-Step

➤ Build the program shown in Figure 23-2.

1. This is reasonably straightforward.

➤ Create a BankAccount class. Give it a Balance property.

1. Use code similar to the following:

```
// The account balance.
public decimal Balance { get; set; }
```

➤ Add Debit and Credit methods to add and remove money from the account.

1. Start with code similar to the following. You'll modify the Debit method later to raise the Overdrawn event.

```
// Add money to the account.
public void Credit(decimal amount)
{
    Balance += amount;
}

// Remove money from the account.
public void Debit(decimal amount)
{
    Balance -= amount;
}
```

➤ Define the `AccountOverdrawnArgs` class to pass to event handlers.

1. Use code similar to the following:

```
// Define the OverdrawnEventArgs type.
public class OverdrawnEventArgs
{
    public decimal currentBalance, invalidBalance;
}
```

➤ Define the `OverdrawnEventHandler` delegate type.

1. Use code similar to the following:

```
// Define the OverdrawnEventHandler delegate type.
public delegate void OverdrawnEventHandler(
    object sender, OverdrawnEventArgs args);
```

➤ Declare the `Overdrawn` event itself.

1. Use code similar to the following:

```
// Declare the Overdrawn event.
public event OverdrawnEventHandler Overdrawn;
```

➤ Make the `Debit` method raise the event when necessary.

1. Modify the simple initial version of the method so it raises the event when necessary. Use code similar to the following:

```
// Remove money from the account.
public void Debit(decimal amount)
{
    // See if there is enough money.
    if (Balance < amount)
    {
        // Not enough money. Raise the Overdrawn event.
        if (Overdrawn != null)
        {
            OverdrawnEventArgs args = new OverdrawnEventArgs();
            args.currentBalance = Balance;
            args.invalidBalance = Balance - amount;
            Overdrawn(this, args);
        }
    }
    else
    {
        // There's enough money.
        Balance -= amount;
    }
}
```

➤ In the main program, register to receive the `Overdrawn` event so it can display a message box.

1. Use code similar to the following:

```
// Declare an account.
BankAccount MyAccount;
```

```
    // Initialize the account.
    private void Form1_Load(object sender, EventArgs e)
    {
        // Initialize the account.
        MyAccount = new BankAccount();
        MyAccount.Balance = 100M;

        // Register to receive the Overdrawn event.
        MyAccount.Overdrawn += MyAccount_Overdrawn;

        // Display the current balance.
        balanceTextBox.Text = MyAccount.Balance.ToString("C");
    }

    // We're overdrawn.
    private void MyAccount_Overdrawn(object sender,
        BankAccount.OverdrawnEventArgs args)
    {
        MessageBox.Show("Insufficient funds.");
    }
```

INHERITANCE

Often when you build one class, you end up building a bunch of other closely related classes. For example, suppose you're building a program that models your company's organization. You might build an `Employee` class to represent employees. After a while, you may realize that there are different kinds of employees: managers, supervisors, project leaders, and so forth.

You could build each of those classes individually but you'd find that these classes have a lot in common. They all probably have `FirstName`, `LastName`, `Address`, `EmployeeId`, and other properties. Depending on the kinds of operations you need the objects to perform, you might also find that they share a lot of methods: `ScheduleVacation`, `PrintTimesheet`, `RecordHours`, and so forth. Though you could build each of these classes individually, you would end up duplicating a lot of code in each class to handle these common features.

Fortunately, C# allows you to make one class inherit from another and that lets them share common code. When you make one class inherit from another one, you *derive* the new class from the existing class. In that case, the new class is called the *child class* and the class from which it inherits is called the *parent class*.

In this example, you could build a `Person` class with properties that all people have: `FirstName`, `LastName`, `Street`, `City`, `State`, and `Zip`. You could then derive the `Employee` class from `Person` and add the new property `EmployeeId`.

Next you could derive the `Manager` class from `Employee` (because all `Managers` are also `Employees`) and add new manager-related properties such as `DepartmentName` and `DirectReports`.

Syntactically, to make a class that inherits from another you add a colon and the parent class's name after the child class. For example, the following code defines the `Manager` class, which inherits from `Employee`. In addition to whatever features the `Employee` class provides, `Manager` adds new `DepartmentName` and `DirectReports` properties.

```
class Employee : Person
{
    public string DepartmentName { get; set; }
    public List<Employee> DirectReports = new List<Employee>();
}
```

 Note that C# only supports single inheritance. That means a class can inherit from at most one parent class. For example, if you define a House *class and a* Boat *class, you cannot make a* HouseBoat *class that inherits from both.*

POLYMORPHISM

Polymorphism is a rather confusing concept that basically means a program can treat an object as if it were any class that it inherits. Another way to think of this is that polymorphism lets you treat an object as if it were any of the classes that it *is*. For example, an `Employee` is a kind of `Person` so you should be able to treat an `Employee` as a `Person`.

Note that the reverse is not true. A `Person` is not necessarily an `Employee` (it could be a `Customer` or some other unrelated person).

For a more detailed example, suppose you make the `Person`, `Employee`, and `Manager` classes and they inherit from each other in the natural progression: `Employee` inherits from `Person` and `Manager` inherits from `Employee`.

Now suppose you write a method that takes a `Person` as a parameter. `Employee` inherits from `Person` so you should be able to pass an `Employee` into this method and the method should be able to treat it as a `Person`. This makes intuitive sense because an `Employee` *is* a `Person`, just a particular kind of `Person`.

Similarly, `Manager` inherits from `Employee` so a `Manager` is a kind of `Employee`. If an `Employee` is a kind of `Person` and a `Manager` is a kind of `Employee`, then a `Manager` must also be a kind of `Person` so the same method should be able to take a `Manager` as its parameter.

This feature allows you to reuse code in ways that makes sense. For example, if you write a method that addresses letters for a `Person`, it can also address letters to `Employees` and `Managers`.

TRY IT

In this final Try It of this lesson, you get to experiment with classes, inheritance, and polymorphism. You build `Person`, `Employee`, and `Manager` classes. To test the classes, you build a simple program that creates instances of each class and passes them to a method that takes a `Person` as a parameter.

You can download the code and resources for this Try It from the book's web page at www.wrox.com *or* www.CSharpHelper.com/24hour.html. *You can find them in the TryIt23c folder in the Lesson23 folder of the download.*

Lesson Requirements

➤ Create a `Person` class with properties `FirstName`, `LastName`, `Street`, `City`, `State`, and `Zip`. Give the `Person` class a `GetAddress` method that returns the `Person`'s name and address properties as a string of the form:

   Alice Archer

   100 Ash Ave

   Bugsville   CO   82010

➤ Derive an `Employee` class from `Person`. Add the properties `EmployeeId` and `MailStop`.

➤ Derive a `Manager` class from `Employee`. Add a `DepartmentName` property and a `DirectReports` property of type `List<Employee>`. Make a `GetDirectReportsList` method that returns the names of the `Manager`'s `Employees` separated by newlines.

➤ Make the main program create two `Employees` named Alice and Bob, a `Manager` named Cindy who has Alice and Bob in her department, and a `Person` named Dan.

➤ Make a `ShowAddress` method that takes a `Person` as a parameter and displays the `Person`'s address.

➤ On the main form, make buttons that call `ShowAddress` for each of the people, passing the method the appropriate object.

➤ Make a final button that displays Cindy's list of direct reports.

Hints

➤ This example doesn't do anything fancy with the class's properties so you can use auto-implemented properties.

➤ The `ShowAddress` method should take a `Person` parameter even though some of the objects it will be passed are `Employees` or `Managers`.

Step-by-Step

➤ Create a `Person` class with properties `FirstName`, `LastName`, `Street`, `City`, `State`, and `Zip`. Give the `Person` class a `GetAddress` method that returns the `Person`'s name and address properties as a string of the form:

   Alice Archer

   100 Ash Ave

   Bugsville   CO   82010

1. Make a new `Person` class with code similar to the following:

```
class Person
{
    public string FirstName { get; set; }
    public string LastName { get; set; }
    public string Street { get; set; }
    public string City { get; set; }
    public string State { get; set; }
    public string Zip { get; set; }

    // Display the person's address.
    // A real application might print this on an envelope.
    public string GetAddress()
    {
        return FirstName + " " + LastName +
            "\n" + Street + "\n" + City +
            "     " + State + "     " + Zip;
    }
}
```

➤ Derive an `Employee` class from `Person`. Add the properties `EmployeeId` and `MailStop`.

1. Make the `Employee` class similar to the following:

```
class Employee : Person
{
    public int EmployeeId { get; set; }
    public string MailStop { get; set; }
}
```

➤ Derive a `Manager` class from `Employee`. Add a `DepartmentName` property and a `DirectReports` property of type `List<Employee>`. Make a `GetDirectReportsList` method that returns the names of the `Manager`'s `Employees` separated by newlines.

1. Make the `Manager` class similar to the following:

```
class Manager : Employee
{
    public string DepartmentName { get; set; }
    public List<Employee> DirectReports = new List<Employee>();

    // Return a list of this manager's direct reports.
    public string GetDirectReportsList()
    {
        string result = "";
        foreach (Employee emp in DirectReports)
        {
            result += emp.FirstName + " " + emp.LastName + "\n";
        }
        return result;
    }
}
```

➤ Make the main program create two `Employees` named Alice and Bob, a `Manager` named Cindy who has Alice and Bob in her department, and a `Person` named Dan.

1. Because the program's buttons need to access the objects, these objects should be stored in fields as in the following code:

```
// Define some people of various types.
private Person Dan;
private Employee Alice, Bob;
private Manager Cindy;
```

2. Add code to the main form's `Load` event handler to initialize the objects. The following code shows how the program might create Alice's `Employee` object:

```
// Make an Employee named Alice.
Alice = new Employee();
Alice.FirstName = "Alice";
Alice.LastName = "Archer";
Alice.Street = "100 Ash Ave";
Alice.City = "Bugsville";
Alice.State = "CO";
Alice.Zip = "82010";
Alice.EmployeeId = 1001;
Alice.MailStop = "A-1";
```

3. Creating and initializing the other objects is similar. The only odd case is adding Alice and Bob as Cindy's employees as in the following code:

```
Cindy.DirectReports.Add(Alice);
Cindy.DirectReports.Add(Bob);
```

➤ Make a `ShowAddress` method that takes a `Person` as a parameter and displays the `Person`'s address.

1. Use code similar to the following:

```
// Display this Person's address.
private void ShowAddress(Person per)
{
    MessageBox.Show(per.GetAddress());
}
```

➤ On the main form, make buttons that call `ShowAddress` for each of the people, passing the method the appropriate object.

1. Create the buttons' `Click` event handlers. The following code shows the event handler that displays Cindy's address:

```
private void cindyAddressButton_Click(object sender, EventArgs e)
{
    ShowAddress(Cindy);
}
```

Note that the variable `Cindy` is a `Manager` but the `ShowAddress` method treats it as a `Person`. That's okay because `Manager` inherits indirectly from `Person`.

➤ Make a final button that displays Cindy's list of direct reports.

1. This method simply calls the `Cindy` object's `GetDirectReportsList` method and displays the result.

```
// Display Cindy's direct reports.
private void cindyReportsButton_Click(object sender, EventArgs e)
{
    MessageBox.Show(Cindy.GetDirectReportsList());
}
```

 Please select Lesson 23 links on the DVD to view the videos that accompany the Try Its in this lesson.

EXERCISES

1. Write a program similar to the one shown in Figure 23-3 to manipulate complex numbers. When you enter the complex numbers' real and imaginary parts in the textboxes and click Calculate, the program should display the sum, difference, and product of the two complex numbers.

Make a `ComplexNumber` class with properties `Real` and `Imaginary` to hold a number's real and imaginary parts. Give the class `AddTo`, `MultiplyBy`, and `SubtractFrom` methods that combine the current `ComplexNumber` with another taken as a parameter and return the result as a new `ComplexNumber`.

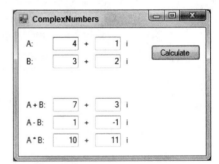

FIGURE 23-3

Hints: Recall from school these equations for calculating with complex numbers:

```
(A + Bi) + (C + Di) = (A + C) + (B + D)i
(A + Bi) - (C + Di) = (A - C) + (B - D)i
(A + Bi) * (C + Di) = (A * C - B * D) + (A * D + B * C)i
```

For more review of complex numbers, see en.wikipedia.org/wiki/Complex_numbers or mathworld.wolfram.com/ComplexNumber.html.

 You can download the solution to this exercise from the book's web page at www.wrox.com or www.CSharpHelper.com/24hour.html. You can find this solution in the Lesson23 folder.

24

Initializing Objects

Most of the time when you create an object, you need to initialize its properties. You generally wouldn't create an `Employee` object without at least setting its `FirstName` and `LastName` properties. The following code shows how you might initialize an `Employee` object:

```
// Make an Employee named Alice.
Employee alice = new Employee();
alice.FirstName = "Alice";
alice.LastName = "Archer";
alice.Street = "100 Ash Ave";
alice.City = "Bugsville";
alice.State = "CO";
alice.Zip = "82010";
alice.EmployeeId = 1001;
alice.MailStop = "A-1";
```

Though this is relatively straightforward, it is a bit tedious. Creating and initializing a bunch of `Employees` would take a lot of repetitive code. Fortunately C# provides alternatives that make this task a little easier.

In this lesson you learn how to initialize an object's properties as you create it. You also learn how to make constructors that make initializing objects easier, and how to make destructors that clean up after an object.

INITIALIZING OBJECTS

C# provides a simple syntax for initializing an object's properties as you create it. Create the object as usual but follow the `new` keyword and the class's name with braces. Inside the braces, place comma-separated statements that initialize the object's properties.

For example, the following code creates an `Employee` object named `Bob`. The statements inside the braces initialize the object's properties.

```
// Make an Employee named Bob.
Employee bob = new Employee()
{
```

```
            FirstName = "Bob",
            LastName = "Baker",
            Street = "200 Beach Blvd",
            City = "Bugsville",
            State = "CO",
            Zip = "82010",
            EmployeeId = 1002,
            MailStop = "B-2"
    };
```

 Note that an initializer can only initialize properties that the code can access. For example, if a property is private, the initializer cannot set its value.

CONSTRUCTORS

Initializers are handy and easy to use but sometimes you might like some extra control over how an object is created. Constructors give you that extra control.

A *constructor* is a routine that is executed when an object is created. The constructor executes before the code that creates the object gets hold of it. The constructor can perform any setup tasks that you want to get the object ready to use. It can look up data in databases, prepare data structures, and initialize properties.

The next two sections describe two kinds of constructors: parameterless constructors and parameterized constructors. The section after those explains how one constructor can invoke another to avoid duplicated work.

Parameterless Constructors

A constructor can take parameters just like any other method to help it in its setup tasks. A *parameterless constructor* takes no parameters, so it's somewhat limited in what it can do.

 Parameterless constructors are also sometimes called empty constructors.

When you first create a class, C# defines a parameterless constructor for it called the default constructor. If you create your own parameterless constructor, the default constructor is not created.

For example, suppose the `Manager` class has a `DirectReports` property, which is a list of `Employees` that report to a given manager. A parameterless constructor cannot build that list because it doesn't know what employees to put in it. It can, however, initialize the `DirectReports` to an empty list as shown in the following code:

```
class Manager : Person
{
    List<Employee> DirectReports;

    // Initialize the Manager.
    public Manager()
    {
        DirectReports = new List<Employee>();
    }
}
```

You implicitly invoke a parameterless constructor any time you create an object without using any parameters. For example, the following code creates a new `Person` object. When this code executes, control jumps briefly to the parameterless constructor so it can prepare the object for use.

```
Person Fred = new Person();
```

Note that C# creates a default public parameterless constructor for you if you make a class that doesn't define any constructors explicitly. If you do give the class *any* constructors, however, C# doesn't create the default constructor. In that case, if you want a parameterless constructor, you must make it yourself.

Parameterized Constructors

Parameterless constructors are useful but fairly limited because they don't have much information to go by. To give a constructor more information, you can make it take parameters just like you can with any other method.

One simple type of parameterized constructor uses its parameters to initialize properties. For example, you could make a constructor for the `Person` class that takes the person's first and last names as parameters. The constructor could then set the object's `FirstName` and `LastName` properties.

Why would you bother doing this when you could use an initializer? First, the syntax for using a constructor is slightly more concise than initializer syntax. The following code uses a constructor that takes eight parameters to initialize an `Employee`'s properties:

```
Employee bob = new Employee("Bob", "Baker", "200 Beach Blvd",
    "Bugsville", "CO", "82010", 1002, "B-2");
```

Compare this code to the earlier snippet that used initializers. This version is more concise, although it's less self-documenting because it doesn't explicitly list the property names.

The second reason you might prefer to use a parameterized constructor instead of an initializer is that a constructor can perform all sorts of checks that an initializer cannot. For example, a constructor can validate its parameters against each other or against a database. An `Employee` class's constructor could take an employee ID as a parameter and check in a database to verify that the employee really exists.

A constructor can also require that certain parameters be provided. For example, a `Person` constructor could require that the first and last name parameters be provided. If you rely on initializers, the program could create a `Person` that has no first or last name.

To make a constructor that takes parameters, simply add the parameters as you would for any other method. The following code shows a constructor for the Person class that uses its parameters to initialize the new Person object's properties:

```
// Make an Employee named Cindy.
Person cindy = new Person("Cindy", "Carstairs",
    "1750 Cedar Ct", "Bugsville", "CO", "82010");
```

DESTRUCTORS

Constructors execute when a new object is created to perform initialization chores. Destructors execute when an object is being destroyed to perform cleanup chores. For example, a destructor might close database connections, close files, free memory, and do whatever else is necessary before the object gets carted off to the electronic recycle center.

Destructors are simpler than constructors because:

➤ A class can have only one destructor.

➤ You cannot call a destructor directly; they are only called automatically.

➤ A destructor cannot invoke another destructor.

➤ Destructors cannot take parameters.

The following code shows a simple destructor for the Person class:

```
~Person()
{
    // Perform cleanup chores here...
}
```

Destructors are a fairly specialized topic and you are unlikely to need to build one until you have more experience programming, but I wanted to describe them for an important reason: so you know when destructors execute and you can help them perform well.

You might think that so far destructors are fairly simple and that would be the end of the story except for one remaining question: "When are destructors called?" This turns out to be a trickier question than you might imagine. To understand when a destructor runs, you need to understand the garbage collector.

Normally a C# program runs merrily along, creating variables and objects as needed. Sometimes all of the references to an object disappear so the program no longer has access to the object. In that case, the memory (and any other resources) used by that object are lost to the program.

If the program makes a lot of objects and then discards them in this way, the program will eventually use up a lot of memory.

Eventually the program may start to run out of memory. At that point, the garbage collector springs into action. The *garbage collector* runs when it thinks the program may have used a lot of inaccessible memory such as these Employee objects. When the garbage collector runs, it reclaims the memory wasted by objects that are inaccessible and makes that memory available for future objects.

It is only when the garbage collector reclaims an object's memory that the object's destructors execute. So the answer to the question "When are destructors called?" is: "Whenever the garbage collector runs." So when does the garbage collector run? The answer to this new question is: "Whenever it feels like it."

The end result is that you cannot really know when a destructor will run. The fancy name for this is *non-deterministic finalization*. Many programs never run low on memory so the garbage collector doesn't run until the program ends.

The moral of the story is that you can use destructors to clean up after an object but you shouldn't rely on them to handle tasks that must be done in a timely fashion. For example, if a destructor closes a file so other programs can use it, the file may not actually be closed until the program ends.

If you want to perform actions such as this in a timely fashion, give the class a CleanUp or Dispose function that the program can call explicitly to take care of business.

 The IDisposable *interface formalizes the notion of providing a* Dispose *method that cleans up an object. It's a fairly advanced topic, however, so it isn't covered here. For more information, see* msdn.microsoft.com/en-us/library/ b1yfkh5e%28VS.71%29.aspx *and* msdn.microsoft.com/en-us/library/system .idisposable.aspx.

If an object does provide a Dispose method, you should probably use it when you are done with the object. To prevent you from forgetting to call Dispose, C# provides the using statement.

The using statement is followed by the object that it manages and, when the using block ends, the program automatically calls the object's Dispose method.

The usual syntax for a using block is:

```
using (variableInitialization)
{
    ... Statements ...
}
```

In this syntax, the *variableInitialization* declares and initializes the variable that the block controls. (You can declare the object outside of the using block but putting it inside the block usually makes it easier to read and restricts its scope to the block.)

For example, the Graphics class uses system resources that should be released when you're done with a Graphics object so it provides a Dispose method. The following code creates a Graphics object named gr associated with the bitmap bigBitmap. The using block ensures that the program executes the gr object's Dispose method when it finishes the block.

```
using (Graphics gr = Graphics.FromImage(bigBitmap))
{
    // Draw stuff...
}
```

Note that the object's `Dispose` method is called even if the program exits from the block due to an exception.

INVOKING OTHER CONSTRUCTORS

You can give a class many different constructors as long as they have different parameter lists (so C# can tell them apart). For example, you might give the `Person` class a parameterless constructor; a second constructor that takes first name and last name as parameters; and a third constructor that takes first and last name, street, city, state, and ZIP Code as parameters.

Often when you give a class multiple constructors, some of them perform the same actions. In the `Person` example, the constructor that initializes first name, last name, street, city, state, and ZIP Code probably does the same things that the second constructor does to initialize just first and last name (plus more).

You can also find overlapping constructor functionality when one class inherits from another. For example, suppose the `Person` class has `FirstName` and `LastName` properties. The `Employee` class inherits from `Person` and adds some other properties such as `EmployeeId` and `MailStop`. The `Person` class's constructor initializes the `FirstName` and `LastName` properties, something that the `Employee` class's constructors should also do.

Having several methods perform the same tasks makes debugging and maintaining code harder. Fortunately, C# provides a way you can make one constructor invoke another.

To make a constructor invoke another in the same class, follow the constructor's parameter declarations with a colon and the keyword `this`, passing `this` any parameters that the other constructor should receive. For example, the following code shows three constructors for the `Person` class that invoke each other with the code that invokes other constructors is shown in bold:

```
// Parameterless constructor.
public Person()
{
    // General initialization if needed ...
}

// Initialize first and last name.
public Person(string firstName, string lastName)
    : this()
{
    FirstName = firstName;
    LastName = lastName;
}

// Initialize all values.
public Person(string firstName, string lastName, string street,
    string city, string state, string zip)
    : this(firstName, lastName)
{
    FirstName = firstName;
    LastName = lastName;
    Street = street;
```

```
        City = city;
        State = state;
        Zip = zip;
    }
```

The first constructor is a parameterless constructor. In this example it doesn't do anything.

The second constructor takes first and last names as parameters. The ": `this()`" at the end of the declaration means the constructor should invoke the parameterless constructor when it starts.

The third constructor takes name and address parameters. Its declaration ends with ": `this(firstName, lastName)`" to indicate that the constructor should begin by calling the second constructor, passing it the `firstName` and `lastName` parameters. (That constructor in turn invokes the parameterless constructor.)

You can use a similar syntax to invoke a parent class constructor by simply replacing the keyword `this` with the keyword `base`.

For example, the `Employee` class inherits from the `Person` class. The following code shows two of the class's constructors:

```
// Parameterless constructor.
public Employee()
    : base()
{
}

// Initialize first and last name.
public Employee(string firstName, string lastName)
    : base(firstName, lastName)
{
}
```

The first constructor is parameterless. It invokes its parent class's parameterless constructor by using ": `base()`."

The second constructor takes first and last name parameters and invokes the `Person` class's constructor that takes two strings as parameters.

Notice how the constructors invoke other constructors by using the keyword `this` *or* `base` *followed by a parameter list. C# uses the parameter list to decide which constructor to invoke. That's why you cannot have more than one constructor with the same kinds of parameters. For example, if two constructors took a single* `string` *as a parameter, how would C# know which one to use?*

TRY IT

In this Try It, you enhance the `Person`, `Employee`, and `Manager` classes you built in one of the Lesson 23 Try Its. You add constructors to make initializing objects easier and you add destructors so you can trace object destruction when the program ends.

> *You can download the code and resources for this Try It from the book's web page at* www.wrox.com *or* www.CSharpHelper.com/24hour.html. *You can find the files in the Lesson24 folder.*

Lesson Requirements

➤ Copy the program you built in the third Try It in Lesson 23 (or download the TryIt23c program from the book's web site).

➤ Give the `Person` class a parameterless constructor. Make it print a message to the Console window indicating that a new `Person` is being created.

➤ Give the `Person` class a constructor that initializes all of the class's properties. Make it invoke the parameterless constructor and display its own message.

➤ Give the `Person` class a destructor that displays a message in the Console window.

➤ Make similar constructors and destructors for the `Employee` and `Manager` classes.

➤ Remove the buttons from the main form and make the program create `Person`, `Employee`, and `Manager` objects using each of the constructors.

➤ Run the program, close it, and examine the Console window messages to see if they make sense.

Hints

➤ Make the constructors invoke each other where possible to avoid duplicate work.

➤ When you use parameterless constructors, use object initialization to set the objects' properties.

Step-by-Step

➤ Copy the program you built in the third Try It in Lesson 23 (or download the TrytIt23c program from the book's web site).

   1. This is relatively straightforward.

➤ Give the `Person` class a parameterless constructor. Make it print a message to the Console window indicating that a new `Person` is being created.

1. The `Person` class's parameterless constructor should look something like this:

```
public Person()
{
    Console.WriteLine("Person()");
}
```

➤ Give the `Person` class a constructor that initializes all of the class's properties. Make it invoke the parameterless constructor and display its own message.

1. This constructor should look something like this:

```
public Person(string firstName, string lastName,
    string street, string city, string state, string zip)
    : this()
{
    FirstName = firstName;
    LastName = lastName;
    Street = street;
    City = city;
    State = state;
    Zip = zip;
    Console.WriteLine("Person(parameters)");
}
```

➤ Give the `Person` class a destructor that displays a message in the Console window.

1. This destructor should look something like this:

```
~Person()
{
    Console.WriteLine("~Person");
}
```

➤ Make similar constructors and destructors for the `Employee` and `Manager` classes.

1. The following code shows the `Employee` class's constructors and destructor:

```
public Employee()
    : base()
{
    Console.WriteLine("Employee()");
}

public Employee(int employeeId, string mailStop,
    string firstName, string lastName, string street,
    string city, string state, string zip)
    : base(firstName, lastName, street, city, state, zip)
{
    EmployeeId = employeeId;
    MailStop = mailStop;
    Console.WriteLine("Employee(parameters)");
}
```

```
~Employee()
{
    Console.WriteLine("~Employee");
}
```

2. The following code shows the `Manager` class's constructors and destructor:

```
public Manager()
    : base()
{
    DirectReports = new List<Employee>();
    Console.WriteLine("Manager()");
}

public Manager(string departmentName, int employeeId,
    string mailStop, string firstName, string lastName,
    string street, string city, string state, string zip)
    : base(employeeId, mailStop, firstName, lastName, street,
    city, state, zip)
{
    DepartmentName = departmentName;
    Console.WriteLine("Manager(parameters)");
}

~Manager()
{
    Console.WriteLine("~Manager");
}
```

➤ Remove the buttons from the main form and make the main program create `Person`, `Employee`, and `Manager` objects using each of the constructors.

1. The following code creates objects in this way:

```
// Make the people.
private void Form1_Load(object sender, EventArgs e)
{
    // Persons.
    Console.WriteLine("Creating Paula");
    Person paula = new Person()
    {
        FirstName = "Paula",
        LastName = "Perch",
        Street = "100 Ash Ave",
        City = "Bugsville",
        State = "CO",
        Zip = "82010",
    };

    Console.WriteLine("Creating Pete");
    Person pete = new Person("Pete", "Pearson",
        "2871 Arc St", "Bugsville ", "CO", "82010");

    // Employees.
    Console.WriteLine("Creating Edna");
    Employee edna = new Employee()
```

```
        {
            FirstName = "Edna",
            LastName = "Evers",
            Street = "200 Beach Blvd",
            City = "Bugsville",
            State = "CO",
            Zip = "82010",
            EmployeeId = 1002,
            MailStop = "B-2",
        };

        Console.WriteLine("Creating Edward");
        Employee edward = new Employee(1002, "B-2", "Edward",
            "Evers", "129 Bold Blvd", "Bugsville", "CO", "82010");

        // Managers.
        Console.WriteLine("Creating Mindy");
        Manager mindy = new Manager()
        {
            DepartmentName = "Research",
            EmployeeId = 1001,
            MailStop = "MS-10",
            FirstName = "Mindy",
            LastName = "Marvel",
            Street = "2981 East Westlake Blvd",
            City = "Bugsville",
            State = "CO",
            Zip = "82010",
        };

        Console.WriteLine("Creating Mike");
        Manager mike = new Manager("Development", 1002, "MS-20",
            "Mike", "Masco", "1298 Elm St", "Bugsville", "CO", "82010");
    }
```

➤ Run the program, close it, and examine the Console window messages to see if they make sense.

   1. The following text shows the program's output. You can see which constructors and destructors were executed for each object.

```
Creating Paula
Person()
Creating Pete
Person()
Person(parameters)
Creating Edna
Person()
Employee()
Creating Edward
Person()
Person(parameters)
Employee(parameters)
Creating Mindy
```

```
Person()
Employee()
Manager()
Creating Mike
Person()
Person(parameters)
Employee(parameters)
Manager(parameters)
~Manager
~Employee
~Person
~Manager
~Employee
~Person
~Employee
~Person
~Employee
~Person
~Person
~Person
```

Please select Lesson 24 on the DVD to view the video that accompanies this lesson.

EXERCISES

1. Copy the program you built in Lesson 23, Exercise 1 (or download Lesson 23's version from the book's web site). Change the main program so it uses initializers to prepare its `ComplexNumber` objects. Be sure to update new instances created inside the `ComplexNumber` class.

2. Copy the program you built for Exercise 1. Give the `ComplexNumber` class a constructor that initializes the new number's real and imaginary parts. Modify the program as needed to use this constructor.

3. Copy the program you built for Lesson 23's second Try It (or download the TryIt23b program from the book's web site). Give the `BankAccount` class a constructor that guarantees that you cannot create an instance with an initial balance under $10. Change the main program so it uses this constructor.

You can download the solutions to these exercises from the book's web page at www.wrox.com or www.CSharpHelper.com/24hour.html. You can find the solutions in the Lesson24 folder of the download.

25

Fine-Tuning Classes

In Lesson 24 you learned how to build constructors and destructors, special methods that execute when an object is created or destroyed. In this lesson you learn about other special methods you can give a class. You learn how to overload and override class methods.

OVERLOADING METHODS

Lesson 24 mentioned that you can give a class any number of constructors as long as they have different parameter lists. For example, it's common to give a class a parameterless constructor that takes no parameters and one or more other constructors that take parameters.

Making multiple methods with the same name but different parameter lists is called *overloading*. C# uses the parameter list to decide which version to use when you invoke the method.

For example, suppose you're building a course assignment application and you have built `Student`, `Course`, and `Instructor` classes. You could give the `Student` class two versions of the `Enroll` method, one that takes as a parameter the name of the class in which the student should be enrolled and a second that takes a `Course` object as a parameter.

You could give the `Instructor` class similar versions of the `Teach` method to make the instructor teach a class by name or `Course` object.

Finally, you could give the `Course` class different `Report` methods that:

➤ Display a report in a dialog if there are no parameters

➤ Append a report to the end of a file if the method receives a `FileStream` as a parameter

➤ Save the report into a new file if the method receives a `string` (the file name) as a parameter

Making overloaded methods is so easy that there's little else to say. Just remember to give each version of the method different kinds of parameters.

OVERRIDING METHODS

When a class inherits from another you can add new properties, methods, and events to the new class to give it new features that were not provided by the parent class.

Once in a while it's also useful to replace a method provided by the parent class with a new version. This is called *overriding* the parent's method.

Before you can override a method, you should mark the method in the parent class with the `virtual` keyword so it allows itself to be overridden. Next add the keyword `override` to the derived class's version of the method to indicate that it overrides the parent class's version.

For example, suppose the `Person` class defines the usual assortment of properties: `FirstName`, `LastName`, `Street`, `City`, and so on. Suppose it also provides the following `GetAddress` function that returns the `Person`'s name and address formatted for printing on an envelope:

```
// Return the Person's address.
public virtual string GetAddress()
{
    return FirstName + " " + LastName + "\n" +
        Street + "\n" + City + "    " + State + "    " + Zip;
}
```

Now suppose you derive the `Employee` class from `Person`. An `Employee`'s address looks just like a `Person`'s except it also includes `MailStop`. The `MailStop` property was added by the `Employee` class to indicate where to deliver mail within the company.

The following code shows how the `Employee` class can override the `GetAddress` function to return an `Employee`-style address:

```
// Return the Employee's address.
public override string GetAddress()
{
    return base.GetAddress() + "\n" + MailStop;
}
```

Notice how the function calls the base class's version of `GetAddress` to reuse that version of the function and avoid duplicated work.

IntelliSense can help you build overridden methods. For example, when you type "public override" and a space in the `Employee` *class, IntelliSense lists the virtual methods that you might be trying to override. If you select one, IntelliSense fills in a default implementation for the new method. The following code shows the code IntelliSense generated for the* `GetAddress` *function:*

```
public override string GetAddress()
{
    return base.GetAddress();
}
```

The most miraculous thing about overriding a virtual method is that the object uses the method even if you invoke it from the base class. For example, suppose you have a `Person` variable pointing to an `Employee` object. Remember that an `Employee` is a kind of `Person` so a `Person` variable can refer to an `Employee` as in the following code:

```
Employee bob = new Employee();
Person bobAsAPerson = bob;
```

Now if the code calls `bobAsAPerson.GetAddress()`, the result is the `Employee` version of `GetAddress`.

You can think of the `virtual` *keyword as making a slot in the base class for the method. When you override the method, the derived class fills this slot with a new version of the method. Now even if you call the method from the base class, it uses whatever is in the slot.*

Overriding a class's `ToString` function is particularly useful. All classes inherit a `ToString` method from `System.Object`, the ultimate ancestor of all other classes, but the default implementation of `ToString` isn't always useful. By default, for classes that you defined such as `Person` and `Employee`, `ToString` returns the class's name.

For example, in the ListPeople program the `Employee` class's `ToString` function returns "ListPeople. Employee." Though this correctly reports the object's class, it might be nice if it returned something that contained information about the object's properties. In this example, it might be nice if it returned the `Employee` object's first and last names.

The following code shows how you can override the `ToString` function to return an `Employee`'s first and last name:

```
// Return first and last name.
public override string ToString()
{
    return FirstName + " " + LastName;
}
```

This makes more sense. Now your program can use an `Employee` object's `ToString` method to learn about the object.

Overriding `ToString` also has a nice side benefit for Windows Forms development. Certain controls and parts of Visual Studio use an object's `ToString` method to decide what to display. For example, the `ListBox` and `ComboBox` controls display lists of items. If those items are not simple strings, the controls use the items' `ToString` methods to generate output.

If the list is full of `Employee` objects and you've overridden the `Employee` class's `ToString` method, then a `ListBox` or `ComboBox` can display the employees' names.

FIGURE 25-1

The ListPeople example program shown in Figure 25-1 (and available as part of this lesson's code download) demonstrates method overriding.

When it starts, the ListPeople program uses the following code to fill its `ListBox` with two `Student` objects and two `Employee` objects. Both of these classes inherit from `Person`.

```
private void Form1_Load(object sender, EventArgs e)
{
    // Make some people.
    peopleListBox.Items.Add(new Student("Ann", "Archer", "101 Ash Ave",
        "Debugger", "NV", "72837"));
    peopleListBox.Items.Add(new Student("Bob", "Best", "222 Beach Blvd",
        "Debugger", "NV", "72837"));
    peopleListBox.Items.Add(new Employee("Cat", "Carter", "300 Cedar Ct",
        "Debugger", "NV", "72837", "MS-1"));
    peopleListBox.Items.Add(new Employee("Dan", "Dental", "404 Date Dr",
        "Debugger", "NV", "72837", "MS-2"));
}
```

The `Employee` class overrides its `ToString` method so you can see the `Employees`' names in Figure 25-1 instead of their class names. The `Student` class does not override its `ToString` method so Figure 25-1 shows class names for the `Student` objects.

If you select a person in this program and click the Show Address button, the program executes the following code:

```
// Display the selected Person's address.
private void showAddressButton_Click(object sender, EventArgs e)
{
    Person person = (Person)peopleListBox.SelectedItem;
    if (person != null) MessageBox.Show(person.GetAddress());
}
```

This code casts the `ListBox`'s selected item into a `Person` object. The item is actually either a `Student` or an `Employee` but those both of those inherit from `Person` (they are kinds of `Person`) so the program can treat them as `Persons`.

If the `Person` is not `null`, then something was selected. The program calls the object's `GetAddress` function and displays the result. If the object was actually a `Student`, the result is a basic name and address. If the object was actually an `Employee`, the result is a name and address plus mailstop.

In addition to `ListBoxes` and `ComboBoxes`, some parts of Visual Studio use an object's `ToString` method, too. For example, if you stop an executing program and hover the mouse over an object in the debugger, a tooltip appears that displays the results of the object's `ToString` function. Similarly if you type an object's name in the Immediate window and press [Enter], the result is whatever is returned by the object's `ToString` method.

TRY IT

In this Try It, you build a simple drawing application. You build a Shape class to represent a drawn shape and then derive the ShapeRectangle and ShapeEllipse classes from that one.

You give the Shape class a virtual Draw method that takes as a parameter a Graphics object and draws the shape on the object. The Shape class's version of Draw simply draws a rectangle with a big X in it.

You make the ShapeRectangle and ShapeEllipse classes override Draw to produce their own shapes.

Finally, you add overloaded versions of Draw that take pen and brush objects as parameters to use when drawing.

> *You can download the code and resources for this Try It from the book's web page at* www.wrox.com *or* www.CSharpHelper.com/24hour.html. *You can find the programs in the Lesson25 folder.*

Lesson Requirements

➤ Start a new program and create the Shape class.

    ➤ Give the class a using System.Drawing directive.

    ➤ Give the class a property named Bounds of type Rectangle. A Rectangle has properties X, Y, Width, and Height.

    ➤ Make a constructor that takes x, y, width, and height parameters and uses them to initialize the Bounds property.

    ➤ Make a virtual Draw method that takes three parameters of type Graphics, Pen, and Brush. Make this method draw a box with an X in it on the Graphics object using the Pen and Brush.

    ➤ Make a virtual overloaded Draw method that takes only a Graphics object as a parameter. Make it invoke the other Draw method, passing it the pen and brush Pens.Red and Brushes.Transparent.

➤ Derive the ShapeRectangle class from the Shape class.

    ➤ Make a constructor that takes x, y, width, and height parameters and invokes the base class's constructor.

    ➤ Override the Shape class's version of the Draw method that takes four parameters so it draws a rectangle.

    ➤ Override the second Draw method so it calls the first, passing it the pen and brush Pens.Black and Brushes.Transparent.

➤ Repeat the previous steps for the ShapeEllipse class.

➤ In the main form, create a List<Shape>.

➤ In the form's `Load` event handler, create some `ShapeRectangles` and `ShapeEllipses` and add them to the list.

➤ Give the form a `CheckBox` labeled Colored. In its `CheckedChanged` event handler, invalidate the form to force a redraw.

➤ In the form's `Paint` event handler, redraw the form by looping through the `Shapes` in the list. If the `CheckBox` is checked, invoke the `Shape` objects' `Draw` method, passing it the pen and brush `Pens.Blue` and `Brushes.LightBlue`. If the `CheckBox` is not checked, invoke the `Draw` method with no parameters.

Hints

If `gr` is the `Graphics` object, then you can use these methods to draw:

➤ `gr.Clear(this.BackColor)` — Clears the object with the form's background color.

➤ `gr.FillRectangle(brush, rect)` — Fills a rectangle defined by the `Rectangle` *rect* with *brush*.

➤ `gr.DrawRectangle(pen, rect)` — Outlines a rectangle defined by the `Rectangle` *rect* with *pen*.

➤ `gr.FillEllipse(brush, rect)` — Fills an ellipse defined by the `Rectangle` *rect* with *brush*.

➤ `gr.DrawEllipse(pen, rect)` — Outlines an ellipse defined by the `Rectangle` *rect* with *pen*.

In the `Paint` event handler, draw on the `Graphics` object provided by the event handler's `e.Graphics` parameter.

Step-by-Step

➤ Start a new program and create the `Shape` class.

➤ Give the class a using `System.Drawing` directive.

1. Simply place the `using` directive at the top of the file.

➤ Give the class a property named `Bounds` of type `Rectangle`. A `Rectangle` has properties X, Y, `Width`, and `Height`.

1. Use code similar to the following:

```
public Rectangle Bounds { get; set; }
```

➤ Make a constructor that takes x, y, `width`, and `height` parameters and uses them to initialize the `Bounds` property.

1. Use code similar to the following:

```
public Shape(int x, int y, int width, int height)
{
    Bounds = new Rectangle(x, y, width, height);
}
```

➤   Make a virtual Draw method that takes three parameters of type Graphics, Pen, and Brush. Make this method draw a box with an X in it on the Graphics object using the Pen and Brush.

   1.   Use code similar to the following:

```
// Draw a box with an X in it using a pen and brush.
public virtual void Draw(Graphics gr, Pen pen, Brush brush)
{
    gr.FillRectangle(brush, Bounds);
    gr.DrawRectangle(pen, Bounds);
    gr.DrawLine(pen, Bounds.Left, Bounds.Top,
        Bounds.Right, Bounds.Bottom);
    gr.DrawLine(pen, Bounds.Right, Bounds.Top,
        Bounds.Left, Bounds.Bottom);
}
```

➤   Make a virtual overloaded Draw method that takes only a Graphics object as a parameter. Make it invoke the other Draw method, passing it the pen and brush Pens.Red and Brushes.Transparent.

   1.   Use code similar to the following:

```
// Draw a box with an X in it.
public virtual void Draw(Graphics gr)
{
    Draw(gr, Pens.Red, Brushes.Transparent);
}
```

➤   Derive the ShapeRectangle class from the Shape class.

   ➤   Make a constructor that takes x, y, width, and height parameters and invokes the base class's constructor.

     1.   Use code similar to the following:

```
public ShapeRectangle(int x, int y, int width, int height)
    : base(x, y, width, height)
{
}
```

   ➤   Override the Shape class's version of the Draw method that takes four parameters so it draws a rectangle.

     1.   Use code similar to the following:

```
public override void Draw(Graphics gr, Pen pen, Brush brush)
{
    gr.FillRectangle(brush, Bounds);
    gr.DrawRectangle(pen, Bounds);
}
```

   ➤   Override the second Draw method so it calls the first, passing it the pen and brush Pens.Black and Brushes.Transparent.

     1.   Use code similar to the following:

```
public override void Draw(Graphics gr)
{
    Draw(gr, Pens.Black, Brushes.Transparent);
}
```

➤ Repeat the previous steps for the `ShapeEllipse` class.

1. The following code shows the `ShapeEllipse` class's code:

```
class ShapeEllipse : Shape
{
    public ShapeEllipse(int x, int y, int width, int height)
        : base(x, y, width, height)
    {
    }

    public override void Draw(Graphics gr, Pen pen, Brush brush)
    {
        gr.FillEllipse(brush, Bounds);
        gr.DrawEllipse(pen, Bounds);
    }

    public override void Draw(Graphics gr)
    {
        Draw(gr, Pens.Black, Brushes.Transparent);
    }
}
```

➤ In the main form, create a `List<Shape>`.

1. Use code similar to the following:

```
// Our list of shapes to draw.
List<Shape> Shapes = new List<Shape>();
```

➤ In the form's `Load` event handler, create some `ShapeRectangles` and `ShapeEllipses` and add them to the list.

1. You can use code similar to the following, or you can create any `ShapeEllipse` and `ShapeRectangle` objects that you like:

```
// Make some shapes.
private void Form1_Load(object sender, EventArgs e)
{
    Shapes.Add(new ShapeEllipse(50, 50, 200, 200));
    Shapes.Add(new ShapeEllipse(100, 80, 40, 60));
    Shapes.Add(new ShapeEllipse(100, 80, 40, 60));
    Shapes.Add(new ShapeEllipse(120, 100, 20, 30));
    Shapes.Add(new ShapeEllipse(160, 80, 40, 60));
    Shapes.Add(new ShapeEllipse(180, 100, 20, 30));
    Shapes.Add(new ShapeEllipse(135, 130, 30, 50));
    Shapes.Add(new ShapeRectangle(120, 190, 60, 5));
    Shapes.Add(new ShapeRectangle(75, 25, 150, 50));
    Shapes.Add(new ShapeRectangle(50, 75, 200, 10));
}
```

➤ Give the form a `CheckBox`. In its `CheckedChanged` event handler, invalidate the form to force a redraw.

   1. The following code shows this event handler:

```
// Force a redraw.
private void coloredCheckBox_CheckedChanged(object sender, EventArgs e)
{
    this.Invalidate();
}
```

➤ In the form's `Paint` event handler, redraw the form by looping through the `Shapes` in the list. If the `CheckBox` is checked, invoke the `Shape` objects' `Draw` method, passing it the pen and brush `Pens.Blue` and `Brushes.LightBlue`. If the `CheckBox` is not checked, invoke the `Draw` method with no parameters.

   1. Use code similar to the following:

```
// Redraw the objects.
private void Form1_Paint(object sender, PaintEventArgs e)
{
    e.Graphics.Clear(this.BackColor);

    // Loop through all of the shapes.
    foreach (Shape shape in Shapes)
    {
        if (coloredCheckBox.Checked)
        {
            // Draw with a pen and brush.
            shape.Draw(e.Graphics, Pens.Blue, Brushes.LightBlue);
        }
        else
        {
            // Draw with no pen or brush.
            shape.Draw(e.Graphics);
        }
    }
}
```

Figure 25-2 shows the result for the objects I created. A more useful drawing program would save edge and fill colors in the objects so they could each have different colors.

FIGURE 25-2

Please select Lesson 25 on the DVD to view the video that accompanies this lesson.

EXERCISES

1. Copy the complex number program you built in Lesson 24, Exercise 2 (or download Lesson 24's version from the book's web site). Override the class's ToString method so it returns the number in a form similar to "2 + 3i." Overload the ComplexNumber class's AddTo, MultiplyBy, and SubtractFrom methods so you can pass them a single double parameter representing a real number with no imaginary part. Modify the form so you can test the new methods.

2. Copy the bank account program you built in Lesson 24, Exercise 3 (or download Lesson 24's version from the book's web site). Derive a new OverdraftAccount class from the Account class. Give it a constructor that simply invokes the base class's constructor. Override the Debit method to allow the account to have a negative balance and charge a $50 fee if any debit leaves the account with a negative balance. Change the main program so the Account variable is still declared to be of type Account but initialize it as an OverdraftAccount. (Hint: Don't forget to make the Account class's version of Debit virtual.)

3. Copy Lesson 23's Turtle program. The Turtle class has a Move method that moves the turtle a specified distance in the object's current direction. Overload this method by making a second version that takes as parameters the X and Y coordinates where the turtle should move. Be sure to raise the OutOfBounds event if the point is not on the canvas. (Hint: Can you reuse code somehow between the two Move methods?)

 You can download the solutions to these exercises from the book's web page at www.wrox.com *or* www.CSharpHelper.com/24hour.html. *You can find those solutions in the Lesson25 folder.*

26

Overloading Operators

In Lesson 25 you learned how to overload a class's methods. C# also lets you overload operators such as + and * to give them new meanings when working with the structures and classes that you create. For example, you could overload the + operator so the program would know how to add a Student object and a Course object. Sometimes that allows you to use a more natural syntax when you're working with objects.

In this lesson, you learn how to overload operators so you can use them to manipulate objects.

Before you jump into operator overloading, be warned that just because you can overload an operator doesn't mean you should. You should only overload operators in intuitive ways.

For example, it makes sense to overload the + operator so you can add two ComplexNumber objects. It might also make sense to overload + so you can add an item to a purchase order.

It probably doesn't make sense to define + between two Employee objects to return a list of projects that included both employees. You could do that but you probably shouldn't because it would be confusing.

OVERLOADABLE OPERATORS

In C#, you can overload unary, binary, and logical operators. Table 26-1 summarizes the operators that you can overload.

TABLE 26-1

TYPE	OPERATORS
Unary	+, -, !, ~, ++, --
Binary	+, -, *, /, %, &, |, ^, <<, >>
Comparison	==, !=, <, >, <=, >=

The comparison operators come in pairs. For example, if you overload the < operator then you must also overload the > operator.

The compound assignment operators (+=, -=, *=, /=, %=, &=, |=, ^=, <<=, and >>=) are automatically overloaded when you overload the corresponding binary operator. For example, if you overload *, then C# automatically overloads *=.

The syntax for overloading operators is easiest to understand by looking at examples. The following sections explain how to overload the different types of operators.

UNARY OPERATORS

The following code shows how you can overload the unary - operator for the ComplexNumber class:

```
public static ComplexNumber operator -(ComplexNumber me)
{
    return new ComplexNumber(-me.Real, -me.Imaginary);
}
```

The method begins with public static followed by the operator's return type. In this case the operator returns a ComplexNumber because the negation of a complex number is another complex number.

Next comes the keyword operator and the operator's symbol, in this case -.

The parameter list tells on which class the operator should be defined. Because this code is defining an operator for the ComplexNumber class, that's the parameter's data type.

I often name this parameter me to help me remember that this is the object to which the operator is being applied.

Note that the overload must be declared inside the class used by the parameter. In this case, because the parameter is a ComplexNumber, this code must be in the ComplexNumber class.

The code inside this method simply negates the ComplexNumber's real and imaginary parts and returns a new ComplexNumber.

The following code shows how a program might use this operator:

```
ComplexNumber a = new ComplexNumber(1, 2);        //  1 + 2i
ComplexNumber minusA = -a;                        // -1 - 2i
```

BINARY OPERATORS

Overloading binary operators is similar to overloading unary operators except the operator takes a second parameter. The first parameter is still the object to which the operator is being applied.

For example, the following code overloads the binary - operator to add two ComplexNumbers:

```
public static ComplexNumber operator -(ComplexNumber me, ComplexNumber other)
{
    return new ComplexNumber(me.Real - other.Real,
        me.Imaginary - other.Imaginary);
}
```

The first parameter gives the object on the left of the – sign and the second parameter gives the object on the right. To help keep them straight, I often name the parameters me and other.

Note that the overload must be declared inside a class or structure used by one of the parameters. In this case, because both parameters are ComplexNumbers, this code must be in the ComplexNumber class.

While this example subtracts two ComplexNumbers, the parameters do not need to have the same data types. The following code defines the binary – operator for subtracting a double from a ComplexNumber:

```
public static ComplexNumber operator -(ComplexNumber me, double x)
{
    return new ComplexNumber(me.Real - x, me.Imaginary);
}
```

Note that this is not the same as subtracting a ComplexNumber from a double. If you want to handle that situation as well, you need the following separate overload:

```
public static ComplexNumber operator -(double me, ComplexNumber other)
{
    return new ComplexNumber(me - other.Real, other.Imaginary);
}
```

With these overloads, a program could execute the following code:

```
ComplexNumber a = new ComplexNumber(2, 3);
ComplexNumber b = new ComplexNumber(4, 5);
ComplexNumber c = a - b;                    // ComplexNumber - ComplexNumber

ComplexNumber d = a - 10;                   // ComplexNumber - double
ComplexNumber e = 10 - a;                   // double - ComplexNumber
```

 The shift operators << and >> are a little different from the other binary operators because the second parameter must always be an integer.

COMPARISON OPERATORS

The comparison operators are simply binary operators that return a Boolean result. The only oddity to these is that they come in pairs. For example, if you define ==, then you must also define !=. The pairs are == and !=, < and >, and <= and >=.

The following code shows how you could overload the < and > operators for the ComplexNumber class:

```
public static bool operator <(ComplexNumber me, ComplexNumber other)
{
    return (me.Magnitude() < other.Magnitude());
}

public static bool operator >(ComplexNumber me, ComplexNumber other)
{
    return (me.Magnitude() > other.Magnitude());
}
```

The Object *class provides* Equals *and* GetHashCode *methods that are tied closely to an object's notion of equality because* Equals *should return true if two objects are equal and* GetHashCode *should return the same value for two objects that are considered equal. To avoid confusion, you should not overload* == *and* != *unless you also override* Equals *and* GetHashCode. *In fact, Visual Studio flags an error if you overload* == *or* != *but not these two methods.*

TRY IT

In this Try It, you extend the ComplexNumber class you built in Lesson 25, Exercise 1. That version of the class included methods such as AddTo and SubtractFrom to perform simple operations. Now you'll replace those cumbersome methods with overloaded +, -, *, and unary - operators.

You can download the code and resources for this Try It from the book's web page at www.wrox.com *or* www.CSharpHelper.com/24hour.html. *You can find them in the Lesson26 folder of the download.*

Lesson Requirements

➤ Copy the ComplexNumber program you built for Lesson 25, Exercise 1 (or download Lesson 25's version from the book's web site). Remove the ComplexNumber class's AddTo, MultiplyBy, and SubtractFrom methods.

➤ Give the class new overloaded operators to handle these cases:

  ➤ ComplexNumber + ComplexNumber

  ➤ ComplexNumber + double

  ➤ double + ComplexNumber

  ➤ ComplexNumber * ComplexNumber

  ➤ ComplexNumber * double

  ➤ double * ComplexNumber

  ➤ -ComplexNumber

  ➤ ComplexNumber - ComplexNumber

  ➤ ComplexNumber - double

  ➤ double - ComplexNumber

➤ Revise the main form's code to use the new operators.

Hints

➤ You can use operators to define other operators. For example, if you define the unary - operator, then the following two operations have the same result:

```
ComplexNumber - ComplexNumber
ComplexNumber + -ComplexNumber
```

Step-by-Step

➤ Copy the ComplexNumber program you built for Lesson 25, Exercise 1 (or download Lesson 25's version from the book's web site). Remove the ComplexNumber class's AddTo, MultiplyBy, and SubtractFrom methods.

1. This is reasonably straightforward.

➤ Give the class new overloaded operators to handle these cases:

  ➤ ComplexNumber + ComplexNumber

  ➤ ComplexNumber + double

  ➤ double + ComplexNumber

  ➤ ComplexNumber * ComplexNumber

  ➤ ComplexNumber * double

  ➤ double * ComplexNumber

  ➤ -ComplexNumber

  ➤ ComplexNumber - ComplexNumber

➤ ComplexNumber - double

➤ double - ComplexNumber

1. You can use code similar to the following:

```
// ComplexNumber + ComplexNumber.
public static ComplexNumber operator +(ComplexNumber me, ComplexNumber other)
{
    return new ComplexNumber(
        me.Real + other.Real,
        me.Imaginary + other.Imaginary);
}

// ComplexNumber + double.
public static ComplexNumber operator +(ComplexNumber me, double x)
{
    return new ComplexNumber(me.Real + x, me.Imaginary);
}

// double + ComplexNumber.
public static ComplexNumber operator +(double x, ComplexNumber other)
{
    return other + x;
}

// ComplexNumber * ComplexNumber.
public static ComplexNumber operator *(ComplexNumber me, ComplexNumber other)
{
    return new ComplexNumber(
        me.Real * other.Real - me.Imaginary * other.Imaginary,
        me.Real * other.Imaginary + me.Imaginary * other.Real);
}

// ComplexNumber * double.
public static ComplexNumber operator *(ComplexNumber me, double x)
{
    return new ComplexNumber(me.Real * x, me.Imaginary * x);
}

// double * ComplexNumber.
public static ComplexNumber operator *(double x, ComplexNumber other)
{
    return other * x;
}

// Unary -.
public static ComplexNumber operator -(ComplexNumber me)
{
    return new ComplexNumber(-me.Real, -me.Imaginary);
}
```

```
// ComplexNumber - ComplexNumber.
public static ComplexNumber operator -(ComplexNumber me, ComplexNumber other)
{
    return me + -other;
}

// ComplexNumber - double.
public static ComplexNumber operator -(ComplexNumber me, double x)
{
    return new ComplexNumber(me.Real - x, me.Imaginary);
}

// double - ComplexNumber.
public static ComplexNumber operator -(double x, ComplexNumber other)
{
    return -other + x;
}
```

➤ Revise the main form's code to use the new operators.

1. You can use code similar to the following:

```
// Perform the calculations between two ComplexNumbers.
private void calculateButton_Click(object sender, EventArgs e)
{
    ComplexNumber a = new ComplexNumber(
        double.Parse(real1TextBox.Text),
        double.Parse(imaginary1TextBox.Text));
    ComplexNumber b = new ComplexNumber(
        double.Parse(real2TextBox.Text),
        double.Parse(imaginary2TextBox.Text));

    ComplexNumber aPlusB = a + b;
    aPlusBTextBox.Text = aPlusB.ToString();

    ComplexNumber aMinusB = a - b;
    aMinusBTextBox.Text = aMinusB.ToString();

    ComplexNumber aTimesB = a * b;
    aTimesBTextBox.Text = aTimesB.ToString();
}

// Perform the calculations with a real number.
private void calculateRealOnlyButton_Click(
    object sender, EventArgs e)
{
    double x = double.Parse(realOnlyTextBox.Text);
    ComplexNumber b = new ComplexNumber(
        double.Parse(real2TextBox.Text),
        double.Parse(imaginary2TextBox.Text));

    ComplexNumber xPlusB = x + b;
    aPlusBTextBox.Text = xPlusB.ToString();
```

```
ComplexNumber xMinusB = x - b;
aMinusBTextBox.Text = xMinusB.ToString();

ComplexNumber xTimesB = x * b;
aTimesBTextBox.Text = xTimesB.ToString();
}
```

 Please select Lesson 26 on the DVD to view the video that accompanies this lesson.

EXERCISES

1. Copy the complex number program you built in this lesson's Try It and overload the
    `ComplexNumber` class's / operator to perform division using this equation:

    $$\left(\frac{a+bi}{c+di}\right) = \left(\frac{ac+bd}{c^2+d^2}\right) + \left(\frac{bc-ad}{c^2+d^2}\right)i$$

    Use this operator to define operators for `ComplexNumber` / `double` and `double` /
    `ComplexNumber`. (Hint: Don't perform all of the calculations for these. Convert the `double`
    into a `ComplexNumber` and then use the previous definition of /.)

    Change the main program to calculate A / B. Verify these calculations:

    (10+11i) / (3+2i) = 4 + 1i
    (15+24i) / 3 = 5 + 8i
    4 / (1+1i) = 2 - 2i

 *You can download the solution to this exercise from the book's web page
at* www.wrox.com *or* www.CSharpHelper.com/24hour.html. *You can find the
solution in the Lesson26 folder.*

27

Using Interfaces

In .NET programming, an *interface* is like a contract. It defines the public properties, methods, and events that a class must provide to satisfy the contract. It doesn't indicate how the class must provide these features, however. That's left up to the class's code. It only defines an interface that the class must show to the rest of the world.

In this lesson, you learn how to implement interfaces that are predefined by .NET namespaces. You also learn how to define your own interfaces to make your code safer and more efficient.

INTERFACE ADVANTAGES

The following sections discuss two of the most important advantages provided by interfaces: multiple inheritance and code generalization.

Multiple Inheritance

Suppose you define a Vehicle class with properties such as NumberOfPassengers, MilesPerGallon, and NumberOfCupHolders. From this class you can derive other classes such as Car, PickupTruck, and Bicycle.

Suppose you also define a Domicile class that has properties such as SquareFeet, NumberOfBedrooms, and NumberOfBathrooms. From this class you can derive Apartment, Condo, and VacationHome.

Next you might like to derive the MotorHome class from both Vehicle and Domicile so it has the properties and methods of both parent classes. Unfortunately you can't do that in C#. In C# a class can inherit from only a single parent class.

Though a class can have only one parent, it can implement any number of interfaces. For example, if you turn the Domicile class into the IDomicile interface, the MotorHome class can inherit from Vehicle and implement IDomicile. The interface doesn't provide the code needed to implement such features as the HasAnnoyingNeighbor property, but at least it defines that property so code that uses a MotorHome object knows the property is available.

To make recognizing interface names easy, you should begin interface names with I *as in* IDomicile, IComparable, *and* IWhatever.

Defining the property but not implementing it may seem like no big deal, but it lets your code treat all IDomicile objects in a uniform way. Instead of writing separate functions to work with Duplex, RusticCabin, and HouseBoat objects, you can write a single function that manipulates objects that implement IDomicile.

That brings us to the second big advantage provided by interfaces: code generalization.

Code Generalization

Interfaces can make your code more general while still providing type checking. They let you treat objects that have common features as if they were of the interface type rather than their true individual types.

For example, suppose you write the following method that displays an array of strings in a ListBox:

```
private void DisplayValues(string[] items)
{
    itemsListBox.Items.Clear();
    foreach (string item in items)
    {
        itemsListBox.Items.Add(item);
    }
}
```

This function works reasonably well, but suppose you later decide that you need to display the items that are in a List<string> instead of an array. You could write a new version of the function that was nearly identical to this one but that works with a list instead of an array as in the following code:

```
private void DisplayValues(List<string> items)
{
    itemsListBox.Items.Clear();
    foreach (string item in items)
    {
        itemsListBox.Items.Add(item);
    }
}
```

If you compare these two functions you'll see that they are practically identical, so if you use them you must write, debug, and maintain two pieces of code that do almost exactly the same thing.

This is where interfaces can help.

Look again at the two functions. They differ only in their parameter definitions and the rest of their code is the same. The reason is that the functions don't really care that the parameters are arrays or lists. All they really care about is that you can use a foreach loop to iterate through them.

The IList<> interface requires that a class provide various list-like features such as Clear, Add, and RemoveAt methods. It also requires support for foreach.

This is a generic interface so you must provide a type parameter for it to indicate the type of items over which the interface can loop.

Both `string[]` and `List<string>` implement `IList<string>` so you can combine and generalize the functions by making their list parameter have the type `IList<string>` instead of `string[]` or `List<string>`.

The following code shows the new version of the method. This version can display the items in a `string[]`, `List<string>`, or any other object that implements `IList<string>`.

```
private void DisplayValues(IList<string> items)
{
    itemsListBox.Items.Clear();
    foreach (string item in items)
    {
        itemsListBox.Items.Add(item.ToString());
    }
}
```

IMPLEMENTING INTERFACES

To make a class that implements an interface, add the interface name in the class's declaration as if the class were inheriting from the interface. For example, the following code shows the declaration for a `Person` class that implements `IComparable`:

```
class Person : IComparable
{
    ...
}
```

You can include a class and multiple interfaces in the inheritance list. For example, the `Manager` class could inherit from `Person` and implement the interfaces `IComparable` and `IDisposable`.

The only other thing you need to do is implement the properties, methods, and events defined by the interface. The `IComparable` interface defines a `CompareTo` function that takes an object as a parameter and returns an integer that is less than, equal to, or greater than zero to indicate whether the object should be considered less than, equal to, or greater than the parameter.

For example, suppose the `Person` class defines `FirstName` and `LastName` properties. The following code implements a version of `CompareTo` that orders `Person` objects according to their last names first:

```
// Compare this Person to another Person.
public int CompareTo(object obj)
{
    // Make sure the object is a Person.
    if (!(obj is Person))
        throw new ArgumentOutOfRangeException("obj",
            "Argument to CompareTo is not a Person");

    // Convert the object into a Person.
    Person other = (Person)obj;
```

```
        // If our last name comes first, we come first.
        if (LastName.CompareTo(other.LastName) < 0) return -1;

        // If our last name comes second, we come second.
        if (LastName.CompareTo(other.LastName) > 0) return 1;

        // If our last names are the same, compare first names.
        return FirstName.CompareTo(other.FirstName);
    }
```

The method first checks whether its parameter is actually a `Person` and throws an exception if it is really something else. Next it casts its parameter from a non-specific `object` into a `Person`, and compares the current object's `LastName` to that of the parameter `Person`. If the current object's `LastName` comes alphabetically before the other object's `LastName`, the function returns –1. If the current object's `LastName` comes alphabetically after the other object's `LastName`, the function returns 1.

If the two objects' `LastNames` are the same, the function compares their `FirstNames` similarly and returns the result.

The easiest way to implement an interface is to let Visual Studio build a default implementation for you. Click on the interface in the class declaration and look for the change suggestion bar to appear. You can see it under the "I" in `IComparable` in Figure 27-1.

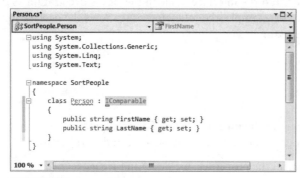

FIGURE 27-1

Move the mouse over this bar and wait until a small icon arrow with a dropdown arrow appears. Click the arrow and select the Implement Interface command, as shown in Figure 27-2.

FIGURE 27-2

When you select that command, Visual Studio adds placeholder code to satisfy the interface. The following code shows the placeholder method for the ICompare interface.

```
public int CompareTo(object obj)
{
    throw new NotImplementedException();
}
```

Now you can fill in the code you want to use.

There are several ways you can learn more about what an interface is for and what it does. You can always search the online help. You can also right-click on the interface's name and select Go To Definition to see information as shown in Figure 27-3. Click the plus signs on the left to view detailed comments describing the purposes of the pieces of code.

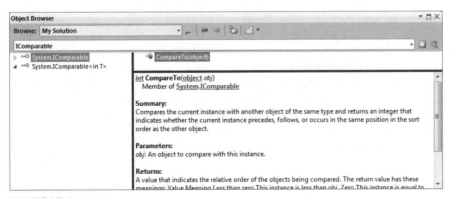

```
IComparable [from metadata]

System.IComparable                                           CompareTo(object obj)

    Assembly mscorlib.dll, v4.0.30128

    using System.Runtime.InteropServices;

    namespace System
    {
        // Summary:
        //     Defines a generalized type-specific comparison method that a value type or
        //     class implements to order or sort its instances.
        [ComVisible(true)]
        public interface IComparable
        {
            ...int CompareTo(object obj);
        }
    }

100 %
```

FIGURE 27-3

Finally you can open the Object Browser (use the View menu's Object Browser command) and search for the interface's name. Select the interface in the browser's left panel. Click an item in the right panel for more details, as shown in Figure 27-4.

```
Object Browser

Browse: My Solution

IComparable

  System.IComparable                    CompareTo(object)
  System.IComparable<in T>
                                        int CompareTo(object obj)
                                            Member of System.IComparable

                                        Summary:
                                        Compares the current instance with another object of the same type and returns an integer that
                                        indicates whether the current instance precedes, follows, or occurs in the same position in the sort
                                        order as the other object.

                                        Parameters:
                                        obj: An object to compare with this instance.

                                        Returns:
                                        A value that indicates the relative order of the objects being compared. The return value has these
                                        meanings: Value Meaning Less than zero This instance is less than obi. Zero This instance is equal to
```

FIGURE 27-4

[handwritten notes:] Define Interface / F-Pairable / Define method as / 'int idFromName (F-Pairable) / List<IPairable> / for each (F-Pairable) / pin List / 4

DEFINING INTERFACES

The preceding sections give examples that implement predefined interfaces. This section explains how you can define your own.

Defining an interface is a lot like defining a class with two main differences:

➤ First, you use the keyword `interface` instead of `class` in the declaration.

➤ Second, you don't provide any code for the properties, methods, and events that you declare in the interface.

The following code shows a simple `IDrawable` interface. The code includes a `using System.Graphics` directive at the top of the file to make working with `Brush`, `Pen`, and `Graphics` objects easier.

```
interface IDrawable
{
    int X { get; set; }
    int Y { get; set; }
    Brush Background { get; set; }
    Pen Foreground { get; set; }
    void Draw(Graphics gr);
}
```

A class that implements `IDrawable` must provide X, Y, `Background`, and `Foreground` properties, and a `Draw` method.

You cannot provide an accessibility modifier such as `private` to the items defined by an interface. They are always assumed to be public, and a class that implements the interface must declare these items as `public`.

The declarations for the properties look like they are providing a default implementation for them, but they actually only define the required accessors. A class that implements `IDrawable` must still provide its own implementations, although that can use auto-implemented properties. For example, the following code shows how the `DrawableCircle` class implements its X property:

```
public int X { get; set; }
```

> *This example might work better with true inheritance instead of an interface. If you make a* Drawable *class that implements the* X, Y, Background, *and* Foreground *properties, other classes such as* DrawableCircle *could inherit them. In this example an interface makes sense only if the classes already inherit from some other class so they cannot also inherit from* Drawable.

TRY IT

In this Try It, you build the `Vehicle` class and the `IDomicile` interface described earlier in this lesson. You then make a `MotorHome` class that inherits from the first and implements the second. Finally, you create an instance of the derived class.

You can download the code and resources for this Try It from the book's web page at www.wrox.com *or* www.CSharpHelper.com/24hour.html. *You can find them in the Lesson27 folder of the download.*

Lesson Requirements

➤ Start a new project. Create a `Vehicle` class with the properties `NumberOfPassengers`, `MilesPerGallon`, and `NumberOfCupHolders`. Give it a constructor to make it easy to initialize a new object's properties. Override its `ToString` method so it returns the object's property values separated by the escape sequence \r\n.

➤ Make an `IDomicile` interface that defines the properties `SquareFeet`, `NumberOfBedrooms`, and `NumberOfBathrooms`. Also make it define a `ToString` method that returns a string as usual.

➤ Derive the `MotorHome` class from `Vehicle`, making it implement `IDomicile`. Give it a constructor to make it easy to initialize a new object's properties. Override its `ToString` method so it returns the object's property values separated by the escape sequence \r\n.

➤ Create an instance of the `MotorHome` class. Then use its `ToString` method to display its properties in a textbox.

Hints

➤ Don't forget to make the `MotorHome` class's constructor invoke the base class's constructor. If you don't remember how, see the section "Invoking Other Constructors" in Lesson 24.

➤ Also save a little work by making the `MotorHome` class's `ToString` method call the `Vehicle` class's version.

Step-by-Step

➤ Start a new project. Create a `Vehicle` class with the properties `NumberOfPassengers`, `MilesPerGallon`, and `NumberOfCupHolders`. Give it a constructor to make it easy to initialize a new object's properties. Override its `ToString` method so it returns the object's property values separated by the escape sequence \r\n.

1. Use code similar to the following:

```
class Vehicle
{
    // Properties.
    public int NumberOfPassengers { get; set; }
    public double MilesPerGallon { get; set; }
    public int NumberOfCupHolders { get; set; }
```

```
            // Initializing constructor.
            public Vehicle(int numberOfPassengers, double milesPerGallon,
                int numberOfCupHolders)
            {
                NumberOfPassengers = numberOfPassengers;
                MilesPerGallon = milesPerGallon;
                NumberOfCupHolders = numberOfCupHolders;
            }

            // Return the object's properties.
            public override string ToString()
            {
                return
                    "NumberOfPassengers: " + NumberOfPassengers +
                    "\r\nMilesPerGallon : " + MilesPerGallon +
                    "\r\nNumberOfCupHolders: " + NumberOfCupHolders;
            }
        }
```

➤ Make an `IDomicile` interface that defines the properties `SquareFeet`, `NumberOfBedrooms`, and `NumberOfBathrooms`. Also make it define a `ToString` method that returns a string as usual.

1. Use code similar to the following:

```
interface IDomicile
{
    int SquareFeet { get; set; }
    int NumberOfBedrooms { get; set; }
    double NumberOfBathrooms { get; set; }
    string ToString();
}
```

➤ Derive the `MotorHome` class from `Vehicle`, making it implement `IDomicile`. Give it a constructor to make it easy to initialize a new object's properties. Override its `ToString` method so it returns the object's property values separated by the escape sequence `\r\n`.

1. Use code similar to the following:

```
class MotorHome : Vehicle, IDomicile
{
    // IDomicile methods.
    public int SquareFeet { get; set; }
    public int NumberOfBedrooms { get; set; }
    public double NumberOfBathrooms { get; set; }

    // Initializing constructor.
    public MotorHome(int numberOfPassengers, double milesPerGallon,
        int numberOfCupHolders, int squareFeet,
        int numberOfBedrooms, double numberOfBathrooms)
        : base(numberOfPassengers, milesPerGallon,
        numberOfCupHolders)
    {
        SquareFeet = squareFeet;
```

```
            NumberOfBedrooms = numberOfBedrooms;
            NumberOfBathrooms = numberOfBathrooms;
        }

        // Return the object's properties.
        public override string ToString()
        {
            return base.ToString() +
                "\r\nSquareFeet: " + SquareFeet +
                "\r\nNumberOfBedrooms: " + NumberOfBedrooms +
                "\r\nNumberOfBathrooms: " + NumberOfBathrooms;
        }
    }
```

➤ Create an instance of the `MotorHome` class. Then use its `ToString` method to display its properties in a textbox.

1. The following code creates an instance of the `MotorHome` class and displays its properties in `resultTextBox`:

```
private void Form1_Load(object sender, EventArgs e)
{
    // Make a MotorHome.
    MotorHome motorHome = new MotorHome(6, 8.25, 32, 150, 3, 0.5);

    // Display its properties.
    resultTextBox.Text = motorHome.ToString();
}
```

 Please select Lesson 27 on the DVD to view the video that accompanies this lesson.

EXERCISES

1. Build a program that defines the `IDrawable` interface described earlier in this lesson. Make the `DrawableCircle` and `DrawableRectangle` classes implement the interface. Hints: Give `DrawableCircle` an additional `Radius` property and give `DrawableRectangle` additional `Width` and `Height` properties. Use code similar to the following to draw the circle centered at the point (X, Y):

```
// Draw the circle centered at (X, Y).
public void Draw(Graphics gr)
{
    gr.FillEllipse(Background, X - Radius, Y - Radius,
        2 * Radius, 2 * Radius);
    gr.DrawEllipse(Foreground, X - Radius, Y - Radius,
        2 * Radius, 2 * Radius);
}
```

Use code similar to the following to draw the rectangle with upper-left corner (X, Y):

```
// Draw the rectangle.
public void Draw(Graphics gr)
{
    gr.FillRectangle(Background, X, Y, Width, Height);
    gr.DrawRectangle(Foreground, X, Y, Width, Height);
}
```

(For bonus points, make a `DrawableStar` class that has a `NumberOfPoints` property and draws a star with that number of points.)

2. An array's `Sort` method can take as a parameter an object that implements the generic `IComparer` interface. Because this interface is generic, you can tell it what kinds of objects the class can compare. For example, `IComparer<Car>` means the class can compare `Car` objects.

Build a `Car` class with the properties `Name`, `MaxSpeed`, `Horsepower`, and `Price`. Override the `ToString` method to display the object's properties formatted with fixed column widths so the values for different `Cars` in a listbox will line up nicely as shown in Figure 27-5. (The listbox uses the fixed-width font Courier New so all of the letters have the same width.)

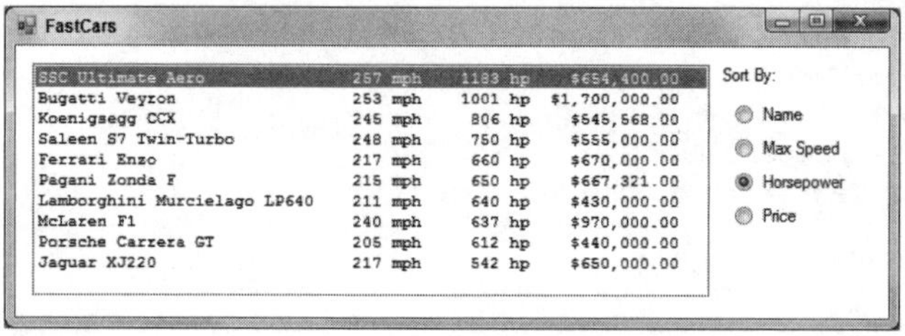

FIGURE 27-5

Build a `CarComparer` class that implements `IComparer<Car>`. Give it the following `SortType` enum:

```
// Different kinds of sorts.
public enum SortType
{
    ByName,
    ByMaxSpeed,
    ByHorsepower,
    ByPrice,
}
```

Next give `CarComparer` a `Sort` property that has type `SortType`.

Finally give the `CarComparer` a `Compare` method to satisfy the `IComparer<Car>` interface. Use a switch statement to make the function return a value that depends on the `Sort` value. For example, if `Sort` is `ByPrice`, then compare the two `Cars`' prices. Make the function sort the `MaxSpeed`, `Horsepower`, and `Price` values in decreasing order.

Note that there are many ways to do this sort of thing. For example, Lesson 37 explains how you can use LINQ to sort items. As with all of the examples and exercises in this book, these examples are primarily designed to demonstrate particular topics, in this case interfaces, rather than to provide the perfect solution.

3. If you set a `ListView` control's `ListViewItemSorter` property equal to an object that implements the `System.Collections.IComparer` interface, then the `ListView` uses that object to sort its rows. To sort the rows, the control calls the object's `Compare` method, passing it two `ListViewItem` objects. (Unfortunately the `ListView` control's `ListViewItemSorter` property is a non-generic `IComparer`, so it works with non-specific `objects` instead of something more concrete like `ListViewItems`.)

For this exercise, make a program with a `ListView` control similar to the one shown in Figure 27-6. At design time, edit the `ListView`'s `Columns` collection to define the columns. Edit its `Items` collection to define the data and set the control's `View` property to `Details`.

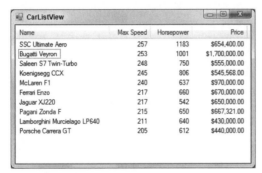

FIGURE 27-6

Next make a `ListViewComparer` class that implements `System.Collections.IComparer`. Give it a `ColumnNumber` property that indicates the number of the column in the `ListView` that the object should use when sorting.

Finally give the `ListView` a `ColumnClick` event handler. The event handler should create a new `ListViewComparer` object to sort on the clicked column and then set the control's `ListViewItemSorter` property to that object.

You can download the solutions to these exercises from the book's web page at www.wrox.com or www.CSharpHelper.com/24hour.html. You can find those solutions in the Lesson27 folder.

28

Making Generic Classes

The section on collection classes in Lesson 16 explained how to use generic collection classes. For example, the following code defines a list that holds `Employee` objects:

```
public List<Employee> Employees = new List<Employee>();
```

This list can only hold `Employee` objects, and when you get an object out of the list, it has the `Employee` type instead of the less specific `object` type.

Lesson 16 also described the main advantages of generic classes: code reuse and specific type checking. You can use the same generic `List<>` class to hold a list of `strings`, `doubles`, or `Person` objects. By requiring a specific data type, the class prevents you from accidentally adding an `Employee` object to a list of `Order` objects, and when you get an object from the list you know it is an `Order`.

In this lesson, you learn how to build your own generic classes so you can raise code reuse to a whole new level.

 Many other things can be generic. You can probably guess that you can build generic structures because structures are so similar to classes. You can also build generic methods (in either generic or non-generic classes), generic interfaces, generic delegate types, and so on. This lesson focuses on generic classes.

DEFINING GENERIC CLASSES

A generic class declaration looks a lot like a normal class declaration with one or more generic type variables added in angled brackets. For example, the following code shows the basic declaration for a generic `TreeNode` class:

```
class TreeNode<T>
{
    ...
}
```

The <T> means the class takes one type parameter, T. Within the class's code, the type T means whatever type the program used when creating the instance of the class. For example, the following code declares a variable named rootNode that is a TreeNode that handles strings:

```
TreeNode<string> rootNode = new TreeNode<string>();
```

If you want the class to use multiple type parameters, separate them with commas. For example, suppose you want to make a Matcher class that takes two kinds of objects and matches objects in the two kinds. It might match Employee objects with Job objects to assign employees to jobs. The following code shows how you might declare the Matcher class:

```
public class Matcher<T1, T2>
{
    ...
}
```

The following code shows how you might create an instance of the class to match Employees with Jobs:

```
Matcher<Employee, Job> jobAssigner = new Matcher<Employee, Job>();
```

> *Many developers use T for name of the type in generic classes that take only one type.*
>
> *If the class takes more than one type, you should use more descriptive names so it's easy to tell the types apart. For example, the generic Dictionary class has two type variables named TKey and TValue that represent the types of the keys and values that the Dictionary will hold.*

Inside the class's code, you can use the types freely. For example, the following code shows more of the TreeNode class's code. A TreeNode object represents a node in a tree, with an associated piece of data attached to it. The places where the class uses the data type T are highlighted in bold.

```
class TreeNode<T>
{
    // This node's data.
    public T Data { get; set; }

    // This node's children.
    private List<TreeNode<T>> children = new List<TreeNode<T>>();

    // Constructor.
    public TreeNode(T data)
    {
        Data = data;
    }

    // Override ToString to display the data.
    public override string ToString()
```

```
    {
        if (Data == null) return "";
        return Data.ToString();
    }

    ...
}
```

Notice how the class uses the type T throughout its code. The class starts with a Data property of type T. This is the data (of whatever data type) associated with the node.

Each node also has a list of child nodes. To hold the right kind of TreeNode objects, the children variable is a generic List<TreeNode<T>>, meaning it can hold only TreeNode<T> objects.

The class's constructor takes a parameter of type T and saves it in the object's Data property.

To make displaying a TreeNode easier, the class overrides its ToString method so it calls the ToString method provided by the Data object. For example, if the object is a TreeNode<string>, then this simply returns the string's value.

USING GENERIC CONSTRAINTS

The previous example overrides the TreeNode class's ToString method so it calls the Data object's ToString method. Fortunately all objects have a ToString method so you know this is possible, but what if you want to call some other method provided by the object?

For example, suppose you want to create a new instance of type T. How do you know that type T provides a constructor that takes no parameters? What if you want to compare two objects of type T to see which is greater? Or what if you want to compare two type T objects to see if they are the same? (An important test for the Dictionary class.) How do you know whether two type T objects are comparable?

You can use *generic constraints* to require that the types used by the program meet certain criteria such as comparability or providing a parameterless constructor.

To use a generic constraint, follow the normal class declaration with the keyword where, the name of the type parameter that you want to constrain, a colon, and the constraint. Some typical constraints include:

➤   A class from which the type must inherit

➤   An interface (or interfaces) that the type must implement

➤   new() to indicate that the type must provide a parameterless constructor

➤   struct to indicate that the type must be a value type such as the built-in value types (int, bool) or a structure

➤   class to indicate that the type must be a reference type

Separate multiple constraints for the same type parameter with commas. If you want to constrain more than one type parameter, place a new `where` clause on a new line.

For example, the following code defines the generic `Matcher` class, which takes two generic type parameters `T1` and `T2`. (Note that this code skips important error handling such as checking for null values to keep things simple.)

```
public class Matcher<T1, T2>
    where T1 : IComparable<T2>, new()
    where T2 : new()
{
    private void test()
    {
        T1 t1 = new T1();
        T2 t2 = new T2();
        ...

        if (t1.CompareTo(t2) < 0)
        {
            // t1 is "less than" t2.
            ...
        }
    }
    ...
}
```

The first constraint requires that type parameter `T1` implement the `IComparable` interface for the type `T2` so the code can compare `T1` objects to `T2` objects. The next constraint requires that the `T1` type also provide a parameterless constructor. You can see that the code creates a new `T1` object and uses its `CompareTo` method (which is defined by `IComparable`).

The second `where` clause requires that the type `T2` also provide a parameterless constructor. The code needs that because it also creates a new `T2` instance.

In general you should use as few constraints as possible because that makes your class usable in as many circumstances as possible. If your code won't need to create new instances of a data type, don't use the `new` constraint. If your code won't need to compare objects, don't use the `IComparable` constraint.

MAKING GENERIC METHODS

In addition to building generic classes, you can also build generic methods inside either a generic class or a regular non-generic class.

For example, suppose you want to rearrange the items in a list so the new order alternately picks items from each end of the list. If the list originally contains the numbers 1, 2, 3, 4, 5, 6, then the alternated list contains 1, 6, 2, 5, 3, 4.

The following code shows how a program could declare an `Alternate` method to return an alternated list. Note that you could put this method in any class, generic or not.

```
public List<T> Alternate<T>(List<T> list)
{
```

```
        // Make a new list to hold the results.
        List<T> newList = new List<T>();
        ...
        return newList;
    }
```

The `Alternate` method takes a generic type parameter `T`. It takes as a regular parameter a `List` that holds items of type `T` and it returns a new `List` containing items of type `T`.

This snippet creates a new `List<T>` to hold the results. (Note that it does not need to require the type `T` to have a default constructor because the code is creating a new `List`, not a new `T`.) The code then builds the new list (not shown here) and returns it.

The following code shows how a program might use this method:

```
List<string> strings = new List<string>(stringsTextBox.Text.Split(' '));
List<string> alternatedStrings = Alternate<string>(strings);
alternatedStringsTextBox.Text = string.Join(" ", alternatedStrings);
```

The first statement defines a `List<string>` and initializes it with the space-separated values in the textbox `stringsTextBox`.

The second statement calls `Alternate<string>` to create an alternated `List<string>`. Notice how the code uses `<string>` to indicate the data type that `Alternate` will manipulate. (This is actually optional and the program will figure out which version of `Alternate` to use if you omit it. However, this makes the code more explicit and may catch a bug if you try to alternate a list containing something unexpected such as `Person` objects.)

The third statement joins the values in the new list separated by spaces and displays the result.

Generic methods can be quite useful for the same reasons that generic classes are. They allow code reuse without the extra hassle of converting values to and from the non-specific `object` class. They also perform type checking, so in this example, the program cannot try to alternate a `List<int>` by calling `Alternate<string>`.

TRY IT

In this Try It, you build a generic `Randomize` method that randomizes an array of objects of any type. To make it easy to add the method to any project, you add the method to an `ArrayMethods` class. To make the method easy to use, you make it `static`, so the main program doesn't need to instantiate the class to use it.

You can download the code and resources for this Try It from the book's web page at www.wrox.com *or* www.CSharpHelper.com/24hour.html. *You can find them in the Lesson28 folder of the download.*

Lesson Requirements

➤ Start a new project and give it an `ArrayMethods` class.

➤ Create a generic `Randomize` method with one generic type parameter `T`. The method should take as a parameter an array of `T` and return an array of `T`.

➤ Make the main program test the method.

Hints

➤ Use the following code for the method's body. Try to figure out the method's declaration yourself before you read the step-by-step instructions that follow.

```
// Make a Random object to use to pick random items.
Random rand = new Random();

// Make a copy of the array so we don't mess up the original.
T[] randomizedItems = (T[])items.Clone();

// For each spot in the array, pick
// a random item to swap into that spot.
for (int i = 0; i < items.Length - 1; i++)
{
    // Pick a random item j between i and the last item.
    int j = rand.Next(i, items.Length);

    // Swap item j into position i.
    T temp = randomizedItems[i];
    randomizedItems[i] = randomizedItems[j];
    randomizedItems[j] = temp;
}

// Return the randomized array.
return randomizedItems;
```

Step-by-Step

➤ Start a new project and give it an `ArrayMethods` class.

1. This is reasonably straightforward. You don't need to make the `ArrayMethods` class generic.

➤ Create a generic `Randomize` method with one generic type parameter `T`. The method should take as a parameter an array of `T` and return an array of `T`.

1. The following code shows how you can implement this method:

```
// Randomize the items in an array.
public static T[] Randomize<T>(T[] items)
{
```

```
        // Make a Random object to use to pick random items.
        Random rand = new Random();

        // Make a copy of the array so we don't mess up the original.
        T[] randomizedItems = (T[])items.Clone();

        // For each spot in the array, pick
        // a random item to swap into that spot.
        for (int i = 0; i < items.Length - 1; i++)
        {
            // Pick a random item j between i and the last item.
            int j = rand.Next(i, items.Length);

            // Swap item j into position i.
            T temp = randomizedItems[i];
            randomizedItems[i] = randomizedItems[j];
            randomizedItems[j] = temp;
        }

        // Return the randomized array.
        return randomizedItems;
    }
```

➤ Make the main program test the method.

1. The program I wrote uses two TextBoxes, one to hold the original items and one to display the randomized items. When you click the Randomize button, the following code executes:

```
// Randomize the list and display the results.
private void randomizeButton_Click(object sender, EventArgs e)
{
    // Get the items as an array of strings.
    string[] items = itemsTextBox.Lines;

    // Randomize the array.
    string[] randomizedItems = ArrayMethods.Randomize<string>(items);

    // Concatenate and display the result.
    randomizedTextBox.Text = string.Join("\r\n", randomizedItems);
}
```

Notice that the code uses the TextBox's Lines property to get the entered values. That property returns the lines in a multiline TextBox as an array of strings.

Also notice that the code doesn't need to make an instance of the ArrayMethods class. That's the advantage of making the Randomize method static.

 Please select Lesson 28 on the DVD to view the video that accompanies this lesson.

EXERCISES

1. Finish building the generic `Alternate` method described earlier in this lesson. Add the code needed to make the alternating version of the list. To make using the method easy, make it static in the `ArrayMethods` class. Make the main program test the method with lists containing odd and even numbers of items.

2. Make the `TreeNode` class to represent a tree node associated with a piece of data of some generic type. In addition to the code shown earlier in this lesson, give the class:

➤ An `AddChild` method that adds a new child node to the node for which the method is invoked. Have the method take a piece of data of the class's generic type as a parameter and return a new `TreeNode` representing that piece of data.

➤ A private `AddToListPreorder` method that adds a node's subtree to a list in pre-order format. The preorder format lists the node's data first and then recursively calls the method to add the data for the node's children. You can use code similar to the following:

```
// Recursively add our subtree to an existing list in preorder.
private void AddToListPreorder(List<TreeNode<T>> list)
{
    // Add this node.
    list.Add(this);

    // Add the children.
    foreach (TreeNode<T> child in Children)
    {
        child.AddToListPreorder(list);
    }
}
```

➤ A public `Preorder` method that returns the node's subtree items in a list in preorder format. The method should call `AddToListPreorder` to do all of the work. You can use code similar to the following:

```
// Return a list containing our subtree in preorder.
public List<TreeNode<T>> Preorder()
{
    List<TreeNode<T>> list = new List<TreeNode<T>>();
    AddToListPreorder(list);
    return list;
}
```

➤ For extra credit, add similar methods to build lists in postorder and inorder. In postorder, a node recursively adds its children to the list and then adds its own data. In inorder, a node recursively adds the first half of its children to the list, then itself, and then the rest of its children.

Make the main program build the tree shown in Figure 28-1, although it doesn't need to display it graphically as in the figure. Make the program display the tree's preorder, postorder, and inorder representations as shown in Figure 28-2.

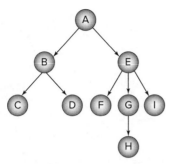

FIGURE 28-1

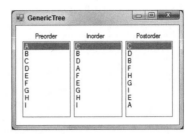

FIGURE 28-2

3. Make a generic `PriorityQueue` class. The class is basically a list holding generic items where each item has an associated priority. Give the class a nested `ItemData` structure similar to the following to hold an item. This structure is defined inside the `PriorityQueue` class and won't be used outside of the class, so it can be `private`. Note that this structure uses the class's generic type parameter `T` for the data it holds.

```
// A structure to hold items.
private struct ItemData
{
    public int itemPriority { get; set; }
    public T data { get; set; }
}
```

The class should store its `ItemData` objects in a generic `List`.

Give the `PriorityQueue` class a public `Count` property that returns the number of items in the list.

Give the class an `AddItem` method that takes as parameters a piece of data and a priority. It should make a new `ItemData` to hold these values and add it to the list.

Finally, give the class a `GetItem` method that searches the list the item with the smallest priority number (priority 1 means top priority), removes that item from the list, and returns the item and its priority via parameters passed by reference. (If there's a tie for lowest priority number, return the first item you find with that priority.) (Hint: Should you use `ref` or `out` to pass the parameters by reference?)

You can download the solutions to these exercises from the book's web page at www.wrox.com *or* www.CSharpHelper.com/24hour.html. *You can find those solutions in the Lesson28 folder.*

SECTION V
System Interactions

The lessons up to this point have explained how you can do some pretty remarkable things. Using their techniques you can read inputs entered by the user, perform intricate calculations, repeat a sequence of commands a huge number of times, and even build your own classes to model complex situations.

All of the programs that you've written so far, however, are self-contained. They get input from the user, but otherwise they don't interact with the computer.

The lessons in this section explain some of the ways a program can interact with the system. They explain how to read and write files, explore the file system, print, and use the clipboard to interact with other applications.

There are lots of other ways a program can interact with the computer. It can interact with hardware through serial ports and special devices and connect to web sites or other programs over a network. There are even many different ways to interact with the same part of the system. For example, there are many ways a program can manipulate files, read and modify the Windows registry, and save and restore program parameters. The chapters in this section describe some of the ways a program can interact with the wider system, but you shouldn't think these are the only ways possible.

29

Reading and Writing Files

Files play an extremely important role on a computer. They hold text, pictures, Microsoft Word documents, spreadsheets, and all sorts of other data. They also hold executable programs including those that provide the operating system itself.

In this lesson you learn some basic techniques for reading and writing text files. Using some fairly simple techniques, you can use text files to store and retrieve data used by a program.

> *This is one of those topics where there are many ways to perform the same tasks. There are lots of approaches to manipulating files, and this lesson describes only one.*

UNDERSTANDING STREAMS

There are many kinds of files: web pages, video, audio, executable, and lots of others. At some level, however, files are all the same. They're just a series of bytes stored on a file system somewhere.

Thinking about files at this very low level lets you treat them uniformly. It lets you define common classes and methods that you can use to manipulate any kind of file.

Many programming languages, including C#, make working with files at a low level easier by defining the concept of a stream. A *stream* is simply an ordered series of bytes.

> *Streams can also represent things other than files. For example, a stream could represent data being sent from one program to another, a series of bytes being downloaded from a web site, or the flow of data as it moves through some complex process such as encryption or compression. This lesson focuses on file streams.*

Stream objects provide methods for manipulating streams at a low level. For example, the `Stream` class provides `Read` and `Write` methods that move bytes of data between the stream and an array of bytes in your program.

Working with streams at this low level is convenient for some programs but it makes day-to-day file handling difficult. You probably don't want to read the bytes from a text file and then reassemble them into characters.

The `StreamReader` and `StreamWriter` classes make reading and writing text streams much easier. As you can probably guess from their names, `StreamReader` lets a program read text from a stream and `StreamWriter` lets a program write text into a stream. If that stream happens to represent a file, then you're reading and writing files.

The `StreamReader` and `StreamWriter` classes are in the `System.IO` namespace. To make it easier to use these classes, you can add the following `using` directive to your code:

```
using System.IO;
```

WRITING FILES

The `StreamWriter` class provides several constructors to build a `StreamWriter` associated with different kinds of streams. One of the simplest constructors takes a filename as a parameter. It opens the file for writing and associates the new `StreamWriter` with it.

Note that `StreamWriter` implements `IDisposable`, so you should use it inside a `using` block to call its `Dispose` automatically.

The following code shows how a program can open the file Memo.txt for writing. If the file already exists, it is overwritten.

```
// Write into the file, overwriting it if it exists.
using (StreamWriter memoWriter = new StreamWriter("Memo.txt"))
{
    // Write into the file.
    ...
}
```

If you pass the constructor a filename without a path such as Memo.txt, the program creates the file in its current directory. You can use a fully qualified filename such as C:\Temp\Memo.txt to create the file in a particular directory.

Another version of the class's constructor takes a second `bool` parameter that indicates whether you want to open the file for appending. If you set this parameter to `true`, the `StreamWriter` opens the existing file and prepares to add text to the end. If the file doesn't exit, the object silently creates a new file and gets ready to append.

The `StreamWriter` class provides a `Write` method to add text to the file. The `WriteLine` method adds text followed by a new line. Both `Write` and `WriteLine` have a bunch of overloaded versions that write various data types into the file: `bool`, `char`, `string`, `int`, `decimal`, and so on. They also provide versions that take a format string and parameters much as the `string.Format` method does.

The `StreamWriter` provides one other very important method that I want to cover here: `Close`. The `Close` method closes the `StreamWriter` and its associated file. When you use the `Write` and `WriteLine` methods, the `StreamWriter` may actually buffer its output in memory and only actually write to the file when it has a bunch of data stored up. The `Close` method forces the `StreamWriter` to flush its buffer into the file. Until that point, the data may not actually be in the file. If your program crashes or ends without calling `Close`, there's a very good chance that some or all of your text may be lost.

The following code shows how a program could save the contents of a textbox in a file:

```
// Write the file, overwriting it if it exists.
using (StreamWriter memoWriter = new StreamWriter("Memo.txt"))
{
    // Write the file.
    memoWriter.Write(memoTextBox.Text);
    memoWriter.Close();
}
```

READING FILES

The `StreamReader` class lets you easily read text from a file. Like the `StreamWriter` class, `StreamReader` provides a constructor that takes a parameter giving the name of the file to open.

Note that the constructor throws an exception if the file doesn't exist, so your program should verify that the file is there before you try to open it. One way to do that is to use the `File` class's static `Exists` method. For example, the code `File.Exists("Memo.txt")` returns true if the file Memo.txt exists in the program's current directory.

The `StreamReader` class provides a `Read` method that lets you read from the file one or more bytes at a time, but usually you'll want to use its `ReadLine` and `ReadToEnd` methods.

As you may be able to guess, `ReadLine` reads the next line from the file and returns it as a string. `ReadToEnd` reads the rest of the file from the current position onward and returns it as a string.

The following code reads the file Memo.txt and displays its contents in a textbox.

```
// Read the file.
using (StreamReader memoReader = new StreamReader("Memo.txt"))
{
    memoTextBox.Text = memoReader.ReadToEnd();
    memoReader.Close();
}
```

The `StreamReader`'s `EndOfStream` property returns `true` if the reader is at the end of the stream. This is particularly useful when you're reading a stream of unknown length. For example, the program can enter a `while` loop that uses `ReadLine` to read lines and continue as long as `EndOfStream` is false.

TRY IT

Available for download on Wrox.com

In this Try It, you build the program shown in Figure 29-1. When the program starts, it loads previously saved values into its textboxes. When it stops, the program saves the values that are currently in the textboxes.

FIGURE 29-1

> *You can download the code and resources for this Try It from the book's web page at* www.wrox.com *or* www.CSharpHelper.com/24hour.html. *You can find them in the Lesson29 folder of the download.*

Lesson Requirements

➤ Start a new project and arrange its form as shown in Figure 29-1.

➤ Give the form a `Load` event handler that uses a `StreamReader` to open the file Values.txt and read the file's lines into the form's textboxes.

➤ Give the form a `Closing` event handler that uses a `StreamWriter` to open the file Values.txt and write the values in the textboxes into the file.

Hints

➤ Don't forget to use the `StreamReader` and `StreamWriter` inside `using` blocks.

➤ Don't forget to make sure the file exists before you try to open it.

Step-by-Step

➤ Start a new project and arrange its form as shown in Figure 29-1.

   1. This is reasonably straightforward.

➤ Give the form a `Load` event handler that uses a `StreamReader` to open the file Values.txt and read the file's lines into the form's textboxes.

   1. Use code similar to the following:

```
// Load saved values.
private void Form1_Load(object sender, EventArgs e)
```

```
    {
        // See if the file exists.
        if (File.Exists("Values.txt"))
        {
            // Open the file.
            using (StreamReader valueReader =
                new StreamReader("Values.txt"))
            {
                firstNameTextBox.Text = valueReader.ReadLine();
                lastNameTextBox.Text = valueReader.ReadLine();
                streetTextBox.Text = valueReader.ReadLine();
                cityTextBox.Text = valueReader.ReadLine();
                stateTextBox.Text = valueReader.ReadLine();
                zipTextBox.Text = valueReader.ReadLine();
                valueReader.Close();
            }
        }
    }
```

➤ Give the form a `FormClosing` event handler that uses a `StreamWriter` to open the file Values.txt and write the values in the textboxes into the file.

1. Use code similar to the following:

```
// Save the values.
private void Form1_FormClosing(object sender, FormClosingEventArgs e)
{
    // Create the file.
    using (StreamWriter valueWriter = new StreamWriter("Values.txt"))
    {
        valueWriter.WriteLine(firstNameTextBox.Text);
        valueWriter.WriteLine(lastNameTextBox.Text);
        valueWriter.WriteLine(streetTextBox.Text);
        valueWriter.WriteLine(cityTextBox.Text);
        valueWriter.WriteLine(stateTextBox.Text);
        valueWriter.WriteLine(zipTextBox.Text);
        valueWriter.Close();
    }
}
```

 Please select Lesson 29 on the DVD to view the video that accompanies this lesson.

EXERCISES

1. Build a Memo program that saves and loads a single memo saved in the file in a multiline textbox. (This is so easy I wouldn't even bother using it as an exercise except it's actually useful. You can use it to record notes during the day and easily read your notes the next day.)

2. Make a program that lets the user select a number from a `NumericUpDown` control and then generates a file containing a multiplication table that goes up to that number times itself. Use formatting to make the numbers line up in columns.

3. Build a program with a `TextBox`, a `ListBox`, an Add button, and a Save button. When the user enters a value in the `TextBox` and clicks Add, add the value to the `ListBox`. When the user clicks Save, write the values from the `ListBox` into a file and then clear the `ListBox`. When the form loads, make it read the values back into the `ListBox`.

4. Build a simple text editor. Give it a `MenuStrip` with Open and Save commands and a `TextBox`. Use an `OpenFileDialog` and a `SaveFileDialog` to let the user select the file to open and save. (Don't worry about any of the other things a real editor would need to handle, such as locked files and ensuring that the user doesn't close the program with unsaved changes.)

 You can download the solutions to these exercises from the book's web page at `www.wrox.com` *or* `www.CSharpHelper.com/24hour.html`. *You can find those solutions in the Lesson29 folder.*

30

Using File System Classes

The techniques described in Lesson 29 let you read and write text files. They also demonstrate techniques that you'll find useful when you deal with streams other than text files.

Those techniques don't let you manipulate the file system itself, however. They let you read or write a file, but they don't let you rename a file, move a file to a different directory, or delete a file.

This lesson describes file system classes that make these and other common file manipulation operations easy. In this lesson you learn how to manipulate the file system to rename, move, or delete files and directories. You also learn how to read or write a text file's contents all at once rather than using a `StreamReader`.

 These classes are in the `System.IO` *namespace so you can make using them in your code easier by including the directive:*

```
using System.IO;
```

THE DRIVEINFO CLASS

The `DriveInfo` class provides information about the system's drives. Its static `GetDrives` function returns an array of `DriveInfo` objects describing all of the system's drives.

Table 30-1 summarizes the `DriveInfo`'s most useful properties.

TABLE 30-1

PROPERTY	PURPOSE
AvailableFreeSpace	The total number of bytes available.
DriveFormat	The drive format, as in NTFS or FAT32.

continues

TABLE 30-1 *(continued)*

PROPERTY	PURPOSE
DriveType	The drive type, as in Fixed or CDRom.
IsReady	True if the drive is ready. A drive must be ready before you can use the AvailableFreeSpace, DriveFormat, TotalSize, or VolumeLabel properties.
Name	The drive's name, as in C:\.
RootDirectory	A DirectoryInfo object representing the drive's root directory.
TotalFreeSpace	The number of bytes available, taking quotas into account.
TotalSize	The drive's total size in bytes.
VolumeLabel	The drive's label.

Example program ListDrives (found as part of this lesson's code download and shown in Figure 30-1) uses the following code to describe the system's drives.

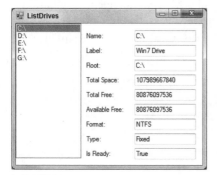

FIGURE 30-1

```
// List the available drives.
private void Form1_Load(object sender, EventArgs e)
{
    drivesListBox.DataSource = DriveInfo.GetDrives();
}

// Display information about the selected drive.
private void drivesListBox_SelectedIndexChanged(object sender, EventArgs e)
{
    DriveInfo info = (DriveInfo)drivesListBox.SelectedItem;
    nameTextBox.Text = info.Name;
    rootTextBox.Text = info.RootDirectory.FullName;
    typeTextBox.Text = info.DriveType.ToString();
    isReadyTextBox.Text = info.IsReady.ToString();
```

```
        // See if the drive is ready.
        if (info.IsReady)
        {
            // Display values.
            labelTextBox.Text = info.VolumeLabel;
            totalSpaceTextBox.Text = info.TotalSize.ToString();
            totalFreeTextBox.Text = info.TotalFreeSpace.ToString();
            availableFreeTextBox.Text = info.AvailableFreeSpace.ToString();
            formatTextBox.Text = info.DriveFormat;
        }
        else
        {
            // Clear values that are unavailable.
            labelTextBox.Clear();
            totalSpaceTextBox.Clear();
            totalFreeTextBox.Clear();
            availableFreeTextBox.Clear();
            formatTextBox.Clear();
        }
    }
```

THE DIRECTORYINFO CLASS

The `DirectoryInfo` class provides information about directories. Table 30-2 summarizes useful `DirectoryInfo` methods for manipulating directories.

TABLE 30-2

METHOD	PURPOSE
Create	Creates a new directory. To use this, make a `DirectoryInfo` object, passing its constructor the name of the directory to create. Then call the `Create` method.
CreateSubdirectory	Creates a subdirectory inside this directory.
Delete	Deletes the directory. If you pass no parameters to this method, it only deletes the directory if it is empty. Alternatively you can pass it a Boolean parameter indicating whether you want to delete all of the directory's files and subdirectories.
GetDirectories	Returns the directory's immediate subdirectories. Optionally you can include a search string to select particular subdirectories.
GetFiles	Returns the directory's files. Optionally you can include a search string to select particular files.
MoveTo	Moves the directory to a new path.

The `DirectoryInfo` class also provides a few useful properties, which are summarized in Table 30-3.

TABLE 30-3

PROPERTY	PURPOSE
Attributes	The directory's attributes, such as `Compressed`, `Hidden`, or `System`.
CreationTime	The time at which the directory was created.
Exists	Returns True if the directory actually exists.
FullName	Gives the directory's fully qualified path.
LastAccessTime	The time at which the directory was last accessed.
LastWriteTime	The time at which the directory was last written.
Name	The directory's name without the path.
Parent	A `DirectoryInfo` representing this directory's parent directory.
Root	The directory's file system root.

Example program UseDirectoryInfo (found in this lesson's code download) uses a `DirectoryInfo` object to display information about directories.

THE DIRECTORY CLASS

The `Directory` class provides static methods for manipulating directories (see Table 30-4). For simple tasks these are sometimes easier to use than the comparable `DirectoryInfo` class methods because you don't need to create a `DirectoryInfo` object to use them.

TABLE 30-4

METHOD	PURPOSE
CreateDirectory	Creates the directory and any missing directories in its path up to the root.
Delete	Deletes a directory.
Exists	Returns `true` if the directory exists.
GetCreationTime	Returns the time at which the file was created.
GetDirectories	Returns a directory's subdirectories.
GetDirectoryRoot	Returns the directory's root.
GetFiles	Returns a directory's files, optionally looking for files matching a pattern.
GetLastAccessTime	Returns the time at which a directory was last accessed.

METHOD	PURPOSE
GetLastWriteTime	Returns the time at which a directory was last written.
GetParent	Returns a `DirectoryInfo` representing a directory's parent directory.
Move	Moves a file or directory to a new location.
SetCreationTime	Sets the directory's creation time.
SetLastAccessTime	Sets the directory's last access time.
SetLastWriteTime	Sets the directory's last write time.

THE FILEINFO CLASS

The `FileInfo` class, as you can probably guess at this point, provides information about files. Table 30-5 summarizes useful `FileInfo` methods for manipulating files.

TABLE 30-5

METHOD	PURPOSE
CopyTo	Copies the file to a new location.
Decrypt	Decrypts a file that was encrypted by the `Encrypt` method.
Delete	Deletes the file.
Encrypt	Encrypts the file so it can only be read by the account used to encrypt it.
MoveTo	Moves the file to a new location.

The `FileInfo` class also provides some useful properties, summarized in Table 30-6.

TABLE 30-6

PROPERTY	PURPOSE
Attributes	The file's attributes, such as `Compressed`, `Hidden`, or `System`.
CreationTime	The time at which the file was created.
Directory	A `DirectoryInfo` object for the directory containing the file.
Exists	Returns `true` if the file actually exists.
Extension	Returns the file's extension.
FullName	Gives the file's fully qualified path.

continues

TABLE 30-6 *(continued)*

PROPERTY	PURPOSE
IsReadOnly	Returns true if the file is marked read-only.
LastAccessTime	The time at which the file was last accessed.
LastWriteTime	The time at which the file was last written.
Length	The file's size in bytes.
Name	The file's name without the path.

Example program UseFileInfo (found in this lesson's code download) uses a FileInfo object to display information about files.

THE FILE CLASS

The File class provides static methods for manipulating files (see Table 30-7). For simple tasks these are sometimes easier to use than the comparable FileInfo class methods because you don't need to create a FileInfo object to use them. The AppendAllText, ReadAllLines, ReadAllText, WriteAllLines, and WriteAllText methods are particularly useful for reading and writing text files all at once, although you may still want to use StreamReader and StreamWriter if you need to manipulate files one line at a time.

TABLE 30-7

METHOD	PURPOSE
AppendAllText	Appends a string to the end of a file.
Copy	Copies a file to a new file.
Create	Creates a file.
Decrypt	Decrypts a file that was encrypted by the Encrypt method.
Delete	Deletes a file.
Encrypt	Encrypts the file so it can only be read by the account used to encrypt it.
Exists	Returns true if a file exists.
GetAttributes	Returns a file's attributes, such as ReadOnly, System, or Hidden.
GetCreationTime	Returns the time at which the file was created.
GetLastAccessTime	Returns the time at which a directory was last accessed.
GetLastWriteTime	Returns the time at which a directory was last written.

METHOD	PURPOSE
Move	Moves a file to a new location.
ReadAllBytes	Returns a file's contents in an array of bytes.
ReadAllLines	Returns the lines in a text file as an array of strings.
ReadAllText	Returns a text file's contents in a string.
SetAttributes	Sets a file's attributes.
SetCreationTime	Sets a directory's creation time.
SetLastAccessTime	Sets a directory's last access time.
SetLastWriteTime	Sets a directory's last write time.
WriteAllBytes	Writes a file's contents from an array of bytes.
WriteAllLines	Writes a text file's contents from an array of strings.
WriteAllText	Writes a text file's contents from a string.

THE PATH CLASS

The Path class provides static methods that perform string operations on file paths. For example, you can use the ChangeExtension method to change the extension part of a filename.

Table 30-8 summarizes the Path class's most useful methods.

TABLE 30-8

METHOD	PURPOSE
ChangeExtension	Changes a filename's extension.
Combine	Combines two path strings, adding a backslash between them if needed.
GetDirectoryName	Returns the directory name part of a path.
GetExtension	Returns the extension part of a filename.
GetFileName	Returns the filename part of a file's path.
GetFileNameWithoutExtension	Returns the filename part of a file's path without the extension.
GetTempFileName	Returns a name for a temporary file.
GetTempPath	Returns the path to the system's temporary folder.

TRY IT

In this Try It, you build the program shown in Figure 30-2 to let the user search for files matching a pattern that contain a target string. Enter a directory at which to start the search, select or enter a file pattern in the Pattern combo box, and enter a target string in the Search For textbox. When you click Search, the program searches for files matching the pattern and containing the target string.

SearchForFiles		
Directory:	D:\Rod\Writing\Books\24-Hour C# Trainer\Src\596906src30\	
Pattern:	*.cs	▼
Search For:	target	
	Search	
Form1.cs		
Form1.Designer.cs		

FIGURE 30-2

You can download the code and resources for this Try It from the book's web page at www.wrox.com *or* www.CSharpHelper.com/24hour.html. *You can find them in the Lesson30 folder of the download.*

Lesson Requirements

➤ Start a new project and arrange its form as shown in Figure 30-2.

  ➤ Give the combo box the choices *.cs, *.txt, *.*, and any other patterns that you think would be useful.

➤ Give the form a `Load` event handler that places the application's startup path in the Directory textbox (just to have somewhere to start).

➤ Give the Search button a `Click` event handler that searches for the desired files.

Hints

➤ Use the `DirectoryInfo` class's `GetFiles` method to search for files matching the pattern.

➤ Use the `FileInfo` class's `ReadAllText` method to get the file's contents. Then use string methods to see if the text contains the target string.

➤ To ignore case, convert the target string and the files' contents to lowercase.

Step-by-Step

➤ Start a new project and arrange its form as shown in Figure 30-2.

    ➤ Give the combo box the choices *.cs, *.txt, *.*, and any other patterns that you think would be useful.

    1. This is reasonably straightforward.

➤ Give the form a `Load` event handler that places the application's startup path in the Directory textbox (just to have somewhere to start).

    1. Use code similar to the following:

```
// Start at the startup directory.
private void Form1_Load(object sender, EventArgs e)
{
    directoryTextBox.Text = Application.StartupPath;
}
```

➤ Give the Search button a `Click` event handler that searches for the desired files.

    1. Use code similar to the following:

```
// Search for files matching the pattern
// and containing the target string.
private void searchButton_Click(object sender, EventArgs e)
{
    // Get the file pattern and target string.
    string pattern = patternComboBox.Text;
    string target = targetTextBox.Text.ToLower();

    // Clear the result list.
    fileListBox.Items.Clear();

    // Search for files.
    DirectoryInfo dirinfo =
        new DirectoryInfo(directoryTextBox.Text);
    foreach (FileInfo fileinfo in
        dirinfo.GetFiles(pattern, SearchOption.AllDirectories))
    {
        // See if we need to look for target text.
        if (target.Length > 0)
        {
            // If this file contains the target string,
            // add it to the list.
            string content =
                File.ReadAllText(fileinfo.FullName).ToLower();
            if (content.Contains(target))
                fileListBox.Items.Add(fileinfo);
        }
        else
```

```
            {
                // Just add this file to the list.
                fileListBox.Items.Add(fileinfo);
            }
        }
    }
```

 Please select Lesson 30 on the DVD to view the video that accompanies this lesson.

EXERCISES

1. Copy the Memo program you built in Lesson 29, Exercise 1 (or download Lesson 29's version from the book's web site). Modify the program to use the `File` class's `ReadAllText` and `WriteAllText` methods instead of using streams.

2. Write a program that sorts a text file. Hint: Load the file's lines of text into an array and use `Array.Sort` to do the actual sorting. Test the program on the file Names.txt included in this lesson's download.

3. Write a program that removes duplicate entries from a text file. Hint: Copy the program you built for Exercise 2. After you sort the array, run through the entries copying them into a new list. If you see a duplicate entry, skip it and write it to the Console window. Test the program on the file Names.txt included in this lesson's download.

 You can download the solutions to these exercises from the book's web page at www.wrox.com *or* www.CSharpHelper.com/24hour.html. *You can find those solutions in the Lesson30 folder.*

31

Printing

Most of the programs described in earlier chapters display output on the computer's screen. Chapters 29 and 30 explain how to save output in files.

This chapter explains a third method for saving output: printing. Using these techniques, you can print text, shapes, images — just about anything you want.

Before you start a printing project, however, be warned that printing in C# isn't trivial. It's easy enough to display some text or a few lines in a printout, but producing a complex formatted document can be a lot of work.

If you need to produce a nicely formatted resume, graph, or grid of values, you should ask yourself whether there's an easier way. For example, Microsoft Word is great at producing nicely formatted text documents, and Microsoft Excel does a wonderful job of making charts and graphs. You can certainly generate these sorts of printouts using C#, but it may be a lot faster if you use another tool such as Word or Excel.

Note that this isn't the only way to print with C# code. For example, a C# program that uses Windows Presentation Foundation (WPF) can build WPF documents for later printing, or it can use the WPF printing techniques described in Lesson 41. A program can also use a reporting tool such as Crystal Reports.

BASIC PRINTING

The `PrintDocument` component sits at the center of the printing process. To print, a program creates an instance of this class either at design time or at run time. It adds event handlers to catch the object's events and then lets the object do its thing. As the object generates pieces of the printout, it raises events to let the program supply graphics for it to print.

The `PrintDocument` object raises four key events:

➤ `BeginPrint` — Raised when the object is about to start printing. The program should do whatever it must to get ready to print.

➤ `QueryPageSettings` — Raised when the object is about to start printing a page. The program can modify the next page's settings. For example, it might adjust the margins so even pages have bigger margins on the left than odd pages or vice versa to allow for a staple in a double-sided document.

➤ `PrintPage` — Raised when the object needs to generate contents for a page. This is where the program does its drawing. It should set the event handler's `e.HasMorePages` value to `false` if this is the last page.

➤ `EndPrint` — Raised after the object has finished printing. The program can perform any necessary clean up here.

The `BeginPrint`, `QueryPageSettings`, and `EndPrint` event handlers are optional. For simple printouts, you may only need the `PrintPage` event handler.

The `PrintPage` event handler gives you a parameter named e of type `PrintPageEventArgs`. This object contains the `HasMorePages` parameter that you use to tell the `PrintDocument` whether this is the last page, a `Graphics` object that you use to draw the page's contents, a `PageBounds` property that tells you how big the page is, and a `MarginBounds` property that tells you where the page's margins are.

Drawing Shapes

The easiest way to generate a printout using the `PrintDocument` object is to place the object on a form and give the object a `PrintPage` event handler to generate the pages. When you're ready to print, simply call the object's `Print` method to send the printout to the default printer. As it builds the pages, the `PrintDocument` raises its `PrintPage` event to find out what to draw.

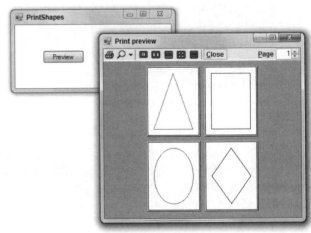

Once you've done this much, it's practically trivial to add a print preview capability to the program. Add a `PrintPreviewDialog` object to the form and set its `Document` property to the `PrintDocument` object that you already created. To display a print preview, simply call the dialog's `ShowDialog` method. The dialog uses the associated `PrintDocument` object to generate the necessary preview and displays the result.

FIGURE 31-1

Figure 31-1 shows the PrintShapes example program (available as part of this lesson's code download) displaying a four-page print preview that contains a triangle, rectangle, ellipse, and diamond.

The following code shows the program's `PrintPage` event handler:

```
// The number of the next page.
private int nextPageNum = 0;

// Print a page.
private void shapesPrintDocument_PrintPage(object sender,
    System.Drawing.Printing.PrintPageEventArgs e)
{
    // These are used to draw the triangle and diamond.
    float xmid = (e.MarginBounds.Left + e.MarginBounds.Right) / 2;
    float ymid = (e.MarginBounds.Top + e.MarginBounds.Bottom) / 2;

    // See which page this is.
    switch (nextPageNum)
    {
        case 0: // Draw a triangle.
            PointF[] trianglePoints =
            {
                new PointF(xmid, e.MarginBounds.Top),
                new PointF(e.MarginBounds.Left, e.MarginBounds.Bottom),
                new PointF(e.MarginBounds.Right, e.MarginBounds.Bottom),
            };
            using (Pen pen = new Pen(Color.Red, 10))
            {
                e.Graphics.DrawPolygon(pen, trianglePoints);
            }
            break;
        case 1: // Draw a rectangle.
            using (Pen pen = new Pen(Color.Blue, 10))
            {
                e.Graphics.DrawRectangle(pen, e.MarginBounds);
            }
            break;
        case 2: // Draw an ellipse.
            using (Pen pen = new Pen(Color.Green, 10))
            {
                e.Graphics.DrawEllipse(pen, e.MarginBounds);
            }
            break;
        case 3: // Draw a diamond.
            PointF[] diamondPoints =
            {
                new PointF(xmid, e.MarginBounds.Top),
                new PointF(e.MarginBounds.Right, ymid),
                new PointF(xmid, e.MarginBounds.Bottom),
                new PointF(e.MarginBounds.Left, ymid),
            };
            using (Pen pen = new Pen(Color.Black, 10))
            {
                e.Graphics.DrawPolygon(pen, diamondPoints);
            }
            break;
    }

    nextPageNum += 1;
```

```
        if (nextPageNum > 3)
        {
            // This is the last page. Start over if we print again.
            e.HasMorePages = false;
            nextPageNum = 0;
        }
        else
        {
            // We have more pages.
            e.HasMorePages = true;
        }
    }
```

The `nextPageNum` variable stores the number of the next page for the program to print.

The event handler uses a `switch` statement to decide which shape it should draw. Depending on the page number, it uses the `e.Graphics` object's `DrawPolygon`, `DrawRectangle`, or `DrawEllipse` method to draw different shapes.

The code uses different `Pen` objects to draw the various shapes. For example, it draws the triangle with a 10-pixel wide red pen. The using statements automatically dispose of the `Pen`'s resources when the program is done with them.

After it draws the current page's shape, the program increments `nextPageNum`. If the new page number is greater than 3, the program has finished drawing all of the pages (there are 4 of them, numbered starting with 0) so it sets `e.HasMorePages` to `false`. It also resets `nextPageNum` to 0 so the program starts over the next time you click one of the buttons.

If the next page number is not greater than 3, the program has more pages to print so it sets `e.HasMorePages` to `true`.

The following code shows how the program displays print previews and generates printouts:

```
// Display a print preview.
private void previewButton_Click(object sender, EventArgs e)
{
    shapesPrintPreviewDialog.ShowDialog();
}

// Print.
private void printButton_Click(object sender, EventArgs e)
{
    shapesPrintDocument.Print();
}
```

Unfortunately there isn't room in this lesson to really get into the drawing routines that you use to generate fancier printouts. See Lesson 39 for more details. For a more complete introduction to graphics programming in C#, see my PDF-format Wrox Blox C# Graphics Programming available at `www.wrox.com/WileyCDA/WroxTitle/productCd-0470343494.html`.

Drawing Text

The PrintShapes program described in the preceding section demonstrates the basic techniques you need to print. It uses a `PrintPage` event handler to draw different shapes on four pages of a printout.

You can print text in much the same way you print shapes. The only real difference is that to draw text you use the `e.Graphics` object's `DrawString` method instead of one of the other `Graphics` methods such as `DrawPolygon` or `DrawEllipse`.

Example program PrintText (available as part of this lesson's code download) uses the following code to print a series of names on a single page:

```
// Print some text on one page.
private void textPrintDocument_PrintPage(object sender,
    System.Drawing.Printing.PrintPageEventArgs e)
{
    // Make a font to use.
    using (Font font = new Font("Times New Roman", 20))
    {
        // Get the coordinates for the first line.
        int x = e.MarginBounds.Left;
        int y = e.MarginBounds.Top;

        // Print some text.
        string[] names =
        {
            "Arsenal", "Burnley", "Chelsea", "Liverpool",
            "Man City", "Portsmouth", "Tottenham", "Wigan",
        };
        foreach (string name in names)
        {
            // Print the name.
            e.Graphics.DrawString(name, font, Brushes.Black, x, y);

            // Move down for the next line.
            y += 30;
        }
    }

    // We only have one page.
    e.HasMorePages = false;
}
```

The program first creates a large font to use when drawing text. It uses a `using` statement to dispose of the font's resources when the program is done with it.

Next the code sets variables `x` and `y` to the coordinates where the first name should appear. In this example, the program displays the first line in the upper-left corner of the page's margin bounds.

The program then loops through an array of names. For each name, the program uses the `e.Graphics` object's `DrawString` method to draw the name. It then adds 30 to the variable `y` so the next name is printed farther down the page.

TRY IT

In this Try It, you build a program that prints and displays a preview of the table shown in Figure 31-2. You build an array of Student objects and then loop through them displaying their values as shown in the figure.

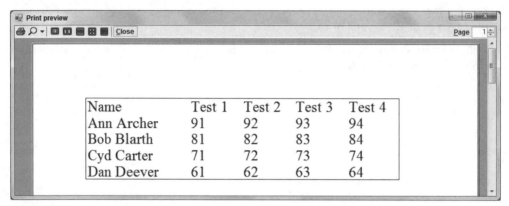

FIGURE 31-2

 You can download the code and resources for this Try It from the book's web page at www.wrox.com *or* www.CSharpHelper.com/24hour.html. *You can find them in the Lesson31 folder of the download.*

Lesson Requirements

➤ Start a new project and create the program's main form. Add PrintDocument and PrintPreviewDialog components to do the printing and previewing.

➤ Add appropriate event handlers to the Preview and Print buttons.

➤ Add a Student class with FirstName and LastName properties. Also give it a TestScores property that is an array of integers.

➤ Create the PrintPage event handler.

> ➤ Create an array of Student objects. Initialize them using array and object initializers.

> ➤ Loop through the Student objects printing them using code similar to the code used by the PrintText example program described earlier.

> ➤ Draw a rectangle around the table.

Hints

➤ Don't forget to set the `PrintPreviewDialog`'s `Document` property to the `PrintDocument` component.

➤ This example doesn't do anything fancy with properties so they can be auto-implemented.

➤ It might help to define variables x0, x1, and so on to keep track of where each column should begin.

Step-by-Step

➤ Start a new project and create the program's main form. Add `PrintDocument` and `PrintPreviewDialog` components to do the printing and previewing.

1. This is reasonably straightforward.

➤ Add appropriate event handlers to the Preview and Print buttons.

1. Use code similar to the following:

```
// Display a print preview.
private void previewButton_Click(object sender, EventArgs e)
{
    textPrintPreviewDialog.ShowDialog();
}

// Print.
private void printButton_Click(object sender, EventArgs e)
{
    textPrintDocument.Print();
}
```

➤ Add a `Student` class with `FirstName` and `LastName` properties. Also give it a `TestScores` property that is an array of integers.

1. Use code similar to the following:

```
class Student
{
    public string FirstName { get; set; }
    public string LastName { get; set; }
    public int[]TestScores { get; set; }
}
```

➤ Create the `PrintPage` event handler.

➤ Create an array of `Student` objects. Initialize them using array and object initializers.

➤ Loop through the Student objects, printing them using code similar to the code used by the PrintText example program described earlier.

➤ Draw a rectangle around the table.

1. Use code similar to the following:

```csharp
// Print the table.
private void textPrintDocument_PrintPage(object sender,
    System.Drawing.Printing.PrintPageEventArgs e)
{
    // Make some data.
    Student[] students =
    {
        new Student() {FirstName="Ann", LastName="Archer",
            TestScores=new int[] {91, 92, 93, 94}},
        new Student() {FirstName="Bob", LastName="Blarth",
            TestScores=new int[] {81, 82, 83, 84}},
        new Student() {FirstName="Cyd", LastName="Carter",
            TestScores=new int[] {71, 72, 73, 74}},
        new Student() {FirstName="Dan", LastName="Deever",
            TestScores=new int[] {61, 62, 63, 64}},
    };

    // Get the coordinates for the first row and the columns.
    int y = e.MarginBounds.Top;
    int x0 = e.MarginBounds.Left;
    int x1 = x0 + 200;
    int x2 = x1 + 100;
    int x3 = x2 + 100;
    int x4 = x3 + 100;

    // Make a font to use.
    using (Font font = new Font("Times New Roman", 20))
    {
        // Draw column headers.
        e.Graphics.DrawString("Name", font, Brushes.Black, x0, y);
        e.Graphics.DrawString("Test 1", font, Brushes.Black, x1, y);
        e.Graphics.DrawString("Test 2", font, Brushes.Black, x2, y);
        e.Graphics.DrawString("Test 3", font, Brushes.Black, x3, y);
        e.Graphics.DrawString("Test 4", font, Brushes.Black, x4, y);
        // Move Y down for the first row.
        y += 30;

        // Loop through the Students displaying their data.
        foreach (Student student in students)
        {
            // Display the Student's values.
            e.Graphics.DrawString(student.FirstName + " " +
                student.LastName, font, Brushes.Black, x0, y);
            e.Graphics.DrawString(student.TestScores[0].ToString(),
                font, Brushes.Black, x1, y);
            e.Graphics.DrawString(student.TestScores[1].ToString(),
                font, Brushes.Black, x2, y);
            e.Graphics.DrawString(student.TestScores[2].ToString(),
                font, Brushes.Black, x3, y);
            e.Graphics.DrawString(student.TestScores[3].ToString(),
                font, Brushes.Black, x4, y);

            // Move Y down for the next row.
            y += 30;
        }
```

```
        }

        // Draw a box around it all.
        e.Graphics.DrawRectangle(Pens.Black,
            x0, e.MarginBounds.Top,
            x4 - x0 + 100,
            y - e.MarginBounds.Top);

        // We're only printing one page.
        e.HasMorePages = false;
    }
}
```

 Please select Lesson 31 on the DVD to view the video that accompanies this lesson.

EXERCISES

1. Copy the program you built in this lesson's Try It and add additional drawing code to produce the result shown in Figure 31-3.

Name	Test 1	Test 2	Test 3	Test 4
Ann Archer	91	92	93	94
Bob Blarth	81	82	83	84
Cyd Carter	71	72	73	74
Dan Deever	61	62	63	64

FIGURE 31-3

2. Make a program that prints a bar chart similar to the one shown in Figure 31-4.

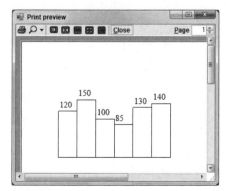

FIGURE 31-4

3. Build the program shown in Figure 31-5. The main form (on the left) contains a DataGridView control where the user can enter values. The File menu contains Preview and Print commands.

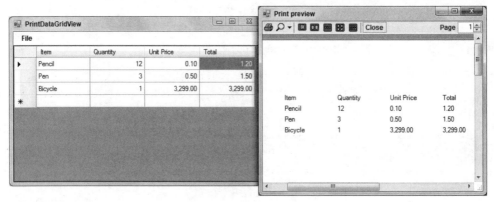

FIGURE 31-5

Add PrintDocument and PrintPreviewDialog controls as usual. The PrintPage event handler should:

1. Call the grid's EndEdit method to commit any current edit.

2. Loop through the grid's Columns collection displaying the column headers. Add each column's Width value to the X coordinate for the next column.

3. Loop through the grid's Rows collection. For each row, loop through the row's Cells collection, displaying the cells' FormattedValue property.

4. For extra credit, draw lines between the values.

You can download the solutions to these exercises from the book's web page at www.wrox.com *or* www.CSharpHelper.com/24hour.html. *You can find those solutions in the Lesson31 folder.*

32

Using the Clipboard

Earlier lessons have explained how to interact with the user (through controls), the file system, and most recently the printer. This lesson explains how your program can interact with other programs via the clipboard.

In this lesson, you learn how to place text, image, and other data on the clipboard so you can paste it into other applications. You also learn how to receive data pasted into your program from the clipboard.

ADDING DATA TO THE CLIPBOARD

Adding data to the clipboard is fairly easy. The `Clipboard` class provides several static methods to place certain kinds of data on the clipboard:

➤ `SetAudio` — Copies an audio stream to the clipboard.

➤ `SetFileDropList` — Copies a list of files to the clipboard as if the user had selected them in Windows Explorer and pressed Ctrl+C.

➤ `SetImage` — Copies an image to the clipboard.

➤ `SetText` — Copies a string to the clipboard.

Example program AddToClipboard, shown in Figure 32-1 and included as part of this lesson's code download, demonstrates these methods. Use the Copy buttons to copy the corresponding content on the left to the clipboard. (When the program starts, it copies the names of the files in its startup directory into the list box. The bottom image represents an audio file.)

FIGURE 32-1

The program uses the following code to copy data to the clipboard:

```
// Copy the text to the clipboard.
// Then manually try pasting into Word, WordPad, etc.
private void copyTextButton_Click(object sender, EventArgs e)
{
    Clipboard.SetText(dataTextBox.Text);

    System.Media.SystemSounds.Beep.Play();
}

// Copy the picture to the clipboard.
// Then try pasting into Word, Paint, etc.
private void copyPictureButton_Click(object sender, EventArgs e)
{
    Clipboard.SetImage(dataPictureBox.Image);

    System.Media.SystemSounds.Beep.Play();
}

// Copy the picture to the clipboard.
// Then try pasting into ReadFromClipboard.
private void copyFilesButton_Click(object sender, EventArgs e)
{
    // Make a StringCollection holding the file names.
    StringCollection files = new StringCollection();
    foreach (string filename in filesListBox.Items)
    {
        files.Add(filename);
    }

    // Save the list to the clipboard.
    Clipboard.SetFileDropList(files);

    System.Media.SystemSounds.Beep.Play();
}

// Copy some audio to the clipboard.
private void copyAudioButton_Click(object sender, EventArgs e)
{
    Clipboard.SetAudio(Properties.Resources.boing);

    using (SoundPlayer player =
        new SoundPlayer(Properties.Resources.boing))
    {
        player.Play();
    }
}
```

The text and image copying event handlers are straightforward. They simply use the appropriate `Clipboard` method to copy data to the clipboard and then play the system's beep sound.

The file list copying button builds a `StringCollection`, adds the files in the list box to it and calls the `Clipboard`'s `SetFileDropList`.

The StringCollection *class is in the* System.Collections *namespace, so the program includes a* using *directive to make using the class easier.*

The audio copying button copies an audio resource to the clipboard.

To add an audio resource to the project at design time, open the Project menu and select Properties at the bottom. Next click the Resources tab. Click the Add Resource dropdown arrow at the top of the page and select Add Existing File. Select the audio file that you want to add to the project and click Open.

Visual Studio adds the audio file to the project and creates a memory stream property that you can use to refer to it. In this example, the file I used was named boing.wav so the program can refer to it as Properties.Resources.boing.

The audio copying button calls the Clipboard's SetAudio method, passing it the audio resource. Then instead of playing the system's beep sound, the program creates a SoundPlayer associated with the audio resource and calls the player's Play method.

 The SoundPlayer *class is in the* System.Media *namespace, so the program includes a* using *directive to make using the class easier.*

 Programs that accept audio pasted from the clipboard are uncommon. To test this program's ability to copy audio to the clipboard, you can use the ReadFromClipboard example program described in the following section.

GETTING DATA FROM THE CLIPBOARD

Getting data from the clipboard is just as easy as putting it there because the Clipboard class provides static methods that return audio streams, file drop lists, images, and text.

Before you try to copy data from the clipboard, however, you should make sure the data you want is present. To let you do that, the Clipboard class also provides a set of functions that tell you whether data in a given format is available.

For example, the following code checks whether text is available on the clipboard and, if it is, copies the text into the textbox named dataTextBox:

```
if (Clipboard.ContainsText()) dataTextBox.Text = Clipboard.GetText();
```

The ReadFromClipboard example program (included in this lesson's code download) uses the following code to paste audio, file drop lists, images, or text from the clipboard:

```csharp
// Paste whatever data is available from the clipboard.
private void pasteButton_Click(object sender, EventArgs e)
{
    // Clear previous results.
    dataTextBox.Clear();
    filesListBox.Items.Clear();
    dataPictureBox.Image = null;

    // Paste the text if available.
    if (Clipboard.ContainsText()) dataTextBox.Text = Clipboard.GetText();

    // Paste the picture if available.
    if (Clipboard.ContainsImage()) dataPictureBox.Image =
        Clipboard.GetImage();

    // Paste file drop list if available.
    if (Clipboard.ContainsFileDropList())
    {
        StringCollection files = Clipboard.GetFileDropList();
        foreach (string filename in files)
        {
            filesListBox.Items.Add(filename);
        }
    }

    // Paste audio if available.
    if (Clipboard.ContainsAudio())
    {
        using (SoundPlayer player =
            new SoundPlayer(Clipboard.GetAudioStream()))
        {
            player.Play();
        }
    }
}
```

The code starts by clearing its current text, file list, and image. It then copies whatever data is available from the clipboard.

If the program finds audio content is available, it makes a `SoundPlayer` associated with the audio stream provided by the clipboard and plays it.

TRY IT

In this Try It, you create a program that backs up files. The program contains a textbox where you can enter a directory name and a button. When you click the button, the program copies any files in the clipboard's file drop list into the backup directory, adding a numeric version number at the end.

You can download the code and resources for this Try It from the book's web page at www.wrox.com *or* www.CSharpHelper.com/24hour.html. *You can find them in the Lesson32 folder of the download.*

Lesson Requirements

➤ Start a new project and add a textbox and button.

➤ When the user clicks the button, see if the clipboard contains a file drop list. If it does:

  ➤ Use the value in the textbox to create a `DirectoryInfo` object. Create the directory if necessary.

  ➤ For each file in the drop list, make a `FileInfo` object. Try adding 001, 002, 003, and so on to the file's name and see if there's already a file with that name in the backup directory. When you find a filename that isn't already in use, copy the file using that name.

Hints

➤ You can use `Path.Combine` to combine the directory's path and the file's name.

Step-by-Step

➤ Start a new project and add a textbox and button.

  1. This is straightforward.

➤ When the user clicks the button, see if the clipboard contains a file drop list. If it does:

  ➤ Use the value in the textbox to create a `DirectoryInfo` object. Create the directory if necessary.

  ➤ For each file in the drop list, make a `FileInfo` object. Try adding 001, 002, 003, and so on to the file's name and see if there's already a file with that name in the backup directory. When you find a filename that isn't already in use, copy the file using that name.

  1. Use code similar to the following:

```
// Back up any files listed on the clipboard's file drop list.
private void backupButton_Click(object sender, EventArgs e)
{
    if (Clipboard.ContainsFileDropList())
    {
        // Get the backup directory.
        DirectoryInfo dirInfo =
            new DirectoryInfo(directoryTextBox.Text);
```

```
        // Create the directory if necessary.
        dirInfo.Create();

        // Process the files.
        foreach (string filename in Clipboard.GetFileDropList())
        {
            FileInfo fileInfo = new FileInfo(filename);

            // Add a version number to the end.
            // Keep trying until we find one that isn't
            // already there.
            for (int i = 0; ; i++)
            {
                // Compose a file name in the backup directory
                // with the file's name and the version number.
                string newFileName =
                    Path.Combine(dirInfo.FullName, fileInfo.Name) +
                    "." + i.ToString("000");

                // See if this file exists.
                if (!File.Exists(newFileName))
                {
                    // Copy the file here.
                    fileInfo.CopyTo(newFileName);

                    // Exit the for loop.
                    break;
                }
            }
        }
    }
    MessageBox.Show("Done");
}
```

 Please select Lesson 32 on the DVD to view the video that accompanies this lesson.

EXERCISES

FIGURE 32-2

1. Build the application shown in Figure 32-2. When the user presses Ctrl+V, display any text or image that the clipboard contains.

Hints: Set the form's `KeyPreview` property to true. Then use code similar to the following to tell when the user presses Ctrl+V. Notice that the code sets `e.Handled = true` to indicate that the key press can be discarded after the event handler is done with it.

```
private void Form1_KeyDown(object sender, KeyEventArgs e)
{
    // See if it's Ctrl+V.
```

```
        if (e.Control && e.KeyCode == Keys.V)
        {
            ...

            // Mark the key press as handled.
            e.Handled = true;
        }
    }
```

2. The Clipboard can contain several different kinds of text. Overloaded versions of the ContainsText and GetText methods take a TextDataFormat parameter that indicates the kind of text you want.

    Build a program with two TextBoxes and a RichTextBox. When the user clicks a button, see what kind of text is available and paste plain text into one TextBox, HTML text into the other, and rich text format (RTF) text into the RichTextBox. Test the program by pasting text copied from programs such as Microsoft Word and WordPad.

 You can download the solutions to these exercises from the book's web page at www.wrox.com or www.CSharpHelper.com/24hour.html. You can find those solutions in the Lesson32 folder.

33

Providing Drag and Drop

In some ways, drag and drop performs the same task as the clipboard. Both allow one application to give data to another. The difference is that the clipboard saves data for later delivery whereas drag and drop delivers the data immediately and is done.

In this lesson, you learn how to add drag and drop to your program so it can interact with other applications.

Note that drag and drop is only useful in some environments. This lesson explains how to provide drag and drop in Windows Forms application (which is the focus of this book). If you're writing an application for some other platform, such as an ASP.NET application that runs in a browser, the techniques described in this chapter won't work. In fact, for some applications drag and drop may not even make sense.

UNDERSTANDING DRAG AND DROP EVENTS

There are two participants in a drag and drop operation: a *drag source* and a *drop target*.

> ➤ The **drag source** initiates a drag, for example when you right-click it. It determines what data is in the drag and what kinds of operations are allowed on the drag such as a copy or cut.

> ➤ The **drop target** is a potential recipient of a drag's data. When the drag moves over it, the target can decide whether it can accept the data in an offered operation such as copy or cut.

To handle all of the potential interactions among the drag source, the drop target, and the user, you can use several event handlers. Some of these events occur in the drag source and others occur in the drop target.

Table 33-1 summarizes the key drag source events.

TABLE 33-1

EVENT	PURPOSE
GiveFeedback	The drag has entered a valid drop target. The source can indicate the type of drop allowed. For example, it might allow Copy if the target is a Label and allow Move or Copy if the target is a TextBox.
QueryContinueDrag	The keyboard or mouse button state has changed. The drag source can decide whether to continue the drag, cancel the drag, or drop the data immediately.

The drop target has more events than the drag source. The drag source merely provides data that drop targets might want to accept. The drop target might need to provide a lot more interaction to tell the user what's happening.

Table 33-2 describes the events received by a drop target when data is dragged over it.

TABLE 33-2

EVENT	PURPOSE
DragEnter	The drag is entering the target. The target can examine the type of data available and set e.Effect to indicate the types of drops it can handle. It can also display some sort of highlight to tell the user that it can accept the data and where it might land.
DragLeave	The drag has left the target. The target should remove any highlighting or other hints that it displayed in DragEnter.
DragOver	The drag is over the target. This event continues to fire a few times per second until the drag leaves. For example, the target could change its appearance to show exactly where the data would land if dropped. It can also check things such as the keyboard state — it might allow a Copy if the Ctrl key is pressed and a Move otherwise.
DragDrop	The user dropped the data on the target so the target should process the data.

STARTING A DRAG

Starting a drag is fairly easy. First create an instance of the DataObject class to indicate the type of data being dragged and to hold the data itself. Then simply call a control's DoDrag method, passing it the DataObject.

The DragSource example program (available in this lesson's code download) uses the following code to start dragging text when you press the right mouse button down over its `dragLabel` control:

```
// Start a drag.
private void dragLabel_MouseDown(object sender, MouseEventArgs e)
{
    // If it's not the right mouse button, do nothing.
    if (e.Button != MouseButtons.Right) return;

    // Make the data object.
    DataObject data = new DataObject(DataFormats.Text, dragLabel.Text);

    // Start the drag allowing only copy.
    dragLabel.DoDragDrop(data, DragDropEffects.Copy);
}
```

The code first checks whether the right mouse button is pressed and exits if it is not. It then creates a `DataObject`. It passes the object's constructor the value `DataFormats.Text` to indicate that it will hold text data and the text that the object should hold.

Finally, the code calls the `Label` control's `DoDrag` method passing it the `DataObject` and the value `DragDropEffects.Copy` to indicate that the drag allows only the copy operation.

This example doesn't bother with the `GiveFeedback` and `QueryContinueDrag` event handlers, so that's the extent of its participation in the drag.

The `DoDrag` function returns a `DragDropEffects` value that indicates what the drop target decided to do with the data. For example, if the function returns `DragDropEffects.Move`, then the user is performing a Move operation so the drag source should remove the data from its application. For example, a file explorer such as Windows Explorer would remove the file from the source location and move it to the drop location.

Note that a drag is completely separate from the drop target. If a drop target can accept the data, it is free to do so. That means you don't need to wait until you read about the DropTarget example program described in the next section to test the DragSource program. You can test the program right now by using it to drag text data into Word, WordPad, or any other program that accepts dropped text. (Notepad doesn't know how to accept dropped text.)

CATCHING A DROP

Before a control can accept a drop, you must set the form's `AllowDrop` property to true. If `AllowDrop` is false, the form will not allow drops no matter what event handlers you create.

The only other thing a drop target must do is provide `DragEnter` and `DragDrop` event handlers.

The `DragEnter` event handler should examine the data available and set the event handler's `e.Effect` parameter to indicate whether it wants to allow the drop. The drag and drop system automatically changes the mouse cursor to indicate the kind of drop that the target allows.

The DropTarget example program (available in this lesson's code download) uses the following `DragEnter` event handler:

```
// A drag entered. List available formats.
private void Form1_DragEnter(object sender, DragEventArgs e)
{
    // Allow text data.
    if (e.Data.GetDataPresent(DataFormats.Text))
    {
        // Only allow the Copy operation.
        e.Effect = DragDropEffects.Copy;
    }
}
```

This code checks whether the drag contains text data and, if it does, sets `e.Effect` to allow the Copy operation.

 The `DragEnter` *event handler's* `e.Effect` *parameter has the value* `DragDropEffects.None` *by default, so you don't need to set it if you want to prevent a drop. In the DropTarget example program, if no text is available, the program doesn't allow any kind of drop operation.*

The `DragDrop` event handler should use its `e.Data` parameter to see what data is available and to get it. It should then set `e.Effect` to indicate what operation it performed, such as Copy or Move so the drag source knows what happened to the data.

The DropTarget example program uses the following `DragDrop` event handler:

```
// Accept dropped data.
private void Form1_DragDrop(object sender, DragEventArgs e)
{
    // Get the dropped data.
    if (e.Data.GetDataPresent(DataFormats.Text))
    {
        dropLabel.Text = (string)e.Data.GetData(DataFormats.Text);

        // Indicate that we copied.
        e.Effect = DragDropEffects.Copy;
    }
}
```

This code checks for text data. If text is available, the code gets it and displays it in a label. It also sets `e.Effect = DragDropEffects.Copy` to tell the drag source that the target performed a Copy operation.

Note that accepting a drop is completely separate from the drag. If data is available in a format that your program can use, you are free to use it. In this case that means you don't need to use the

DragSource example program described in the previous section to test the DropTarget example program. You can also drag text from Word, WordPad, or any other program that knows how to start dragging text. (Notepad doesn't know how to start a drag.)

 ## TRY IT

In this Try It, you elaborate on the DragSource and DropTarget example programs. You modify DragSource so it allows Copy or Move operations.

You make DropTarget perform Copy or Move operations depending on whether the Ctrl key is pressed during the drop. You also provide feedback if the user changes the state of the Ctrl key during the drag.

> *You can download the code and resources for this Try It from the book's web page at* www.wrox.com *or* www.CSharpHelper.com/24hour.html. *You can find them in the Lesson33 folder of the download.*

Lesson Requirements

➤ Copy the DragSource and DropTarget example programs into new directories.

➤ In DragSource, allow Copy and Move operations. Check the result of DoDragDrop and if the operation was a Move, remove the text from the source Label control.

➤ In DropTarget, make the DragEnter event handler allow Copy and Move operations.

➤ In DropTarget, add a DragOver event handler. The value e.KeyState & 8 is nonzero if the Ctrl key is pressed. If Ctrl is pressed, allow Copy. If Ctrl is not pressed, allow Move.

➤ In DropTarget, make the DragDrop event handler check the state of the Ctrl key just as DragOver does. If Ctrl is pressed, tell the drag source that the operation is a Copy. If Ctrl is not pressed, tell the drag source that the operation is a Move.

Hints

➤ To make DragSource allow either Move or Copy operations, use DragDropEffects.Copy | DragDropEffects.Move.

➤ To make DropTarget allow either Move or Copy operations, use DragDropEffects.Copy | DragDropEffects.Move.

Step-by-Step

➤ Copy the DragSource and DropTarget example programs into new directories.

1. This is straightforward.

➤ In DragSource, allow Copy and Move operations. Check the result of DoDragDrop and if the operation was a Move, remove the text from the source Label control.

1. Pass the DoDragDrop function the parameter DragDropEffects.Copy | DragDropEffects.Move for the allowed operations.

2. Check the result returned by DoDragDrop. If the result is DragDropEffects.Move, clear the Label control.

3. The code should look something like this:

```
// Start a drag.
private void dragLabel_MouseDown(object sender, MouseEventArgs e)
{
    // If it's not the right mouse button, do nothing.
    if (e.Button != MouseButtons.Right) return;

    // Make the data object.
    DataObject data = new DataObject(DataFormats.Text, dragLabel.Text);

    // Start the drag allowing copy and move.
    if (dragLabel.DoDragDrop(data,
        DragDropEffects.Copy | DragDropEffects.Move)
            == DragDropEffects.Move)
    {
        // This is a Move. Remove the data from this application.
        dragLabel.Text = "";
    }
}
```

➤ In DropTarget, make the DragEnter event handler allow Copy and Move operations.

1. In the DragEnter event handler, if text data is available set e.Effect = DragDropEffects.Copy | DragDropEffects.Move to allow both Copy and Move operations. The code should look something like this:

```
// A drag entered. List available formats.
private void Form1_DragEnter(object sender, DragEventArgs e)
{
    // Allow text data.
    if (e.Data.GetDataPresent(DataFormats.Text))
    {
        // Only allow the Copy and Move operations.
        e.Effect = DragDropEffects.Copy | DragDropEffects.Move;
    }
}
```

➤ In DropTarget, add a DragOver event handler. The value e.KeyState & 8 is nonzero if the Ctrl key is pressed. If Ctrl is pressed, allow Copy. If Ctrl is not pressed, allow Move.

1. Add the DragOver event handler. If Ctrl is pressed, set e.Effect = DragDropEffects.Copy. If Ctrl is not pressed, set e.Effect = DragDropEffects.Move.

```
// Allow copy or move depending on the Ctrl key state.
private void Form1_DragOver(object sender, DragEventArgs e)
```

```
    {
        const int keyCtrl = 8;

        if ((e.KeyState & keyCtrl) != 0)
        {
            // Ctrl is pressed. Allow Copy.
            e.Effect = DragDropEffects.Copy;
        }
        else
        {
            // Ctrl is not pressed. Allow Move.
            e.Effect = DragDropEffects.Move;
        }
    }
```

➤ In DropTarget, make the `DragDrop` event handler check the state of the Ctrl key just as `DragOver` does. If Ctrl is pressed, tell the drag source that the operation is a Copy. If Ctrl is not pressed, tell the drag source that the operation is a Move.

1. Display the data as before.

2. Determine whether Ctrl is pressed. If Ctrl is pressed, set `e.Effect = DragDropEffects .Copy`. If Ctrl is not pressed, set `e.Effect = DragDropEffects.Move`.

```
// Accept dropped data.
private void Form1_DragDrop(object sender, DragEventArgs e)
{
    const int keyCtrl = 8;

    // Get the dropped data.
    if (e.Data.GetDataPresent(DataFormats.Text))
    {
        dropLabel.Text = (string)e.Data.GetData(DataFormats.Text);

        // Tell the drag source what operation we performed.
        if ((e.KeyState & keyCtrl) != 0)
        {
            // Ctrl is pressed. Allow Copy.
            e.Effect = DragDropEffects.Copy;
        }
        else
        {
            // Ctrl is not pressed. Allow Move.
            e.Effect = DragDropEffects.Move;
        }
    }
}
```

 Please select Lesson 33 on the DVD to view the video that accompanies this lesson.

EXERCISES

1. Copy this lesson's Try It (both the DragSource and DropTarget programs). Modify the DropTarget program in these ways:

> ➤ Add a `ListBox` named `formatsListBox`. In the program's `DragEnter` event handler, loop through the string array returned by `e.Data.GetFormats` and list the available formats in the `ListBox`.

> ➤ In the `DragEnter` event handler, allow the Copy operation for the `Text` and `FileDrop` types of data.

> ➤ Add a `DragLeave` event handler that clears `formatsListBox`.

> ➤ In the `DragDrop` event handler, display text in a `TextBox` as before. If the dropped data is a `FileDrop`, it is an array of strings. Loop through the array and display the dropped filenames in a `ListBox` named `dropListBox`. Test this feature by dragging files from Windows Explorer onto the program.

2. Copy the program you built for the Try It in Lesson 32 (or download Lesson 32's version from the book's web site). Add the ability for the program to accept a dropped file list instead of only getting a file list from the clipboard.

Hint: Don't forget to set the form's `AllowDrop` property to true.

Hint: It would be nice to move the code that backs up the files into a new `BackupFiles` function so you could call it for a file list taken from the clipboard or from drag and drop. Unfortunately the clipboard's file list is a `StringCollection` but drag and drop's file list is an array of strings. Because they have different data types, you cannot make `BackupFiles` handle them both easily.

To solve this problem, make `BackupFiles` take a `filenames` parameter of the non-generic type `System.Collections.IList`. The clipboard data implements this interface, so you can simply pass it to `BackupFiles`. To pass the drag and drop data to `BackupFiles`, simply cast it into the `System.Collections.IList` type.

 You can download the solutions to these exercises from the book's web page at www.wrox.com *or* www.CSharpHelper.com/24hour.html. *You can find those solutions in the Lesson33 folder.*

SECTION VI
Specialized Topics

The lessons so far have dealt with general programming topics. For example, every desktop application needs to use controls and most also need to use variables, classes, and files.

The lessons in this section explain more specialized topics. They describe ideas and techniques that you won't need for every program you write, although you will still find them useful under many circumstances.

34

Localizing Programs

Many programmers write applications that are used only in their countries. It's easy enough to find plenty of customers for a small application without looking for customers long-distance.

However, the world has grown smaller in the past few decades, and it's not too hard to provide programs for people all over the world. Customers can download your software over the web and pay for it using online payment systems in a matter of minutes. Web applications that run in a browser are even more likely to be used by people all over the world.

With such a potentially enormous market, it makes sense in some cases to make programs accessible to people in different countries, particularly since C# and Visual Studio make it relatively easy.

In this lesson, you learn how to make a program accessible to customers in other countries with different cultures. You learn how to make multiple interfaces for a program so users can work in their own languages. You also learn how to work with values such as currency and dates that have different formats in different locales.

Localization is a huge topic so there isn't room to cover everything there is to know about it here. In particular, you should always get a native of a particular locale to help in localizing your application whenever possible. Unless you are extremely well-versed in a locale's language, customs, and idioms, it's very easy to make mistakes.

Note that I am not fluent in all of the locales that this lesson uses. I used the Babel Fish automatic translation tool at `babelfish.yahoo.com` *to make the simple translations shown here. You can use Babel Fish or a similar tool for practice and for this lesson's exercises, but you should get human help before releasing a program to users.*

UNDERSTANDING LOCALIZATION

A computer's *locale* is a setting that defines the user's language, country, and cultural settings that determine such things as how dates and monetary values are formatted. For example, the FormatValues example program shown in Figure 34-1 (and available in this lesson's code download) displays the same values in American, British, German, and French locales.

If you look closely at Figure 34-1, you can see that the same values produce very different results in the different locales. For example, the currency value 1234.56 is displayed variously as:

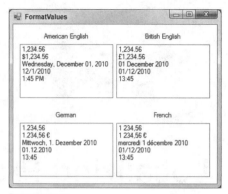

FIGURE 34-1

- ➤ $1,234.56
- ➤ £1,234.56
- ➤ 1.234,56 €
- ➤ 1 234,56 €

Not only do these results use different currency symbols, but they even use different decimal and thousands separators.

> *Globalization is the process of building an application that can be used by users from different cultures.*
>
> *Localization is the process of customizing a globalized application for a specific culture.*
>
> *Localizing an application involves two main steps: building a localized user interface and processing locale-specific values.*

BUILDING LOCALIZED INTERFACES

At first this may seem like a daunting task. How do you build completely separate interfaces for multiple locales? Fortunately this is one thing that C# and Visual Studio do really well.

To build a globalized program, start by creating the form as usual. Add controls and set their properties as you would like them to appear by default.

After you've defined the program's default appearance, you can localize it for a particular locale. Set its `Localizable` property to true. Then select a new locale from the dropdown list provided by the form's `Language` property. Now modify the form to handle the new locale. You can change control properties such as the text they display. You can also move controls around and change their sizes, which is particularly important because the same text may take up a different amount of room in different languages.

At run time, the program automatically checks the computer's locale settings and picks the language that is closest. Note that many languages have several sub-locales. For example, English comes in the varieties used in the India, Ireland, New Zealand, and more than a dozen other locales.

There's also locale listed simply as "English." If the user's computer is set up for one of the English locales that the program doesn't support, the program falls back to the generic English locale. If the program can't support that locale either, it uses the default locale that you used when you initially created the form.

The LocalizedWeekdays example program (available in this lesson's code download) is localized for English (the form's default) and German. Figure 34-2 shows the form's English interface and Figure 34-3 shows its German interface.

FIGURE 34-2   **FIGURE 34-3**

Having the program check the computer's locale automatically at run time is convenient for the user but it makes testing different locales tricky.

One way to force the program to pick a particular locale so you can test it is to select the locale in code. You must do this before the form is initialized because after that point the form's text and other properties are already filled in and setting the locale won't reload the form.

When you create a form, Visual Studio automatically creates a constructor for it that calls the InitializeComponent function. Place your code before the call to InitializeComponent.

The following code shows how the LocalizedWeekdays program explicitly selects either the English or German locale:

```
using System.Threading;
using System.Globalization;
...

public Form1()
{
    // English.
    //Thread.CurrentThread.CurrentCulture =
    //    new CultureInfo("en-US", false);
    //Thread.CurrentThread.CurrentUICulture =
```

```
//    new CultureInfo("en-US", false);

// German.
Thread.CurrentThread.CurrentCulture =
    new CultureInfo("de-DE", false);
Thread.CurrentThread.CurrentUICulture =
    new CultureInfo("de-DE", false);

InitializeComponent();
}
```

This code contains statements that set the locale to English or German. Simply comment out the one that you don't want to use for a given test.

For a list of more than 100 culture values that you can use in code such as en-US and de-DE, see msdn.microsoft.com/library/ee825488(CS.20).aspx.

Setting the CurrentCulture makes the program use locale-specific methods when processing dates, currency, numbers, and other values in the code. Setting the CurrentUICulture makes the program load the appropriate user interface elements for the form.

After you finish testing a form's localized version, be sure to remove the code that selects the culture so the program can use the system's settings. Otherwise you may end up with some very confused users.

PROCESSING LOCALE-SPECIFIC VALUES

Within a C# program, variables are stored in American English formats. To avoid confusion, Microsoft decided to pick one locale for code values and stick with it.

When you move data in and out of the program, however, you need to be aware of the computer's locale. For example, suppose the program uses the following code to display an order's due date:

```
dueDateTextBox.Text = dueDate.ToString("MM/dd/yy")
```

If the date is November 20, 2010, this produces the result "11/20/10," which makes sense in the United States but should be "20/11/10" in France and "20.11.10" in Germany.

The problem is that the program uses a custom date format that is hard-coded to use an American-style date format. To produce a format appropriate for the user's system, you should use predefined date, time, and other formats whenever possible. The following code uses the standard short date format:

```
dueDateTextBox.Text = dueDate.ToString("d")
```

This produces "11/20/2010" on an American system and "20/11/2010" on a French system.

You can run into the same problem if you assume the user will enter values in a particular format. For example, suppose you want to get the whole number part of the value 1,234.56 entered by the user. If you assume the decimal separator is a period and just use whatever comes before it as the integer part, then you'll get the answer 1 when a German user enters "1.234,56" and the program will crash when a French user enters the value "1 234.56."

To avoid this problem, use locale-aware functions such the numeric classes' `Parse` methods to read values entered by the user. In this example, a good solution is to use `float.Parse` to read the value and then truncate it as shown in the following code rather than trying to truncate the value while it's still in its string form:

```
value = (int)float.Parse(valueTextBox.Text);
```

For a list of standard numeric formats, see `msdn.microsoft.com/library/dwhawy9k(VS.100).aspx`.

For a list of standard date and time formats, see `msdn.microsoft.com/library/az4se3k1(VS.100).aspx`.

For more information on parsing strings, see `msdn.microsoft.com/library/b4w53z0y(VS.100).aspx`.

Previous lessons have shown how to use `Parse` *methods to parse currency values. For example, the following statement parses a currency value entered by the user:*

```
value = decimal.Parse(valueLabel.Text, NumberStyles.Any);
```

This isn't completely foolproof. If the user has a German system but types a value in a French format, the program will crash, but it seems reasonable to ask a German user to enter German values.

The LocalizedParsing example program shown in Figure 34-4 (and available in this lesson's code download) parses currency values displayed in labels in different languages, doubles the parsed decimal values, and displays the results. For each language, it selects the appropriate culture so it can parse and display the correct formats.

FIGURE 34-4

Language	Text	Parsed Value
American English	$1,234.56	$2,469.12
British English	£1,234.56	£2,469.12
German	1.234,56 €	2.469,12 €
French	1 234,56 €	2 469,12 €

TRY IT

In this Try It, you write the program shown in Figures 34-5 and 34-6, which let you select foreground and background colors in American English and Mexican Spanish.

FIGURE 34-5   **FIGURE 34-6**

 You can download the code and resources for this Try It from the book's web page at www.wrox.com *or* www.CSharpHelper.com/24hour.html. *You can find them in the Lesson34 folder of the download.*

Lesson Requirements

➤ Build the default interface.

➤ Add code to handle the RadioButtons' Click events.

➤ Localize the application for Mexican Spanish.

➤ Add code to let you test the form for either locale.

Hints

➤ There's no need to build a separate event handler for each RadioButton. Use one event handler for all of the foreground buttons and one for all of the background buttons.

➤ These event handlers must then figure out which button was clicked, but they cannot use the buttons' text because that will change depending on which locale is selected. They could use the buttons' names because they don't change, but it's even easier to store the corresponding colors' names in their Tag properties and then use the Color class's FromName method to get the appropriate Color.

Step-by-Step

➤ Build the default interface.

1. Build a form that looks like the one shown in Figure 34-5.

2. Store the color names (red, green, blue, and so forth) in the radio buttons' `Tag` properties.

➤ Add code to handle the `RadioButtons'` `Click` events.

1. Write an event handler similar to the following. The code converts the `sender` object into a `RadioButton` and uses its `Tag` property to get the appropriate color. It then applies that color to the form and the two `GroupBoxes`.

```
// Set the foreground color.
private void Foreground_Click(object sender, EventArgs e)
{
    // Get the sender as a RadioButton.
    RadioButton rad = sender as RadioButton;

    // Use the color.
    Color clr = Color.FromName(rad.Tag.ToString());
    this.ForeColor = clr;
    fgGroupBox.ForeColor = clr;
    bgGroupBox.ForeColor = clr;
}
```

2. Connect the foreground `RadioButtons` to this event handler.

3. Repeat these steps for the background `RadioButtons`.

➤ Localize the application for Mexican Spanish.

1. Set the form's `Localizable` property to true. Click the Language property, click the dropdown arrow to the right, and select "Spanish (Mexico)."

2. Change the controls' `Text` properties so they have the values shown in Figure 34-6.

➤ Add code to let you test the form for either locale.

1. Use code similar to the following in the form's constructor:

```
// Select a locale for testing.
public Form1()
{
    // English.
    //Thread.CurrentThread.CurrentCulture =
    //    new CultureInfo("en-US", false);
    //Thread.CurrentThread.CurrentUICulture =
    //    new CultureInfo("en-US", false);

    // Spanish.
    Thread.CurrentThread.CurrentCulture =
        new CultureInfo("es-MX", false);
    Thread.CurrentThread.CurrentUICulture =
        new CultureInfo("es-MX", false);

    InitializeComponent();
}
```

 Please select Lesson 34 on the DVD to view the video that accompanies this lesson.

EXERCISES

1. Copy this lesson's Try It and add support for Italian (it-IT) as shown in Figure 34-7. Don't forget to add code to let you test it.

FIGURE 34-7

2. When a program reads data from a file, it must use the correct locale. Download the files Dutch.txt, German.txt, and English.txt from the book's web site and make a program that can read them. The program should let the user select a file, check the file-name to see which locale it should use, and select the correct locale. It should read and parse the values into appropriate data types and then display the values again in a `DataGridView` control.

Hint: Use locale names en-US for English, de-DE for German, and nl-NL for Dutch. Use code similar to the following to select the proper locale before you parse the values:

```
Thread.CurrentThread.CurrentCulture =
    new CultureInfo("en-US", false);
```

Hint: The values within a line in the file are separated by tabs so use `File.ReadAllLines` to get the lines and `Split` to break each line into fields.

The following text shows the values in the file Dutch.txt:

```
Potlood     € 0,10       12    € 1,20
Blocnote    € 1,10       10    € 11,00
Laptop      € 1.239,99    1    € 1.239,99
```

You can download the solutions to these exercises from the book's web page at www.wrox.com *or* www.CSharpHelper.com/24hour.html. *You can find those solutions in the Lesson34 folder.*

35

Programming Databases, Part 1

Database programming is another truly enormous topic, so there isn't room to cover it all here. However, Visual Studio provides tools that make some simple kinds of database programs so easy to write that your education won't be complete until you've written a few.

In this lesson, you learn how to make a simple database application. You learn how to connect to a database, load data, let the user navigate through records, and save any changes.

CONNECTING TO A DATABASE

The first step in building a database program is giving it a connection to the data. You can do this interactively at design time quite easily, although quite a few steps are involved.

1. First open the Data menu and select Add New Data Source to display the dialog shown in Figure 35-1. As you can see in the figure, there are several different places you might want the program to get data.

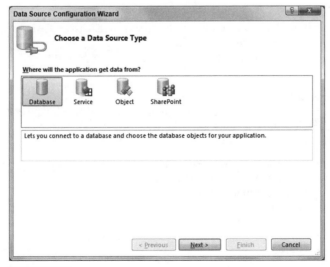

FIGURE 35-1

The data source used in this example is a database, so select Database and click Next.

2. The dialog's next screen lets you decide whether you want to use a dataset or an entity data model for your data. For this example, pick Dataset and click Next to make the dialog display the screen shown in Figure 35-2.

A dataset is an in-memory representation of a data source. A dataset can include multiple tables that are related with complex database relationships, although this example's database contains only a single table.

FIGURE 35-2

3. If you have previously built data connections, you can pick one from the dropdown list. Otherwise, click the New Connection button to display the dialog shown in Figure 35-3.

In this figure, I selected a Microsoft Access database. If you want to use some other kind of database, such as a SQL Server or Oracle database, click the Change button and select the right kind of database.

Enter the name of the database in the textbox or click the Browse button and select it. When you're finished, if you like, you can click Test Connection to see if Visual Studio can connect to the database.

Click OK to create the new connection and return to the dialog shown in Figure 35-2.

FIGURE 35-3

PICKING A DATABASE

Picking the right database product is a tough decision. Access databases have the advantage that a C# program can read and manipulate one even if Access isn't installed. That means you can build a database on one computer that has Access installed and then copy it to another computer without Access and use it there.

SQL Server, Oracle, MySQL, and similar database products tend to provide more database features than Access. For example, they support bigger databases, triggers, views, and other features that Access does not provide.

A common compromise is to start development with SQL Server Express, a free version of SQL Server that has some size restrictions. Later if you decide you need the extra space provided by the full version of SQL Server, you can upgrade relatively easily. You can learn more about SQL Server Express and download it at `www.microsoft.com/express/Database`.

Unfortunately a C# program cannot use these more powerful databases unless you have them installed, an assumption I don't want to make, so this Lesson works with Access databases. You can get the necessary databases from the lesson's code download and use them even if you don't have Access installed.

If you're planning to do more database programming, I encourage you to install one of the more powerful database products, particularly since SQL Server Express and MySQL are free.

---

4. When you click Next, Visual Studio asks whether you want to include the database in the project. Click Yes to copy the database file into the project so it can easily be distributed with the program.

5. The dialog's next page asks whether you want to include the database connection string in the program's configuration file so the program can use that string to connect to the database at run time. This is often convenient because it lets you change the connection string without rebuilding the application. Note, however, that you shouldn't store database passwords in the configuration file, so if the database requires a password, you may want to leave the connection string out of the configuration file.

    When you click Next again, you see the page shown in Figure 35-4.

6. Expand the database object treeview and select the tables and fields that you want the program to use. In this example, the database contains only one table. In Figure 35-4 I selected the Tables entry and that selected the table and all of its fields.

7. When you click Finish, Visual Studio defines a dataset that can hold the data in the database. It also adds some code to make working with the dataset easier.

Now that you've added a data source to the project, Visual Studio provides easy ways to make two kinds of database programs: one that displays data in a grid and one that displays data one record at a time.

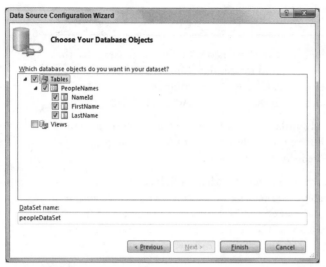

FIGURE 35-4

DISPLAYING RECORDS IN A GRID

To display records in a grid, first open the Data Sources window. If you can't find it, use the Data menu's Show Data Sources command. Figure 35-5 shows the Data Sources window after I connected to a Microsoft Access database named People.mdb.

FIGURE 35-5

To display data in a grid, click a table in the Data Sources window and drag it onto the form. When you drop the table, Visual Studio adds several objects to the form to help manage the table's data. It adds:

➤ **A DataGridView** — This control displays the data.

➤ **A dataset** — This dataset holds the data at run time. The dataset is basically an in-memory copy of the database that the program can manipulate.

➤ **A BindingSource** — This object encapsulates the data source. It provides a link between the form's controls and the data source.

➤ **A data adapter** — This object provides methods to move data between the database and the dataset.

➤ **A table adapter manager** — This object helps coordinate movement of data by the data adapter.

➤ **Binding navigator** — This object provides navigation services for the controls on the form. For example, buttons that move to the next or previous record use these navigation services.

This seems like a confusing assortment of objects. Fortunately you don't need to do much with them for the simple database applications described in this lesson.

Figure 35-6 shows the program created by Visual Studio at run time. The only changes I made were to resize the form and dock the `DataGridView` control to make it fill the form.

PeopleGrid		
NameId	First Name	Last Name
1	Ann	Archer
2	Bob	Baker
3	Cindy	Carruthers
4	Dan	Dweezle
9	Rod	Stephens

FIGURE 34-6

The `DataGridView` and the `BindingNavigator` (which provides the buttons at the top) automatically let the user perform a lot of simple database tasks, such as:

➤ Clicking a cell to change its value

➤ Selecting a row and pressing Delete to delete the corresponding record

➤ Clicking and dragging to the left of the data to select multiple rows, which the user can then delete all at once

➤ Using the navigation buttons to move through the records

➤ Entering values in the last row to create a new record

➤ Resizing rows and columns

➤ Clicking the floppy disk button to save changes to the data

➤ Clicking a column header to sort the records using that column

In this kind of program, changes are made locally to the dataset and are not copied to the database until the user clicks the Save button.

There are only a few things that this automatically generated program doesn't do that you should add for this simple example. The most important of these is to check for unsaved changes before allowing the form to close.

The following `FormClosing` event handler prevents the user from accidentally closing the form with unsaved changes:

```
// Check for unsaved changes.
private void Form1_FormClosing(object sender, FormClosingEventArgs e)
{
    // See if there are unsaved changes.
    if (this.peopleDataSet.HasChanges())
    {
        // Make the user confirm.
        DialogResult result = MessageBox.Show(
            "Do you want to save changes before closing?",
            "Save Changes?",
            MessageBoxButtons.YesNoCancel,
```

```
            MessageBoxIcon.Question);
    if (result == DialogResult.Cancel)
    {
        // Cancel the close.
        e.Cancel = true;
    }
    else if (result == DialogResult.Yes)
    {
        // Save the changes.
        peopleNamesTableAdapter.Update(peopleDataSet);

        // Make sure the save worked.
        // If we still have unsaved changes, cancel.
        e.Cancel = (this.peopleDataSet.HasChanges());
    }

    // Else the user doesn't want to save
    // the changes so just keep going.
    }
}
```

If the dataset has unsaved changes, the code asks the user whether it should save the changes. If the user clicks Cancel, the code sets e.Cancel to true so the program doesn't close the form.

If the user clicks Yes, the code call's the table adapter's Update method to save the dataset's changes back to the database.

If the user clicks No, the code just continues and lets the form close without saving the changes.

DISPLAYING RECORDS ONE ROW AT A TIME

Instead of displaying a table's records in a grid, you can display the data one record at a time as shown in Figure 35-7.

With this kind of interface, you can click the navigation buttons on the BindingNavigator to move through the records. You can use the display controls (TextBoxes in Figure 35-7) to change a record's values.

FIGURE 35-7

To build this interface, first create a data source as before. Then, instead of dragging a table from the Data Sources window onto the form, drag individual fields onto the form. For each field, Visual Studio adds a label and an appropriate display control (such as a TextBox) to the form.

This version of the interface does most of the things the grid-based version does but in different ways. One feature that is missing is the ability to easily add and delete records. In the previous version, the grid lets you add and delete records. In the record-based version, you need to enable the BindingNavigator's Add New and Delete buttons. (You can also enable them in the grid-based version if you like, but because the grid can handle those functions by itself, it's not mandatory.)

Fortunately this is fairly easy. Simply add code to the form's Load event handler to enable the buttons. The following code shows how the PeopleFields example program (available in this lesson's code download) enables its buttons. The first comment and line of code that calls Fill were automatically generated when I dragged the first field from the Data Sources window onto the form. (I reformatted the comment slightly because it was too long to fit in the following listing.)

```
private void Form1_Load(object sender, EventArgs e)
{
    // TODO: This line of code loads data into the
    // 'peopleDataSet.PeopleNames' table. You can move,
    // or remove it, as needed.
    this.peopleNamesTableAdapter.Fill(this.peopleDataSet.PeopleNames);

    // Enable the Add New and Delete buttons.
    this.bindingNavigatorDeleteItem.Enabled = true;
    this.bindingNavigatorAddNewItem.Enabled = true;
}
```

As in the PeopleGrid example program (discussed earlier in this lesson and also available in the lesson's code download), the code created by Visual Studio doesn't check for unsaved changes before the form closes. You can solve this problem by adding a FormClosing event to check for unsaved changes.

This version of the program works a little differently than the previous grid-style version, however. The DataGridView control used by the previous program automatically marks the data as modified when the user starts changing a value. In contrast, the new program marks the data as modified only when the user changes a value and then moves to a new record. That means if the user changes a value and then tries to close the form without moving to a new record, the program doesn't know there is an unsaved change and closes.

To prevent that, you can add the following two lines to the beginning of the FormClosing event handler:

```
this.Validate();
this.peopleNamesBindingSource.EndEdit();
```

These lines make the program officially finish editing any fields that the user is modifying so the dataset knows that it has a pending change.

After that, the FormClosing event handler works exactly as before.

TRY IT

In this Try It, you have a chance to practice the techniques described in this lesson. You create an application that displays contact information in a grid.

> You can download the code and resources for this Try It from the book's web page at www.wrox.com or www.CSharpHelper.com/24hour.html. You can find them in the Lesson35 folder of the download.

Lesson Requirements

➤   Start a new project. Download the Contacts.mdb database from the book's web site and place it in the project directory.

➤   Add a new data source for this database.

➤   Open the Data Sources window and drag the Contacts table onto the form.

➤   Add code to the `FormClosing` event handler to check for unsaved changes.

Hints

➤   Dock the `DataGridView` control so it fills the form. Resize the form so all fields are visible.

Step-by-Step

➤   Start a new project. Download the Contacts.mdb database from the book's web site and place it in the project directory.

   1.   This is straightforward.

➤   Add a new data source for this database.

   1.   Follow the steps described earlier in this lesson.

➤   Open the Data Sources window and drag the Contacts table onto the form.

   1.   This is straightforward.

➤   Add code to the `FormClosing` event handler to check for unsaved changes.

   1.   Use code similar to the following:

```
// Check for unsaved changes.
private void Form1_FormClosing(object sender, FormClosingEventArgs e)
{
    if (this.contactsDataSet.HasChanges())
    {
        // Make the user confirm.
        DialogResult result = MessageBox.Show(
            "Do you want to save changes before closing?",
            "Save Changes?",
            MessageBoxButtons.YesNoCancel,
            MessageBoxIcon.Question);
        if (result == DialogResult.Cancel)
        {
            // Cancel the close.
            e.Cancel = true;
        }
        else if (result == DialogResult.Yes)
        {
            // Save the changes.
            peopleNamesTableAdapter.Update(peopleDataSet);
```

```
            // Make sure the save worked.
            // If we still have unsaved changes, cancel.
            e.Cancel = (this.contactsDataSet.HasChanges());
        }

        // Else the user doesn't want to save
        // the changes so just keep going.
    }
}
```

 Please select Lesson 35 on the DVD to view the video that accompanies this lesson.

EXERCISES

1. Make a program similar to the one you built for the Try It except make it display one record at a time instead of using a grid. Anchor the `TextBoxes` so they widen if the form widens. Don't forget to enable the Add New and Delete buttons, and to add the `FormClosing` event handler.

2. Copy the program you built for this lesson's Try It. That program's grid lets the user navigate through the records, add records, and delete records, so you don't really need all of those buttons on the `BindingNavigator`. Select the `BindingNavigator`. In the Properties window, click the Items property and click the ellipsis to the right. Set the `Visible` property to false for every item except the position, count, and save items.

3. Copy the program you built for Exercise 1. Add a `MenuStrip` with a Data menu that has items First, Prev, Next, Last, Add New, Delete, and Save. Set the `Visible` property on the corresponding `BindingNavigator` buttons to false.

To make the menu items work, use the `BindingSource`'s `CurrencyManager`. That object's properties and methods let you manipulate the current record (hence the name *CurrencyManager*). For example, the following code sets the current position to the first record:

```
this.contactsBindingSource.CurrencyManager.Position = 0;
```

Add or subtract one from `Position` to move to the next or previous record. Set `Position` to the `CurrencyManager`'s `List.Count - 1` value to move to the end of the list.

Use the `RemoveAt` method to delete the current record.

Finally, to save changes to the data, write a `SaveChanges` method similar to this one:

```
private void SaveChanges()
{
    this.Validate();
    this.contactsBindingSource.EndEdit();
    this.tableAdapterManager.UpdateAll(this.contactsDataSet);
}
```

Invoke this function when the user selects the Save menu item. Also invoke it when the FormClosing event handler needs to save changes. (The previous version that invokes the BindingNavigator's Save button no longer works because that button is hidden, so it doesn't do anything.)

You can download the solutions to these exercises from the book's web page at www.wrox.com *or* www.CSharpHelper.com/24hour.html. *You can find those solutions in the Lesson35 folder.*

36

Programming Databases, Part 2

The simple programs described in the previous lesson are hardly commercial-caliber database applications, but they do let you perform basic database operations with amazingly little code.

In this lesson, you learn how to add a few new features to the programs described in Lesson 35. You learn how to add searching, filtering, and sorting to the programs to make finding data easier.

SEARCHING

In a large database, it can be hard to locate a particular value. A program can make finding records easier by using the `BindingContext`'s `Find` method. This method takes as parameters the name of a field and the value that it should find. It returns the index of the first record that has the desired value.

For example, the following code searches the data in the `BindingSource` named `contacts-BindingSource` for a record with FirstName value equal to Kim:

```
int recordNumber = this.contactsBindingSource.Find("FirstName", "Kim");
```

Having found the index of the target record, you can then highlight it in some way for the user to see. For example, recall that a `BindingSource`'s `CurrencyManager` controls the current position within the data. The following code makes the current record be the record found by `Find` so any controls displaying the data will show this record:

```
this.contactsBindingSource.CurrencyManager.Position = recordNumber;
```

 Find *returns –1 if it cannot find the target string. Be careful not to try to do anything explicitly with record number –1 or your program may crash.*

If the program is displaying data in a grid, focus moves to the found record's row. If the program is displaying data in field controls, those controls now show the found record's data.

FILTERING

The `Find` method is somewhat restrictive. It only searches for exact matches in a single field and only returns the index of the first record that matches. Often you might prefer more flexibility such as searches that can check conditions (Age >= 21), look for partial matches (LastName begins with S), and combine multiple tests (State is VA or DC). It might also be nice to see all of the records that meet a condition instead of just the first record.

Filters let you perform these kinds of searches. A *filter* tests each record in a `BindingSource`'s data and selects those that satisfy the test. Any display controls attached to the `BindingSource` show only the selected records.

To use a filter, set the `BindingSource`'s `Filter` property to a string describing the records that you want to select. The filter compares each record's fields to values and selects the records that match. For example, the clause `State='FL'` selects records where the State field has the value FL.

String values should be delimited with single or double quotes. (Single quotes are generally easier to type into a string that is itself delimited by double quotes.) Numeric values should not have delimiters.

Table 36-1 lists the operators that you can use to compare fields to values.

TABLE 36-1

OPERATOR	PURPOSE
=	Equal to
<>	Not equal to
<	Less than
>	Greater than
<=	Less than or equal to
>=	Greater than or equal to
LIKE	Matches a pattern
IN	Is in a list of values

The `LIKE` operator performs pattern matching. Use * or % as a wildcard that matches zero or more characters.

You can use the AND, OR, and NOT logical operators to combine the results of multiple comparisons. Use parentheses to determine the evaluation order if necessary.

Table 36-2 lists some example filters.

TABLE 36-2

FILTER	SELECTS
LastName = 'Johnson'	Records where LastName is Johnson
FirstName = 'Ann' OR FirstName = 'Anne'	Records where FirstName is Ann or Anne
FirstName LIKE 'Pam%'	Records where FirstName begins with Pam
State IN('NY','NC','NJ')	Records where State is NY, NC, or NJ
(Balance < -50) OR ((Balance < 0) AND (DaysOverdue > 30))	Records where the account is overdrawn by more than $50 or where the account has been overdrawn by any amount for more than 30 days

You can use the BindingSource's RemoveFilter method to remove the filter and display all of the records again.

SORTING

If you display data in a DataGridView, you can click a column's header to sort the records based on the values in that column. Clicking again reverses the sort order. Sorting doesn't get much easier than that.

If you're displaying the data in fields rather than a grid, however, you don't get automatic sorting. Fortunately, you can make a BindingSource sort simply by setting its Sort property to the name of the field on which you want to sort. Use its RemoveSort method to cancel the sort and display the records in their original order.

TRY IT

Available for
download on
Wrox.com

In this Try It, you add filtering to a program that displays records in a grid. You let the user enter a state abbreviation and you make the program display only records with that state value.

> *You can download the code and resources for this Try It from the book's web page at* www.wrox.com *or* www.CSharpHelper.com/24hour.html. *You can find them in the Lesson36 folder of the download.*

Lesson Requirements

➤ Copy the program you built for the Try It in Lesson 35 (or download Lesson 35's version from the book's web site).

➤ Add a `MenuStrip` with a Data menu that contains the menu item Filter by State.

➤ Create a new form to use as a dialog where the user can enter a state abbreviation.

➤ When the user selects the Filter by State menu item, display the dialog. If the user enters a state and clicks OK, filter the records to find those with the state entered by the user. If the user clicks Cancel, remove any previous filter.

Hints

➤ If you like, you can give the Filter by State menu item the shortcut Ctrl+Shift+F. (Save Ctrl+F for use by the Find menu item that you'll add in Exercise 2 of this lesson.)

➤ The dialog doesn't need to perform any validation so you can use the buttons' `DialogResult` properties to close it.

Step-by-Step

➤ Copy the program you built for the Try It in Lesson 35 (or download Lesson 35's version from the book's web site).

1. This is straightforward.

➤ Add a `MenuStrip` with a Data menu that contains the menu item Filter by State.

1. This is straightforward.

➤ Create a new form to use as a dialog where the user can enter a state abbreviation.

1. This is straightforward.

➤ When the user selects the Filter by State menu item, display the dialog. If the user enters a state and clicks OK, filter the records to find those with the state entered by the user. If the user clicks Cancel, remove any previous filter.

1. Use code similar to the following:

```
// Filter by state.
private void filterByStateToolStripMenuItem_Click( object sender, EventArgs e)
{
    FilterDialog dlg = new FilterDialog();
    if (dlg.ShowDialog() == DialogResult.OK)
    {
        // Filter the records.
        string filter = "State = '" + dlg.stateTextBox.Text + "'";
        this.contactsBindingSource.Filter = filter;
    }
    else
```

```
        {
            this.contactsBindingSource.RemoveFilter();
        }
    }
```

 Please select Lesson 36 on the DVD to view the video that accompanies this lesson.

EXERCISES

1. Copy the program you built for Exercise 1 in Lesson 35. Add `RadioButtons` to the right of the `TextBoxes`, as shown in Figure 36-1. When the user clicks a `RadioButton`, make the program sort its data using the corresponding field.

FIGURE 36-1

2. Copy the program you built for this lesson's Try It and add a Find Name feature. Add a Find Name menu item to the main form's menu. Give it the shortcut Ctrl+F. When the user invokes this item, display a dialog where the user can enter a name. If the user clicks OK, find the record with the correct FirstName value. Use the following code to highlight the first cell holding the name:

```
contactsDataGridView.CurrentCell =
    contactsDataGridView.Rows[recordNumber].Cells[0];
```

3. Copy the program you built for Exercise 1 and add a Find Name feature similar to the one you added for Exercise 2. If you find a record containing the name entered by the user, use the following code to move to that record:

```
contactsBindingSource.CurrencyManager.Position = recordNumber;
```

4. Copy the program you built for Exercise 3 and add a Filter by State feature similar to the one you added for this lesson's Try It.

 You can download the solutions to these exercises from the book's web page at `www.wrox.com` *or* `www.CSharpHelper.com/24hour.html`. *You can find those solutions in the Lesson36 folder.*

37

LINQ to Objects

Lessons 35 and 36 explain how you can use Visual Studio's wizards to build simple database programs. They show one of many ways to connect a program to a data source.

Language-Integrated Query (LINQ) provides another method for bridging the gap between a program and data. Instead of simply providing another way to access data in a database, however, LINQ can help a program access data stored in many places. LINQ lets a program access data stored in databases, arrays, collections, or files in basically the same way.

LINQ provides four basic technologies that give you access to data stored in various places:

- ➤ **LINQ to SQL** — Data stored in SQL Server databases
- ➤ **LINQ to Dataset** — Data stored in other databases
- ➤ **LINQ to XML** — Data stored in XML (eXtensible Markup Language) files
- ➤ **LINQ to Objects** — Data stored in collections, lists, arrays, strings, files, and so forth

In this lesson you learn how to use LINQ to Objects. You learn how to extract data from lists, collections, and arrays, and how to process the results.

LINQ BASICS

Using LINQ to process data takes three steps:

1. Create a data source.
2. Build a query to select data from the data source.
3. Execute the query and process the result.

You might expect the third step to be two separate steps, "Execute the query" and "Process the result." In practice, however, LINQ doesn't actually execute the query until it must — when the program tries to access the results. This is called *deferred execution*.

The following code displays the even numbers between 0 and 99:

```
// Display the even numbers between 0 and 99.
private void Form1_Load(object sender, EventArgs e)
{
    // 1. Create the data source.
    int[] numbers = new int[100];
    for (int i = 0; i < 100; i++)
    {
        numbers[i] = i;
    }

    // 2. Build a query to select data from the data source.
    var evenQuery =
        from int num in numbers
        where (num % 2 == 0)
        select num;

    // 3. Execute the query and process the result.
    foreach (int num in evenQuery)
    {
        Console.WriteLine(num.ToString());
    }
}
```

The program starts by creating the data source: an array containing the numbers 0 through 99. In this example the data source is quite simple, but in other programs it could be much more complex. Instead of an array of numbers, it could be a list of Customer objects, or an array of Order objects that contain lists of OrderItem objects.

Next the program builds a query to select the even numbers from the list. I explain queries in more detail later, but the following list describes the key pieces of this query:

➤ var — This is the data type of whatever is returned by the query. In this example, the result will be an IEnumerable<int> but in general the results of LINQ queries can have some very strange data types. Rather than trying to figure out what a query will return, most developers use the implicit data type var. The var keyword tells the C# compiler to figure out what the data type is and use that so you don't need to use a specific data type.

➤ evenQuery — This is the name the code is giving to the query. You can think of it as a variable that represents the result that LINQ will later produce.

➤ from int num in numbers — This means the query will select data from the numbers array. It will use the int variable num to range over the values in the array. Because num ranges over the values, it is called the query's *range variable*. (If you omit the int data type, the compiler will implicitly figure out its data type.)

➤ where (num % 2 == 0) — This is the query's *where clause*. It determines which items are selected from the array. This example selects the even numbers where num mod 2 is 0.

➤ select num — This tells the query to return whatever is in the range variable num for the values that are selected. Often you will want to return the value of the range variable but you could return something else such as 2 * num or a new object created with a constructor that takes num as a parameter.

I don't recommend using var *for variables in general if you can easily figure out a more specific data type. When you use* var, *you can't be sure what data type the compiler will use. That can lead to confusion if the compiler picks different data types for variables that must later work together.*

For example, in the following code the third statement is allowed because you can store an int *value in a* double *but the fourth statement is not allowed because a* double *may not fit in an* int:

```
var x = 1.2;    // double.
var y = 1;      // int.
x = y;          // Allowed.
y = x;          // Not allowed.
```

So, if you do know the data type, just use that instead of var.

In the final step to performing the query, the code loops through the result produced by LINQ. The code displays each int value in the Console window.

The following sections provide more detailed descriptions of some of the key pieces of a LINQ query: where clauses, order by clauses, and select clauses.

WHERE CLAUSES

Probably the most common reason to use LINQ is to filter the data with a *where clause.* The where clause can include normal Boolean expressions that use &&, ||, >, and other Boolean operators. It can use the range variable and any properties or methods that it provides (if it's an object). It can even perform calculations and invoke functions.

For example, the following query is similar to the earlier one that selects even numbers, except this one's where clause uses the IsPrime function to select only prime numbers. (How the IsPrime function works isn't important to this discussion, so it isn't shown here. You can see it in the FindPrimes program in this lesson's download.)

The where clause is optional. If you omit it, the query selects all of the items in its range.

```
var primeQuery =
    from int num in numbers
    where (IsPrime(num))
    select num;
```

The FindCustomers example program shown in Figure 37-1 (and available in this chapter's code download on the web site) demonstrates several where clauses.

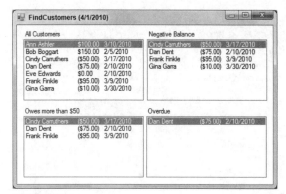

FIGURE 37-1

The following code shows the `Customers` class used by the FindCustomers program. It just includes some auto-implemented properties and an overridden `ToString` method that displays the `Customer`'s values.

```
class Customer
{
    public string FirstName { get; set; }
    public string LastName { get; set; }
    public decimal Balance { get; set; }
    public DateTime DueDate { get; set; }

    public override string ToString()
    {
        return FirstName + " " + LastName + "\t" +
            Balance.ToString("C") + "\t" + DueDate.ToString("d");
    }
}
```

The following code shows how the FindCustomers program displays the same customer data selected with different where clauses:

```
// Display customers selected in various ways.
private void Form1_Load(object sender, EventArgs e)
{
    DateTime today = new DateTime(2010, 4, 1);
    //DateTime today = DateTime.Today;

    this.Text = "FindCustomers (" + today.ToString("d") + ")";

    // Make the customers.
    Customer[] customers =
    {
        new Customer() { FirstName="Ann", LastName="Ashler",
            Balance = 100, DueDate = new DateTime(2010, 3, 10)},
        new Customer() { FirstName="Bob", LastName="Boggart",
            Balance = 150, DueDate = new DateTime(2010, 2, 5)},
        // ... Other Customers omitted ...
    };
```

```
        // Display all customers.
        allListBox.DataSource = customers;

        // Display customers with negative balances.
        var negativeQuery =
            from Customer cust in customers
            where cust.Balance < 0
            select cust;
        negativeListBox.DataSource = negativeQuery.ToArray();

        // Display customers who owe at least $50.
        var owes50Query =
            from Customer cust in customers
            where cust.Balance <= -50
            select cust;
        owes50listBox.DataSource = owes50Query.ToArray();

        // Display customers who owe at least $50
        // and are overdue at least 30 days.
        var overdueQuery =
            from Customer cust in customers
            where (cust.Balance <= -50) &&
                  (DateTime.Now.Subtract(cust.DueDate).TotalDays > 30)
            select cust;
        overdueListBox.DataSource = overdueQuery.ToArray();
    }
```

The program starts by creating a `DateTime` named `today` and setting it equal to April 1, 2010. In a real application you would probably use the current date (commented out), but this program uses that specific date so it works well with the sample data. The program then displays the date in its title bar (so you can compare it to the `Customers`' due dates) and creates an array of `Customer` objects.

Next the code sets the `allListBox` control's `DataSource` property to the array so that listbox displays all of the `Customer` objects. The `Customer` class's overridden `ToString` method makes it display each `Customer`'s name, balance, and due date.

The program then executes the following LINQ query:

```
    // Display customers with negative balances.
    var negativeQuery =
        from Customer cust in customers
        where cust.Balance < 0
        select cust;
    negativeListBox.DataSource = negativeQuery.ToArray();
```

This query's where clause selects `Customers` with `Balance` properties less than 0. The query returns an `IEnumerable`, but a `ListBox`'s `DataSource` property requires an `IList` or `IListSource` so the program calls the result's `ToArray` method to convert it into an array that the `DataSource` property can handle.

After displaying this result, the program executes two other LINQ queries and displays their results similarly. The first query selects `Customers` who owe at least $50. The final query selects `Customers` who owe at least $50 and who have a `DueDate` more than 30 days in the past.

ORDER BY CLAUSES

Often the result of a query is easier to read if you sort the selected values. You can do this by inserting an *order by clause* between the where clause and the select clause.

The order by clause begins with the keyword `orderby` followed by one or more values separated by commas that determine how the results are ordered.

Optionally you can follow a value by the keyword `ascending` (the default) or `descending` to determine whether the results are ordered in ascending (1-2-3 or A-B-C) or descending (3-2-1 or C-B-A) order.

For example, the following query selects `Customers` with negative balances and orders them so those with the smallest (most negative) values come first:

```
var negativeQuery =
    from Customer cust in customers
    where cust.Balance < 0
    orderby cust.Balance ascending
    select cust;
```

The following version orders the results first by balance and then, if two customers have the same balance, by last name:

```
var negativeQuery =
    from Customer cust in customers
    where cust.Balance < 0
    orderby cust.Balance, cust.LastName
    select cust;
```

SELECT CLAUSES

The select clause determines what data is pulled from the data source and stored in the result. All of the previous examples select the data over which they are ranging. For example, the FindCustomers example program ranges over an array of `Customer` objects and selects certain `Customer` objects.

Instead of selecting the objects in the query's range, a program can select only some properties of those objects, a result calculated from those properties, or even completely new objects. Selecting a new kind of data from the existing data is called *projecting* or *transforming* the data.

The FindStudents example program shown in Figure 37-2 (and available in this chapter's code download on the web site) uses the following simple `Student` class:

```
class Student
{
    public string FirstName { get; set; }
    public string LastName { get; set; }
    public List<int> TestScores { get; set; }
}
```

The program uses the following query to select all of the students' names and test averages ordered by name:

```
// Select all students and their test averages ordered by name.
var allStudents =
```

```
        from Student student in students
        orderby student.LastName, student.FirstName
        select String.Format("{0} {1}\t{2:0.00}",
            student.FirstName, student.LastName,
            student.TestScores.Average());
    allListBox.DataSource = allStudents.ToArray();
```

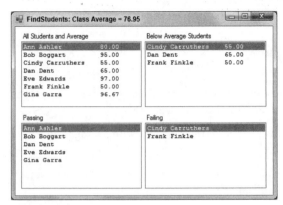

FIGURE 37-2

This query's select statement does not select the range variable `student`. Instead it selects a string that holds the student's first and last names and the student's test score average. (Notice how the code calls the `TestScore` list's `Average` method to get the average of the test scores.) The result of the query is a `List<string>` instead of a `List<Student>`.

The program next uses the following code to list the students who have averages of at least 60, giving them passing grades:

```
// Select passing students ordered by name.
var passingStudents =
    from Student student in students
    orderby student.LastName, student.FirstName
    where student.TestScores.Average() >= 60
    select student.FirstName + " " + student.LastName;
passingListBox.DataSource = passingStudents.ToArray();
```

This code again selects a string instead of a `Customer` object. The code that selects failing students is similar, so it isn't shown here.

The program uses the following code to select students with averages below the class average:

```
// Select all scores and compute a class average.
var allAverages =
    from Student student in students
    orderby student.LastName, student.FirstName
    select student.TestScores.Average();
double classAverage = allAverages.Average();

// Display the average.
this.Text = "FindStudents: Class Average = " + classAverage.ToString("0.00");
```

```
    // Select students with average below the class average ordered by average.
    var belowAverageStudents =
        from Student student in students
        orderby student.TestScores.Average()
        where student.TestScores.Average() < classAverage
        select new {Name = student.FirstName + " " + student.LastName,
            Average = student.TestScores.Average()};

    foreach (var info in belowAverageStudents)
    {
        belowAverageListBox.Items.Add(info.Name + "\t" + info.Average);
    }
```

This snippet starts by selecting all of the students' test score averages. This returns a List<double>. The program calls that list's Average function to get the class average.

Next the code queries the student data again, this time selecting students with averages below the class average.

This query demonstrates a new kind of select clause that creates a list of objects. The new objects have two properties, Name and Average, that are given values by the select clause.

The data type of these new objects is created automatically and isn't given an explicit name so this is known as an *anonymous type*.

After creating the query, the code loops through its results, using each object's Name and Average property to display the below average students in a ListBox. Notice that the code gives the looping variable info the implicit data type var so it doesn't need to figure out what data type it really has.

Objects with anonymous data types actually have a true data type, just not one that you want to have to figure out. For example, you can add the following statement inside the previous code's foreach *loop to see what data type the objects actually have:*

```
        Console.WriteLine(info.GetType().ToString());
```

If you look in the Output window, you'll see that these objects have the ungainly data type:

```
        <>f__AnonymousType0`2[System.String,System.Double]
```

Though you can sort of see what's going on here (note that the object contains a string and a double), you probably wouldn't want to type this mess into your code even if you could. In this case, the var *type is a lot easier to read.*

LINQ provides plenty of other features that won't fit in this lesson. It lets you:

➤ Group results to produce output lists that contain other lists

➤ Take only a certain number of results or take results while a certain condition is true

> ➤ Skip a certain number of results or skip results while a certain condition is true

> ➤ Join objects selected from multiple data sources

> ➤ Use aggregate functions such as Average (which you've already seen), Count, Min, Max, and Sum

Microsoft's "Language-Integrated Query (LINQ)" page at msdn.microsoft.com/library/bb397926.aspx provides a good starting point for learning more about LINQ.

TRY IT

In Lesson 30's Try It, you built a program that used the DirectoryInfo class's GetFiles method to search for files matching a pattern and containing a target string. For example, the program could search the directory hierarchy starting at C:\C#Projects to find files with the .cs extension and containing the string "DirectoryInfo."

In this Try It, you modify that program to perform the same search with LINQ. Instead of writing code to loop through the files returned by GetFiles and examining each, you make LINQ examine the files for you.

> *You can download the code and resources for this Try It from the book's web page at* www.wrox.com *or* www.CSharpHelper.com/24hour.html. *You can find them in the Lesson37 folder of the download.*

Lesson Requirements

> ➤ Copy the program you built for Lesson 30's Try It (or download Lesson 30's version from the book's web site) and modify the code to use LINQ to search for files.

Hints

> ➤ Use the DirectoryInfo object's GetFiles method in the query's from clause.

> ➤ In the query's where clause, use the File class's ReadAllText method to get the file's contents. Convert it to lowercase and use Contains to see if the file holds the target string.

Step-by-Step

> ➤ Copy the program you built for Lesson 30's Try It (or download Lesson 30's version from the book's web site) and modify the code to use LINQ to search for files.

> **1.** Copying the program is reasonably straightforward. To use LINQ to search for files, modify the Search button's Click event handler so it looks like the following. The lines in bold show the modified code.

```
// Search for files matching the pattern
// and containing the target string.
private void searchButton_Click(object sender, EventArgs e)
{
    // Get the file pattern and target string.
    string pattern = patternComboBox.Text;
    string target = targetTextBox.Text.ToLower();

    // Search for the files.
    DirectoryInfo dirinfo =
        new DirectoryInfo(directoryTextBox.Text);
    var fileQuery =
        from FileInfo fileinfo
            in dirinfo.GetFiles(pattern,
                SearchOption.AllDirectories)
        where
            File.ReadAllText(fileinfo.FullName).ToLower().Contains(target)
        select fileinfo.FullName;

    // Display the result.
    fileListBox.DataSource = fileQuery.ToArray();
}
```

 Please select Lesson 37 on the DVD to view the video that accompanies this lesson.

EXERCISES

1. Build a program that lists the names of the files in a directory together with their sizes, ordered with the biggest files first.

2. Copy the program you built for Exercise 1 and modify it so it searches for files in the directory hierarchy starting at the specified directory.

3. Make a program that lists the perfect squares between 0 and 999.

For Exercises 4 through 8 download the CustomerOrders program. This program defines the following classes:

```
class Person
{
    public string Name { get; set; }
}

class OrderItem
{
    public string Description { get; set; }
    public int Quantity { get; set; }
    public decimal UnitPrice { get; set; }
```

```
    }

    class Order
    {
        public int OrderId { get; set; }
        public Person Customer { get; set; }
        public List<OrderItem> OrderItems { get; set; }
    }
```

The program's `Form_Load` event handler creates an array of `Order` objects. The program's buttons, which are shown in Figure 37-3, let the user display the data in various ways although initially they don't contain any code. In Exercises 4 through 8, you add that code to give the program its features.

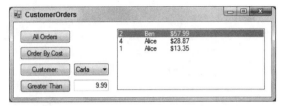

FIGURE 37-3

4. The CustomerOrders program creates several `Order` objects, but it doesn't fill in those objects' `TotalCosts` properties. Use LINQ to do that. (Use a `foreach` loop to loop through the objects. For each object, use a LINQ query to go through the order's `OrderItems` list and select each `OrderItem`'s `UnitPrice` times its `Quantity`. After you define the query, call its `Sum` function to get the total cost for the order.)

5. Copy the program you built for Exercise 4 and add code behind the All Orders button. That code should use a LINQ query to select the orders' ID, customer name, and total costs. Display the results in the `resultListBox` by setting that control's `DataSource` property to the query.

6. Copy the program you built for Exercise 5 and add code behind the Order By Cost button. That code should use a query similar to the one used by Exercise 5, but it should order the results by cost so the orders with the largest costs are listed first.

7. Copy the program you built for Exercise 6 and add code behind the Customer button. That code should use a LINQ query to list orders placed by the customer selected in the combobox. (Hint: Get the customer's name from the combobox's `Text` property. If the name is blank, exit the method without doing anything.)

8. Copy the program you built for Exercise 7 and add code behind the Greater Than button. That code should use a LINQ query to list orders with total costs greater than the value entered in the textbox.

You can download the solutions to these exercises from the book's web page at `www.wrox.com` *or* `www.CSharpHelper.com/24hour.html`. *You can find those solutions in the Lesson37 folder.*

38

LINQ to SQL

Lesson 37 provided an introduction to LINQ to Objects. This lesson gives a brief introduction to another of the LINQ family of technologies: LINQ to SQL.

LINQ to SQL lets you use queries similar to those provided by LINQ to Objects to manipulate SQL Server databases. It uses a set of classes to represent database objects such as tables and records. The classes provide intuitive methods for adding, modifying, deleting, and otherwise manipulating the records.

In this lesson you learn the basics of LINQ to SQL. You learn how to make LINQ objects representing a SQL Server database and how to add records to the database. You also learn how to perform queries similar to those described in Lesson 37 to filter and sort data taken from the database.

The basic steps for making a LINQ to SQL application are connecting to the database, making LINQ to SQL classes, and writing code to manipulate the data.

Note that the programs and techniques described in this chapter demonstrate only very simple uses of LINQ to SQL. For more information, search the Web. Microsoft's "Language-Integrated Query (LINQ)" page at msdn.microsoft.com/library/bb386976. aspx provides a good starting point for learning more about LINQ to SQL.

CONNECTING TO THE DATABASE

The first step in creating a LINQ to SQL program is connecting to the database. Create a Windows Forms application as usual. Then open the Server Explorer shown in Figure 38-1. Use the View menu's Server Explorer command if you can't find it.

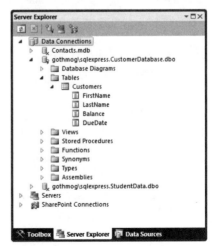

FIGURE 38-1

To run most of the programs described in this chapter, you need to have SQL Server installed on your computer. The Visual Studio installation software comes with SQL Server (at least the versions I've seen) or you can download the free SQL Server Express edition at www.microsoft.com/express/Database. You should probably download the management tools, too. You may find SQL Server Management Studio particularly useful for building databases.

Unfortunately there isn't room here to say too much about SQL Server and how to use it. You'll have to rely on the Web or get a book about SQL Server to do much with it.

To make using the examples described in this lesson a bit easier, the download includes a program named BuildCustomerDatabase. This program connects to your SQL Server instance, deletes the database named CustomerDatabase if it exists, and creates a new CustomerDatabase containing a few records for the examples described in this lesson to use.

Obviously don't run this program if you already have a database named CustomerDatabase that you want to preserve because that database will be destroyed.

Click the Connect to Database button (third from the left at the top in Figure 38-1) to display the Add Connection dialog shown in Figure 38-2.

Initially the Add Connection dialog may have some type of database other than SQL Server selected. The dialog shown in Figure 38-2 is ready to connect to a Microsoft Access database. To switch to SQL Server, click the Change button to display the dialog shown in Figure 38-3.

FIGURE 38-2   **FIGURE 38-3**

Select the Microsoft SQL Server entry and click OK. When you return to the Add Connection dialog, it should look like Figure 38-4.

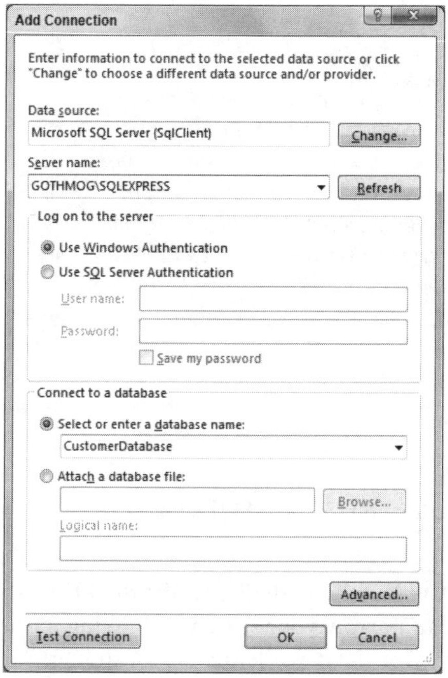

FIGURE 38-4

Enter your server name in the indicated textbox. If you are running SQL Server Express Edition, follow the server's name with \SQLEXPRESS as shown in the figure.

Enter the name of the database on the server (I entered CustomerDatabase in Figure 38-4) and click OK.

In the dialog shown in Figure 38-4, if you enter the name of a database that doesn't exist on the server, Visual Studio tells you that the database doesn't exist and asks if you want to create it. If you click Yes, you can use the Server Explorer to build the database. The Server Explorer doesn't provide as many features as a database management tool such as SQL Server Management Studio, but it's handy if you don't have easy access to those tools.

If you go back to Figure 38-1, you can see the Server Explorer with the GOTHMOG\SQLEXPRESS server's CustomerDatabase expanded to show its single table, Customers, and its columns.

You can use similar steps to connect to other kinds of databases such as Oracle, MySql, or Microsoft Access databases. Only the details needed to connect to the database in the Add Connection dialog are different. For example, Figure 38-2 shows the details needed for a Microsoft Access database, and Figure 38-4 shows the details needed for a SQL Server database.

Note that LINQ to SQL is intended to work with SQL Server and making it work with other types of databases takes some extra work. The section "Using LINQ to SQL with Access" later in this lesson explains how to use LINQ to SQL classes with Access databases, but there's no guarantee that the same techniques will work with every kind of database or that those techniques will keep working in later versions of Visual Studio.

MAKING LINQ TO SQL CLASSES

After you make a database connection, you're ready to build the LINQ to SQL classes that you can use to manipulate the database.

Open the Project menu and select Add New Item. In the Add New Item dialog, select the LINQ to SQL Classes template. If you have trouble finding it, you can narrow your search by looking in the Data template category on the left. Enter a descriptive name for the new file such as CustomerClasses and click Add.

At this point Visual Studio creates a .dbml file to manage the new LINQ to SQL classes. It opens that file in the entity-relationship designer shown in Figure 38-5, although initially the designer is blank.

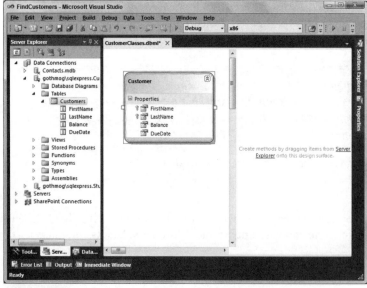

FIGURE 38-5

In the Server Explorer, expand your database until you find its tables, and drag the tables that you want to manage onto the designer surface. In Figure 38-5, I dragged the Customers table onto the surface so the designer created a class to represent the table. Each instance of the class will represent a row in the table.

The designer represents the table's fields as properties. If you look closely at Figure 38-5, you can see that the table's primary key fields FirstName and LastName have little key symbols on the left.

If you click a field in the designer, the Properties window shows the field's properties. Figure 38-6 shows the properties for the table's FirstName field.

A few key values include:

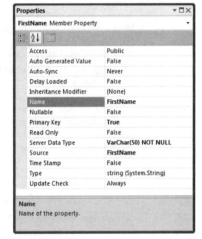

➤ **Name** — The name of the field in the class

➤ **Nullable** — Indicates whether the field can hold null values

➤ **Server Data Type** — The data type of the field in the database

➤ **Source** — The name of the field in the database

When you save your changes, Visual Studio automatically generates a `CustomerClassesDataContext` class to represent the database. (CustomerClasses is the name I gave the new LINQ to SQL file.) This object has a `Customers` property that represents the database's Customers table.

FIGURE 38-6

Visual Studio also creates a `Customer` class to represent the records in the table.

You can look at these classes (although don't modify them) in the file CustomerClasses.designer.cs.

Note that this is an extremely simple example. Most real databases contain multiple tables. In that case, you can use the entity-relationship designer to model the relationships between the tables.

To add a relationship, right-click the designer's surface, open the Add menu, and select Association. Select the parent and child classes from the dropdown lists and then select the fields that match up in the two classes.

For example, an Orders table might hold an OrderId *field that you can use to find corresponding* OrderItems *records that make up the order. In that case, the parent class would be* Orders, *the child class would be* OrderItems, *and the fields that match up would be the* OrderId *fields in both classes.*

After you build the association, the designer displays an arrow to represent the one-to-many relationship between the two classes (one Order *may hold many* OrderItems).

WRITING CODE

FIGURE 38-7

Now that you've built the LINQ to SQL classes, you can use them to manipulate the database. For example, the MakeCustomerData example program shown in Figure 38-7 and available as part of this lesson's code download uses the following code to add a new record to the database.

```
// Add a new Customers record.
private void addButton_Click(object sender, EventArgs e)
{
    // Get the database.
    using (CustomerClassesDataContext db =
        new CustomerClassesDataContext())
    {
        // Make a new Customer object.
        Customer cust = new Customer();
        cust.FirstName = firstNameTextBox.Text;
        cust.LastName = lastNameTextBox.Text;
        cust.Balance = decimal.Parse(balanceTextBox.Text);
        cust.DueDate = DateTime.Parse(dueDateTextBox.Text);

        // Add it to the table.
        db.Customers.InsertOnSubmit(cust);

        // Submit the changes.
        db.SubmitChanges();
    }

    // Prepare to add the next customer.
    firstNameTextBox.Clear();
    lastNameTextBox.Clear();
    balanceTextBox.Clear();
    dueDateTextBox.Clear();
    firstNameTextBox.Focus();
}
```

The code starts with what is probably its least obvious step: creating a new instance of the `CustomerClassesDataContext`. This object represents the database and provides access to its tables. It provides a `Dispose` method so the program creates it in a `using` block to call `Dispose` automatically.

Next the code creates a new `Customer` object to represent a new row in the Customers table. The code initializes this object's properties.

The program then calls the Customers table's `InsertOnSubmit` method, passing it the new `Customer` object. The following statement calls the database object's `SubmitChanges` method to send any pending changes (in this case, the new `Customer`) to the database.

The code finishes by clearing the textboxes so the form is ready for you to enter another customer's data.

USING LINQ QUERIES

The MakeCustomerData program described in the previous section uses the LINQ to SQL classes to manage the database but it doesn't actually use LINQ queries.

You can use LINQ queries with these classes much as you can use them with lists, arrays, and classes that you build yourself in code. For example, you can use a query to select particular records from a table.

The following code shows how the FindCustomers program described in Lesson 37 displayed customers with negative account balances:

```
// Display customers with negative balances.
var negativeQuery =
    from Customer cust in customers
    where cust.Balance < 0
    //orderby cust.Balance ascending, cust.FirstName
    select cust;
negativeListBox.DataSource = negativeQuery.ToArray();
```

The following code shows how the FindCustomers program available for this lesson displays the same customers from the Customers table:

```
// Display customers with negative balances.
var negativeQuery =
    from Customer cust in db.Customers
    where cust.Balance < 0
    //orderby cust.Balance ascending, cust.FirstName
    select String.Format("{0} {1}\t{2:C}\t{3:d}",
        cust.FirstName, cust.LastName,
        cust.Balance, cust.DueDate);
negativeListBox.DataSource = negativeQuery.ToArray();
```

There are only two real differences between these two queries. First, the second query ranges over items in the db.Customers LINQ to SQL object instead of a customers array created by the program's code.

The second difference is that the new version's select clause doesn't select Customer objects. Instead it concatenates certain fields taken from those objects. I made this change because the Customer class generated by Visual Studio doesn't override its ToString method to display a nice representation of the object as the earlier version of the class did in Lesson 37. The new version builds strings that the ListBox can display directly.

UNDERSTANDING NULLABLE FIELDS

While LINQ to Objects and LINQ to SQL queries work mostly in the same way, behind the scenes there are some important differences.

One difference that you are likely to run into immediately is that values provided by LINQ to SQL classes are often nullable. A *nullable type* is a data type that can hold the special value null in addition to whatever other values it normally holds. The value null represents "no value."

For example, a nullable `int` can hold an integer or it can hold the special value `null`, which means it doesn't contain any real integer value.

 Only value types (such as structures, enumerated types, `ints`, and `doubles`) can be nullable because reference types can already hold the value `null`. The only surprising case is `string`, which looks a lot like a value type but which is really a reference type.

 You can declare your own nullable variables by following their data types with a question mark. For example, the following code declares a nullable integer variable named `numCourses` and assigns it the initial value `null`:

```
int? numCourses = null;
```

Databases often have fields that are allowed to have no value and the LINQ to SQL classes represent them as nullable properties. In the database's Customers table, the `Balance` and `DueDate` fields are not required so the `Customer` LINQ to SQL class makes its `Balance` and `DueDate` fields nullable. That means when the program's C# code looks at those fields, they may not contain any value.

To decide whether a field contains a value, you can compare it to `null` or use its `HasValue` property. Once you know that the value exists, you can use its `Value` property to get the value.

For example, the following code checks whether a `Customer`'s `Balance` field is null and, if the value exists, displays it:

```
if (cust.Balance != null)
{
    // There is a Balance. Display it.
    MessageBox.Show("Balance: " + cust.Balance.Value.ToString());
}
```

UNDERSTANDING QUERY EXECUTION

While LINQ to SQL looks a lot like LINQ to Objects in your C# code, behind the scenes there is a huge difference in the way the two kinds of queries are executed.

The C# compiler converts a LINQ to Objects query into a series of method calls to do all of the work. The code does nothing that you couldn't do yourself in C# code, so it works more or less the way you would expect C# code to work.

In contrast, the compiler converts a LINQ to SQL query into code that can execute within the database. Instead of executing code within your program, it sends commands to the database to make it do all of the work. With a bit of work, you could come up with similar database commands yourself and make your program execute them on the database, but LINQ to SQL does that for you.

Why should LINQ to SQL handle this differently?

Suppose you want to find a customer with a particular name in a `customers` array that holds 100,000 objects. LINQ to Objects can zip through the array fairly quickly and find the right customer with little problem.

Now suppose you want to find the same customer in a database containing 100,000 records. To perform that search in C# code, the program would need to fetch 100,000 records from the database. Moving that much data from the database into the program would take quite a bit of time and memory. In contrast, the database itself has great tools for finding specific records, particularly if the table uses name as an index. In that case, the database may need to perform only a few disk accesses to search through its index structure for the right customer, a much more efficient operation than moving 100,000 records into the program and then searching them sequentially.

For many reasonably simple queries, the translation from LINQ query syntax into something the database can understand works and there's no problem. Sometimes, however, your query code doesn't translate easily into database-speak and the database cannot execute it.

For example, the following code shows how the FindCustomer program described in Lesson 37 displayed customers who owe more than $50 and who are more than 30 days overdue. (In this code the variable `today` holds the current date and is used to simplify the code.)

```
// Display customers who owe at least $50
// and are overdue at least 30 days.
var overdueQuery =
    from Customer cust in customers
    where (cust.Balance <= -50) &&
        (today.Subtract(cust.DueDate).TotalDays > 30)
    select cust;
overdueListBox.DataSource = overdueQuery.ToList<Customer>();
```

Unfortunately, SQL Server doesn't have a function that subtracts one date from another, so this query doesn't translate perfectly into database commands and at run time the program throws the following error:

```
Method 'System.TimeSpan Subtract(System.DateTime)' has no supported
translation to SQL.
```

One solution is to rewrite the query in terms that the database can understand. The following code shows a query that LINQ to SQL can translate successfully:

```
// Display customers who owe at least $50
// and are overdue at least 30 days.
var overdueQuery =
    from Customer cust in db.Customers
    where (cust.Balance == null || cust.Balance.Value < -50) &&
        (cust.DueDate == null || today > cust.DueDate.Value.AddDays(30))
    //orderby cust.Balance ascending, cust.FirstName
    select String.Format("{0} {1}\t{2:C}\t{3:d}",
        cust.FirstName, cust.LastName,
        cust.Balance, cust.DueDate);
overdueListBox.DataSource = overdueQuery.ToArray();
```

Although the translation to database code doesn't know how to subtract dates, it does know how to add days to a date so this query uses that capability. It selects records where the customer:

➤ Has no balance or has a balance less than $50, and

➤ Has no due date or today's date is greater than the due date plus 30 days

USING LINQ TO SQL WITH ACCESS

LINQ to SQL is intended to let you use objects to manage SQL Server databases, but with a little extra work you can also use it to manage other kinds of databases.

> *Why would you want to use LINQ to SQL to manage other kinds of databases? One reason is that the LINQ to SQL classes are convenient. They allow you to use fairly intuitive objects to manipulate the data.*
>
> *Another reason for using LINQ to SQL classes with other databases is that it lets me give you examples in Microsoft Access databases. Though SQL Server is generally more powerful, you cannot use it without installing SQL Server (at least the Express Edition). The .NET Framework includes all of the classes you need to interact with an Access database so you can connect to one and use it without installing anything else.*

Create a normal Windows Forms project, open the Project menu, and select Add New Item. Select the LINQ to SQL Classes template as before, give the file a good name, and click Add.

If you were working with SQL Server, you would then drag tables from the Server Explorer onto the design surface to define the classes. Visual Studio won't let you drag tables from other kinds of databases onto the entity-relationship designer, but you can build the classes manually.

Open the Toolbox as shown in Figure 38-8 and use the tools it holds to build the classes.

To get the model to work, you need to set a few properties correctly.

For a table class, set the `Source` property to the name of the table in the database. For example, if you want to represent the Customers table's records with `Customer` objects, then create a `Customer` class and set its `Source` property to `Customers`.

FIGURE 38-8

For each property in a class, set:

➤ `Primary Key` — True if the field is part of the table's primary key

➤ `Nullable` — True if the database field allows nulls

➤ `Server Data Type` — The field's data type in the database (for example, `VARCHAR(50) NOT NULL`)

➤   Source — The name of the field in the database (probably the same as the property's name in the class)

➤   Type — The property's type in the class (for example, string)

After you build the model, Visual Studio generates the classes you need. Now you just need to add code to use them.

If you are using a Microsoft Access database, start by adding the following line at the top of the file. The connection object that you need to open the database is defined in this namespace. (For other kinds of databases, you may need to use different database objects in other namespaces.)

```
using System.Data.OleDb;
```

Next build a database connection. The LinqToSqlAccess example program that is available in this lesson's download uses the following code to build its connection:

```
// Get the database's location.
string filename = Path.GetFullPath(
    Application.StartupPath + @"\..\..\CustomerData.mdb");

// Connect to the database.
using (OleDbConnection conn = new OleDbConnection(
    "Provider=Microsoft.Jet.OLEDB.4.0;" +
    "Data Source=" + filename))
{
```

This program assumes the CustomerData.mdb database is located two directory levels above where the program is executing. This is true if the program is running from its bin\Debug directory.

The program gets the location of the database file. It creates a new OleDbConnection object, passing its constructor a connect string that includes the location of the database file. (Connect strings for different kinds of databases hold different fields. If you're using some other kinds of database, you'll need to build an appropriate connect string.)

Having connected to the database, the program should create an instance of the LINQ to SQL database class, passing its constructor the database connection. The LinqToSqlAccess example program uses the following code:

```
// Get the database.
using (CustomerClassesDataContext db =
    new CustomerClassesDataContext(conn))
{
```

From this point on, the code is the same as it is for working with SQL Server. The only complication is that not all databases are created equal. Different databases may provide different features and the automatically generated database code may not work properly for all databases.

The LinqToSqlAccess example program executes the same queries as the FindCustomers example and has no trouble until the final query, which adds 30 days to the customer's due date. Access cannot understand the automatically generated code for that query and throws an error.

In this case, you can fix the query by subtracting 30 days from the current date and seeing if the result is after the customer's due date as shown in the following code:

```
DateTime todayMinus30 = today.Subtract(new TimeSpan(30, 0, 0, 0));
var overdueQuery =
    from Customer cust in db.Customers
    where (cust.Balance == null || cust.Balance.Value < -50) &&
        (cust.DueDate == null || todayMinus30 > cust.DueDate.Value)
    //orderby cust.Balance ascending, cust.FirstName
    select String.Format("{0} {1}\t{2:C}\t{3:d}",
        cust.FirstName, cust.LastName,
        cust.Balance, cust.DueDate);
overdueListBox.DataSource = overdueQuery.ToArray();
```

TRY IT

In this Try It, you extend the FindCustomers program to find customers that are missing data. You add a new `ListBox` to display customers that are missing first name, last name, balance, or due date values.

> *You can download the code and resources for this Try It from the book's web page at* www.wrox.com *or* www.CSharpHelper.com/24hour.html. *You can find them in the Lesson38 folder of the download.*

Lesson Requirements

➤ Copy the FindCustomers program available in this lesson's download. Add a new `ListBox` to hold customers with missing data.

➤ Use a LINQ to SQL query to display customers that have missing values.

Hints

➤ Remember that a blank string (a string with no characters) is not the same as a null value. You don't need to check the `FirstName` and `LastName` fields for `null` values, but you should check them for blank values.

Step-by-Step

➤ Copy the FindCustomers program available in this lesson's download. Add a new `ListBox` to hold customers with missing data.

   1. This is straightforward.

➤ Use a LINQ to SQL query to display customers that have missing values.

1. You can use code similar to the following.

```
// List customers with missing data.
var missingDataQuery =
    from Customer cust in db.Customers
    where (cust.FirstName == "" ||
           cust.LastName == "" ||
           cust.Balance == null ||
           cust.DueDate == null)
    select String.Format("{0} {1}\t{2:C}\t{3:d}",
        cust.FirstName, cust.LastName,
        cust.Balance, cust.DueDate);
missingDataListBox.DataSource = missingDataQuery.ToArray();
```

 Please select Lesson 38 on the DVD to view the video that accompanies this lesson.

EXERCISES

For these exercises, use the customer database built by program BuildCustomerDatabase. (If you don't want to install SQL Server, you can use the Access database CustomerData.mdb included in the LinqToSqlAccess example program in this lesson's download.)

1. Build the user interface shown in Figure 38-9. Make the First and Last Name `TextBoxes` read-only. (Don't worry about the data yet. Just build the user interface.)

FIGURE 38-9

2. Copy the program you built for Exercise 1 and make it display the list of customers. To do that:

a. Add LINQ to SQL classes to the program.

b. Override the `Customer` class's `ToString` method so it displays the customer's name. Instead of modifying the automatically generated `Customer` class, however, add a new class named `Customer`. Modify the class definition as follows:

```
// Add a ToString override to Customer.
public partial class Customer
```

```
    {
        public override string ToString()
        {
            return FirstName + " " + LastName;
        }
    }
```

The `partial` keyword indicates that this class is part of a class that may have pieces elsewhere. In this case, it means the `ToString` method should be added to the `Customer` class built by LINQ to SQL so you don't need to modify the automatically generated code.

c. Declare a field name `Db` with your `DataContext` class's type.

d. Write a method `LoadData` that queries the database and sets the `ListBox`'s `DataSource` property to the result.

e. In the form's `Load` event handler, initialize the `Db` variable and call function `LoadData`.

3. Copy the program you built for Exercise 2 and make it display the currently selected customer's properties. To do that:

a. Write a `ShowSelectedCustomer` method. It should get the `ListBox`'s `SelectedItem` property as a `Customer` object. It should then display the object's properties in the textboxes.

b. In the listbox's `SelectedIndexChanged` event handler, call `ShowSelectedCustomer`.

4. Copy the program you built for Exercise 3 and make it update the `Customer` objects when the user modifies the balance or due date. To do that, give the textboxes `TextChanged` event handlers. They should get the current customer object, parse the value in the textbox, and save the value in the customer object. Use a `try catch` statement to protect against invalid data and, if a value is invalid, store `null` in the object.

5. Copy the program you built for Exercise 4 and finish it by making the Save and Cancel buttons work. To do that:

a. Make the Save button call `Db.SubmitChanges`. That saves any changes pending in the `DataContext` back to the SQL Server database.

b. Make the Cancel button execute the following statement to cancel any changes pending in the `DataContext`:

```
Db.Refresh(System.Data.Linq.RefreshMode.OverwriteCurrentValues,
    customerListBox.Items);
```

Then make the button's event handler call `ShowSelectedCustomer` to redisplay the currently selected customer.

You can download the solutions to these exercises from the book's web page at www.wrox.com *or* www.CSharpHelper.com/24hour.html. *You can find those solutions in the Lesson38 folder.*

39

Drawing with GDI+

Previous lessons have touched upon drawing graphics in a couple of places. For example, Lesson 23 uses a `Turtle` class that provides drawing methods, and Lesson 31 explains printing, which requires that you draw text, lines, and whatever other shapes you want to print.

However, I've mostly avoided discussing graphics code. While I find graphics code a lot of fun, I have to admit that it's usually not a high priority for most business applications (aside from printing).

This lesson explains the basics of graphics programming in C#. It explains the objects that you use to produce graphics and shows how to use those objects to draw on bitmaps or controls at run time.

Before you can start drawing bar charts or building a new painting application, however, you need to know about three classes: `Graphics`, `Pen`, and `Brush`.

GRAPHICS

The `Graphics` class represents the drawing surface, whether it is a bitmap stored in memory, a control's surface on the screen, or a printed page (you saw printing in Lesson 31). In many ways you can think of `Graphics` as the "paper" on which you're drawing.

The `Graphics` class provides the methods that do the actual drawing. Many of them come in two flavors: one for drawing and one for filling. For example, `DrawRectangle` draws a hollow rectangle and `FillRectangle` fills in a rectangle's interior.

Table 39-1 summarizes some of the most useful of those methods. Missing entries mean the `Graphics` class doesn't provide the method. For example, there is a `DrawArc` method but no `FillArc` method.

TABLE 39-1

DRAW METHOD	FILL METHOD	PURPOSE
DrawArc		Draw an arc of an ellipse
DrawBezier		Draw a smooth Bézier curve defined by a set of control points
DrawBeziers		Draw a series of connected smooth Bézier curves defined by a set of control points
DrawClosedCurve	FillClosedCurve	Draw/fill a smooth curve through a series of points
DrawCurve		Draw a smooth curve through a series of points
DrawEllipse	FillEllipse	Draw/fill an ellipse
DrawImage		Draw part of an image at a specific location
DrawLine		Draw a line
DrawLines		Draw a series of connected lines
DrawPie	FillPie	Draw/fill a pie slice defined by an ellipse
DrawPolygon	FillPolygon	Draw/fill a polygon
DrawRectangle	FillRectangle	Draw/fill a rectangle
DrawRectangles	FillRectangles	Draw/fill many rectangles
DrawString		Draw text

See the online help for information about specific drawing or filling methods. The page msdn.microsoft.com/library/system.drawing.graphics_members.aspx describes the Graphics object's methods.

All of the filling methods take a Brush as a parameter. For example, the following code fills a yellow rectangle with an upper-left corner at the point (10, 20), 200 pixels wide, and 100 pixels tall on the Graphics object named gr:

```
gr.FillRectangle(Brushes.Yellow, 10, 20, 200, 100);
```

Most of the drawing methods take a Pen as a parameter. For example, if gr is a Graphics object, then the following code outlines the preceding rectangle in blue:

```
gr.DrawRectangle(Pens.Blue, 10, 20, 200, 100);
```

The two methods that don't fit the pattern are DrawString, which takes a Brush as a parameter instead of a Pen, and DrawImage, which draws an image and doesn't use either a Pen or Brush. Despite their names, these two don't really draw in the sense that the others do. The DrawString method produces text, which is much more complicated than drawing lines and curves, and the DrawImage method fills an area with part of an image.

You learn more about pens and brushes in the following sections, but before I leave the topic of `Graphics` objects, there's one more thing you need to know: where do they come from? There are four main ways you can get a `Graphics` object.

➤ First, you can catch a control's `Paint` event. The event handler receives a parameter named `e` that contains a `Graphics` object representing the surface of the control that raised the event. For example, the following code draws a rectangle on a form whenever the form repaints:

```
// Draw a yellow rectangle with a blue border.
private void Form1_Paint(object sender, PaintEventArgs e)
{
    e.Graphics.FillRectangle(Brushes.Yellow, 10, 20, 200, 100);
    e.Graphics.DrawRectangle(Pens.Blue, 10, 20, 200, 100);
}
```

➤ The second way to get a `Graphics` object is to catch a `PrintDocument`'s `PrintPage` event. A `PrintPage` event handler also has an `e` parameter that is similar to the `Paint` event handler's. See Lesson 31 for more information on printing.

➤ The third way to get a `Graphics` object is to create one using a control's `CreateGraphics` method. Note that this method creates a `Graphics` object for use immediately on the control as it sits on the screen. Anything you draw using this object is not permanent, and the next time the control refreshes (for example, if the form is minimized and then restored), whatever you drew disappears.

The following code draws a filled and outlined circle on the form:

```
// Draw a circle on the form.
private void drawCircleButton_Click(object sender, EventArgs e)
{
    using (Graphics gr = this.CreateGraphics())
    {
        gr.FillEllipse(Brushes.LightGreen, 30, 80, 75, 75);
        gr.DrawEllipse(Pens.Green, 30, 80, 75, 75);
    }
}
```

 Notice that the code using `CreateGraphics` *includes a* using *statement to automatically dispose of the* `Graphics` *object when it has finished drawing with it. The graphics classes* `Graphics`, `Pen`, *and* `Brush` *all use relatively scarce resources, so you should always dispose of them when you are finished with them.*

This rule applies only to objects that you create yourself, not to stock objects such as `Pens.Red` *and* `Brushes.Blue`, *or to* `Graphics` *objects passed into an event handler as in* `e.Graphics`.

➤ The fourth way to get a `Graphics` object is to make one associated with a bitmap. Create a `Bitmap` object and use the `Graphics` class's static `FromImage` method to create a `Graphics` object associated with it. Then when you use the `Graphics` object's drawing and filling methods, the results are applied to the `Bitmap`.

When should you use the Paint *event handler and when should you use a* Bitmap?

A Bitmap *can take up a lot of memory, but the time it needs to redraw doesn't depend on how complex its image is. In contrast, a* Paint *event handler doesn't use any extra memory, but it can take a long time to draw a very complex image.*

If an image is simple so redrawing it is very fast, you should consider redrawing in the Paint *event handler. If an image takes a noticeable amount of time to draw, you should consider saving it in a* Bitmap.

For example, drawing a few hundred lines or rectangles is fast, so you can easily do it in a Paint *event handler.*

In contrast, to draw the Mandelbrot set a program must perform hundreds of calculations for each pixel in the image. Redrawing a big image could take several seconds in a Paint *event handler, so the program should draw it into a* Bitmap *instead and then display the result in a* PictureBox *or some other control.*

The following code creates a Bitmap, draws on it, and then sets the form's BackgroundImage property to the Bitmap. This is a convenient way to make a permanent picture that you don't need to redraw in a Paint event handler.

```
// Make a bitmap and draw on it.
private void makeBitmapButton_Click(object sender, EventArgs e)
{
    // Make the Bitmap.
    Bitmap bm = new Bitmap(100, 100);

    // Make an associated Graphics object.
    using (Graphics gr = Graphics.FromImage(bm))
    {
        // Make some points to define a polygon.
        Point[] points =
        {
            new Point(50, 10),
            new Point(60, 40),
            new Point(90, 50),
            new Point(60, 60),
            new Point(50, 90),
            new Point(40, 60),
            new Point(10, 50),
            new Point(40, 40),
        };
        // Draw on it.
        gr.FillPolygon(Brushes.HotPink, points);
        gr.DrawPolygon(Pens.Red, points);
    }

    // Display the bitmap on the form's background.
    this.BackgroundImage = bm;
}
```

Note that the code includes a using *statement to dispose of the* Graphics *object, but it does* not *dispose of the* Bitmap *object. This is important! The program uses the* Bitmap *object whenever it needs to refresh the form's background image. If you dispose of it (perhaps with a* using *statement), the program crashes the next time it needs to refresh the image.*

Figure 39-1 shows the DrawShapes example program (available as part of this lesson's code download) using the code snippets described in this section. The Make Bitmap button created the star shape in the background. The form's Paint event handler draws the large rectangle whenever the form repaints. The Draw Circle button draws the circle on top of everything else. If you minimize and then restore the form, the background and rectangle remain but the circle disappears.

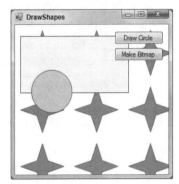

FIGURE 39-1

The Graphics class has three properties that determine how smoothly its methods draw. You can change the smoothness by setting these properties before you draw. Generally smoother drawing is slower, although you usually won't notice a difference in speed for simple drawings.

The following list summarizes these three properties.

➤ SmoothingMode — Determines how smoothly lines and shapes are drawn

➤ TextRenderingHint — Determines how smoothly text is rendered

➤ InterpolationMode — Determines how smoothly images are enlarged or reduced

The Smoothness example program, which is shown in Figure 39-2 and available in this lesson's download, demonstrates some of the possible values for these properties.

The three lines of text use TextRenderingHint values SingleBitPerPixel (not very good), SystemDefault (slightly better), and AntiAliasGridFit (very smooth).

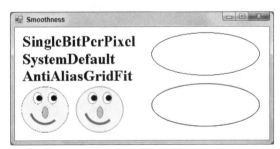

FIGURE 39-2

The two ellipses use the SmoothingMode values Default (a little rough) and AntiAlias (smooth).

The two smiley face images were drawn smaller than the original using the InterpolationMode values Default (on the left) and HighQualityBilinear (on the right).

PEN

The `Pen` class represents a linear feature such as a line or curve. This object determines such properties as a line's color, thickness, dash style, and cap style (the shape of the ends of the line and its dashes).

There are two main ways to get a `Pen`. First, you can use the `Pens` class's static color properties. (The `Pen` and `Pens` classes are two different classes.) For example, the value `Pens.Black` returns a simple black `Pen`. All of these pens are one pixel wide, and you cannot change their properties (such as dash style). The shapes drawn in Figure 39-1 use this kind of stock pen.

The second way to get a `Pen` is to make an instance of the `Pen` class. The simplest constructors can take a color or a color and thickness as parameters. For example, the following code makes a 10-pixel wide blue `Pen` and uses it to draw an ellipse:

```
// Use a thick blue pen.
using (Pen thickPen = new Pen(Color.Blue, 10))
{
    e.Graphics.DrawEllipse(thickPen, 10, 70, 100, 50);
}
```

When you create your own `Pen` object, you can change its properties. For example, the following code creates a `Pen` and sets its `DashStyle` property before drawing with it:

```
// Use a dashed pen.
using (Pen dashedPen = new Pen(Color.Red, 5))
{
    dashedPen.DashStyle = System.Drawing.Drawing2D.DashStyle.Dash;
    e.Graphics.DrawEllipse(dashedPen, 10, 130, 100, 50);
}
```

Table 39-2 summarizes the `Pen` class's most useful properties. The descriptions refer to drawing lines but the same properties apply to any linear feature.

TABLE 39-2

PROPERTY	PURPOSE
Brush	A `Brush` that determines the `Pen`'s appearance
Color	The `Pen`'s color
CompoundArray	An array of values that splits lines drawn with the pen lengthwise
CustomEndCap[1]	Determines the shape of a line's end point
CustomStartCap[1]	Determines the shape of a line's start point
DashCap	Determines the shape of the ends of a line's dashes
DashOffset	Determines the distance from the start of a line to its first dash
DashPattern	An array of `floats` that determines the pattern of pixels drawn and skipped by a line's dash pattern

PROPERTY	PURPOSE
DashStyle	Selects a standard dash style
EndCap	Selects a standard end point shape
LineJoin	Determines whether the corners where lines meet (for example, in a polygon) are mitered, beveled, or rounded
StartCap	Selects a standard start point shape
Width	The line's thickness in pixels

[1] These are cool features but are fairly advanced and complicated so they're not covered further here.

The UsePens example program shown in Figure 39-3 and available as part of this lesson's code download demonstrates some of the Pen class's features. The form's Paint event handler draws an ellipse with a stock pen, an ellipse with a thick pen, a dashed ellipse, an ellipse with a custom dash pattern, a polygon with a pen that uses a CompoundArray property, and two lines with start and end caps.

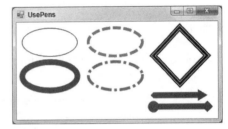

FIGURE 39-3

You can learn more about the Pen class's properties by looking at the UsePens program's code or at msdn.microsoft.com/library/system.drawing.pen_members.aspx.

BRUSH

The Brush class determines the way in which an area is filled. This object determines such properties as the fill color, fill pattern, or color gradient.

As is the case with Pens, you can use stock Brushes or you can create your own. Unlike the case with the Pen class, however, there are several different Brush classes:

➤ **HatchBrush** — Fills an area with a hatch pattern

➤ **LinearGradientBrush** — Fills an area with a color gradient that shades from one color to another, possibly multiple times

➤ **PathGradientBrush** — Fills an area defined by a path with a color gradient

➤ **SolidBrush** — Fills an area with a solid color

➤ **TextureBrush** — Fills an area with an image

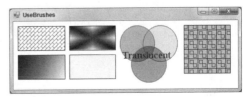

Example program UseBrushes shown in Figure 39-4 and available as part of this lesson's code download demonstrates several kinds of brushes.

FIGURE 39-4

The four rectangles on the left demonstrate a `TextureBrush`, `PathGradientBrush`, `LinearGradientBrush`, and `SolidBrush`. The three overlapping circles demonstrate transparent `SolidBrushes`, and the square on the right demonstrates a `TextureBrush` filled with a small repeating image.

For example, the following code shows how the program draws the hatched rectangle in the upper left corner.

```
// Use a HatchBrush.
using (HatchBrush br = new HatchBrush(
    HatchStyle.DiagonalBrick,
    Color.Green,
    Color.White))
{
    e.Graphics.FillRectangle(br, 10, 10, 100, 50);
    e.Graphics.DrawRectangle(Pens.Black, 10, 10, 100, 50);
}
```

You can look at the code for additional details, but I will mention a few extra facts about the different kinds of brushes.

➤ The `HatchBrush` provides more than 50 hatch patterns. If you want a pattern that isn't in the list, use a `TextureBrush`. Parameters to the `HatchBrush`'s constructor give the pattern's foreground and background colors.

➤ The `LinearGradientBrush` shades from one color at one point to another color at another point. More complicated versions of the brush can shade between several colors and points and let you change the way colors drop off.

➤ The `PathGradientBrush` makes colors shade from points along a path to another color at a "center point," although you can move the "center point" so it isn't actually in the center.

➤ Stock `SolidBrushes` use predefined, solid, opaque colors. You can also define `SolidBrushes` by specifying the brush's color and that color can be translucent.

➤ By default the `TextureBrush` tiles the area it is filling with copies of its image. You can change that behavior so the brush fills the area with different kinds of reflections of the image if you like. For example, it could flip copies that are adjacent in the X direction horizontally so they look like mirror images.

Instead of passing x, y, width, and height parameters to rectangle or ellipse methods, you can pass a `Rectangle` *or* `RectangleF`*.*

If you are going to fill a shape and then outline it, use the same `Rectangle` *or* `RectangleF` *for both so you're guaranteed that the fill and draw methods line up properly, even if you need to change the location later.*

You can learn more about the `Brush` class's properties by looking at the following web pages:

➤ **HatchBrush** — msdn.microsoft.com/library/system.drawing.drawing2d .hatchbrush.aspx

➤ **LinearGradientBrush** — `msdn.microsoft.com/library/system.drawing.drawing2d.lineargradientbrush.aspx`

➤ **PathGradientBrush** — `msdn.microsoft.com/library/system.drawing.drawing2d.pathgradientbrush.aspx`

➤ **SolidBrush** — `msdn.microsoft.com/library/system.drawing.solidbrush.aspx`

➤ **TextureBrush** — `msdn.microsoft.com/library/system.drawing.texturebrush.aspx`

TRY IT

Available for
download on
Wrox.com

In this Try It, you build the program shown in Figure 39-5. The program's `DrawLineGraph` function takes as parameters a `PictureBox`, a `Graphics` object, and an array of values and draws the graph on the `PictureBox`.

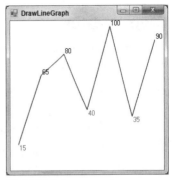

FIGURE 39-5

> You can download the code and resources for this Try It from the book's web page at www.wrox.com or www.CSharpHelper.com/24hour.html. You can find those solutions in the Lesson39 folder.

Lesson Requirements

➤ Start a new program and make a `PictureBox` named `graphPictureBox` that is docked to fill the form.

➤ Give the `PictureBox` a `Paint` event handler that makes an array of `floats` and invokes the `DrawLineGraph` method.

➤ Make the `DrawLineGraph` method loop through the values drawing lines between them.

Hints

➤ Calculate the width and height of the `PictureBox` minus a margin.

➤ Divide the width by the number of values minus one to get a horizontal scale factor.

➤ Divide the width by the maximum value to get a vertical scale factor.

➤ Make variables `x0` and `y0` to record the location of the graph's previous point. Initially set those equal to the location of the first point. Use the scale factors to figure out where to put the point. Remember the margins and that Y coordinates increase downward in a `PictureBox`.

➤ Loop through the values drawing lines from the previous point to the next one. After each value, update the x0 and y0 variables to hold the location of the point you just handled.

➤ As you draw each point, draw its value below or above the point, depending on whether the value is less than 50.

Step-by-Step

➤ Start a new program and make a PictureBox named graphPictureBox that is docked to fill the form.

1. This is straightforward.

➤ Give the PictureBox a Paint event handler that makes an array of floats and invokes the DrawLineGraph method.

1. Use code similar to the following:

```
// Draw the graph.
private void graphPictureBox_Paint(object sender, PaintEventArgs e)
{
    float[] values = { 15, 65, 80, 40, 100, 35, 90 };
    DrawLineGraph(graphPictureBox, e.Graphics, values);
}
```

➤ Make the DrawLineGraph method loop through the values drawing lines between them.

1. Use code similar to the following:

```
// Draw a line graph that fills the PictureBox
// (except for a margin).
private void DrawLineGraph(PictureBox graphPictureBox,
    Graphics graphics, float[] values)
{
    // Make things smooth.
    graphics.SmoothingMode =
        System.Drawing.Drawing2D.SmoothingMode.AntiAlias;
    graphics.TextRenderingHint =
        System.Drawing.Text.TextRenderingHint.AntiAliasGridFit;

    // Figure out the geometry of the drawable area.
    const int marginX = 15;
    const int marginY = 10;
    int width = graphPictureBox.ClientSize.Width - 2 * marginX;
    int height = graphPictureBox.ClientSize.Height - 2 * marginY;

    // Calculate scale factors.
    float scaleX = width / (values.Length - 1);
    float scaleY = height / values.Max();

    // Find the first point's coordinates.
    float x0 = marginX + scaleX * 0;
    float y0 = graphPictureBox.ClientSize.Height -
        marginY - scaleY * values[0];

    for (int i = 0; i < values.Length; i++)
```

```
        {
            // Find the next point's coordinates.
            float x1 = marginX + scaleX * i;
            float y1 = graphPictureBox.ClientSize.Height -
                marginY - scaleY * values[i];

            // Draw a line from the previous point to this one.
            graphics.DrawLine(Pens.Black, x0, y0, x1, y1);

            // Draw this point's value in text.
            if (values[i] >= 50)
            {
                graphics.DrawString(values[i].ToString(),
                    this.Font, Brushes.Black, x1, y1 - 12);
            }
            else
            {
                graphics.DrawString(values[i].ToString(),
                    this.Font, Brushes.Red, x1, y1);
            }

            // Update (x0, y0).
            x0 = x1;
            y0 = y1;
        }
    }
```

 Please select Lesson 39 on the DVD to view the video that accompanies this lesson.

EXERCISES

1. Build a program that uses a `Paint` event handler to draw a picture similar to the one shown in Figure 39-6. (Feel free to embellish with ears, a hat, a scarf, or anything else you like.)

2. Build a program that uses a `Paint` event handler to draw a bar chart similar to the one shown in Figure 39-7. (Hint: Use the program you built for the Try It as a starting point.)

FIGURE 39-6

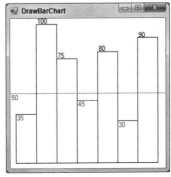

FIGURE 39-7

3. Build a Scribble program similar to the one shown in Figure 39-8. Hints: Make fields `isDrawing` (true when drawing) and `lastPoint` (the last point drawn). Make a `MouseDown` event handler that sets `isDrawing` to `true` and records the current point. In the `MouseMove` event handler, verify that the user is drawing, draw between the last and current points, and update `lastPoint`. In the `MouseUp` event handler, set `isDrawing` to false. Do all drawing on a `Bitmap` that is created when the program starts and if the user selects the File menu's New command. Finally, be sure to call the `PictureBox`'s `Refresh` method any time you draw.

4. (Hard) Make a program that uses a `Paint` event handler to draw a star as shown in Figure 39-9. Make the number of points a constant and allocate arrays big enough to hold the star's corner points and the `PathGradientBrush`'s `SurroundColors`. (Hint: If the star has 7 points as in Figure 39-9, you'll need 14 corner points in the polygon and 14 colors for the brush.) Use `Math.Cos` and `Math.Sin` to calculate positions for the points.

FIGURE 39-8

FIGURE 39-9

 You can download the solutions to these exercises from the book's web page at www.wrox.com *or* www.CSharpHelper.com/24hour.html. *You can find those solutions in the Lesson39 folder.*

40

Making WPF Applications

Up to this point, this book has dealt only with Windows Forms applications. The programs have displayed forms and used Windows Forms controls such as Buttons, TextBoxes, and Labels.

In .NET 3.0, Microsoft released Windows Presentation Foundation (WPF). WPF uses a whole new set of controls, a new presentation system, and a whole new approach to user interface programming. New features provide support for property animation (making property values vary over time), simpler multimedia control, easier graphical transformations (for example, to rotate or scale controls), and much more.

WPF uses a whole new set of controls, some of which correspond to Windows Forms controls and some of which are completely new. For example, WPF has Label, TextBox, Button, and CheckBox controls that serve similar purposes to their Windows Forms counterparts. It also has Grid, Expander, Ellipse, Rectangle, and DocumentViewer controls that don't have Windows Forms counterparts.

In this lesson, you learn a little bit about WPF. You learn some of its advantages and disadvantages. You also build some simple WPF programs to get a firsthand glimpse of some of the differences between WPF and Windows Forms.

Note that although there's room in this book to give you an idea about some of the things that WPF can do, WPF is much too big a topic to cover in one or two lessons. For more detailed information, see a book about WPF such as my Wrox book *WPF Programmer's Reference* (Wiley, 2010).

In addition to Visual Studio, Expression Blend is another tool you can use to build WPF applications. It includes some tools that Visual Studio lacks, such as the ability to record property animations. For more information, see www.microsoft.com/expression.

WEIGHING WPF'S BENEFITS AND WEAKNESSES

Although WPF and Windows Forms controls provide many of the same features (buttons, labels, textboxes, and so on), they also have many large differences. One of the biggest architectural differences is in the way they render their content.

Windows Forms controls use Graphics Device Interface (GDI) functions to display their output. Though these functions are effective, they are also very old. They were first developed when computer hardware was much less powerful than it is today, so they don't take full advantage of modern graphics processors.

In contrast, WPF controls use the DirectX Application Programming Interface (API) to render their content. *DirectX* is a collection of high-performance multimedia APIs that provide much better access to graphics hardware than GDI does. That gives WPF controls a lot of benefits practically for free.

For example, DirectX includes a 3D drawing library that makes drawing three-dimensional scenes in a WPF application a lot easier than it is in a Windows Forms application. DirectX also provides transformations that can translate, rotate, scale, and skew a drawing. WPF controls inherit that capability to make it easy to do things like display a button or textbox that is rotated or scaled.

The following list summarizes the biggest benefits WPF gets due to its use of DirectX:

➤ **High-performance graphics** — WPF controls take better advantage of graphics hardware than Windows Forms controls.

➤ **Transformations** — You can easily translate, rotate, scale, and skew WPF controls.

➤ **Multimedia support** — Multimedia WPF controls such as `MediaPlayer` make it very easy to play media such as audio and video.

➤ **3D drawing** — 3D drawing support makes it relatively easy to draw three-dimensional scenes.

In addition to these benefits, WPF controls provide some other advantages:

➤ **Property animations** — WPF provides classes that let you animate a control's property as it changes from one value to another. For example, when the mouse moves over it, a button could grow to twice its normal size.

➤ **Retained-mode graphics** — A Windows Forms application needs to redraw any drawings that it should display whenever it receives a `Paint` event. WPF provides objects that represent drawing components and they redraw themselves automatically whenever necessary.

➤ **More uniform content model** — Many Windows Forms controls can hold only text or an image. WPF controls can hold just about anything (with some exceptions). For example, a WPF button can hold a grid that contains images, labels, textboxes, and even video.

➤ **Styles** — Styles let you define a package of property values that you can then apply to many controls, giving them a consistent appearance and allowing you to make changes easily.

➤ **Templates** — Templates let you determine what controls make up other controls. For example, you can make a button use an ellipse instead of a rectangle to draw itself.

➤ **Data templates** — Data templates let you bind data to control properties in ways that are not possible in Windows Forms controls. For example, you can make a listbox display several pieces of text and a picture for each of the items it contains.

➤ **Scalable controls** — A program can scale WPF controls to any degree without distorting them. For example, you can zoom in on a curve or a string as much as you want and the result will still appear smooth, not pixelated as it would if you zoomed in on a bitmapped image.

Although WPF has many advantages, it also has some disadvantages, the biggest of which is its complexity. To really get the most out of it, you need to learn about its controls, pens, brushes, styles, templates, data templates, flow documents, resources, property triggers, event triggers, animations, themes, printing, data binding, commanding, transformations, page navigation, and many other topics. WPF has some amazing capabilities but taking advantage of them can be challenging.

The good news is that building simple programs is relatively easy. Most of what you've already learned in this book still applies, and as the following section explains, you can use it fairly easily to build basic WPF applications.

BUILDING WPF APPLICATIONS

Building a simple WPF application in Visual Studio is a lot like building a Windows Forms application. To start a new WPF application, open the File menu, expand the New submenu, and select Project. On the New Project dialog, expand the Visual C# category, open the Windows subcategory, and select WPF Application. Enter a name for the new project, select a directory to hold it, and click OK.

So far this is almost exactly like building a Windows Forms application. When the new project appears, however, the main object you see is a `Window` not a `Form`.

Figure 40-1 shows Visual Studio displaying a new project. Much of this should look familiar. The Toolbox is still on the left, the Solution Explorer is on the upper right, and the Properties window is on the lower right.

The main editing area displays tabs much as a Windows Forms project does. The tab labeled MainWindow.xaml.cs is a C# code window much like those that contain event handlers for a `Form`.

The designer window shown in Figure 40-1 allows you to edit the WPF controls on the `Window`. You can use the Toolbox to place WPF controls on the `Window` much as you place Windows Forms controls on a `Form`. Select a control (or the `Window`) and then use the Properties window to set the selected object's properties.

To make an event handler for a control, select the control in the designer. Then click the Events button on the Properties window and double-click the event just as you would in a Windows Forms application. Visual Studio creates an empty event handler in the MainWindow.xaml.cs file and opens it in the code editor.

The event handlers and other code that sits behind the user interface is called code-behind.

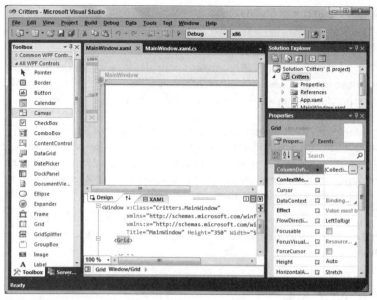

FIGURE 40-1

The area below the main designer is a XAML code editor. *eXtensible Application Markup Language* (XAML) is a language that defines the user interface for WPF applications. XAML (pronounced *zammel*) is a user interface definition language used by WPF to define the controls that make up an application. As you use the design surface to modify the application, Visual Studio builds a corresponding XAML file. Conversely if you modify the XAML code (and don't make any mistakes), the design surface updates to show the changes you made.

You don't need to understand XAML to build simple interfaces, but it's helpful when you want to do something more advanced.

 XAML is a form of eXtensible Markup Language (XML), a flexible text-based language used to hold hierarchical data. You can find a brief overview of XML at www.w3schools.com/XML/xml_whatis.asp *or* en.wikipedia.org/wiki/XML.

I built the program shown in Figure 40-2 by placing several `Image` controls on the `Window` and setting a few properties.

FIGURE 40-2

After adding the controls to the `Window`, I set the `Window`'s `Title` property to "Critters." I then set the properties for the `Image` controls shown in Table 40-1.

TABLE 40-1

PROPERTY	VALUE
Name	A name, such as *butterflyImage*
Image	The picture the control should display
Width	100
Height	100
Stretch	Uniform

Notice that these are not the same properties that you would set for a Windows Forms application. In Windows Forms you would probably use `PictureBox` controls, and set their `Image`, `ScaleMode`, and `Size` properties.

When you are editing a WPF application, the Properties window handles a control's name specially. Instead of treating Name *as just another property, the window displays the name above the other properties and the Properties and Events buttons. It's not obvious when you look at the Properties window but if you click the control's name, you can change it.*

At the top of the Properties window in Figure 40-1, you can see the control's type Grid and just to the right the faint text <no name>. In this case, that means the control doesn't have any name.

After creating the basic interface, I added a `MouseDown` event handler to each of the `Images`. The following code shows the code-behind for the frog image. This looks more or less like a normal C# event handler.

```
private void frogImage_MouseDown(object sender, MouseButtonEventArgs e)
{
    MessageBox.Show("Frog");
}
```

The following code shows the XAML code that Visual Studio produced to define the user interface. I didn't type this; Visual Studio built it to represent the controls that I placed on the Window. The definitions for the `Image` controls are all very similar so only the first is shown here.

```
<Window x:Class="Critters.MainWindow"
        xmlns="http://schemas.microsoft.com/winfx/2006/xaml/presentation"
        xmlns:x="http://schemas.microsoft.com/winfx/2006/xaml"
        Title="Critters" Height="164" Width="569">
```

```
<Grid>
    <Image Height="100" HorizontalAlignment="Left" Margin="12,12,0,0"
     Name="butterflyImage" Source="/Critters;component/Butterfly.jpg"
     Stretch="Uniform" VerticalAlignment="Top" Width="100"
     MouseDown="butterflyImage_MouseDown" />

     ... Other Image controls omitted ...
    </Grid>
</Window>
```

If you study this code, you'll see that the `Window` contains a `Grid` and the `Grid` contains the `Image` controls. You'll also notice that the XAML code gives the name of the code-behind event handlers that should execute when the user presses the mouse down on an `Image`. In the code shown here, the `MouseDown` event handler is called `butterflyImage_MouseDown`.

 A `Window` can contain only a single child control. Normally that is a container such as a `Grid` that holds all of the other controls.

Although this simple application works, it could use some improvements. For example, the images are not centered vertically. They also do not resize to take advantage of the form's current size.

One of the philosophical goals of WPF is to make controls arrange themselves to make the best use of whatever spaces is available. In a Windows Forms application you might use `Anchor` properties to do this. In a WPF application, you generally use container controls that help arrange their children.

The following section shows how you can improve the way this program arranges its controls.

ARRANGING WPF CONTROLS

The first version of the Critters program placed `Image` controls directly inside the `Window`'s `Grid`. The `Grid` control arranges its children in rows and columns, although the designer creates only one row and column by default. A better arrangement for this program would use five columns: one for each `Image`.

To make the columns, select the `Grid` control. In the Properties window, click the ellipsis button to the right of the `ColumnDefinitions` property and use the dialog that appears to create five columns. By default the columns have `Width` set to *, which means they divide the `Grid`'s area evenly.

Because the `Image` controls were originally placed in the `Grid`'s first column, they are still contained in that column. To move the controls into their proper columns, set their `Grid.Column` properties. Note that the columns are numbered starting with 0 so the column indexes should be 0, 1, 2, 3, and 4.

Originally the `Image` controls used their `Margin` properties to position themselves within the `Grid`'s first row and column. Now those values move them to strange locations within their new columns. For example, the frog `Image`'s `Margin` value of 118,12,0,0 moves the image 118 pixels to the right so it isn't visible in its column.

The Margin *property supports three different formats that hold one, two, or four values. One value represents all of the control's margins. Two values represent the left/right and top/bottom margins. Four values represent the left, top, right, and bottom margins.*

To make the Images appear centered in their Grid cells, set their Margin properties to 4.

Right now the controls' Width and Height properties are 100 so the controls always have the same size. If you change these property values to Auto, the controls will resize themselves to fit their Grid cells (minus their margins).

Finally, to ensure that the Image controls are centered in their cells, set their HorizontalAlignment and VerticalAlignment properties to Center.

The following XAML code shows how the program defines the new interface. This code shows only the frog image's definition. The others are similar.

```
<Window x:Class="Critters.MainWindow"
        xmlns="http://schemas.microsoft.com/winfx/2006/xaml/presentation"
        xmlns:x="http://schemas.microsoft.com/winfx/2006/xaml"
        Title="Critters" Height="164" Width="569">
    <Grid>
        <Grid.ColumnDefinitions>
            <ColumnDefinition />
            <ColumnDefinition />
            <ColumnDefinition />
            <ColumnDefinition />
            <ColumnDefinition />
        </Grid.ColumnDefinitions>

        ... Other Image controls omitted ...

        <Image HorizontalAlignment="Center" Margin="4"
         Name="frogImage" Source="/Critters;component/Frog.jpg"
         Stretch="Uniform" VerticalAlignment="Center"
         MouseDown="frogImage_MouseDown"
         Grid.Column="1" />

        ... Other Image controls omitted ...
    </Grid>
</Window>
```

Now when you resize the Window, the Grid resizes. Its columns divide the Grid's space evenly so they resize. The Image controls then resize to fill their cells (minus their margins).

Figure 40-3 shows the new program when the form has been shrunk. Notice that the Image controls are also shrunk so they fit in their Grid cells. If you shrink the first version of this program, the Image controls do not resize so they are clipped off.

FIGURE 40-3

EDITING XAML CODE

The next change I'd like to make to the program is to give the images drop shadows, as shown in Figure 40-4.

FIGURE 40-4

Unfortunately the Properties window won't let you add this kind of effect so you must type in the appropriate code in the XAML editor.

To display a drop shadow, you must set the `Image` control's `BitmapEffect` property to a `DropShadowBitmapEffect` object. Because this value is an object and not a simple value like a string or number, you need to use a special syntax for setting it.

Inside the `Image` element, you need to add an `Image.BitmapEffect` element to indicate the property you are setting. Inside that you need to add a `DropShadowBitmapEffect` object.

The following XAML code shows the new definition of the frog `Image` control with the control's `BitmapEffect` property highlighted in bold. Here I've also changed the `Margin` property to 8, so there's more room for the drop shadows between the controls. The code for the other controls is similar.

```
<Image HorizontalAlignment="Center" Margin="8" Name="frogImage"
 Source="/Critters;component/Frog.jpg" Stretch="Uniform"
 VerticalAlignment="Center" MouseDown="frogImage_MouseDown"
 Grid.Column="1">
    <Image.BitmapEffect>
        <DropShadowBitmapEffect/>
    </Image.BitmapEffect>
</Image>
```

USING WPF STYLES

The last change I want to make to this program is to simplify the code. The preceding XAML snippet shows the definition for the first `Image` control. The code that defines the others is omitted because it is very similar.

In fact, the code for those other controls is so similar that the XAML file contains a lot of duplicate code. All of the controls have the same `HorizontalAlignment`, `Margin`, `Stretch`, `VerticalAlignment`, and `BitmapEffect` values. Repeating those values for every control makes the code cluttered and makes it hard to change the values for every control. For example, if you decide that you'd rather give the images a beveled edge instead of a drop shadow, you have to make the change in five places.

You can simplify the code and its maintenance by creating a style. A *style* is a set of specific property values that you can then assign in a group to other controls.

You can create a style inside an object's Resources section. For this example, I've placed the style in the Window's Resources section.

The style itself is represented by a Style element. That element's TargetType property tells the kind of object to which the style will apply (Image controls for this example). Its x:Key property gives the style a name.

Within the Style element, Setter elements define property values. The Setter element's Property and Value attributes determine which property is set to what value.

After you define a style, you can set a control's Style property to it. If the style is named imageStyle, then the syntax for assigning the Style property is:

```
Style="{StaticResource imageStyle}"
```

The following code shows the revised XAML file. The new Window.Resources section defines the style. The Image controls' definitions now use the style instead of setting all of their common properties individually. In this snippet the style's definition and the places where it is used are highlighted in bold.

```
<Window x:Class="Critters.MainWindow"
        xmlns="http://schemas.microsoft.com/winfx/2006/xaml/presentation"
        xmlns:x="http://schemas.microsoft.com/winfx/2006/xaml"
        Title="Critters" Height="164" Width="569">
    <Window.Resources>
        <Style TargetType="Image" x:Key="imageStyle">
            <Setter Property="HorizontalAlignment" Value="Center"/>
            <Setter Property="VerticalAlignment" Value="Center"/>
            <Setter Property="Margin" Value="8"/>
            <Setter Property="Stretch" Value="Uniform"/>
            <Setter Property="BitmapEffect">
                <Setter.Value>
                    <DropShadowBitmapEffect/>
                </Setter.Value>
            </Setter>
        </Style>
    </Window.Resources>
    <Grid>
        <Grid.ColumnDefinitions>
            <ColumnDefinition />
            <ColumnDefinition />
            <ColumnDefinition />
            <ColumnDefinition />
            <ColumnDefinition />
        </Grid.ColumnDefinitions>
        <Image Style="{StaticResource imageStyle}" Name="butterflyImage"
         Source="/Critters;component/Butterfly.jpg"
         MouseDown="butterflyImage_MouseDown" />
        <Image Style="{StaticResource imageStyle}" Name="frogImage"
         Source="/Critters;component/Frog.jpg"
         MouseDown="frogImage_MouseDown" Grid.Column="1" />
        <Image Style="{StaticResource imageStyle}" Name="platypusImage"
```

```
                    Source="/Critters;component/Platypus.jpg"
                    MouseDown="platypusImage_MouseDown" Grid.Column="2" />
                <Image Style="{StaticResource imageStyle}" Name="sharkImage"
                    Source="/Critters;component/Shark.jpg"
                    MouseDown="sharkImage_MouseDown" Grid.Column="3" />
                <Image Style="{StaticResource imageStyle}" Name="tigerImage"
                    Source="/Critters;component/Tiger.jpg"
                    MouseDown="tigerImage_MouseDown" Grid.Column="4" />
        </Grid>
    </Window>
```

Now that you've built the style, you can easily make changes that apply to all of the images. For example, if you want to change the `BitmapEffect` property to a `BevelBitmapEffect` object, you can do so in one place.

TRY IT

By now you probably understand what I meant when I said that WPF's biggest weakness is its complexity. The syntax is sometimes odd and inconsistent. The way you need to use different syntax to set property values with different types, the unusual way you define styles, the odd syntax you use to refer to a style, and a host of other differences between WPF programming and Windows Forms programming make mastering WPF difficult.

However, building simple applications isn't too hard.

In this Try It, you get to practice some of the techniques described in this lesson while you build a program similar to the Critters program described earlier in this lesson. In this program, however, you'll remove the initially created `Grid` control and replace it with a horizontally oriented `StackPanel`.

The `StackPanel` control allows the controls it contains to take their preferred sizes. It allows an `Image` control to take whatever size it needs to hold its picture at full scale. In contrast, the `Grid` control requests that its children resize themselves to use the available space. That means the `Images` in this Try It must be given fixed sizes so they have a reasonable size.

You can download the code and resources for this Try It from the book's web page at www.wrox.com *or* www.CSharpHelper.com/24hour.html. *You can find them in the Lesson40 folder of the download.*

Lesson Requirements

➤ Create a new WPF application. Copy the critter images from the Critters4 directory in this lesson's download into the project directory (or use images of your own).

➤ Remove the initially created `Grid` control and add a `StackPanel`.

➤ Use the Properties window to give the `StackPanel` the properties shown in Table 40-2:

TABLE 40-2

PROPERTY	VALUE
Height	Auto
Orientation	Horizontal
Width	Auto

➤ Add five Image controls to the StackPanel.

➤ Use the Properties window or the XAML code editor to give the Image controls the property values shown in Table 40-3:

TABLE 40-3

PROPERTY	VALUE
HorizontalAlignment	Center
Margin	4
Source	An appropriate picture
Stretch	Uniform
VerticalAlignment	Center
Width	100

➤ Resize the Window so it fits the images nicely.

Hints

➤ Sometimes it's easier to edit XAML code directly instead of using the designer to modify the user interface. In this example, you can simply replace the Grid control with a StackPanel in the XAML code if you like.

➤ If you like, you can make a style to hold common properties.

Step-by-Step

The steps required for this Try It are all fairly straightforward exercises in using Visual Studio. If you have trouble figuring out how to perform a step, skim this lesson again or watch the lesson's screencast.

The basic steps are:

1. Create the new program.

2. Remove the initially created Grid control and replace it with a StackPanel. Set the StackPanel's properties. (In particular, set Orientation to Horizontal.)

3. Add five `Image` controls. Set their properties. (In particular, set `Stretch` to `Uniform` and set their `Source` properties.)

4. If you like, move common `Image` properties into a style.

 Please select Lesson 40 on the DVD to view the video that accompanies this lesson.

EXERCISES

1. Copy the program you built for this lesson's Try It and replace the `StackPanel` with a `WrapPanel`. (Hint: Instead of removing the `StackPanel` and all the controls that it contains and then rebuilding everything inside a `WrapPanel`, edit the XAML code and replace the `StackPanel` element with a `WrapPanel` element. Be sure to also change the closing `</StackPanel>` tag.) Run the program and see what happens if you make the program's window taller and narrower.

2. Make the program shown in Figure 40-5. Replace the initially created `Grid` with a `UniformGrid`. Set the new control's `Rows` property to 2 and its `Columns` property to 3.

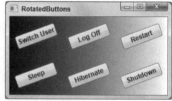

FIGURE 40-5

Add a button to the `UniformGrid`. Then add a `LayoutTransform` property to it as shown in the following code:

```
<Button Content="Switch User" Height="23" Width="75">
    <Button.LayoutTransform>
        <RotateTransform Angle="-20"/>
    </Button.LayoutTransform>
</Button>
```

Copy and paste this button several times and edit each button's `Content` property to determine the text it displays.

If you like, experiment with the `UniformGrid`'s background brush and move common properties into a style.

 You can download the solutions to these exercises from the book's web page at www.wrox.com *or* www.CSharpHelper.com/24hour.html. *You can find them in the Lesson40 folder of the download.*

41

Printing with WPF

Lesson 31 explained how to print in a Windows Forms application. Your program catches a `PrintDocument` object's `PrintPage` event handler and uses its `e.Graphics` parameter to generate graphics for each page of the printout.

Windows Presentation Foundation (WPF) uses a different printing model that many programmers find more intuitive. Instead of making your program respond to `PrintPage` events to generate printed pages, a WPF program's code can directly print visual objects that it draws using WPF controls such as `Label` and `TextBox`.

In addition to being easier to understand, this approach has a couple of other benefits.

For example, it lets the program use the same kind of code to display and print data. In Windows Forms, a program uses controls such as `TextBox` and `Label` to display text on the screen but it uses a `Graphics` object's `DrawString` method to draw text on a printout. WPF uses the same kinds of `TextBoxes` and `Labels` for both display and printing.

WPF also allows you to zoom in as much as you like without creating a pixellated result. That means, for example, you can enlarge a window as much as you like for a printout and you'll still see a smooth result.

In this lesson, you learn how to produce printouts in WPF. You learn how to print images of windows and other visual objects displayed on the screen centered and scaled to fill the printed page.

PRINTING VISUALS

In WPF, a `PrintDialog` object starts the printing process. This object can display a printer selection dialog and provides a `PrintVisual` method that prints visual objects.

Although your code can simply call `PrintVisual` to send output to the default printer immediately, most programs first display the dialog so the user can select a printer. To do that, the program creates a `PrintDialog` object and calls its `ShowDialog` method. If the user selects a printer and clicks Print, `ShowDialog` returns `true` and the program can then call the dialog's `PrintVisual` method, passing it the visual object to print.

For example, the PrintWindow program shown in Figure 41-1 (and available as part of this lesson's code download) uses the following code to print an image of its window:

```
// Print the window.
private void printButton_Click(object sender, RoutedEventArgs e)
{
    // Display the print dialog and check the result.
    PrintDialog printDialog = new PrintDialog();
    if (printDialog.ShowDialog() == true)
    {
        // Print.
        printDialog.PrintVisual(this, "PrintWindow Image");
    }
}
```

The code creates a `PrintDialog` object and calls its `ShowDialog` method. If `ShowDialog` returns `true`, the code calls the dialog's `PrintVisual` method, passing it the window variable `this`. It also passes `PrintVisual` a descriptive title for the printer to display in its user interface.

This code is simple and produces a high-resolution result but it has a big drawback: it makes poor use of the printer's area. The result appears too close to the page's upper-left corner for the printer to actually print all of it so you get an image with the top and left edges trimmed off about a quarter inch.

FIGURE 41-1

In addition to moving the result away from the corner, it would also be nice to center the image and possibly scale it to use up more of the paper.

The simplicity of the previous code may make it seem like fixing these problems would be hard. Where in that code is there room for these sorts of changes?

Fortunately WPF provides two features that make this problem much easier to solve than you might think.

➤ First, it provides transformations that let you scale, rotate, and translate images easily.

➤ Second, it lets you easily place most graphical objects inside other graphical objects.

Instead of trying to modify the window's image, you can place an image of it inside other controls such as `Grids` and `Viewboxes`. Then you can transform those controls to fit properly on the printed page.

Example program PrintWindowCentered (also available as part of this lesson's code download) uses the following code to print an image of the window centered on the page. Admittedly this code is a lot longer than the previous version, but it's simpler than it looks at first glance.

```
// Print an image of the window centered.
private void printButton_Click(object sender, RoutedEventArgs e)
{
    PrintDialog printDialog = new PrintDialog();
    if (printDialog.ShowDialog() == true)
```

```
        {
            PrintWindowCentered(printDialog, this, "New Customer", null);
        }
    }

    // Print a Window centered on the printer.
    private void PrintWindowCentered(PrintDialog printDialog, Window win,
        String title, Thickness? margin)
    {
        // Make a Grid to hold the contents.
        Grid drawingGrid = new Grid();
        drawingGrid.Width = printDialog.PrintableAreaWidth;
        drawingGrid.Height = printDialog.PrintableAreaHeight;

        // Make a Viewbox to stretch the result if necessary.
        Viewbox viewBox = new Viewbox();
        drawingGrid.Children.Add(viewBox);
        viewBox.HorizontalAlignment = HorizontalAlignment.Center;
        viewBox.VerticalAlignment = VerticalAlignment.Center;

        if (margin == null)
        {
            // Center without resizing.
            viewBox.Stretch = Stretch.None;
        }
        else
        {
            // Resize to fit the margin.
            viewBox.Margin = margin.Value;
            viewBox.Stretch = Stretch.Uniform;
        }

        // Make a VisualBrush holding an image of the Window's contents.
        VisualBrush br = new VisualBrush(win);

        // Make a Rectangle the size of the Window.
        Rectangle windowRect = new Rectangle();
        viewBox.Child = windowRect;
        windowRect.Width = win.Width;
        windowRect.Height = win.Height;
        windowRect.Fill = br;
        windowRect.Stroke = Brushes.Black;
        windowRect.Effect = new DropShadowEffect();

        // Arrange to produce output.
        Rect rect = new Rect(0, 0,
            printDialog.PrintableAreaWidth, printDialog.PrintableAreaHeight);
        drawingGrid.Arrange(rect);

        // Print it.
        printDialog.PrintVisual(drawingGrid, title);
    }
```

This code adds a DropShadowEffect below the grid. That class is defined in the System.Windows.Media.Effects *namespace, so to make using it easier, the program includes the following* using *directive:*

```
using System.Windows.Media.Effects;
```

When you click the Print button, the program displays a `PrintDialog`. If you select a printer and click Print, the program calls the `PrintWindowCentered` method passing it the `PrintDialog` object and the `Window` to print. It also passes the method a title to use for the printout and a margin, which can be null.

The `PrintWindowCentered` function makes a `Grid` that fills the printer's printable area. Inside the `Grid` it places a `Viewbox` named viewBox. A `Viewbox` displays a single object that it can optionally stretch in various ways.

If the method receives a margin parameter, the program sets the `ViewBox`'s margin appropriately and makes the control stretch its contents so they are as large as possible without changing shape. If the margin parameter is `null`, the code makes the `ViewBox` not stretch its contents.

Next the code makes a `VisualBrush` from the `Window`. A `VisualBrush` fills an area with the image of some visual object such as a control or, in this case, the program's main `Window`. The code creates a `Rectangle`, places it inside the `ViewBox`, and fills it with the brush.

At this point, all of the objects needed to display the `Window` appropriately sized and centered on the printed page are in place. The code only needs to perform two more steps.

First, it calls the `Grid`'s `Arrange` method to make its children arrange themselves. Finally the code calls the `PrintDialog`'s `PrintVisual` method to print the `Grid`.

Figure 41-2 shows the printout. To make this figure, I printed the `Window` into an XML Paper Specification (XPS) file by selecting the Microsoft XPS Document Writer from the `PrintDialog`. I then double-clicked the XPS file to display it in the XPS Viewer shown in Figure 41-2. You can see in the figure that the `Window`'s image is centered.

In Figure 41-2 the image of the window looks a bit grainy and pixilated, but that's caused by the way the XPS Viewer displays the document. The document itself was generated at a very high resolution. In Figure 41-3 the viewer has enlarged the document by 227%, so you can see that the result is actually very smooth and the final printout can take advantage of the printer's relatively high resolution.

The PrintWindowEnlarged example program (also available as part of this lesson's code download) is similar to the PrintWindowCentered example program except it uses the following code to pass a `Thickness` object to the `PrintWindowCentered` method to use as a margin. That makes the function stretch the `Window`'s image to fill the printable area minus a 50-pixel margin.

```
// Print an image of the window centered and stretched to fill the page.
private void printButton_Click(object sender, RoutedEventArgs e)
{
    PrintDialog printDialog = new PrintDialog();
```

```
        if (printDialog.ShowDialog() == true)
        {
            PrintWindowCentered(printDialog, this, "New Customer",
                new Thickness(50));
        }
    }
```

FIGURE 41-2

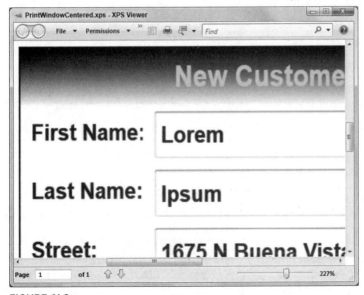

FIGURE 41-3

Figure 41-4 shows the result. Notice that the `Window`'s image is centered and enlarged to fill most of the printable area.

FIGURE 41-4

In addition to the `PrintVisual` method, the `PrintDialog` class provides a `PrintDocument` method that prints multipage output or document objects such as `FlowDocuments` or `FixedDocuments`. Unfortunately these topics are fairly complex, so they're not described here. If you need those capabilities, you can find more information online at:

➤   `PrintDocument` — `msdn.microsoft.com/library/system.windows.controls` `.printdialog.printdocument.aspx`

➤   `FixedDocument` — `msdn.microsoft.com/library/system.windows.documents` `.fixeddocument.aspx`

➤   `FlowDocument` — `msdn.microsoft.com/library/system.windows.documents` `.flowdocument.aspx`

 TRY IT

In this Try It, you modify the example programs described in this lesson to print an image of a window rotated sideways so it fills even more of the printed page. Figure 41-5 shows the result.

 You can download the code and resources for this Try It from the book's web page at www.wrox.com *or* www.CSharpHelper.com/24hour.html. *You can find them in the Lesson41 folder of the download.*

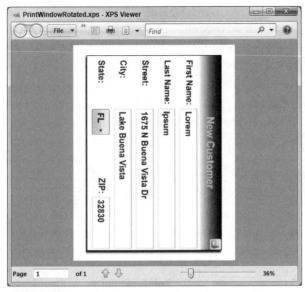

FIGURE 41-5

Lesson Requirements

➤ Copy the PrintWindowEnlarged example program, which is available in this lesson's download.

➤ Modify the `PrintWindowCentered` method so it rotates its result, stretching it appropriately as shown in Figure 41-5.

Hints

➤ This is a *lot* easier than you might think. Simply add a layout transformation to the `Grid` to rotate it 90 degrees.

➤ Think about how the `Grid`'s width and height will match up with the paper's dimensions after you rotate the `Grid`.

Step-by-Step

➤ Copy the PrintWindowEnlarged example program, which is available in this lesson's download.

    1. This is straightforward.

➤ Modify the `PrintWindowCentered` method so it rotates its result, stretching it appropriately as shown in Figure 41-5.

    1. There are several ways you could try to do this. You could try to rotate the brush that copies the `Window`'s image into the `Rectangle`. You could try rotating the `Rectangle`. The method that gave me the best result was to rotate the `Grid` that holds everything.

2. After you rotate the `Grid`, you want its width to be the same as the printable area's height and vice versa. The following code shows how the program shown in Figure 41-5 makes its `Grid` control. The rest of the program's code is the same as it is in the PrintWindowEnlarged example program.

```
// Make a Grid to hold the contents.
Grid drawingGrid = new Grid();
drawingGrid.Width = printDialog.PrintableAreaHeight;
drawingGrid.Height = printDialog.PrintableAreaWidth;
drawingGrid.LayoutTransform = new RotateTransform(90);
```

 Please select Lesson 41 on the DVD to view the video that accompanies this lesson.

EXERCISES

1. The examples in this lesson print images of a `Window` but similar techniques work with any visual object such as a `Grid`, `StackPanel`, or `TextBox`.

For this exercise, build a program similar to the one shown in Figure 41-6. Each of the program's tabs has a Print button in the lower-right corner. When you click the button, the program should print an image of the `Grid` control on the current tab.

FIGURE 41-6

You can use the Ex41-1a program available in this lesson's download as a starting point. That project defines the user interface, but none of the code.

You can use the `PrintWindowCentered` method used by the earlier example programs with a few changes:

➤ Change the method's name to `PrintGridCentered`.

➤ Instead of taking a `Window` as a parameter, make the method take a `Grid` as a parameter.

➤ The `Grid` control doesn't have a set width or height, so its `Width` and `Height` properties don't return meaningful values. Use the `Grid`'s `ActualWidth` and `ActualHeight` properties instead.

➤ To avoid repeating code, write a `PrintGrid` method that takes as parameters a `Grid`, title string, and `Thickness`. It should display a `PrintDialog` and, if the user clicks Print, it should call `PrintGridCentered` to do the actual printing.

 You can download the solution to this exercise from the book's web page at www.wrox.com *or* www.CSharpHelper.com/24hour.html. *You can find it in the* Lesson41 *folder of the download.*

Glossary

This appendix provides a glossary of key terms that you may encounter while studying C# programs.

accelerator   Underlined character, usually in a menu item, that activates that menu item when the user presses [Alt] plus the letter.

AcceptButton   The button triggered in a dialog when the user presses [Enter].

accessibility   Determines which code is allowed to access a class's fields, properties, methods, and other members. This can be `public`, `private`, `protected`, `internal`, or `protected internal`.

accessor   The `get` and `set` methods that allow a class to save and return a property's value.

Anchor   Property that lets a control attach its left, right, top, and bottom edges to those of its container.

anonymous type   A data type that is automatically created by LINQ and never given a name for your code to use.

API   Application Programming Interface. A library of methods, classes, and other programming tools.

array   A group of values stored together in a single variable and accessed by index.

assembly   The smallest independent unit of compiled code. Typically this is a DLL or executable program.

assertion   A statement that the code claims is true. If the statement is false, the program stops running so you can decide whether a bug occurred.

backing field   A private field used to store the value of a property. The property's accessors get and set the backing field's value.

bit   A single binary digit. A bit can hold the value 0 or 1.

breakpoint   A marked piece of code that stops execution when running in the IDE.

bug   A programming error that makes a program fail to produce the correct result. A bug may make the program crash, produce an incorrect result, or perform the wrong action.

by reference   When you pass a parameter to a method by reference, C# passes the location of the value's memory into the method. If the method modifies the parameter, the value is changed in the calling code as well. In C#, use the `ref` and `out` keywords to pass values by reference.

by value   When you pass a parameter by value, C# makes a copy of the value and passes the copy to the method. Changes that the method makes to the value do not affect the value in the calling code.

byte   Eight bits. When considered as an unsigned integer, a byte can hold values between 0 and 255. When considered as a signed integer, a byte can hold values between -127 and 128

C#   Pronounced "see sharp." A general-purpose high-level programming language. It is one of the programming languages that can run in the powerful Visual Studio integrated development environment (IDE).

CAD   See *computer aided design.*

camel casing   A naming convention where multiple words are strung together with the first letter of each word except the first capitalized as in `firstNameTextBox` or `numberOfEmployees`.

CancelButton   The button triggered in a dialog when the user presses [Esc].

catch   When an exception occurs, a program can *catch* the exception to take control and perform some remedial action (or just tell the user that something's wrong). Also when an object raises an event, the program can *catch* the event and take action.

class   Defines a data type with properties, methods, events, and other code encapsulated in a package. After you define a class, you can make as many instances of that class as you like. Very similar to a structure except classes are reference types while structures are value types.

code-behind   The event handlers and other code that sits behind a WPF user interface.

comment   Text within the program that is not executed by the program. Use comments to make the code easier to understand.

component   A programming entity similar to a control except it has only code and doesn't have a visible appearance on the screen. You still place it on a form at design time, however, and the program's code can interact with it. Some components such as `ErrorProvider` and `ToolTip` may display visible effects on the screen.

Component Tray   The area below the form where components sit.

compound assignment operators   Operators such as += and &= that combine a variable's current value with a new value.

computer aided design   A program that helps the user design something, often something graphical such as an architectural drawing or an electronic circuit. Many CAD systems do more than just draw. For example, they may produce lists of materials, validate electronic circuits, or calculate physical properties of the system designed.

concatenate   Join two strings together.

constant Similar to a variable, but you must assign it a value when you declare it and you cannot change the value later. You can use constants to make your code easier to read.

constructor A method that executes when an object is created.

control A programming entity that combines a visible appearance on the screen with code that defines its appearance and behavior.

Coordinated Universal Time (UTC) Basically Greenwich Mean Time (GMT), the time at the Royal Observatory in Greenwich, London. (See `en.wikipedia.org/wiki/Coordinated_Universal_Time` for details and history.)

data type A particular kind of data such as `int`, `string`, `DateTime`, or `TextBox`. All variables must have a data type.

dataset An in-memory representation of a data source.

default constructor The parameterless constructor that is created by default when you create a class.

deferred execution When a program delays performing some task until a later time. LINQ uses deferred execution when it delays performing a query until the results of the query are actually needed.

derive To make one class that inherits from another.

design time The time when you are editing a program in Visual Studio. During this time, you use the Form Designer, Code Editor, Properties window, and other IDE features to build the program. Contrast this with *run time*.

DialogResult The result returned by a dialog to tell the calling code which button was clicked.

DirectX A collection of high-performance multimedia APIs that provide much better access to graphics hardware than GDI does.

Dock Property that lets a control fill the left, right, top, bottom, or remaining area of its container.

dominant control When you select a group of controls in the Form Designer, one is marked as the dominant control. Arranging tools use this control to determine how the controls are arranged. For example, the Format ⇨ Align ⇨ Lefts tool aligns the selected controls' left edges to the dominant control's left edge.

drag source An object that initiates a drag-and-drop operation.

drop target An object that is a candidate to receive data dropped in a drag-and-drop operation.

edit-and-continue A debugger feature that lets you modify a stopped program's code and continue running without stopping and restarting the program.

empty constructor A parameterless constructor.

encapsulation Detail hiding. A class hides its internal details so the rest of the program doesn't need to understand how they work, just how to use them.

enumerated type See *enumeration*.

enumeration A data type that can take one of a list of specific values.

escape sequence   A sequence of characters that represent a special character such as carriage return or tab.

Euclid's algorithm   Also called the Euclidean algorithm. An efficient algorithm for finding the greatest common divisor (GCD) of two numbers.

event   An object *raises* an event to tell the program that something interesting has occurred. The program can *catch* the event to take action.

event handler   An event handler *catches* an event and takes appropriate action.

exception   Object that represents some kind of error such as an attempt to divide by zero or an attempt to parse a string that has an invalid number format.

eXtensible Application Markup Language   See *XAML*.

factorial   The factorial of a number N is written N! and equals 1 * 2 * 3 * ... * N.

Fibonacci number   The Nth Fibonacci number Fib(N) is defined recursively by Fib(0) = 0, Fib(1) = 1, and Fib(N) = Fib(N − 1) + Fib(N − 2).

field   A variable defined in a class or structure not inside any method defined by the class or structure.

filter   A condition on data that filters out some of the records. If you place a filter on a binding source, the source selects only records that satisfy the filter and any display controls associated with the source display only those records.

garbage collector   A behind-the-scenes process that runs to reclaim inaccessible memory.

GDI   Graphics Device Interface. A library of methods for rendering graphics in Windows used by Windows Forms controls.

GDI+   The .NET version of GDI.

generic class   A class that takes as a parameter one or more data types that it uses to work more closely with those data types.

generic constraint   A constraint on the types passed to a generic class such as requiring the type to have a parameterless constructor or requiring that it implement the `IComparable` interface.

gigabyte (GB)   1,024 megabytes.

globalization   The process of building an application that can be used by users from different cultures.

greatest common divisor (GCD)   The largest integer that evenly divides two other integers.

IDE   See *integrated development environment*.

index   A value that selects an item from a group. For example, in an array, the index is an integer between 0 and one less than the number of elements in the array used to identify a specific item in the array.

integrated development environment   An environment for building, testing, and debugging programs, such as Visual Studio.

interface   Defines public properties, methods, and events that a class must provide to satisfy the interface.

kilobyte (KB)   1,024 bytes.

LINQ   Language Integrated Query.

locale   A setting that defines the user's language, country, and cultural settings that determine such things as how dates and monetary values are formatted.

localization   The process of customizing a globalized application for a specific culture.

lower bound   An array's smallest index (always 0 in C#).

machine language   A low-level language that gives instructions directly to the computer's central processing unit to perform tasks on the machine's hardware. Machine language is much harder for humans to read and understand than a higher level programming language such as C#.

magic number   A value hard-coded into a program that is difficult to remember. To make code clearer, use constants such as `taxRate` instead of magic numbers such as `0.65M`.

megabyte (MB)   1,024 kilobytes.

method   A group of programming statements wrapped in a neat package so you can invoke it as needed. A method can take parameters and can return a value.

method scope   A variable declared inside a method and not inside any other code block has method scope. It is visible to all of the following code within that method.

modal   When the program displays a modal form, the user cannot interact with any other part of the application until closing that form. Dialogs are generally modal. A form's `ShowDialog` method displays the form modally.

modeless   When the program displays a modeless form, the user can interact with other parts of the application while the modeless form is still visible. A form's `Show` method displays a modeless form.

namespace   A classification of classes with a common purpose. Include `using` directives at the top of a code file to tell C# which namespaces to search for classes that the code uses.

nibble   Half a byte.

nondeterministic finalization   The idea that you cannot tell when an object will be finalized and its destructor run because objects are destroyed when the garbage collector runs.

nullable type   A data type that can hold the special value `null` in addition to whatever other values it normally holds.

NumberStyles.Any   Passed as a second parameter to `decimal.Parse`, this allows that method to correctly interpret values formatted as currency.

operator overloading   Defining a new meaning for an operator such as + or * when working with arguments of specific data types.

order by clause   A clause in a LINQ query that orders the returned data.

overloading   Giving a class more than one method with the same name but different parameter lists.

overriding   Replacing a parent class method with a new version.

parameterless constructor   A constructor that takes no parameters.

parse   To try to find structure and meaning in text.

Pascal casing   A naming convention where multiple words are strung together with the first letter of each word capitalized as in `TextBox` and `ProgressBar`.

pixel   A single point on the screen or in an image. The word pixel comes from "picture element."

polymorphism   The ability to treat an object as if it were of another parent class.

precision specifier   Number that affects the way a formatting character works. For example, the format D10 formats an integer value with digits only (no thousands separators) padded on the left with zeros if necessary so it is 10 digits long.

programming language   A language used by programmers to build programs. Contrast this with machine language, which is at a much lower level intended for use by the computer.

projecting LINQ query   A LINQ query that uses a select clause to return data other than the values over which the query ranges.

queue   A list that lets you add items at the front and remove them from the back. Also called a *FIFO list* or *FIFO*. (FIFO stands for *first-in-first-out*.)

raise   An object *raises* an event to tell the program that something interesting occurred.

range variable   The variable that a LINQ query uses to range over the data in the data source.

recursion   The process of a method calling itself.

recursive method   A method that calls itself.

refactoring   Restructuring a program to make it more reliable, easier to read, or easier to maintain without changing its outward behavior.

reference type   A data type such as a class reference that refers to an item instead of holding the item itself. Variables referring to class instances are reference variables. Contrast this with a *value type*.

relatively prime   Two numbers are relatively prime if their greatest common divisor is 1.

run time   The time when the program is running. Contrast this with *design time*.

scope   A variable's scope is the code that can "see" or access the variable.

select clause   A clause in a LINQ query that determines what data is returned for the selected data.

shortcut   Key combination such as [Ctrl]+S or [Ctrl]+N that immediately activates a menu command.

side effects   Consequences that last after a method has finished. Side effects make code harder to understand and debug, so you should try to avoid writing methods with nonobvious side effects.

splitter   An area that you can click and drag to adjust the sizes of the areas on either side of the splitter.

stack   A list that lets you add items at the front and remove them from the front. Also called a *LIFO list* or *LIFO*. (LIFO stands for *last-in-first-out*.)

static method   A shared method that is provided by the class itself rather than an instance of the class. You invoke it as in `ClassName.MethodName()`.

stream   An ordered series of bytes, sometimes representing a file.

strong type checking   Requiring values to have specific data types such as `Person` or `string` instead of more general types such as `object`.

structure   Defines a data type with properties, methods, events, and other code encapsulated in a package. After you define a class, you can make as many instances of that class as you like. Very similar to a class except classes are reference types while structures are value types.

terabyte (TB)   1,024 gigabytes.

this   A special object reference that means "the object that is currently executing this code."

throw   A program *throws* an exception to indicate that something bad has happened that it cannot handle. Other code higher up in the call stack can *catch* the exception and take action.

transforming LINQ query   See *projecting LINQ query.*

upper bound   An array's largest index. Because C# arrays start with lower bound 0, the upper bound (for one-dimensional arrays) is one less than the array's length.

value type   A data type that holds its data, not a reference to it. Primitive data types such as `int` and `float`, as well as structures, are value types. Contrast this with a *reference type.*

variable   A named piece of memory that can hold a piece of data.

verbatim string literal   A string literal that begins with `@"` and ends with a corresponding closing quote `"`. It doesn't process escape sequences so it can contain special characters such as \, carriage returns, and tabs.

virtual   Keyword that marks a method so it can be overridden in a derived class.

Visual C#   The combination of C# used in the Visual Studio development environment. It's what this book is all about.

Visual Studio   A development environment for building programs in several programming languages including Visual C#, Visual Basic, Visual C++, and F#. Home page: `msdn.microsoft.com/vstudio`.

where clause   A clause in a LINQ query that filters the data to return only selected items.

XAML (eXtensible Application Markup Language)   A language that defines the user interface for WPF applications.

B

Control Summary

This appendix summarizes the purposes of the most common Windows Forms controls. The intent of this appendix is to let you know what kinds of controls are available, not to provide an exhaustive reference.

For additional details on how to use a control, see the online documentation. The web page describing a control is named after the control including its namespace. For example, the web page describing the `ComboBox` class is `msdn.microsoft.com/library/system.windows .forms.combobox.aspx`.

All of the controls listed here are in the `System.Windows.Forms` namespace (which you need to know to enter the correct URL) unless otherwise noted.

CONTROL	PURPOSE
BackgroundWorker	Executes a background task in parallel on a separate thread. Events provide notification of progress and completion (`System. ComponentModel` namespace).
BindingNavigator	Provides a user interface for controls bound to a data source.
BindingSource	Encapsulates a data source for a form. Provides methods for manipulating the data.
Button	A button.
CheckBox	A checkbox.
CheckedListBox	A list of items with checkboxes that let the user easily select one or more items without needing the Click/Shift+Click/Ctrl+Click techniques used by the regular `ListBox` control.
ColorDialog	A dialog that lets the user select a color.
ComboBox	A combo box.

continues

(continued)

CONTROL	PURPOSE
ContextMenuStrip	A context menu. Assign this object to another control's ContextMenu property and the menu automatically appears when the user right-clicks the control.
DataGridView	Displays a grid of data, possibly bound to a data source.
DataSet	An in-memory representation of a database.
DateTimePicker	Allows the user to select a date and a time.
DomainUpDown	Displays a spin box (up-down control) that lets the user scroll through a list of predefined choices.
ErrorProvider	Displays an error indicator for other controls.
EventLog	Allows a program to interact with system event logs (System.Diagnostics namespace).
FileSystemWatcher	Raises events when a directory or file changes so you can keep track of it (although I've had mixed success with this control) (System.IO namespace).
FlowLayoutPanel	A panel that dynamically arranges its contents in either rows or columns.
FolderBrowserDialog	A dialog that lets the user select a folder (directory).
FontDialog	A dialog that lets the user select a font.
Form	Displays a window on the desktop.
GroupBox	Groups controls inside an outline and displays a header for the group.
HelpProvider	Provides a tooltip or online help for other controls.
HScrollBar	A horizontal scrollbar.
ImageList	Stores a list of images for use by other controls.
Label	Displays non-editable text in a single font.
LinkLabel	Displays a label that contains a hyperlink. When the user clicks the hyperlink, the control raises an event so the program can take action.
ListBox	Displays a list of items.
ListView	Displays a group of items in four different views: LargeIcon, SmallIcon, Details, and Tile.

CONTROL	PURPOSE
MaskedTextBox	Similar to a `TextBox` except it displays an input mask to prompt the user and restrict entry. For example, a telephone mask might look like (___)-___-____.
MenuStrip	A form's main menu.
MessageQueue	Provides tools for creating and interacting with message queues (`System.Messaging` namespace).
MonthCalendar	Allows the user to select a date or date range from a calendar.
NotifyIcon	Displays an icon in the notification area or system tray (usually on the right end of the taskbar). Can provide a context menu, and the program can use the icon to indicate status to the user.
NumericUpDown	Displays a spin box (up-down control) that lets the user pick a numeric value.
OpenFileDialog	A dialog that lets the user select a file for opening. Can require that the file actually exists.
PageSetupDialog	A dialog that allows the user to define printer page settings, such as margins and printout orientation.
Panel	A simple container that holds other controls. Set `AutoScroll` = true to make the `Panel` automatically display scrollbars if needed. (This is its coolest feature!)
PerformanceCounter	Provides access to Windows NT performance counters (`System.Diagnostics` namespace).
PictureBox	Displays an image. The `SizeMode` property determines how the image is sized and can take the values `Normal` (clip the image if it doesn't fit), `StretchImage` (make the image fit the `PictureBox` even if that distorts it), `AutoSize` (size the `PictureBox` to fit the image), `CenterImage` (center the image, clipping it if it is too big), and `Zoom` (make the image as large as possible without distorting its shape).
PrintDialog	A dialog that allows the user to select a printer, set printer properties, and pick the pages to print.
PrintDocument	Represents a printed document. Catch the `PrintPage` event to generate output.
PrintPreviewControl	Displays a preview of a `PrintDocument` in a control.
PrintPreviewDialog	Displays a preview of a `PrintDocument` in a dialog.

continues

(continued)

CONTROL	PURPOSE
Process	Lets a program control processes running on the system. You can use the `Start` method to run the default application for a file. For example, the following code opens the CSharpHelper web site in the system's default browser: `System.Diagnostics.process.Start ("http://www.csharphelper.com")` (`System.Diagnostics` namespace).
ProgressBar	Indicates the progress of some task to the user.
PropertyGrid	Displays an object's properties at run time and lets the user edit them much as the Properties window lets you change a control's properties at design time.
RadioButton	A radio button.
RichTextBox	Lets the user edit text. Can display multiple fonts, images, bulleted and numbered lists, and other formats.
SaveFileDialog	A dialog that lets the user select a file for saving. Can prompt the user to overwrite the file if it already actually exists.
SerialPort	Allows a program to control serial ports (`System.IO.Ports` namespace).
ServiceController	Allows a program to control Windows services (`System.ServiceProcess` namespace).
SplitContainer	Displays two `Panels` separated by a `Splitter` to let the user easily resize the panels.
StatusStrip	A status bar, usually displayed at the bottom of a form.
TabControl	Displays a series of tabs holding groups of controls.
TableLayoutPanel	A panel that arranges its contents in rows and columns.
TextBox	Lets the user edit text in a single font.
Timer	A component that raises a `Tick` event at regular repeating intervals.
ToolStrip	A toolbar.
ToolStripContainer	A container that can hold `ToolStrips`. The user can drag the `ToolStrips` to new positions within the `ToolStripContainer`.
ToolTip	Displays a tooltip for other controls when the mouse hovers over them.

CONTROL	PURPOSE
TrackBar	Displays a trackbar that lets the user select a numeric value. It behaves much as a scrollbar does but with a different appearance.
TreeView	Displays a hierarchical set of items much as the left panel in Windows Explorer normally does (if you haven't customized its appearance).
VScrollBar	A vertical scrollbar.
WebBrowser	A web browser control. You can use this to control a browser inside your application. For example, your program can go to specific sites, examine URLs and cancel navigation for some URLs, examine the links and images on a web page, and so on.

What's on the DVD?

This appendix provides you with information on the contents of the DVD that accompanies this book. For the latest and greatest information, please refer to the ReadMe file located at the root of the DVD. Here is what you will find in this appendix:

➤ System Requirements

➤ Using the DVD

➤ What's on the DVD

➤ Troubleshooting

SYSTEM REQUIREMENTS

Most reasonably up-to-date computers with a DVD drive should be able to play the screencasts that are included on the DVD. You may also find an Internet connection helpful for searching Microsoft's online help and for downloading updates to this book. Finally, the system requirements for running Visual Studio are much greater than those for simply running a DVD.

If your computer doesn't meet the following requirements then you may have some problems using Visual Studio.

➤ PC running Windows XP, Windows Vista, Windows 7, or later

➤ A processor running at 1.6GHz or faster

➤ An Internet connection

➤ At least 1GB of RAM

➤ At least 3GB of available hard disk space

➤ A DVD-ROM drive

You may be able to run Visual Studio using a slower processor or with less memory, but things may be slow. I highly recommend more memory, 2GB or even more if possible. (I do fairly well with an Intel Core 2 system running Windows 7 at 1.83 GHz with 2GB of memory and a 500GB hard drive.)

USING THE DVD

To access the content from the DVD, follow these steps.

1. Insert the DVD into your computer's DVD-ROM drive. The license agreement appears.

> *The interface won't launch if you have autorun disabled. In that case, click Start ⇨ Run (For Windows 7, Start ⇨ All Programs ⇨ Accessories ⇨ Run). In the dialog box that appears, type D:\Start.exe. (Replace D with the proper letter if your DVD drive uses a different letter. If you don't know the letter, see how your DVD drive is listed under My Computer.) Click OK.*

2. Read through the license agreement, and then click the Accept button if you want to use the DVD.

    The DVD interface appears. Simply select the lesson number for the video you want to view.

WHAT'S ON THE DVD

Each of this book's lessons contains one or more Try It sections that lets you practice the concepts covered by that lesson. The Try It includes a high-level overview, requirements, and step-by-step instructions explaining how to build the example program.

This DVD contains video screencasts showing my computer screen as I work through key pieces of the Try Its from each lesson. In the audio I explain what I'm doing step-by-step so you can see how the techniques described in the lesson translate into actions performed in Visual Studio.

I don't always show how to build every last piece of a Try It's program. For example, if the requirements ask you to build 10 controls and set their properties, I may only do the first few and let you do the rest so you don't need waste time watching me do the same thing again and again.

I recommend using the following steps when reading a lesson:

1. Read the lesson's text.

2. Read the Try It's overview, requirements, and hints.

3. Try to write a program that satisfies the requirements.

4. Read the step-by-step instructions. If the program you wrote doesn't satisfy all of the requirements, use these instructions to improve it. Also look for places where my solution differs from yours. In programming there's always more than one way to solve a problem, and it's good to know about several different approaches.

5. Watch the screencast to see how I handle the key issues.

Sometimes a screencast mentions useful techniques and shortcuts that didn't fit in the book, so you may want to watch the screencast even if you feel completely confident in your solution.

After finishing with the Try It section, I recommend that you work through the exercises or at least skim them and figure out how you would solve them.

You can also download all of the book's examples, solutions to the Try Its, and solutions to the exercises at the book's web sites.

Finally, if you're stuck and don't know what to do next, e-mail me at `RodStephens@CSharpHelper.com`, and I'll try to point you in the right direction.

TROUBLESHOOTING

If you have difficulty installing or using any of the materials on the companion DVD, try the following solutions:

➤ **Reboot if necessary.** As with many troubleshooting situations, it may make sense to reboot your machine to reset any faults in your environment.

➤ **Turn off any anti-virus software that you may have running.** Installers sometimes mimic virus activity and can make your computer incorrectly believe that it is being infected by a virus. (Be sure to turn the anti-virus software back on later.)

➤ **Close all running programs.** The more programs you're running, the less memory is available to other programs. Installers also typically update files and programs; if you keep other programs running, installation may not work properly.

➤ **Reference the ReadMe:** Please refer to the ReadMe file located at the root of the DVD for the latest product information at the time of publication.

CUSTOMER CARE

If you have trouble with the DVD, please call the Wiley Product Technical Support phone number at (800) 762-2974. Outside the United States, call 1(317) 572-3994. You can also contact Wiley Product Technical Support at `http://support.wiley.com`. John Wiley & Sons will provide technical support only for installation and other general quality control items. For technical support on the applications themselves, consult the program's vendor or author.

To place additional orders or to request information about other Wiley products, please call (877) 762-2974.

INDEX

WILEY PUBLISHING, INC. END-USER LICENSE AGREEMENT